Introducing the MySQL 8 Document Store

Charles Bell

Apress®

Introducing the MySQL 8 Document Store

Charles Bell
Warsaw, Virginia, USA

ISBN-13 (pbk): 978-1-4842-2724-4   ISBN-13 (electronic): 978-1-4842-2725-1
https://doi.org/10.1007/978-1-4842-2725-1

Library of Congress Control Number: 2018945864

Managing Director, Apress Media LLC: Welmoed Spahr
Acquisitions Editor: Jonathan Gennick
Development Editor: Laura Berendson
Coordinating Editor: Jill Balzano

Cover designed by eStudioCalamar

Cover image designed by Freepik (www.freepik.com)

Distributed to the book trade worldwide by Springer Science+Business Media New York, 233 Spring Street, 6th Floor, New York, NY 10013. Phone 1-800-SPRINGER, fax (201) 348-4505, e-mail orders-ny@springer-sbm.com, or visit www.springeronline.com. Apress Media, LLC is a California LLC and the sole member (owner) is Springer Science + Business Media Finance Inc (SSBM Finance Inc). SSBM Finance Inc is a **Delaware** corporation.

For information on translations, please e-mail rights@apress.com, or visit http://www.apress.com/rights-permissions.

Apress titles may be purchased in bulk for academic, corporate, or promotional use. eBook versions and licenses are also available for most titles. For more information, reference our Print and eBook Bulk Sales web page at http://www.apress.com/bulk-sales.

Any source code or other supplementary material referenced by the author in this book is available to readers on GitHub via the book's product page, located at www.apress.com/9781484227244. For more detailed information, please visit http://www.apress.com/source-code.

Printed on acid-free paper

I dedicate this book to the open source enthusiasts of the world who make the MySQL ecosystem strong. Live long and prosper, Sakila!

Table of Contents

About the Author

Charles Bell conducts research in emerging technologies. He is a member of the Oracle MySQL Development team, and is a senior software developer for the MySQL Enterprise Backup team. He lives in a small town in rural Virginia with his wife. He received his doctor of philosophy in engineering from the Virginia Commonwealth University in 2005.

Charles is an expert in the database field and has extensive knowledge and experience in software development and systems engineering. His research interests include 3D printers, microcontrollers, three-dimensional printing, database systems, software engineering, and sensor networks. He spends his limited free time as a practicing maker, focusing on microcontroller projects and refinement of three-dimensional printers.

About the Technical Reviewer

Paulo Jesus is currently a principal software developer at Oracle, in the MySQL Engineering Team. He obtained his PhD in distributed systems in 2012, from the MAP-i doctoral program in computer science by the Universities of Minho, Aveiro, and Porto (Portugal). He also has a MSc degree in mobile systems (2007). His research interests include distributed algorithms, fault tolerance, and mobile systems.

Acknowledgments

I thank all the many talented and energetic professionals at Apress. I appreciate the understanding and patience of my acquisition editor, Jonathan Gennick, and coordinating editor, Jill Balzano. They were instrumental in the success of this project. I also thank the army of publishing professionals at Apress for making me look so good in print with a special thank you to the reviewers for their wise council and gentle nudges in the right direction. Thank you all very much!

I also am indebted to the technical reviewer for his insight and guidance in making this book the best book on the new MySQL Document Store.

Most important, I thank my wife, Annette, for her unending patience and understanding while I spent so much time with my laptop.

Introduction

NoSQL has been given a lot of hype in recent years. As with most new technologies, the underlying principles are rarely truly new, rather, it is the unique combination of known technologies that forms and transforms the whole to become more than the sum of its parts. This is especially true for MySQL 8 and the new MySQL Document Store. Never has MySQL offered so much for so many. Whether you want a traditional relational database solution with a strong foundation or you want the ultimate flexibility to store JSON documents in a document store—or anywhere in between, MySQL can do it.

The trick then is learning how to migrate your applications using each of these technologies: whether you use traditional tables with fixed schemas or you have some JSON fields to allow some freedom from rigid structure or you employ the flexibility of a JSON-based document store.

This book will give you the knowledge you seek to navigate the MySQL Document Store including how to migrate existing applications and best practices for using a document store solution.

Intended Audience

I wrote this book to share my passion for the new MySQL Document Store and Python. I especially wanted to show how anyone can write document store solutions without investing in learning a large, complex language and development environment. The intended audience therefore includes anyone interested in learning about the MySQL Document Store such as database administrators, developers, and information technology managers and strategic planners.

How This Book Is Structured

The book was written to guide the reader from a general knowledge of the new features in MySQL 8 to detailed explanations of the components that make up the MySQL Document Store. The first several chapters cover general topics including a short introduction to MySQL 8, how to install MySQL 8, and how to configure the new document store components. Later chapters present more detailed coverage of the MySQL Document Store components including the MySQL Shell, X DevAPI, X Plugin, and more. Following those chapters is a pair of chapters that present an example application for storing information on books written as a relational database, a hybrid, and a document store. Thus, you can see how to migrate a single application through those variants. The book concludes with some notes about upgrading to MySQL 8 and best practices for using the MySQL Document Store including a recap of the migration process. The following is a brief overview of each chapter included in this book.

- Chapter 1, "Introducing MySQL 8—A New Beginning": This chapter explores some of the highlights of the new MySQL server version 8.0. You will discover those features originally introduced in earlier versions that have been adapted to the new paradigm that is version 8.0, features that are new, and those new features that are truly revolutionary such as the document store, Group Replication, and InnoDB Cluster.

- Chapter 2, "Getting Started with MySQL": This chapter presents a tutorial on MySQL discussing the power of using the MySQL database server in its traditional role using the SQL interface; how to issue commands for creating databases and tables for storing data as well as commands for retrieving that data. Although this chapter presents only a small primer on MySQL, you will learn how to get started with your own installation of MySQL.

- Chapter 3, "JSON Documents": This chapter explores the JSON data type in more detail. You will see examples of how to work with the JSON data in relational tables via the numerous built-in JSON functions provided in MySQL. The JSON data type is key to allowing users to develop hybrid solutions that span the gulf of SQL and NoSQL applications.

- Chapter 4, "The MySQL Shell": This chapter demonstrates how to use the MySQL Shell including a look at the startup options, shell commands, connections, sessions, and we even how to do a bit of interactive scripting in JavaScript and Python. This chapter therefore is the key chapter for learning how to get started with the MySQL Shell and working with JSON and relational data. Although this chapter is not an exhaustive coverage of all the features of the MySQL Shell, it provides a broad tutorial for how to use it for the most common tasks.

- Chapter 5, "X Developer API": This chapter explores the X DevAPI and examines the major classes and methods available for connecting to the MySQL server, creating collections, working with results, and even how to work with relational data. Finally, you will see a set of quick references tables that you can use as the primary reference for developing document store applications.

- Chapter 6, "X Plugin": This chapter discusses the X Plugin and how it works. In particular, you will see how to configure the X Plugin such as changing the port and enabling secure connections via SSL that are separate from the server. The chapter also presents some of the other system variables as well as a lengthy list of status variables that you can use to monitor the X Plugin.

- Chapter 7, "X Protocol": This chapter examines the X Protocol starting with the motivations for why it was created, the chief tenets or goals of the design, and how it was implemented using protobuf as the foundation. You will see a walkthrough of how portions of the X Protocol work for simple use cases. The chapter also presents an example of how to use protobuf in our applications for moving data (messages) around in the code (on disk, over the wire, etc.), which illustrates the power of protobuf.

- Chapter 8, "Library Application: User Interface": This chapter presents a web application library for Python named Flask. You will learn how Flask is built as an extensible framework that is easily augmented with components to make your application more robust. The chapter also presents an introduction to the user interface for the library application built on the foundations of what we learned about Flask.

- Chapter 9, "Library Application: Database Implementations": This chapter explores the differences between a relational database solution and a relational database solution augmented with JSON fields, and finally a pure document store solution. This chapter demonstrates how to build applications for any of these solutions with complete code that demonstrates many of the tenets of the X DevAPI and the MySQL Document Store.

- Chapter 10, "Planning for MySQL 8 and the Document Store": This chapter presents some strategies for migrating to MySQL 8 including considerations and best practices for migrating applications to use the document store with another example of migrating existing database applications. The chapter concludes with some tips and tricks for working with MySQL 8.

How to Use This Book

This book is designed to guide you through learning more about MySQL 8, JSON, the MySQL Document Store, discovering the power of X DevAPI, and learning how to migrate existing and building new document store applications.

If you are new to MySQL, you should spend some time going through the first four chapters including installing MySQL on your own system and learning how to use the MySQL Shell.

If you are familiar with Python and have used the X DevAPI via the MySQL Shell, you may want to read the chapters on the X DevAPI skimming through the examples. On the other hand, if you have not used the X DevAPI or Python, you should attempt to reproduce all the code examples in the chapters.

Once you are familiar with MySQL and the X DevAPI from reading the first seven chapters, you can work through Chapters 8 and 9 that present a complete solution that demonstrates how to build a relational database solution, the same solution as a hybrid relational table with JSON columns, and a migration to a full document store solution.

Planners may find Chapter 10 especially helpful in planning to upgrade to MySQL 8 and to adapt the MySQL Document Store to your infrastructure.

Downloading the Code

The code for the examples shown in this book is available on the Apress web site, www.apress.com. You can find a link on the book's information page on the Source Code/Downloads tab. This tab is in the *Related Titles* section of the page.

Contacting the Author

Should you have any questions or comments—or even spot a mistake you think I should know about—you can contact me at drcharlesbell@gmail.com.

## CHAPTER 1

Introducing MySQL 8—A New Beginning

It is a testament to the dedication of the Oracle MySQL engineers (and Oracle itself) that MySQL continues to improve with new features. The drive within the MySQL engineering division is to continue to develop disruptive database technologies for the Internet. Oracle has not only fostered this aggressiveness but has continued to live up to its promise to invest in and expand their MySQL business. The newest version, MySQL 8, proves conclusively that Oracle has fulfilled the promise to ensure MySQL will remain the world's most popular open source database system.

Previous versions of MySQL have added some new and interesting features since MySQL 5.0[1] making MySQL a better product. Although the features have been well received and used to solve a lot of problems, the changes were largely evolutionary improvements rather than revolutionary changes.

This tendency is not unique to MySQL nor is it unusual in a stable, mature product. That doesn't mean evolutionary development is bad—it isn't. However, given that several competitive technologies have emerged, the MySQL engineers realized they must reach higher and further if they are to continue to dominate the industry.

Thus, this new release of MySQL breaks many of the molds of previous versions adding new, revolutionary features that change the firmament of how some will use MySQL. Indeed, the version number alone has jumped from 5.x to 8.0[2] signifying the jump in technological sophistication and the break from continuous development of the 5.x codebase, which lasted for over 13 years.

---

[1]MySQL 5.0 was first released (alpha) in December 2003.

[2]Some would say the change in version number is not only welcome but also long overdue.

© Charles Bell 2018
C. Bell, *Introducing the MySQL 8 Document Store*, https://doi.org/10.1007/978-1-4842-2725-1_1

The changes to MySQL 8.0 include changes to existing features as well as some new, game changing features. This book examines one of the most important and newest features: the MySQL Document Store. However, there are other equally as important features such as Group Replication and the InnoDB Cluster. Although I focus on the document store, I will also see how these other features can be leveraged to take your MySQL installation into the future.

MYSQL—WHAT DOES IT MEAN?

The name *MySQL* is a combination of a proper name and an acronym. SQL is structured query language. The *My* part isn't a possessive form—it is a name. In this case, *My* is the name of the founder's daughter. As for pronunciation, MySQL experts pronounce it "My-S-Q-L"—not "my sequel."

In this chapter, I examine some of the new features of MySQL 8 including a short introduction to some of the features that were emerging technologies from previous versions, new features unique to MySQL 8, and those revolutionary features that make MySQL 8 the greatest MySQL release to date.

Note   This book is based on the MySQL 8.0.11 release with a focus on the document store. There are many more new features than those that are listed in this chapter. Be sure to consult the latest MySQL online MySQL reference manual (https://dev.mysql.com/doc/refman/8.0/en/) for a complete list of the new, updated, and removed features.[3]

The new features have a great deal of sophistication. As you will see, some of the features are designed to work together and others are designed as add-ons. Rather than explain every minor detail or list features and benefits, the following sections present the basics of the various features available today in MySQL 8 so that you can get an idea of what is available. You will also see just how far the new version has advanced beyond the traditional MySQL mechanism of storage and retrieval.

Let's begin with a look at some of the features that were part of earlier releases but are now refined and more fully integrated into the server.

---

[3]The online MySQL reference manual refers to the reference manual for MySQL Server. References to other such manuals are prefaced with the product name.

Old Features New Again

The first category of features includes those under development in MySQL 5.7 either as a separate, experimental development project; a plugin; or as a planned feature for a later stable release. Thus, these features had already been released in some limited form. Most were considered "development releases" and were accompanied with a disclaimer that strongly suggested they not be used in a production environment. Some had been included in the latest release candidate (RC) versions of the server.

To be more precise, Oracle released these features as early releases so that systems and database administrators, information technology architects, and other planners could try out the features and provide feedback to help the feature mature. It also allows customers to adapt the technologies early in development environments in case the features required changes to the infrastructure or applications.

WHAT IS A PLUGIN?

Plugins are means that add functionality to the server without having to compile and rebuild the server proper to incorporate the new features. Plugin technology has been around for a long time. In fact, MySQL originally supported pluggable storage engines that allowed you to add and remove storage engine options on the fly. The MySQL plugin technology has evolved since those days, but the concept is the same. As long as the plugin is compatible with the server version, you can download MySQL plugins from Oracle and install them on your server for immediate use.

Plugins are also a convenient way for Oracle to release new features into existing, stable releases. For example, new features, such as Group Replication, have been introduced as plugins (but are included in the latest release). Even if a plugin is released as a development release (think early beta), you could still use it with the compatible GA (generally available) release of the server. This allows Oracle to produce features much more quickly than having to bundle them with a major server release. In the case of Group Replication and similar technologies, this has saved Oracle years of development work by making the features available to users in near record time.

There are several features that have evolved in the MySQL 5.7 code base. The following are some of the key features that I explore in this book. These include the JSON data type and the MySQL Shell.

JSON Data Type

As of MySQL version 5.7.8, MySQL supports a native JSON data type that enables efficient access to data in JSON documents in a table row. Thus, you can have columns in your table of the JSON data type. JSON stands for JavaScript Object Notation.[4] The new JSON data type is a key component to using MySQL as a document store. In short, JSON is a markup language used to exchange data. Not only is it human readable, it can be used directly in your applications to store and retrieve data to and from other applications, servers, and even MySQL.

Note   I give a very brief overview of the JSON data type and JSON documents in this section. I give an in-depth look at JSON in Chapter 3.

In fact, JSON looks familiar to programmers because it resembles other markup schemes. JSON is also very simple in that it supports only two types of structures: 1) a collection containing pairs (name, value), and 2) an ordered list (or array). Of course, you can also mix and match the structures in an object. When we create a JSON object, we call it a JSON document.

The JSON data type, unlike the normal data types in MySQL, allows you to store JSON formatted objects (documents) in a column for a row. You can have more than one JSON column (field) in a single table. Although you could do this with TEXT or BLOB fields (and many people do), there is no facility built into MySQL to interact with the data in TEXT and BLOB fields. Thus, manipulation of the data is largely application dependent. In addition, the data is normally structured such that every row has the same "format" for the column. Storing data in TEXT and BLOB fields is not new and has been done for years.

This could work by using a single string or even a binary representation of data and storing it in the TEXT or BLOB field. If the data is small enough, you could store it in a VARCHAR and similar string column. To store and retrieve data in this manner, you have to encode then decode the data—something that could be tedious—especially if you're trying to ingest data from someone else.

---

[4]http://www.json.org/

With the JSON data type, you don't have to write specialized code to store and retrieve data. This is because JSON documents are well understood and many programming environments and scripting languages support it natively. Think of JSON as an outgrowth or extension of what XML documents were supposed to be. That is, they offer a flexible way to store data that may differ from one application to another. JSON allows you to store the data that you have at the time. Unlike a typical database table, you don't have to worry about default values (they're not allowed) or whether you have enough columns or even master/detail relationships to normalize and store all of the data in a nice, neat, structured package.

Let's take a look at a simple JSON document that we can store in MySQL. Let's say we have a contact list in which each contact may or may not have an address on file, may or may not have an email, multiple phone numbers, and so forth. If you were to create a typical database table to store this information, you may go so far as to store a lot of empty columns for entries that you only have a name and a single phone number.

In fact, we can add new data items any time we want without having to alter the underlining table structure. For example, if you find you later need to add a Skype Id to some of the records, you can do that in your code adding the key for those entries you want without having to go back and change any existing data. The only catch is that your code for reading the data will have to change to test for the existence of the key before accessing it. I show an example of this in Chapters 8 and 9.

Let's consider an example contact list that contains several people who perform a service for me who live in my area. All I need to store is their name and phone number. Sometimes I only know (or care to store) their first name. I don't need their address because I never send them anything and they're just down the street after all. Listing 1-1 demonstrates what some of the entries could look like. I chose to demonstrate what JSON looks like by using SQL INSERT statements so that you can see one way unstructured data can be inserted in our database.

Listing 1-1. Example of JSON Documents

```
INSERT INTO rolodex.contacts (contact_info) VALUES ('
{
  "name": "Allen",
  "phones": [
    {
      "work": "212-555-1212"
    }
```

```
  ]
}
');

INSERT INTO rolodex.contacts (contact_info) VALUES ('
{ "name": {
    "first": "Joe",
    "last": "Wheelerton"
  },
  "phones": [
    {
      "work": "212-555-1213"
    },
    {
      "home": "212-555-1253"
    }
  ],
  "address": {
      "street": "123 main",
      "city": "oxnard",
      "state": "ca",
      "zip": "90125"
  },
  "notes": "Excellent car detailer. Referrals get $20 off next detail!"
}
');
```

Note that I used a bit of formatting with newlines and whitespace to make the JSON easier to read. However, that is not necessary. Indeed, if we query a table with JSON data as in the rows in Listing 1-1, we would see the data would display a bit differently. Listing 1-2 shows the output of a typical SELECT query.

Listing 1-2. SELECT with JSON Columns

```
mysql> SELECT * FROM rolodex.contacts \G
*************************** 1. row ***************************
        id: 1
contact_info: {"name": "Allen", "phones": [{"work": "212-555-1212"}]}
*************************** 2. row ***************************
        id: 2
contact_info: {"name": {"last": "Wheelerton", "first": "Joe"}, "notes":
"Excellent car detailer. Referrals get $20 off next detail!", "phones":
[{"work": "212-555-1213"}, {"home": "212-555-1253"}], "address": {"zip":
"90125", "city": "oxnard", "state": "ca", "street": "123 main"}}
2 rows in set (0.00 sec)
```

That isn't very easy to read, is it? Not to worry because your applications can ingest this data easily (those languages that support JSON) so it doesn't matter so much.

If you want to experiment with this example, you will need to create the structure and data. In this case, you will need a schema (think database) and collection (think table). The following are the SQL statements that you need to create the schema and collection. However, you normally would not use SQL statements with the document store, but you can since the underlining storage for a collection in MySQL is a specially formed table shown in the following.

```
CREATE DATABASE `rolodex`;
CREATE TABLE `rolodex`.`contacts` (
    `id` INT NOT NULL AUTO_INCREMENT,
    `contact_info` json DEFAULT NULL,
  PRIMARY KEY (`id`)
) ENGINE=InnoDB DEFAULT CHARSET=utf8mb4;
```

The JSON data type enables you to build flexibility into your data storage through the support built into MySQL for working with the JSON documents as well as additional facilities to enable interaction with JSON through the MySQL Shell, X Plugin, and X Protocol. Let's look at the MySQL Shell.

MySQL Shell

The MySQL Shell is another feature that was added during the MySQL 5.7 timeframe. In this case, it was in the form of a new, separate product. The MySQL Shell is the next generation of command-line client for MySQL. Not only can you execute traditional SQL commands, you can also interact with the server using one of several programming languages including Python and JavaScript. Furthermore, if you also have the X Plugin installed, you can use MySQL Shell to work with both traditional relational data as well as JSON documents. How cool is that?

Tip   You can download the MySQL Shell from `http://dev.mysql.com/downloads/shell/`.

If you're thinking, "It is about time!" that Oracle has made a new MySQL client, you're not alone. The MySQL Shell represents a bold new way to interact with MySQL. There are many options and even different ways to configure and use the shell. And although we will see more about the shell in Chapter 4, let's see how to use the shell to execute the same query shown previously. Figure 1-1 shows a snapshot of the new MySQL Shell. Note that it provides a very familiar interface albeit a bit more modern and far more powerful.

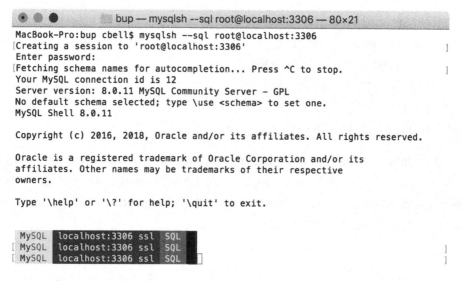

```
● ● ●              bup — mysqlsh --sql root@localhost:3306 — 80×21
MacBook-Pro:bup cbell$ mysqlsh --sql root@localhost:3306
Creating a session to 'root@localhost:3306'
Enter password:
Fetching schema names for autocompletion... Press ^C to stop.
Your MySQL connection id is 12
Server version: 8.0.11 MySQL Community Server - GPL
No default schema selected; type \use <schema> to set one.
MySQL Shell 8.0.11

Copyright (c) 2016, 2018, Oracle and/or its affiliates. All rights reserved.

Oracle is a registered trademark of Oracle Corporation and/or its
affiliates. Other names may be trademarks of their respective
owners.

Type '\help' or '\?' for help; '\quit' to exit.


MySQL  localhost:3306 ssl  SQL
 MySQL  localhost:3306 ssl  SQL
 MySQL  localhost:3306 ssl  SQL
```

Figure 1-1.   *The MySQL Shell*

Listing 1-3 shows how to start the shell and execute a SELECT statement displaying the results. Note that the command used to launch the shell. In this case, we specify that we want to use the shell in a manner that resembles the old client in SQL mode (--sql).

Listing 1-3. Querying JSON data in the MySQL Shell

```
$ mysqlsh -uroot --sql
Creating a session to 'root@localhost'
Enter password:
Your MySQL connection id is 281 (X protocol)
Server version: 8.0.11 MySQL Community Server (GPL)
No default schema selected; type \use <schema> to set one.
MySQL Shell 8.0.11

Copyright (c) 2016, 2018, Oracle and/or its affiliates. All rights reserved.

Oracle is a registered trademark of Oracle Corporation and/or its
affiliates. Other names may be trademarks of their respective
owners.

Type '\help' or '\?' for help; '\quit' to exit.

 MySQL  localhost:33060+ ssl  SQL > SELECT * FROM rolodex.contacts \G
*************************** 1. row ***************************
doc: {"_id": "9801A79DE093991311E7FFCB243C3451", "name": {"first":
"Allen"}, "phones": [{"work": "212-555-1212"}]}
_id: 9801A79DE093991311E7FFCB243C3451
*************************** 2. row ***************************
doc: {"_id": "9801A79DE0939E0411E7FFCB243DCDE3", "name": {"last":
"Wheelerton", "first": "Joe"}, "notes": "Excellent car detailer. Referrals
get $20 off next detail!", "phones": [{"work": "212-555-1213"}, {"home":
"212-555-1253"}], "address": {"zip": "90125", "city": "oxnard", "state":
"ca", "street": "123 main"}}
_id: 9801A79DE0939E0411E7FFCB243DCDE3
2 rows in set (0.00 sec)
 MySQL  localhost:33060+ ssl  SQL > \exit
Bye!
```

9

> **Note**   These examples are executed with a server that has the X Plugin installed
> and enabled. Chapter 2 demonstrates how to do this.

Although that is indeed nice, it is not so different than the old client. What makes the
shell really powerful is you can use a scripting language to process the data. Listing 1-4
shows how to launch the shell in Python mode (`--python`) and execute Python code to
retrieve the same result set. I also demonstrate a nice option that allows us to improve
the JSON output format (`--json=pretty`). Aha, so now we see that there is a nicer way
to see JSON in results! This option does tend to be rather verbose. I've suppressed some
of the more verbose output for clarity.

Listing 1-4.   Using the MySQL Shell with Python

```
$ mysqlsh -uroot --python --json=pretty
...
MySQL  localhost:33060+ ssl  Py > \use rolodex
MySQL  localhost:33060+ ssl  rolodex  Py > contacts = db.get_
collection("contacts")
MySQL  localhost:33060+ ssl  rolodex  Py > contacts.find()
{
    "documents": [
        {
            "_id": "9801A79DE093991311E7FFCB243C3451",
            "name": {
                "first": "Allen"
            },
            "phones": [
                {
                    "work": "212-555-1212"
                }
            ]
        },
        {
            "_id": "9801A79DE0939E0411E7FFCB243DCDE3",
            "address": {
```

```
            "city": "oxnard",
            "state": "ca",
            "street": "123 main",
            "zip": "90125"
        },
        "name": {
            "first": "Joe",
            "last": "Wheelerton"
        },
        "notes": "Excellent car detailer. Referrals get $20 off next
        detail!",
        "phones": [
            {
                "work": "212-555-1213"
            },
            {
                "home": "212-555-1253"
            }
        ]
    }
],
"executionTime": "0.00 sec",
"warningCount": 0,
"warnings": []
}
 MySQL  localhost:33060+ ssl  rolodex  Py > \exit
Bye!
```

Ok, now we're starting to see how much the shell changes our MySQL experience. Note that the output is formatted to make it read better and the commands we used were quite a bit different than the SQL commands previously. If you're thinking, that looks like application code, you're on the right track! We'll see more about the MySQL Shell in Chapter 4. Let's now discover what makes the shell powerful by examining the new X Plugin and X Protocol.

X Plugin, X Protocol, and X DevAPI

MySQL has introduced a new protocol and API to work with JSON documents. Along with supporting the JSON data type, we have three technologies prefixed with the simple name "X": the X Plugin, X Protocol, and X DevAPI. The X Plugin is a plugin that enables the X Protocol. The X Protocol is designed to communicate with the server using the X DevAPI. The X DevAPI is an application programming interface that (among other things) permits you to develop NoSQL solutions for MySQL and use MySQL as a document store.

I KNOW SQL, BUT WHAT IS NOSQL?

If you have worked with relational databases systems, you are no doubt very familiar with SQL (structured query language) in which we use special statements (commands) to interact with the data. In fact, most database systems have their own version of SQL that includes commands to manipulating the data (DML; data manipulation language) as well as defining the objects to store data (DDL; data definition language) and even administrative commands to manage the server.[5]

That is, you get result sets that have to use commands to search for the data then convert results into internal programming structures making the data seem like an auxiliary component rather than an integral part of the solution. NoSQL interfaces break this mold by allowing you to use APIs (application programming interfaces) to work with the data. More specific, you use programming interfaces rather than command based interfaces.

It is unfortunate that NoSQL can mean a number of things depending on your perspective including "non-SQL," "not only SQL," or "nonrelational." But they all refer to the fact that the mechanism you're using is not using a command based interface and most uses of the term indicate you're using a programming interface. For MySQL 8, access to JSON documents can be either through SQL or NoSQL using the X Protocol and X DevAPI through the X Plugin.

---

[5]Such as those in Oracle database: https://docs.oracle.com/cd/B14117_01/server.101/b10759/statements_1001.htm

The X Plugin is a great example of how Oracle makes use of the plugin technology to enable new features. In this case, the X Plugin is a gateway from within the server to allow communication using the X Protocol. The MySQL X Plugin comes with the server, and is enabled by default. If you have an older release of MySQL Server, you can use the MySQL Shell to enable the plugin with the following command.

```
$ mysqlsh -u root -h localhost --mysql --dba enableXProtocol
Creating a Classic session to 'root@localhost'
Enter password:
Your MySQL connection id is 527
Server version: 8.0.11 MySQL Community Server (GPL)
No default schema selected; type \use <schema> to set one.
enableXProtocol: X Protocol plugin is already enabled and listening for
connections on port 33060
```

Any client (not just the MySQL Shell) that supports the X Protocol can use the associated X DevAPI to use MySQL as a document store. In fact, the X Protocol is designed to expose the ACID (atomicity, consistency, isolation, and durability) compliant storage abilities of MySQL as a document store enabling you to execute Create, Read, Update, and Delete (CRUD) operations against JSON documents. The X Protocol also supports the normal SQL interface to MySQL so you can build your applications to use both SQL and NoSQL interfaces!

You may have wondered how the shell and the plugin interact with the server. Figure 1-2 demonstrates how the components are "stacked."

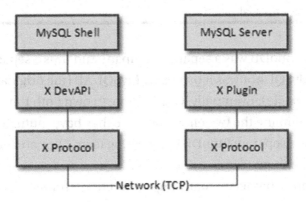

Figure 1-2. *X Protocol stack*

Note that the shell permits the use of the X DevAPI, which is communicated over the wire to the server via the X Plugin. Thus, the X Plugin is an enabling technology with the real power consisting of X Protocol and X DevAPI.

Now that we've seen the technologies that enable using MySQL as a document store, let's look at how the InnoDB storage engine has changed in recent releases.

InnoDB Improvements

Since MySQL 5.6, InnoDB has been the flagship storage engine (and the default engine) for MySQL. Oracle has slowly evolved away from the multiple storage engine model focusing on what a modern database server should do—support transactional storage mechanisms. InnoDB is the answer to that requirement and much more.

WHAT IS A STORAGE ENGINE?

A storage engine is a mechanism to store data in various ways. For example, there is a storage engine that allows you to interact with comma separated values (text) files (CSV), another that is optimized for writing log files (Archive), one that stores data in memory only (Memory), and even one that doesn't store anything at all (Blackhole). You can use them with your tables by using the ENGINE= table option. Along with InnoDB, the MySQL server ships with the Archive, Blackhole, CSV, Memory, MyISAM storage engines. The InnoDB storage engine is the only one that supports transactions. For more information about the other storage engines including the features of each and how they are used, see the "Alternative Storage Engines" section in the online MySQL reference manual.

In the early days, InnoDB was a separate company and thus a separate product that was neither part of MySQL nor was it owned by MySQL AB (the original owner of MySQL now fully owned by Oracle). Eventually, Oracle came to own both InnoDB and MySQL so it made sense to combine the two efforts because they have mutually inclusive goals. Although there still is a separate InnoDB engineering team, they are fully integrated with the core server development team.

This tight integration has led to many improvements in InnoDB including a host of performance enhancements. This is readily apparent in how InnoDB continues to evolve with those refinements.

The list of refinements has grown since the 5.6 releases and although most of the improvements are rather subtle in the sense you won't notice them (except through better performance and reliability, which are not to be taken lightly), most show a dedication to making InnoDB the best transactional storage mechanism and through extension MySQL a strong transactional database system. The following list a number of the more interesting improvements to InnoDB that you will find in MySQL 8. Some of these may seem to be very deep into the depths of the code, but those who have optimized or otherwise tuned their InnoDB installation may need to take note of these when planning to move to MySQL 8. What is not listed here are dozens of minor improvements in reliability and performance.

- *Crash recovery*: Should the index tree become corrupt, InnoDB writes a corruption flag to the redo log. This makes the corruption flag crash safe (it is not lost on a forced restart). Likewise, InnoDB also writes an in-memory corruption flag on each checkpoint. When crash recovery is initiated, InnoDB can read the flags and use them to adjust recovery operations.

- *InnoDB memcached Plugin*: Has been improved by permitting fetching of multiple (key, value) pairs in a single memcached query.

- *Deadlock detection*: There are several new options, but the most promising includes an option to dynamically configure deadlock detection (`innodb_deadlock_detect`). This could permit additional tuning control for high usage systems in which deadlock detection is a detriment to performance.

- *New INFORMATION_SCHEMA views*: There are new views for InnoDB, which includes the following:

  - `INNODB_CACHED_INDEXES` is used to discover the number of index pages cached in the InnoDB buffer pool for each index.

  - `INNODB_TABLESPACES_BRIEF` is used to see the space, name, path, flags, and space type for tablespaces.

- `AUTO_INCREMENT`: There are several minor improvements with auto-increment fields including the following:

  - The current maximum auto-increment value is now persistent across server restarts.

- A restart no longer cancels the effect of the AUTO_INCREMENT = N table option.

- A server restart immediately following a ROLLBACK operation no longer results in the reuse of auto-increment values that were allocated to the rolled-back transaction.

- Setting an AUTO_INCREMENT column value to a value larger than the current maximum is persisted and later new values (say after a restart) start with the new, larger value.

- *Temporary tables*: All temporary tables are now created in the shared temporary tablespace named ibtmp1.

Although this list seems focused on minor improvements, some of these are very important to system administrators looking for help tuning and planning their database server installations. If you would like to know more about any of these improvements or see a list of all the latest changes, see the online MySQL reference manual.[6]

I also should note that this list is likely to grow as MySQL 8 matures and new features are added. Indeed, the InnoDB Cluster is one such new feature that we discuss in the section "InnoDB Cluster."

The next section describes those features that have been added to and are unique to MySQL 8.

New Features

Aside from those features that have been in development during the 5.7 server releases, there are features that are unique to MySQL 8. That is to say, they are not currently (or even likely to be incorporated) in the older releases. Part of this is because of how much the server code base was changed to accommodate the new features. Those new features available in MySQL 8.0 include the new data dictionary and a new account management system.

Note   Some features are available as a separate download as a plugin that you can install and may be released separately with a different rating than the server. Some, such as Group Replication, can also be used with MySQL 5.7.

---

[6]http://downloads.mysql.com/docs/refman-8.0-en.pdf.

Data Dictionary

If you have ever worked with MySQL trying to get information about the objects contained in the databases; either to discover which objects are there, searching for objects with a specific name prefix, or trying to discover which indexes exist, chances are you have had to access the numerous tables in the mysql database or you've had to navigate the views in INFORMATION_SCHEMA.

Although this has been the default for many years, there are a number of problems with this mechanism. Most notable, there is no easy way to find things (you have to "learn" where things are and then how to search them). More important, because the data was in nontransactional tables (and metadata files), the mechanisms were not transactional and, by extension, not crash safe.

Indeed, many a MySQL DBA has earned their salary by recovering data in the mysql database, fixing corrupt or missing .frm files, and a host of other small plagues that can visit a large MySQL installation. Happily, those days are gone with the addition of the data dictionary!

WHAT'S AN FRM FILE?

If you examine the data directory of a MySQL installation for version 5.7 and earlier, you will see a folder named data that contains subfolders named for each database created. In these folders, you will see files named with the table names and a file extension of .frm. Many MySQL developers call these files "FRM files." The file is a specially formatted binary file that describes the table's format (definition). Thus, a table named table1 in database1 has an FRM file named /data/database1/table1.frm.

Sadly, because FRM files are binary files, they are not readable by normal means. In fact, the format has been a mystery for many years (it uses a layout called *Unireg*). Because the FRM files contain the metadata for the table, all the column definitions and table options, including index definitions, are stored in the file. This means it should be possible to extract the data needed to reconstruct the CREATE TABLE statement from a FRM file. Unfortunately, given the interface and uniqueness of Unireg, it is not easy to parse these files for the information.

Fortunately, you can decipher the FRM files via a Python utility that is part of the MySQL Utilities product. If you need to read an FRM file to recover a table, see the online MySQL Utilities documentation for more details: http://dev.mysql.com/doc/mysql-utilities/1.6/en/utils-task-get-structure.html.

What you may find curious and even a bit strange is the fact that the data dictionary implementation is hidden and very much behind the scenes. That is, data dictionary tables are invisible and cannot be accessed directly. You won't find the data dictionary tables easily (although it is possible if you look hard enough). This was done primarily to make the data dictionary crash safe and something you don't have to manage. Fortunately, you can access the information stored in the data dictionary via the INFORMATION_SCHEMA database and even the SHOW commands. The mysql database still exists, but it mainly contains extra information such as time zones, help, and similar nonvital information.

Tip   The data dictionary is one of the key factors that you must understand when planning any upgrades from older versions of MySQL. I examine a number of these issues in Chapter 10.

For more information about the data dictionary, see the section "MySQL Data Dictionary" in the online MySQL reference manual.

Adding the data dictionary has finally made possible a number of features that many have wanted to implement for some time. One of the newest is a change in account management.

Account Management

If you have ever managed a MySQL database server (or many servers), chances are you have encountered a situation where you need to assign the same privileges to a group of users. For example, your server may support several applications or databases with sets (groups) of users that have specific rights to database objects. In most cases, savvy database administrators (DBAs) make a copy of the user privileges (often in the form of GRANT statements) so that they can reuse them when they need to create another user with the same privileges.

Although the MySQL Utilities product has a Python utility to help manage this tedium (see "mysqluserclone" in http://dev.mysql.com/doc/mysql-utilities/1.6/en/), having to create dozens of different "types" of users can be quite a challenge. What is really needed is a way to create a role and tailor the privileges to the role then grant the role to users. Fortunately, with the advent of the data dictionary, supporting roles in MySQL has become a reality in MySQL 8!

Roles can be created, dropped, privileges granted or revoked. We also can grant or revoke roles to/from users. Roles finally make the tedium of managing user accounts on MySQL much easier. For more information about roles, see Using Roles in the online MySQL reference manual.

There also have been changes in the SSL (secure sockets layer) support in the server.

Removed Options, Variables, and Features

The first thing you may notice about MySQL 8 is a host of small changes to startup options, variables, and so forth. Fortunately, most of these are related to supporting the newest features and the removal of old and obsolete settings. Also, many of those options, variables, and features marked as deprecated in MySQL 5.7 (and prior) are officially removed in MySQL 8. Some of the more familiar items removed in MySQL 8 include the following.

- `--bootstrap`: was used to control how the server started and was typically used to create the MySQL privilege tables without having to start a full MySQL server.

- `--innodb_file_format_*`: was used to configure the file format for the InnoDB storage engine.

- `--partition` and `--skip partition`: was used to control user-defined partitioning support in the MySQL server.

One of the consequences of the new data dictionary is removal of the need for `.frm` files (FRM). Because the data dictionary contains all of the information about every object in all of the databases hosted in a reliable, recoverable storage mechanism, there is no longer a need to store such information in a separate file. Those of us who have often fought with or otherwise had the unique frustration to attempt to repair a server whose FRM files were lost or corrupt, the removal of the FRM files is a long overdue and most welcome omission.

For those using SSL, one area that may be of concern is the removal of some of the SSL options and the introduction of a new authentication plugin (`caching_sha2_password`) to improve secure connections. The new authentication plugin was introduced in release 8.0.4. Most installation packages give you the option to choose the older authentication method should you require it, but it is strongly recommended that you use the new authentication plugin.

Error codes are another area where you will see some changes. Many error codes were changed in the latest release including the removal of dozens of lesser known (used) error codes. If your applications use the MySQL server error codes, you should check the documentation to ensure the error codes have not changed or been removed.

There were also many minor items removed including the mysql_plugin utility,[7] the embedded server (`libmysqld`), the generic partition engine (InnoDB now has native partitioning), the `mysql_install_db` script (this has been replaced with the `--initialize` option), and more.

As I mentioned in the previous sections, the list of features that were removed in MySQL 8 will likely grow as more features become mature and are added. If you have defined tuning procedures, stored procedures, DevOps,[8] or other mechanisms that use or interact with options and variables, you should carefully examine the entry in the MySQL 8 documentation to ensure you can modify your tools.

Tip   See `http://dev.mysql.com/doc/refman/8.0/en/added-removed-variables-options.html` for a complete list of features to be removed in MySQL 8.

Paradigm Shifting Features

When the MySQL engineers and product management teams decided to develop ground breaking high availability features and a new way to store unstructured data, they knew they were on to something that would change the MySQL world in dramatic fashion.

In this section, we look at two high availability features that are poised to change MySQL high availability in a new and dramatic way. We will also see how the new structured storage mechanism will change what you can store and indeed how you can interact with MySQL to store data for applications where data can change allowing your application to adapt without having to rebuild the storage layers.

Let's begin with the high availability solutions.

---

[7]I was the original designer and implementer of this utility. Improvements in plugin handling in the server have made the utility unnecessary.

[8]`https://en.wikipedia.org/wiki/DevOps`

Group Replication

If you have used MySQL replication, you are no doubt very familiar with how to leverage it when building high availability solutions. Indeed, it is likely you have discovered a host of ways to improve availability in your applications with MySQL replication.

WHAT IS REPLICATION? AND HOW DOES IT WORK?

MySQL replication is an easy-to-use feature and yet a complex and major component of the MySQL server. This section presents a bird's-eye view of replication for the purpose of explaining how it works and how to set up a simple replication topology. For more information about replication and its many features and commands, see the online MySQL reference manual (http://dev.mysql.com/doc/refman/8.0/en/replication.html).

Replication requires two or more servers. One server must be designated as the origin or master. The master role means all data changes (writes) to the data are sent to the master and only the master. All other servers in the topology maintain a copy of the master data and are by design and requirement read-only servers. Thus, when your sensors send data for storage, they send it to the master. Applications you write to use the sensor data can read it from the slaves.

The copy mechanism works using a technology called the binary log that stores the changes in a special format, thereby keeping a record of all the changes. These changes are then shipped to the slaves and executed there. Thus, once the slave executes the changes (called *events*), the slave has an exact copy of the data.

The master maintains a binary log of the changes, and the slave maintains a copy of that binary log called the *relay log*. When a slave requests data changes from the master, it reads the events from the master and writes them to its relay log; then another thread in the slave executes those events from the relay log. As you can imagine, there is a slight delay from the time a change is made on the master to the time it is made on the slave. Fortunately, this delay is almost unnoticeable except in topologies with high traffic (lots of changes).

Moreover, it has become apparent that the more your high availability needs and your solution expands (grows in sophistication), the more you need to employ better ways to manage the loss of nodes, data integrity, and general maintenance of the clusters (groups of servers replicating data—sometimes called *replicasets*). In fact, most high availability solutions have outgrown the base master and slaves topology evolving into tiers consisting of clusters of servers. Some have replicated a portion of the data for faster throughput and for compartmental storage. All of these have led many to discover they need more from MySQL replication. Oracle has answered these needs and more with Group Replication.

Group Replication was released as GA in December 2016 and is bundled with the server in the form of a plugin. Although it is a GA release, I list it here as a paradigm-shifting feature because of the promise it provides for allowing MySQL high availability to grow well beyond the confines of the original MySQL replication feature and thus empower MySQL 8 to become an important component in high availability database solutions.

Note   I touch on only the very basics of Group Replication to give you an idea of its complexity and benefits. A deeper dive into using Group Replication and its implementation is beyond the scope of this book.

Group Replication makes the topology eventually synchronous replication (among the nodes belonging to the same group) a reality, whereas the existing MySQL Replication feature is asynchronous (or at most semi-synchronous). Therefore, better high availability guaranties can be provided, because transactions are delivered to all members in the same order (despite being applied at its own pace in each member after being accepted).

Group Replication does this via a distributed state machine with strong coordination among the servers assigned to a group. This communication allows the servers to coordinate replication automatically within the group. More specific, groups maintain membership so that the data replication among the servers is always consistent at any point in time. Even if servers are removed from the group, when they are added, the consistency is initiated automatically. Further, there is also a failure detection mechanism for servers that go offline or become unreachable. Figure 1-3 shows how you would use Group Replication with our applications to achieve high availability.

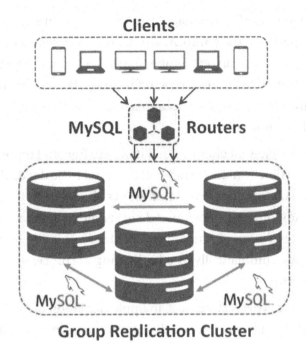

Group Replication Cluster

Figure 1-3. *Using Group Replication with applications for high availability (Courtesy of Oracle)*

Note that Group Replication can be used with the MySQL Router to allow your applications to have a layer of isolation from the cluster. We will see a bit about the router when we examine the InnoDB Cluster.

Another important distinction between Group Replication and standard replication is that all of the servers in the group can participate in updating the data with conflicts resolved automatically. Yes, you no longer have to carefully craft your application to send writes (updates) to a specific server! However, you can configure Group Replication to allow updates by only one server (called the *primary*) with the other servers acting as secondary servers or as a backup (for failover).

All of these capabilities and more are made possible using three specific technologies built into Group Replication: group membership, failure detection, and fault tolerance.[9]

---

[9]Failure detection and fault tolerance are required for successful high availability solutions.

- *Group membership*: This manages whether servers are active (online) and participating in the group. Also, ensures every server in the group has a consistent view of the membership set. That is, every server knows the complete list of servers in the group. When servers are added to the group, the group membership service reconfigures the membership automatically.

- *Failure detection*: A mechanism that is able to find and report which servers are offline (unreachable) and assumed to be dead. The failure detector is a distributed service that allows all servers in the group to test the condition of the presumed dead server and in that way, the group decides if a server is unreachable (dead). This allows the group to reconfigure automatically by coordinating the process of excluding the failed server.

- *Fault tolerance*: This service uses an implementation of the Paxos[10] distributed algorithm to provide distributed coordination among the servers. In short, the algorithm allows for automatic promotion of roles within the group to ensure the group remains consistent (data is consistent and available) even if a server (or several) fail or leave the group. As with similar fault tolerance mechanisms, the number of failures (servers that fail) is limited. Currently, Group Replication fault tolerance is defined as $n = 2f + 1$, where n is the number of servers needed to tolerate f failures. For example, if you want to tolerate up to 5 servers failing, you need at least 11 servers in the group.

Although Group Replication is a plugin, it is bundled with the server installation today with MySQL 5.7 (starting with the 5.7.17 release) as well as MySQL 8.[11]

---

[10]See https://en.wikipedia.org/wiki/Paxos_(computer_science).

[11]See http://www.mysql.com/downloads/ for more information about downloading the server. For more information about Group Replication, see the "Group Replication" section in the online MySQL reference manual at http://dev.mysql.com/doc or visit http://dev.mysql.com/doc/refman/8.0/en/group-replication.html.

Tip   To learn more about the internal mechanisms, designs, implementation as well as how to setup and use Group Replication, see the developer documentation at `http://mysqlhighavailability.com/mysqlha/gr/doc/index.html`.

Rather than demonstrate Group Replication by itself, we will see just how powerful this feature is when we explore another new feature named InnoDB Cluster in the following section. As you will see in the demonstration of InnoDB Cluster, Group Replication is easy to use and when part of InnoDB Cluster, both technologies change the way we use MySQL replication in a most dramatic way.

InnoDB Cluster

Another new and emerging feature is called InnoDB Cluster. It is designed to make high availability easier to setup, use, and maintain. InnoDB Cluster works with the X AdminAPI via the MySQL Shell and the Admin API, Group Replication, and the MySQL Router[12] to take high availability and read scalability to a new level. That is, it combines new features in InnoDB for cloning data with Group Replication and the MySQL Shell and MySQL Router to provide a new way to setup and manage high availability.

Note   The AdminAPI is a special API available via the MySQL Shell for configuring and interacting with InnoDB Cluster. Therefore, the Admin API has features designed to make working with InnoDB Cluster easier.

In this use case, the cluster is setup with a single primary (think master in standard replication parlance), which is the target for all write (updates). Multiple secondary servers (slaves) maintain replicas of the data, which can be read from and thus enable reading data without burdening the primary thus enabling read out scalability (but all servers participate in consensus and coordination). The incorporation of Group Replication means the cluster is fault tolerant and group membership is managed automatically. The MySQL router caches the metadata of the InnoDB Cluster and performs high availability routing to the MySQL server instances making it easier to write applications to interact with the cluster.

---

[12]`http://dev.mysql.com/doc/mysql-router/en/`

You may wonder what makes this different from a readout scalability setup with standard replication. At a high level, it may seem that the solutions are solving the same use case. However, with InnoDB Cluster, you can create, deploy, and configure servers in your cluster from the MySQL Shell providing a complete high availability solution that can be managed easily. That is, you can use the InnoDB Cluster AdminAPI via the shell to create and administer an InnoDB Cluster programmatically using either JavaScript or Python.

Let us now see these new technologies in action. What follows is a demonstration of deploying three servers, configuring them as a cluster via Group Replication using JavaScript commands in the new MySQL Shell. Although that sounds like a lot of effort, it really isn't and in fact is really easy.

Note   The following commands were run using InnoDB Cluster on a system with MySQL 8.0.11, InnoDB Cluster, and MySQL Router installed.

Let's begin by starting the shell and deploying three servers using the AdminAPI. In this case, we will use the deploySandboxInstance() method in the dba object to create new instances for each server. All of these will run on our localhost. Listing 1-5 demonstrates how to deploy three servers. I highlight the commands used to help identify the commands from the messages.

Listing 1-5. Creating Local Server Instances

```
$ mysqlsh
MySQL Shell 8.0.11

Copyright (c) 2016, 2018, Oracle and/or its affiliates. All rights
reserved.

Oracle is a registered trademark of Oracle Corporation and/or its
affiliates. Other names may be trademarks of their respective
owners.

Type '\help' or '\?' for help; '\quit' to exit.

 MySQL   JS > dba.deploySandboxInstance(3307)
A new MySQL sandbox instance will be created on this host in
/Users/cbell/mysql-sandboxes/3307
```

```
Please enter a MySQL root password for the new instance:
Deploying new MySQL instance...

Instance localhost:3307 successfully deployed and started.
Use shell.connect('root@localhost:3307'); to connect to the instance.

 MySQL   JS > dba.deploySandboxInstance(3308)
A new MySQL sandbox instance will be created on this host in
/Users/cbell/mysql-sandboxes/3308

Please enter a MySQL root password for the new instance:
Deploying new MySQL instance...

Instance localhost:3308 successfully deployed and started.
Use shell.connect('root@localhost:3308'); to connect to the instance.

 MySQL   JS > dba.deploySandboxInstance(3309)
A new MySQL sandbox instance will be created on this host in
/Users/cbell/mysql-sandboxes/3309

Please enter a MySQL root password for the new instance:
Deploying new MySQL instance...

Instance localhost:3309 successfully deployed and started.
Use shell.connect('root@localhost:3309'); to connect to the instance.

 MySQL   JS >
```

Note that the text explains that we are using a *sandbox*, which is a term applied to running servers on the localhost in a special directory: the mysql-sandboxes folder in the user home. In particular in this case, we use /Users/cbell/mysql-sandboxes. Note that we now have three servers running on ports 3307, 3308, and 3309. Note also that the shell will prompt you for the new password.

Tip   JavaScript is case sensitive so make sure you use the correct spelling for variables, objects, and methods. That is, a variable named abc is not the same variable named Abc.

The next thing we need to do is setup a new cluster. We do this with the createCluster() method in the dba object. But first, we must connect to the server we want to make our primary server. Listing 1-6 demonstrates how to create the cluster. Note that this is a continuation of our shell session and demonstrates how to create a new cluster.

Listing 1-6. Creating a Cluster in InnoDB Cluster

```
MySQL   JS > \connect root@localhost:3307
Creating a session to 'root@localhost:3307'
Enter password:
Your MySQL connection id is 12
Server version: 8.0.11 MySQL Community Server (GPL)
No default schema selected; type \use <schema> to set one.
 MySQL  localhost:3307 ssl  JS > my_cluster = dba.createCluster('my_cluster')
A new InnoDB cluster will be created on instance 'root@localhost:3307'.

Creating InnoDB cluster 'my_cluster' on 'root@localhost:3307'...
Adding Seed Instance...

Cluster successfully created. Use Cluster.addInstance() to add MySQL
instances.
At least 3 instances are needed for the cluster to be able to withstand up to
one server failure.

<Cluster:my_cluster>
```

Note that we named the cluster my_cluster and used a variable of the same name to store the object returned from the createCluster() method. Note that the first server we connected has become the primary (master).

Next, we add the other two server instances to complete the cluster using the addInstance() of our new my_cluster object. These servers automatically become secondary servers (slaves) in the group. Listing 1-7 shows how to add the instances to the cluster.

Listing 1-7. Adding Instances to the Cluster

```
MySQL  localhost:3307 ssl  JS > my_cluster = dba.getCluster('my_cluster')
<Cluster:my_cluster>
MySQL  localhost:3307 ssl  JS > my_cluster.addInstance('root@
localhost:3308')
A new instance will be added to the InnoDB cluster. Depending on the amount
of data on the cluster this might take from a few seconds to several hours.

Please provide the password for 'root@localhost:3308':
Adding instance to the cluster ...

The instance 'root@localhost:3308' was successfully added to the cluster.

 MySQL  localhost:3307 ssl  JS > my_cluster.addInstance('root@
localhost:3309')
A new instance will be added to the InnoDB cluster. Depending on the amount
of data on the cluster this might take from a few seconds to several hours.

Please provide the password for 'root@localhost:3309':
Adding instance to the cluster ...

The instance 'root@localhost:3309' was successfully added to the cluster.
```

Once the cluster is created and the instances are added, we can get the status of the cluster using the status() method of our my_cluster object as shown in Listing 1-8.

Listing 1-8. Getting the Status of the Cluster

```
MySQL  localhost:3307 ssl  JS > my_cluster.status()
{
    "clusterName": "my_cluster",
    "defaultReplicaSet": {
        "name": "default",
        "primary": "localhost:3307",
        "ssl": "REQUIRED",
        "status": "OK",
        "statusText": "Cluster is ONLINE and can tolerate up to ONE failure.",
```

```
        "topology": {
            "localhost:3307": {
                "address": "localhost:3307",
                "mode": "R/W",
                "readReplicas": {},
                "role": "HA",
                "status": "ONLINE"
            },
            "localhost:3308": {
                "address": "localhost:3308",
                "mode": "R/O",
                "readReplicas": {},
                "role": "HA",
                "status": "ONLINE"
            },
            "localhost:3309": {
                "address": "localhost:3309",
                "mode": "R/O",
                "readReplicas": {},
                "role": "HA",
                "status": "ONLINE"
            }
        }
    }
}
 MySQL  localhost:3307 ssl  JS > \exit
Bye!
```

At this point, we've seen how InnoDB Cluster can setup servers and add them to the group. What you do not see behind the scenes is all of the Group Replication mechanisms—you get them for free! How cool is that?

Now that we have a cluster, there is one more thing we need to do to enable applications to use the fault tolerance features of Group Replication. That is, we need to be able to connect to the cluster and interact with MySQL even if one of the servers fails. Note that because we only have three servers, we can only tolerate one failure. For example, solving for f in the number of faults tolerated by Group Replication, we get $3 = 2f + 1$ or $f = 1$.

We must now use MySQL Router to manage the connections for our application. Although we don't have an application to demonstrate, we can see this in action using the shell. Now let's see how easy it is to set up the router. Listing 1-9 shows how to start the router in bootstrap mode. Note that by connecting to the cluster, the router automatically gets the members of the group. Recall from the previous section, this is one of the tenets of Group Replication via the membership service.

Listing 1-9. Setting Up the MySQL Router

```
& mysqlrouter --bootstrap localhost:3307 --user=cbell
Please enter MySQL password for root:

Bootstrapping system MySQL Router instance...
MySQL Router  has now been configured for the InnoDB cluster 'my_cluster'.

The following connection information can be used to connect to the cluster.

Classic MySQL protocol connections to cluster 'my_cluster':
- Read/Write Connections: localhost:6446
- Read/Only Connections: localhost:6447
X protocol connections to cluster 'my_cluster':
- Read/Write Connections: localhost:64460
- Read/Only Connections: localhost:64470
& mysqlrouter &
```

Okay, now we have the router running. Our applications can use the features of the router to automatically reroute our application connections should something happen to one of the servers in the cluster.

Let's see a short demonstration of this feature. In this case, we will use the shell to connect to the cluster via the router on port 6446 as shown in Listing 1-9. We use this port because the router is used to forward connections automatically. That is, if the server we're connected to goes down—for instance the one on port 3307—we do not have to restart our application to reconnect to a server on another port. Thus, the router, routes the communications for us. Let's see this in action.

Listing 1-10 demonstrates connecting to the cluster via the router. We switch to SQL mode in the shell and use an SQL command to see the port of the server where we're connected. We then switch back to JavaScript and use the AdminAPI to kill the instance. We then attempt to issue the SQL command again and now notice that, once the shell has automatically reconnected, we are now connected to another server. Cool!

Listing 1-10. Fault Tolerance Demonstration

```
$ mysqlsh --uri root@localhost:6446 --sql
Creating a session to 'root@localhost:6446'
Enter password:
Your MySQL connection id is 47
Server version: 8.0.11 MySQL Community Server (GPL)
No default schema selected; type \use <schema> to set one.
MySQL Shell 8.0.11

Copyright (c) 2016, 2018, Oracle and/or its affiliates. All rights
reserved.

Oracle is a registered trademark of Oracle Corporation and/or its
affiliates. Other names may be trademarks of their respective
owners.

Type '\help' or '\?' for help; '\quit' to exit.

 MySQL  localhost:6446 ssl  SQL > SELECT @@port;
+--------+
| @@port |
+--------+
|   3307 |
+--------+
1 row in set (0.00 sec)
 MySQL  localhost:6446 ssl  SQL > \js
Switching to JavaScript mode...
 MySQL  localhost:6446 ssl  JS > dba.killSandboxInstance(3307)
The MySQL sandbox instance on this host in
/Users/cbell/mysql-sandboxes/3307 will be killed

Killing MySQL instance...

Instance localhost:3307 successfully killed.

 MySQL  localhost:6446 ssl  JS > \sql
Switching to SQL mode... Commands end with ;
 MySQL  localhost:6446 ssl  SQL > SELECT @@port;
```

```
ERROR: 2006 (HY000): MySQL server has gone away
The global session got disconnected.
Attempting to reconnect to 'root@localhost:6446'..
The global session was successfully reconnected.
 MySQL  localhost:6446 ssl  SQL > SELECT @@port;
+--------+
| @@port |
+--------+
|   3308 |
+--------+
1 row in set (0.00 sec)
 MySQL  localhost:6446 ssl  SQL > \quit
Bye!
```

Note that although the shell had lost the connection it automatically reconnected so that we can retry the command. Very nice.

Finally, let's discover how to put the instance that failed back into service. In this case, we simulate recovering a downed server adding it back to the cluster where Group Replication ensures that the new server becomes consistent by applying any missing transactions. Listing 1-11 shows the commands you can use to recover the server.

Listing 1-11. Recovering a Lost Server

```
$ mysqlsh --uri root@localhost:6446
 MySQL  localhost:6446 ssl  JS > dba.startSandboxInstance(3307)
The MySQL sandbox instance on this host in
/Users/cbell/mysql-sandboxes/3307 will be started

Starting MySQL instance...

Instance localhost:3307 successfully started.

 MySQL  localhost:6446 ssl  JS > my_cluster = dba.getCluster('my_cluster')
<Cluster:my_cluster>
MySQL  localhost:6446 ssl  JS > my_cluster.rejoinInstance('root
@localhost:3307')
Rejoining the instance to the InnoDB cluster. Depending on the original
problem that made the instance unavailable, the rejoin operation might not be
```

successful and further manual steps will be needed to fix the underlying problem.

Please monitor the output of the rejoin operation and take necessary action if the instance cannot rejoin.

```
Please provide the password for 'root@localhost:3307':
Rejoining instance to the cluster ...
```

```
The instance 'root@localhost:3307' was successfully rejoined on the
cluster.
```

```
The instance 'localhost:3307' was successfully added to the MySQL Cluster.
 MySQL  localhost:6446 ssl  JS > \q
Bye!
```

It is clear that using the shell to setup and manage a cluster is a lot easier than setting up and managing a standard Group Replication setup. In particular, you don't have to manually configure replication! Better still, should a server fail, you don't have to worry about reconfiguring your application or the topology to ensure the solution remains viable—InnoDB Cluster does this automatically for you.

To learn more about InnoDB Cluster, see the online documentation at https://dev.mysql.com/doc/mysql-innodb-cluster/en/.

Summary

MySQL has come a long way since the days when developers downloaded the code, modified it, and put it into use on their rapidly developed platforms. As one who has watched and participated in its evolution, it is with some pride that I look back on the bad old days and see just how far MySQL has come.

The journey hasn't been easy. The engineering team alone has weathered two acquisitions (Sun Microsystems and Oracle) in rapid succession and a host of smaller team development and minor personnel changes. Through all of this, the engineering team continued to improve features and add new technologies remaining dedicated to making MySQL the best possible solution.

Users also have grown in how they use MySQL from stand alone, single database server installations to massive high availability server farms. Through all of this, the MySQL product has remained poised for something greater. Now, with MySQL 8.0, Oracle has shown its hand and it's loaded with top-notch technologies. Indeed, the MySQL world is poised to discover new ways to leverage MySQL in a yet unknown variety of methods. I am certain by the time you read this book you will have your own ideas of how to revamp your use of MySQL.

In this chapter, we explored some of the highlights of the new MySQL server version 8.0. We discovered those features originally introduced in earlier versions that have been adapted to the new paradigm that is version 8.0, features that are new, and those new features that are truly revolutionary such as the document store, Group Replication, and InnoDB Cluster.

In Chapter 2, I take a short detour into a brief primer on installing and using MySQL. If you have not used MySQL before or any form of a relational database system, Chapter 2 will prepare you for how MySQL works in the more traditional manner via SQL commands. If you have been using older versions of MySQL, you may still want to skim the chapter to learn how to install and configure MySQL 8 for use with the document store. I discuss more about the MySQL Shell in Chapter 4 and upgrading to MySQL 8 in Chapter 10.

Getting Started with MySQL

Perhaps you've never used a database system before or maybe you've used one as a user but have never had any need to set up one from scratch. Or perhaps you've decided to discover what all the fuss is about database systems in general. Or maybe you've used MySQL only as a developer never seeing how to setup and configure the server.

In this chapter, I present a short introduction to MySQL in the general SQL interface sense (traditional MySQL). Not only will you see how MySQL 8 is setup, you will also be introduced to some of the basics of the SQL interface, which is necessary and indeed required to fully manage a MySQL server. That is, the new shell, X protocol, X DevAPI, and the features that build on it but do not offer a complete mechanism for managing the server; you will need to continue to use SQL commands for those tasks.

So, although MySQL 8 offers an excellent NoSQL interface for both applications and interactive sessions, you still need to know to use the SQL interface. Fortunately, I present the basics in a short primer on how to use MySQL. Let's begin with a brief foray into what MySQL is and what it can do for us.

Getting to Know MySQL

MySQL is the world's most popular open source database system for many excellent reasons. First, it is open source, which means anyone can use it for a wide variety of tasks for free. Best of all, MySQL is included in many platform repositories this makes it easy to get and install. If your platform doesn't include MySQL in the repository (such as aptitude), you can download it from the MySQL web site (`http://dev.mysql.com`).

© Charles Bell 2018
C. Bell, *Introducing the MySQL 8 Document Store*, https://doi.org/10.1007/978-1-4842-2725-1_2

The Oracle Corporation owns MySQL. Oracle obtained MySQL through an acquisition of Sun Microsystems, which acquired MySQL from its original owners, MySQL AB. Despite fears to the contrary, Oracle has shown excellent stewardship of MySQL by continuing to invest in the evolution and development of new features as well as faithfully maintaining its open source heritage. Although Oracle also offers commercial licenses of MySQL—just as its prior owners did in the past—MySQL is still open source and available to everyone.

IS OPEN SOURCE REALLY FREE?

Open source software grew from a conscious resistance to the corporate property mind-set. Richard Stallman is credited as the father of the free software movement who pioneered a licensing mechanism to help protect ownership of software and yet make the use of the software and to some degree its revision free to all. The goal was to reestablish a community of developers cooperating with a single imperative: to guarantee freedom rather than restrict it.

This ultimately led to the invention of some cleverly worded (read legally binding) licensing agreements that permits the code to be copied and modified without restriction, states that derivative works (the modified copies) must be distributed under the same license as the original version without any additional restrictions. One such license (created by Stallman) is called the GNU Public License (GPL). This is the license that is used by Oracle to license MySQL and as such it is indeed free for anyone to use.

However, GPL and similar licenses are intended to guarantee freedom to use, modify, and distribute; most never intended "free" to mean "no cost" or "free to a good home." To counter this misconception, the Open Source Initiative (OSI) formed and later adopted and promoted the phrase open source to describe the freedoms guaranteed by the GPL license. For more information about open source software and the GPL, visit www.opensource.org.

MySQL runs as a background process (or as a foreground process if you launch it from the command line) on your system. As with most database systems, MySQL supports structured query language (SQL). You can use SQL to create databases and objects (using data definition language; DDL), write or change data (using data manipulation language; DML), and execute various commands for managing the server.

How Do I Connect to MySQL?

We have already seen a brief look at the new MySQL Shell for connecting to and working with MySQL servers, the AdminAPI to configure an InnoDB Cluster, and the X DevAPI to access with data. However, there is another client that has been around in MySQL for decades. It is an application named mysql, which enables you to connect to and run SQL commands on the server. It is interesting that this MySQL client was originally named the MySQL monitor but has long since been called simply the "MySQL client," terminal monitor, or even the MySQL command window.

NEW DEFAULT AUTHENTICATION

Prior to MySQL version 8.0.4, the default authentication mechanism used an authentication plugin called the mysql_native_password plugin, which used the SHA1 algorithm. This mechanism was fast and did not require an encrypted connection. However, since the National Institute of Standards and Technology (NIST) suggested that they should stop using the SHA1 algorithm; Oracle has changed the default authentication plugin in MySQL version 8.0.4 to the cachin_sha2_password plugin.

The consequences of this change should not be an issue to any organizations that install MySQL 8.0.4 but may be a concern for those upgrading to 8.0.4 or those who have older installations of MySQL. The biggest issue is that the older client utilities, such as the mysql client from version 5.7, may not be able to connect to newer installations of MySQL 8.0.4 or later.

Although you can change your MySQL 8.0.4 to use the older authentication mechanism, it is not recommended and you should upgrade all your client tools to 8.0.4 or later to work with the latest versions of MySQL.

If you would like to learn more about the changes including why Oracle made the change and the advantages for users, see https://mysqlserverteam.com/mysql-8-0-4-new-default-authentication-plugin-caching_sha2_password/.

To connect to the server using the MySQL client (mysql), you must specify a user account and the server to which you want to connect. If you are connecting to a server on the same machine, you can omit the server information (host and port) because they default to localhost on port 3306. The user is specified using the --user (or -u) option.

You can specify the password for the user on the command, but the more secure practice is to specify --password (or -p), and the client will prompt you for the password. If you do specify the password on the command line, you will be prompted with a warning encouraging you to not use that practice.

Using the mysql client on the same machine without the --host (or -h) and --port option does not use a network connection. If you want to connect using a network connection or want to connect using a different port, you must use the loopback address. For example, to connect to a server running on port 3307 on the same machine, use the command mysql -uroot -p –h127.0.0.1 --port=3307. Listing 2-1 shows examples of several SQL commands in action using the mysql client.

Tip   To see a list of the commands available in the client, type help; and press Enter at the prompt.

Listing 2-1. Commands Using the mysql Client

```
$ mysql -uroot -proot -h 127.0.0.1 --port=3307
mysql: [Warning] Using a password on the command line interface can be
insecure.
Welcome to the MySQL monitor.  Commands end with ; or \g.
Your MySQL connection id is 14
Server version: 8.0.11 MySQL Community Server (GPL)

Copyright (c) 2000, 2018, Oracle and/or its affiliates. All rights reserved.

Oracle is a registered trademark of Oracle Corporation and/or its
affiliates. Other names may be trademarks of their respective
owners.

Type 'help;' or '\h' for help. Type '\c' to clear the current input statement.

mysql> CREATE DATABASE greenhouse;
Query OK, 1 row affected (0.00 sec)

mysql> CREATE TABLE greenhouse.plants (plant_name char(50), sensor_value
int, sensor_event timestamp);
Query OK, 0 rows affected (0.01 sec)
```

```
mysql> INSERT INTO greenhouse.plants VALUES ('living room', 23, NULL);
Query OK, 1 row affected (0.01 sec)

mysql> SELECT * FROM greenhouse.plants;
+-------------+--------------+--------------+
| plant_name  | sensor_value | sensor_event |
+-------------+--------------+--------------+
| living room |           23 | NULL         |
+-------------+--------------+--------------+
1 row in set (0.00 sec)

mysql> SET @@global.server_id = 106;
Query OK, 0 rows affected (0.00 sec)

mysql> quit
Bye
```

In this example, you see DDL in the form of the CREATE DATABASE and CREATE TABLE statements, DML in the form of the INSERT and SELECT statements, and a simple administrative command to set a global server variable. Next you see the creation of a database and a table to store the data, the addition of a row in the table, and finally the retrieval of the data in the table. Notice how I used capital letters for SQL command keywords. This is a common practice and helps make the SQL commands easier to read and easier to find user-supplied options or data.

Tip   You can exit the MySQL client by typing the command quit. On Linux and Unix systems, you can press Ctrl+D to exit the client.

A great many commands are available in MySQL. Fortunately, you need master only a few of the more common ones. The following are the commands you will use most often. The portions enclosed in <> indicate user-supplied components of the command, and [...] indicates that additional options are needed.

- CREATE DATABASE <database_name>: creates a database
- USE <database>: sets the default database (not an SQL command)

- `CREATE TABLE <table_name> [...]`: creates a table or structure to store data

- `INSERT INTO <table_name> [...]`: adds data to a table

- `UPDATE [...]`: changes one or more values for a specific row

- `DELETE FROM <table_name> [...]`: removes data from a table

- `SELECT [...]`: retrieves data (rows) from the table

- `SHOW [...]`: shows a list of the objects

Note   You must terminate each command with a semicolon (;) or \G.

Although this list is only a short introduction and not a complete syntax guide, there is an excellent online MySQL reference manual that explains every command (and much more) in greater detail. You should refer to the online MySQL reference manual whenever you have a question about anything in MySQL. You can find it at `http://dev.mysql.com/doc/`.

One of the more interesting commands shown allows you to see a list of objects. For example, you can see the databases with `SHOW DATABASES`, a list of tables (once you change to a database) with `SHOW TABLES`, and even the permissions for users with `SHOW GRANTS`. I find myself using these commands frequently.

If you think that there is a lot more to MySQL than a few simple commands, you are correct. Despite its ease of use and fast start-up time, MySQL is a full-fledged relational database management system (RDBMS). There is much more to it than you've seen here. For more information about MySQL, including all the advanced features, see the online MySQL reference manual.

How to Get and Install MySQL

The MySQL server is available for a variety of platforms including most Linux and Unix platforms, Mac OS X, and Windows. As of this writing, MySQL 8 was not a GA release and as such only offered as a development milestone release (DMR). DMRs are an excellent way for you to try out new versions and features before they are released as GA. Generally, non-GA releases are considered developmental or in the case of early release candidates such as MySQL 8.0.4, a release candidate. Thus, you should not install and use DMR releases on your production machines.

To download GA releases of MySQL 8, visit `http://dev.mysql.com/downloads/` and click *Community*, then *MySQL Community*. You can also click on the link near the bottom of the downloads page named *Community (GPL) Downloads*, then click *MySQL Community Server*. This is the GPLv2 license of MySQL. The page will automatically detect your operating system. If you want to download for another platform, you can select it from the dropdown list.

The download page will list several files for download. Depending on your platform, you may see several options including compressed files, source code, and installation packages. Most will choose the installation package for installation on a laptop or desktop computer. Figure 2-1 shows an example of the various download options for macOS platforms.

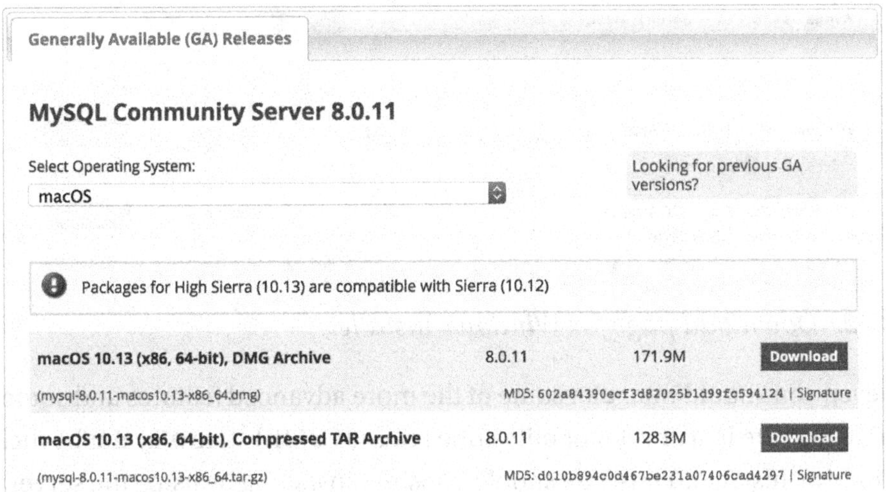

Figure 2-1. Download page for macOS

One of the most popular platforms is Microsoft Windows. Oracle has provided a special installation packaging for Windows named the Windows Installer. This package includes all the MySQL products available under the community license including MySQL Server, Workbench, Utilities, and all of the available connectors (program libraries for connecting to MySQL). This makes installing on Windows a one-stop, one-installation affair. Figure 2-2 shows the download page for the Windows installer.

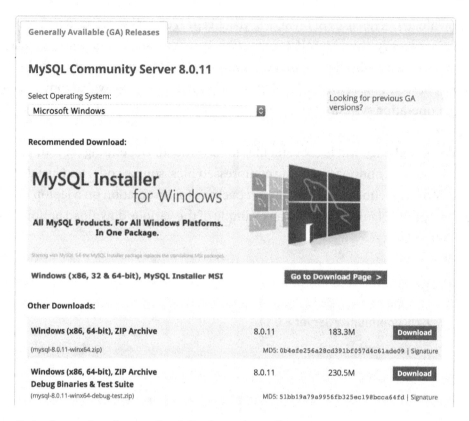

Figure 2-2. Download page for Windows Installer

However, you should note that some of the more advanced features and some of the plugins that also are in a developer milestone release (DMR) state may not be included in the Windows Installer. Thus, you should consider installing by using the server package. We see these below the Windows Installer download link in Figure 2-2. You can choose either the Windows Installer 32- or 64-bit installation. Note that the package may be nothing more than a .zip file containing the server code. In this case, you may need to either run the server from the unzipped folder or do a local, manual install.

Fortunately, as MySQL 8 matures, more packaging options will become available allowing you to use a semi-automated installation mechanism. Let's see one of those in action. In this scenario, we will install MySQL 8 on a macOS Sierra machine. In this case, I have downloaded the file mysql-8.0.11-macos10.13-x86_64.dmg, which is a compressed file containing a package installation program named mysql-8.0.11-macos10.13-x86_64.pkg for macOS. Once I launch the installer, the first step is agreeing to the license. Figure 2-3 shows the license agreement panel of the installation dialog.

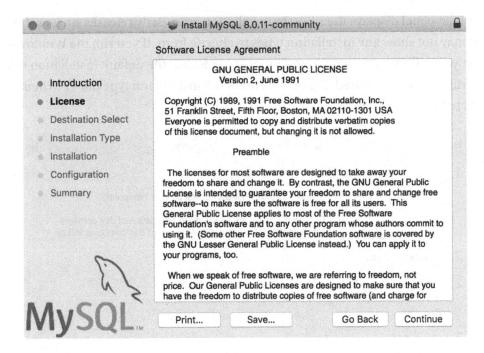

Figure 2-3. *License agreement*

The license shown is the GPLv2 license for the community edition. You can read the license and when ready, click *Continue*. You will see an acceptance dialog open, which will give you another chance to read the license.[1] When you're ready to accept the license, click *Accept*. Figure 2-4 shows the license acceptance dialog.

To continue installing the software you must agree to the terms of the software license agreement.

Click Agree to continue or click Disagree to cancel the installation and quit the Installer.

| Read License | | Disagree | Agree |

Figure 2-4. *Accept license*

---

[1]You really should read the license at least once.

The next panel displays the setup or installation type. Early releases such as this version may not show any installation types to choose from. If you run the Windows Installer, you will see several options. For most platforms, the default installation type is all you will need to get started. Figure 2-5 shows the installation type panel. When ready, click *Install*.

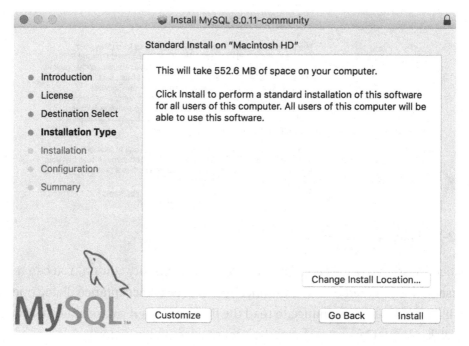

Figure 2-5. *Installation type*

The installation may ask you to authorize the installation and once done, it will proceed rather quickly installing MySQL in the /usr/local/mysql folder (e.g., on Sierra).

If this is the first time you've installed MySQL 8, you will see a dialog that displays the default password for the root account. This was a change made in MySQL 5.7, which eliminated anonymous accounts and made server installations more secure. You should take note of this password, as it is a general random collection of characters and symbols that you won't be able to guess. Figure 2-6 shows one such example dialog.

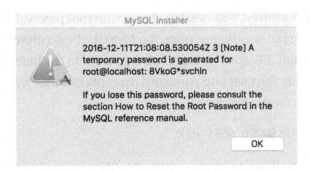

Figure 2-6. *Root password notice*

Figure 2-7 shows how you can recover this dialog on macOS from the notification center if you, like me, tend to dismiss dialogs without fully reading them.[2]

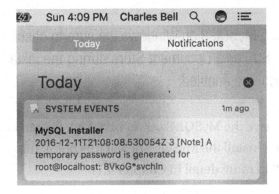

Figure 2-7. *Root password notice in macOS notification center*

Once complete, you will get a completion dialog, which you can safely dismiss. Finally, you will be asked whether you want to keep the installation file (the .dmg) or delete it. If you are experimenting with MySQL 8 or think you may want to install it some other place, do not delete the file.

Tip   It may be a good idea to add the path /usr/local/mysql/bin to your default PATH variable if it is not already set. It makes starting the MySQL client tools much easier.

---

[2]Yes, I know. A shameful practice for which I must do penance. Admit it. You do it too, don't you?

As you may have surmised, you need to change the root password as your first action after installation. Doing so is easy. Just open the MySQL client (mysql) and issue the following SQL statement. Because we installed the server in the default location, we can start the client with only the user and password prompts like this: `mysql -uroot -p`. The client will prompt you for the password.

```
SET PASSWORD='NEW_PASSWORD_GOES_HERE';
```

If you get a message that you cannot connect to the server, it may mean the server has not been started. You can start the server on macOS with the following command.

```
sudo launchctl load -F /Library/LaunchDaemons/com.oracle.oss.mysql.mysqld.plist
```

Note   When installing MySQL 8 on Windows, be sure to check the box marked Enable X Protocol/MySQL as a Document Store during the installation to ensure the X Plugin and X Protocol are enabled.

Okay, now that we have the MySQL 8 server installed, we can begin configuring the server for use. You could install the MySQL Shell at this point, but we will explore how to install the MySQL Shell in more detail in Chapter 4.

Configuring and Managing Access to MySQL

Now that you know how to install MySQL, let's briefly discuss how to configure MySQL and how to grant access to the server (and databases) to others as well as how to setup the X Plugin (the key component to enable the document store). We begin with a look at the configuration file used to define the behavior and configure options in MySQL.

Configuration Files

The primary way to configure start-up options and variables in MySQL is accomplished using a text file named my.cnf (or my.ini on Windows). This file is normally located on Posix systems in the /etc folder. For example, on macOS, the file is named /etc/my.cnf. Listing 2-2 shows the first few dozen lines from a typical MySQL configuration file.

Listing 2-2. MySQL Configuration File Excerpt

```
# Example MySQL config file for small systems.
#
# This is for a system with little memory (<= 64M) where MySQL is only used
# from time to time and it's important that the mysqld daemon
# doesn't use much resources.
#
# MySQL programs look for option files in a set of
# locations which depend on the deployment platform.
# You can copy this option file to one of those
# locations. For information about these locations, see:
# http://dev.mysql.com/doc/mysql/en/option-files.html
#
# In this file, you can use all long options that a program supports.
# If you want to know which options a program supports, run the program
# with the "--help" option.

# The following options will be passed to all MySQL clients
[client]
port            = 3306
socket          = /tmp/mysql.sock

# Here follows entries for some specific programs

# The MySQL server
[mysqld]
port            = 3306
socket          = /tmp/mysql.sock
skip-external-locking
key_buffer_size = 16K
max_allowed_packet = 1M
table_open_cache = 4
sort_buffer_size = 64K
read_buffer_size = 256K
read_rnd_buffer_size = 256K
net_buffer_length = 2K
```

```
thread_stack = 1024K
...
innodb_log_file_size = 5M
innodb_log_buffer_size = 8M
innodb_flush_log_at_trx_commit = 1
innodb_lock_wait_timeout = 50
innodb_log_files_in_group = 2
slow-query-log
general-log
...
```

Note that we have settings grouped by section defined using square brackets [ ]. For example, we see a section named [client], which is used to define options for any MySQL client that reads the configuration file. Likewise, we see a section named [mysqld], which applies to the server process (because the executable is named mysqld). Note that we also see settings for basic options like port, socket, and so forth. However, we also can use the configuration file to set options for InnoDB, replication, and more.

I recommend that you locate and browse the configuration file for your installation so you can see the options and their values. If you encounter a situation in which you need to change an option—say to test the effect or perhaps to experiment—you can use the SET command to change values either as a global setting (affects all connections) or a session setting (applies only to the current connection).

However, if you change a global setting that is also in the configuration file, the value (state) will remain only until the server is rebooted. Thus, if you want to keep global changes, you should consider placing them in the configuration file.

On the other hand, setting a value at the session level could be beneficial for a limited time or may be something you want to do only for a specific task. For example, the following turns off the binary log, executes a SQL command, and then turns the binary log back on. The following is a simple but profound example of how to perform actions on a server that participate in replication without having the actions affect other servers.[3]

```
SET sql_log_bin=0;
CREATE USER 'hvac_user1'@'%' IDENTIFIED BY 'secret';
SET sql_log_bin=1;
```

---

[3]Or worse, introduce errant transactions. See https://dev.mysql.com/doc/mysql-utilities/1.6/en/utils-task-slavetrx.html.

For more information about the configuration file and how to use it to configure MySQL 8 including using multiple option files and where the files exist on each platform, see the section, "Using Option Files" in the online MySQL reference manual (http://dev.mysql.com/doc/refman/8.0/en/).

Creating Users and Granting Access

There are two additional administrative operations you need to understand before working with MySQL: creating user accounts and granting access to databases. MySQL can perform both with the GRANT statement, which automatically creates a user if one does not exist. But the more pedantic method is first to issue a CREATE USER command followed by one or more GRANT commands. For example, the following shows the creation of a user named hvac_user1 and grants the user access to the database room_temp:

```
CREATE USER 'hvac_user1'@'%' IDENTIFIED BY 'secret';
GRANT SELECT, INSERT, UPDATE ON room_temp.* TO 'hvac_user1'@'%';
```

The first command creates the user named hvac_user1, but the name also has an @ followed by another string. This second string is the host name of the machine with which the user is associated. That is, each user in MySQL has both a user name and a host name, in the form user@host, to uniquely identify them. That means the user and host hvac_user1@10.0.1.16 and the user and host hvac_user1@10.0.1.17 are not the same. However, the % symbol can be used as a wildcard to associate the user with any host. The IDENTIFIED BY clause sets the password for the user.

A NOTE ABOUT SECURITY

It is always a good idea to create a user for your application that does not have full access to the MySQL system. This is so you can minimize any accidental changes and also to prevent exploitation. For example, it is recommended that you create a user with access only to those databases in which you store (or retrieve) data.

Also be careful about using the wildcard % for the host. Although it makes it easier to create a single user and let the user access the database server from any host, it also makes it much easier for someone bent on malice to access your server (once they discover the password).

The second command allows access to databases. There are many privileges that you can give a user. The example shows the most likely set that you would want to give a user of a sensor network database: read (SELECT), add data (INSERT), and change data (UPDATE). See the online MySQL reference manual for more about security and account access privileges.

The command also specifies a database and objects where to grant the privilege. Thus, it is possible to give a user read (SELECT) privileges to some tables and write (INSERT, UPDATE) privileges to other tables. This example gives the user access to all objects (tables, views, and so on) in the room_temp database.

As mentioned, you can combine these two commands into a single command. You are likely to see this form more often in the literature. The following shows the combined syntax. In this case, all you need to do is add the IDENTIFIED BY clause to the GRANT statement. Cool!

```
GRANT SELECT, INSERT, UPDATE ON room_temp.* TO 'hvac_user1'@'%' IDENTIFIED
BY 'secret';
```

Next, let's see how to configure the server for use with the document store; to be more specific by installing the X Plugin.

Configuring the Document Store

The last thing you want to do before exploring the MySQL Document Store is to ensure the X Plugin is installed. If you installed MySQL on Windows, and you chose to enable the Enable X Protocol/MySQL as a Document Store, you can skip this step. However, other platforms may require configuring the server for use with the document store.

To enable the X Protocol on older MySQL servers, we need to install the X Plugin. The X Plugin is named MySQLX and is easily installed with the following command. The INSTALL PLUGIN command takes the name of the plugin (mysqlx) and the name of the shared library. By convention, shared libraries are named the same as the plugin with the .so suffix (Windows machines use .dll).

```
INSTALL PLUGIN mysqlx SONAME 'mysqlx.so';
```

Note   MySQL release 8.0.11 and later enable the X Plugin by default.

You can check to see what plugins are enabled using the following command. You will see all plugins installed and their current state. Note that we see the X Plugin in the list as enabled.

```
mysql> SHOW PLUGINS \G
*************************** 1. row ***************************
   Name: keyring_file
 Status: ACTIVE
   Type: KEYRING
Library: keyring_file.so
License: GPL
*************************** 2. row ***************************
   Name: binlog
 Status: ACTIVE
   Type: STORAGE ENGINE
Library: NULL
License: GPL
...
*************************** 43. row ***************************
   Name: mysqlx
 Status: ACTIVE
   Type: DAEMON
Library: mysqlx.so
License: GPL
43 rows in set (0.00 sec)
```

That's all there is to it. Once enabled, your server will communicate with the X Protocol to the MySQL Shell or any other system, service, or application that uses the X Protocol.

If there is a need to uninstall the X Plugin, you can do so with the following command:

```
UNINSTALL PLUGIN mysqlx;
```

In the following section, I take a longer tour of the MySQL server, to show how to use basic SQL commands. There will be more about the document store in later chapters.

A MySQL Primer

If you have never used a database system, learning and mastering the system requires training, experience, and a good deal of perseverance. Chief among the knowledge needed to become proficient is how to use the common SQL commands and concepts. This section completes the primer on MySQL by introducing the most common MySQL commands and concepts as a foundation for learning how to use the document store.

Note   Rather than regurgitate the online MySQL reference manual, this section introduces the commands and concepts at a higher level. If you decide to use any of the commands or concepts, please refer to the online MySQL reference manual for additional details, complete command syntax, and additional examples.

This section reviews the most common SQL and MySQL-specific commands that you will need to know to get the most out of your MySQL server databases. Although you have already seen some of these in action, this section provides additional information to help you use them.

One important rule to understand is user-supplied variable names are case sensitive and obey case sensitivity of the host platform. For example, resolving last_name versus Last_Name is not consistent across platforms. That is, case-sensitivity behavior is different on Windows than it is on macOS. Check the online MySQL reference manual for your platform to see how case sensitivity affects user-supplied variables.

Creating Databases and Tables

The most basic commands you will need to learn and master are the CREATE DATABASE and CREATE TABLE commands. Recall that database servers such as MySQL allow you to create any number of databases that you can add tables and store data in a logical manner.

To create a database, use CREATE DATABASE followed by a name for the database. If you are using the MySQL client, you must use the USE command to switch to a specific database. The client focus is the latest database specified either at startup (on the command line) or via the USE command.

You can override this by referencing the database name first. For example, `SELECT *` `FROM db1.table1` will execute regardless of the default database set. However, leaving off the database name will cause the mysql client to use the default database. The following shows two commands to create and change the focus of the database:

```
mysql> CREATE DATABASE greenhouse;
mysql> USE greenhouse;
```

Tip   If you want to see all the databases on the server, use the SHOW DATABASES command.

Creating a table requires the, yes, `CREATE TABLE` command. This command has many options allowing you to specify not only the columns and their data types but also additional options such as indexes, foreign keys, and so on. An index also can be created using the `CREATE INDEX` command (see the following code). The following code shows how to create a simple table for storing plant sensor data such as what may be used for monitoring a personal greenhouse.[4]

```
CREATE TABLE `greenhouse`.`plants` (
  `plant_name` char(30) NOT NULL,
  `sensor_value` float DEFAULT NULL,
  `sensor_event` timestamp NOT NULL DEFAULT CURRENT_TIMESTAMP ON UPDATE
  CURRENT_TIMESTAMP,
  `sensor_level` char(5) DEFAULT NULL,
  PRIMARY KEY `plant_name` (`plant_name`)
) ENGINE=InnoDB DEFAULT CHARSET=latin1;
```

Note here that I specified the table name (plants) and four columns (`plant_name`, `sensor_value`, `sensor_event`, and `sensor_level`). I used several data types. For `plant_name`, I used a character field with a maximum of 30 characters, a floating-point data type for `sensor_value`, a timestamp value for `sensor_event`, and another character field for `sensor_level` of five characters.

---

[4]I call it a greenhouse, but it is essentially our sun porch. During the summer there are only a few plants but in winter it becomes a small conservatory.

The TIMESTAMP data type is of particular use any time you want to record the date and time of an event or action. For example, it is often helpful to know when a sensor value is read. By adding a TIMESTAMP column to the table, you do not need to calculate, read, or otherwise format a date and time at the sensor or even aggregate node.

Note also that I specified that the plant_name column be defined as a key, which creates an index. In this case, it is also the primary key. The PRIMARY KEY phrase tells the server to ensure that there exists one and only one row in the table that matches the value of the column. You can specify several columns to be used in the primary key by repeating the keyword. Note that all primary key columns must not permit nulls (NOT NULL).

If you cannot determine a set of columns that uniquely identify a row (and you want such a behavior—some favor tables without this restriction, but a good DBA will not), you can use an artificial data type option for integer fields called AUTO INCREMENT. When used on a column (this must be the first column), the server automatically increases this value for each row inserted. In this way, it creates a default primary key. For more information about auto increment columns, see the online MySQL reference manual.

Tip   Best practices suggest using a primary key on a character field to be suboptimal in some situations such as tables with large values for each column or many unique values. This can make searching and indexing slower. In this case, you could use an auto increment field to artificially add a primary key that is smaller in size (but somewhat more cryptic).

There are far more data types available than those shown in the previous example. You should review the online MySQL reference manual for a complete list of data types. See the section "Data Types." If you want to know the layout or "schema" of a table, use the SHOW CREATE TABLE command.

Tip   Like databases, you can also get a list of all the tables in the database with the SHOW TABLES command.

Searching for Data

The most used basic command you need to know is the command to return the data from the table (also called a result set or rows). To do this, you use the SELECT statement. This SQL statement is the workhorse for a database system. All queries for data will be executed with this command. As such, we will spend a bit more time looking at the various clauses (parts) that can be used starting with the column list.

Note   Although we examine SELECT statements first, if you want to try these out on your system, be sure to run the INSERT statements first.

The SELECT statement allows you to specify which columns you want to choose from the data. The list appears as the first part of the statement. The second part is the FROM clause, which specifies the table(s) you want to retrieve rows from.

Note   The FROM clause can be used to join tables with the JOIN operator.

The order that you specify the columns determines the order shown in the result set. If you want all of the columns, use an asterisks (*) instead. Listing 2-3 demonstrates three statements that generate the same result sets. That is, the same rows will be displayed in the output of each. In fact, I am using a table with only four rows for simplicity.

Listing 2-3. Example SELECT Statements

```
mysql> SELECT plant_name, sensor_value, sensor_event, sensor_level FROM
greenhouse.plants;
+-----------------------+--------------+---------------------+--------------+
| plant_name            | sensor_value | sensor_event        | sensor_level |
+-----------------------+--------------+---------------------+--------------+
| fern in den           |       0.2319 | 2015-09-23 21:04:35 | NULL         |
| fern on deck          |         0.43 | 2015-09-23 21:11:45 | NULL         |
| flowers in bedroom1   |        0.301 | 2015-09-23 21:11:45 | NULL         |
| weird plant in kitchen |       0.677 | 2015-09-23 21:11:45 | NULL         |
+-----------------------+--------------+---------------------+--------------+
4 rows in set (0.00 sec)
```

```
mysql> SELECT * FROM greenhouse.plants;
+-----------------------+--------------+---------------------+--------------+
| plant_name            | sensor_value | sensor_event        | sensor_level |
+-----------------------+--------------+---------------------+--------------+
| fern in den           |       0.2319 | 2015-09-23 21:04:35 | NULL         |
| fern on deck          |         0.43 | 2015-09-23 21:11:45 | NULL         |
| flowers in bedroom1   |        0.301 | 2015-09-23 21:11:45 | NULL         |
| weird plant in kitchen |       0.677 | 2015-09-23 21:11:45 | NULL         |
+-----------------------+--------------+---------------------+--------------+
4 rows in set (0.00 sec)

mysql> SELECT sensor_value, plant_name, sensor_level, sensor_event FROM
greenhouse.plants;
+--------------+-----------------------+--------------+---------------------+
| sensor_value | plant_name            | sensor_level | sensor_event        |
+--------------+-----------------------+--------------+---------------------+
|       0.2319 | fern in den           | NULL         | 2015-09-23 21:04:35 |
|         0.43 | fern on deck          | NULL         | 2015-09-23 21:11:45 |
|        0.301 | flowers in bedroom1   | NULL         | 2015-09-23 21:11:45 |
|        0.677 | weird plant in kitchen | NULL        | 2015-09-23 21:11:45 |
+--------------+-----------------------+--------------+---------------------+
4 rows in set (0.00 sec)
```

Note that the first two statements result in the same rows as well as the same columns in the same order. However, the third statement although it generates the same rows, displays the columns in a different order.

You also can use functions in the column list to perform calculations and similar operations. One special example is using the COUNT() function to determine the number of rows in the result set, as shown here. See the online MySQL reference manual for more examples of functions supplied by MySQL.

```
SELECT COUNT(*) FROM greenhouse.plants;
```

The next clause in the SELECT statement is the WHERE clause. This is where you specify the conditions you want to use to restrict the number of rows in the result set. That is, only those rows that match the conditions. The conditions are based on the columns and can be quite complex. That is, you can specify conditions based on calculations, results from a join, and more. But most conditions will be simple equalities or inequalities on one or more columns to answer a question. For example, suppose you wanted to see the plants where the sensor value read is less than 0.40? In this case, we issue the following query and receive the results. Note that I specified only two columns: the plant name and the value read from sensor.

```
mysql> SELECT plant_name, sensor_value FROM greenhouse.plants WHERE sensor_
value < 0.40;
+----------------------+---------------+
| plant_name           | sensor_value  |
+----------------------+---------------+
| fern in den          |        0.2319 |
| flowers in bedroom1  |         0.301 |
+----------------------+---------------+
2 rows in set (0.01 sec)
```

There are additional clauses you can use including the GROUP BY clause, which is used for grouping rows for aggregation or counting, and the ORDER BY clause, which is used to order the result set. Let's take a quick look at each starting with aggregation.

Suppose you wanted to average the sensor values read in the table for each sensor. In this case, we have a table that contains sensor readings over time for a variety of sensors. Although the example contains only four rows (and thus may not be statistically informative), the example demonstrates the concept of aggregation quite plainly, as shown in Listing 2-4. Note that what we receive is simply the average of the four sensor values read.

Listing 2-4. GROUP BY Example

```
mysql> SELECT plant_name, sensor_value FROM greenhouse.plants WHERE plant_
name = 'fern on deck';
+---------------+---------------+
| plant_name    | sensor_value  |
+---------------+---------------+
| fern on deck  |          0.43 |
| fern on deck  |          0.51 |
| fern on deck  |         0.477 |
| fern on deck  |          0.73 |
+---------------+---------------+
4 rows in set (0.00 sec)
```

```
mysql> SELECT plant_name, AVG(sensor_value) AS avg_value FROM greenhouse.
plants WHERE plant_name = 'fern on deck' GROUP BY plant_name;
+---------------+--------------------+
| plant_name    | avg_value          |
+---------------+--------------------+
| fern on deck  | 0.536750003695488  |
+---------------+--------------------+
1 row in set (0.00 sec)
```

Note that I specified the average function, AVG(), in the column list and passed in the name of the column I wanted to average. There are many such functions available in MySQL to perform some powerful calculations. Clearly, this is another example of how much power exists in the database server that would require many more resources on a typical lightweight sensor or aggregator node in the network.

Also note that I renamed the column with the average using the AS keyword. You can use this to rename any column specified, which changes the name in the result set, as you can see in the listing.

Another use of the GROUP BY clause is counting. In this case, we replaced AVG() with COUNT() and received the number of rows matching the WHERE clause. More specific, we want to know how many sensor values were stored for each plant.

```
mysql> SELECT plant_name, COUNT(sensor_value) as num_values FROM
greenhouse.plants GROUP BY plant_name;
+-------------------------+------------+
| plant_name              | num_values |
+-------------------------+------------+
| fern in den             |          1 |
| fern on deck            |          4 |
| flowers in bedroom1     |          1 |
| weird plant in kitchen  |          1 |
+-------------------------+------------+
4 rows in set (0.00 sec)
```

Now let's say we want to see the results of our result set ordered by sensor value. We use the same query that selected the rows for the fern on the deck, but we order the rows by sensor value in ascending and descending order using the ORDER BY clause. Listing 2-5 shows the results of each option.

Listing 2-5. ORDER BY Examples

```
mysql> SELECT plant_name, sensor_value FROM greenhouse.plants WHERE plant_
name = 'fern on deck' ORDER BY sensor_value ASC;
+--------------+--------------+
| plant_name   | sensor_value |
+--------------+--------------+
| fern on deck |         0.43 |
| fern on deck |        0.477 |
| fern on deck |         0.51 |
| fern on deck |         0.73 |
+--------------+--------------+
4 rows in set (0.00 sec)

mysql> SELECT plant_name, sensor_value FROM greenhouse.plants WHERE plant_
name = 'fern on deck' ORDER BY sensor_value DESC;
+--------------+--------------+
| plant_name   | sensor_value |
+--------------+--------------+
| fern on deck |         0.73 |
| fern on deck |         0.51 |
| fern on deck |        0.477 |
| fern on deck |         0.43 |
+--------------+--------------+
4 rows in set (0.00 sec)
```

As I mentioned, there is a lot more to the SELECT statement than shown here, but what we have seen will get you very far, especially when working with data typical of most small- to medium-sized database solutions.

Creating Data

Now that you have a database and tables created, you will want to load or insert data into the tables. You can do so using the INSERT INTO statement. Here we specify the table and the data for the row. The following shows a simple example:

```
INSERT INTO greenhouse.plants (plant_name, sensor_value) VALUES ('fern in
den', 0.2319);
```

In this example, I am inserting data for one of my plants by specifying the name and value. What about the other columns, you wonder? In this case, the other columns include a timestamp column, which will be filled in by the database server. All other columns (just the one) will be set to NULL, which means no value is available, the value is missing, the value is not zero, or the value is empty.

Note that I specified the columns before the data for the row. This is necessary whenever you want to insert data for fewer columns than what the table contains. To be more specific, leaving the column list off means you must supply data (or NULL) for all columns in the table. Also, the order of the columns listed can be different from the order they are defined in the table. Leaving the column list off will result in the ordering the column data based on how they appear in the table.

You can also insert several rows using the same command by using a comma separated list of the row values, as shown here:

```
INSERT INTO greenhouse.plants (plant_name, sensor_value) VALUES ('flowers
in bedroom1', 0.301), ('weird plant in kitchen', 0.677), ('fern on deck',
0.430);
```

Here I've inserted several rows with the same command. Note that this is just a shorthand mechanism, and except for automatic commits, no different than issuing separate commands.

Updating Data

There are times when you want to change or update data. You may have a case where you need to change the value of one or more columns, replace the values for several rows, or correct formatting or even scale of numerical data. To update data, we use the UPDATE command. You can update a particular column, update a set of columns, perform calculations on one or more columns, and more.

What may be more likely is you or your users will want to rename an object in your database. For example, suppose we determine the plant on the deck is not actually a fern but was an exotic flowering plant. In this case, we want to change all rows that have a plant name of "fern on deck" to "flowers on deck." The following command performs the change:

```
UPDATE greenhouse.plants SET plant_name = 'flowers on deck' WHERE plant_
name = 'fern on deck';
```

Note that the key operator here is the SET operator. This tells the database to assign a new value to the column(s) specified. You can list more than one set operation in the command.

Note I used a WHERE clause here to restrict the UPDATE to a particular set of rows. This is the same WHERE clause as you saw in the SELECT statement, and it does the same thing; it allows you to specify conditions that restrict the rows affected. If you do not use the WHERE clause, the updates will apply to all rows.

Caution   Don't forget the WHERE clause! Issuing an UPDATE command without a WHERE clause will affect all rows in the table!

Deleting Data

Sometimes you end up with data in a table that needs to be removed. Maybe you used test data and want to get rid of the fake rows. Perhaps you want to compact or purge your tables or you want to eliminate rows that no longer apply. To remove rows, use the DELETE FROM command.

Let's look at an example. Suppose you have a plant-monitoring solution under development and you've discovered that one of your sensors or sensor nodes are reading values that are too low because of a coding, wiring, or calibration error. In this case, we want to remove all rows with a sensor value less than 0.20. The following command does this:

```
DELETE FROM plants WHERE sensor_value < 0.20;
```

Caution   Don't forget the WHERE clause! Issuing a DELETE FROM command without a WHERE clause will **permanently delete all rows in the table**!

Note that I used a WHERE clause here. That is, a conditional statement to limit the rows acted on. You can use whatever columns or conditions you want; just be sure you have the correct ones! I like to use the same WHERE clause in a SELECT statement first. For example, I would issue the following first to check that I am about to delete the rows I want and only those rows. Note that it is the same WHERE clause.

```
SELECT * FROM plants WHERE sensor_value < 0.20;
```

Using Indexes

Tables are created without the use of any ordering; that is, they are unordered. Although it is true MySQL will return the data in the same order each time, there is no implied (or reliable) ordering unless you create an index. The ordering I am referring to here is not what you think when sorting (that's possible with the ORDER BY clause in the SELECT statement).

Rather, indexes are mappings that the server uses to read the data when queries are executed. For example, if you had no index on a table and wanted to select all rows with a value greater than a certain value for a column, the server will have to read all rows to find all the matches. However, if we added an index on that column, the server would have to read only those rows that match the criteria.

I should note that there are several forms of indexes. What I am referring to here is a clustered index where the value for column in the index is stored in the index, allowing the server to read the index only and not the rows to do the test for the criteria.

To create an index, you can either specify the index in the CREATE TABLE statement or issue a CREATE INDEX command. The following shows a simple example:

```
CREATE INDEX plant_name ON plants (plant_name);
```

This command adds an index on the plant_name column. Observe how this affects the table.

```
CREATE TABLE `plants` (
  `plant_name` char(30) NOT NULL,
  `sensor_value` float DEFAULT NULL,
  `sensor_event` timestamp NOT NULL DEFAULT CURRENT_TIMESTAMP ON UPDATE
  CURRENT_TIMESTAMP,
  `sensor_level` char(5) DEFAULT NULL,
  PRIMARY KEY (`plant_name`),
  KEY `plant_name` (`plant_name`)
) ENGINE=InnoDB DEFAULT CHARSET=latin1
```

Indexes created like this do not affect the uniqueness of the rows in the table. In other words, make sure that there exists one and only one row that can be accessed by a specific value of a specific column (or columns). What I am referring to is the concept of a primary key (or primary index), which is a special option used in the creation of the table as described earlier.

Views

Views are logical mappings of results of one or more tables. They can be referenced as if they were tables in queries, making them a powerful tool for creating subsets of data to work with. You create a view with CREATE VIEW and give it a name similar to a table. The following shows a simple example where we create a test view to read values from a table. In this case, we limit the size of the view (number of rows), but you could use a wide variety of conditions for your views, including combining data from different tables.

```
CREATE VIEW test_plants AS SELECT * FROM plants LIMIT 5;
```

Views are not normally encountered in small- or medium-sized database solutions, but I include them to make you aware of them in case you decide to do additional analysis and want to organize the data into smaller groups for easier reading.

Triggers

Another advanced concept (and associated SQL command) is the use of an event-driven mechanism that is "triggered" when data is changed. That is, you can create a short set of SQL commands (a procedure) that will execute when data is inserted or changed.

There are several events or conditions under which the trigger will execute. You can set up a trigger either before or after an update, insert, or delete action. A trigger is associated with a single table and has as its body a special construct that allows you to act on the rows affected. The following shows a simple example:

```
DELIMITER //
CREATE TRIGGER set_level BEFORE INSERT ON plants FOR EACH ROW
BEGIN
  IF NEW.sensor_value < 0.40 THEN
    SET NEW.sensor_level = 'LOW';
  ELSEIF NEW.sensor_value < 0.70 THEN
    SET NEW.sensor_level = 'OK';
  ELSE
    SET NEW.sensor_level = 'HIGH';
  END IF;
END //
DELIMITER ;
```

This trigger will execute before each insert into the table. As you can see in the compound statement (BEGIN...END), we set a column called sensor_level to LOW, OK, or HIGH depending on the value of the sensor_value. To see this in action, consider the following command. The FOR EACH ROW syntax allows the trigger to act on all rows in the transaction.

```
INSERT INTO plants (plant_name, sensor_value) VALUES ('plant1', 0.5544);
```

Because the value we supplied is less than the middle value (0.70), we expect the trigger to fill in the sensor_level column for us. The following shows this indeed is what happened when the trigger fired:

```
+------------+--------------+---------------------+--------------+
| plant_name | sensor_value | sensor_event        | sensor_level |
+------------+--------------+---------------------+--------------+
| plant1     |       0.5544 | 2015-09-23 20:00:15 | OK           |
+------------+--------------+---------------------+--------------+
1 row in set (0.00 sec)
```

This demonstrates an interesting and powerful way you can create derived columns with the power of the database server and save the processing power and code in your applications. I encourage you to consider this and similar powerful concepts for leveraging the power of the database server.

Simple Joins

One of the most powerful concepts of database systems is the ability to make relationships (hence the name relational) among the data. That is, data in one table can reference data in another (or several tables). The most simplistic form of this is called a master-detail relationship in which a row in one table references or is related to one or more rows in another.

A common (and classic) example of a master-detail relationship is from an order-tracking system where we have one table containing the data for an order and another table containing the line items for the order. Thus, we store the order information such as customer number and shipping information once and combine or "join" the tables when we retrieve the order proper.

Let's look at an example from the sample database named world. You can find this database on the MySQL web site (http://dev.mysql.com/doc/index-other.html). Feel free to download it and any other sample database. They all demonstrate various designs of database systems. You also will find it handy to practice querying the data as it contains more than a few, simple rows.

Note   If you want to run the following examples, you need to install the world database as described in the documentation for the example (http://dev.mysql.com/doc/world-setup/en/world-setup-installation.html).

Listing 2-6 shows an example of a simple join. There is a lot going on here, so take a moment to examine the parts of the SELECT statement, especially how I specified the JOIN clause. You can ignore the LIMIT option because that simply limits the number of rows in the result set.

Listing 2-6. Simple JOIN Example

```
mysql> USE world;
mysql> SELECT Name, Continent, Language FROM Country JOIN CountryLanguage
ON Country.Code = CountryLanguage.CountryCode LIMIT 10;
+-------------+---------------+------------+
| Name        | Continent     | Language   |
+-------------+---------------+------------+
| Aruba       | North America | Dutch      |
| Aruba       | North America | English    |
| Aruba       | North America | Papiamento |
| Aruba       | North America | Spanish    |
| Afghanistan | Asia          | Balochi    |
| Afghanistan | Asia          | Dari       |
| Afghanistan | Asia          | Pashto     |
| Afghanistan | Asia          | Turkmenia  |
| Afghanistan | Asia          | Uzbek      |
| Angola      | Africa        | Ambo       |
+-------------+---------------+------------+
10 rows in set (0.00 sec)
```

Here I used a JOIN clause that takes two tables specified such that the first table is joined to the second table using a specific column and its values (the ON specifies the match). What the database server does is read each row from the tables and returns only those rows where the value in the columns specified a match. Any rows in one table that are not in the other are not returned.

Tip   You can retrieve those rows with different joins. See the online MySQL reference manual on inner and outer joins for more details.

Note that I included only a few columns. In this case, I specified the country name and continent from the Country table and the language column from the CountryLanguage table. If the column names were not unique (the same column appears in each table), I would have to specify them by table name such as Country. Name. In fact, it is considered good practice to always qualify the columns in this manner.

There is one interesting anomaly in this example that I feel important to point out. In fact, some would consider it a design flaw. Note in the JOIN clause that I specified the table and column for each table. This is normal and correct, but note that the column name does not match in both tables. Although this really doesn't matter, and creates only a bit of extra typing, some DBAs would consider this erroneous and would have a desire to make the common column name the same in both tables.

Another use for a join is to retrieve common, archival, or lookup data. For example, suppose you had a table that stored details about things that do not change (or rarely change) such as cities associated with ZIP codes or names associated with identification numbers (e.g., SSN). You could store this information in a separate table and join the data on a common column (and values) whenever you needed. In this case, that common column can be used as a foreign key, which is another advanced concept.

Foreign keys are used to maintain data integrity (i.e., if you have data in one table that relates to another table but the relationship needs to be consistent). For example, if you wanted to make sure when you delete the master row that all of the detail rows are also deleted, you could declare a foreign key in the master table to a column (or columns) to the detail table. See the online MySQL reference manual for more information about foreign keys.

This discussion on joins touches only the very basics. Indeed, joins are arguably one of the most difficult and often confused areas in database systems. If you find you want to use joins to combine several tables or extend data so that the data is provided from several tables (outer joins), you should spend some time with an in-depth study of database concepts such as Clare Churcher's book *Beginning Database Design* (Apress, 2012).

Stored Routines

There are many more concepts and commands available in MySQL, but two that may be of interest are PROCEDURE and FUNCTION, sometimes called stored routines. I introduce these concepts here so that if you want to explore them, you understand how they are used at a high level.

Suppose you need to run several commands to change data. That is, you need to do some complex changes based on calculations. For these types of operations, MySQL provides the concept of a stored procedure. The stored procedure allows you to execute a compound statement (a series of SQL commands) whenever the procedure is called. Stored procedures are sometimes considered an advanced technique used mainly for periodic maintenance, but they can be handy in even the more simplistic situations.

For example, suppose you want to develop your own database application that uses SQL, but because you are developing it, you need to periodically start over and want to clear out all the data first. If you had only one table, a stored procedure would not help much, but suppose you have several tables spread over several databases (not unusual for larger databases). In this case, a stored procedure may be helpful.

Tip   When entering commands with compound statements in the MySQL client, you need to change the delimiter (the semicolon) temporarily so that the semicolon at the end of the line does not terminate the command entry. For example, use DELIMITER // before writing the command with a compound statement, use // to end the command, and change the delimiter back with DELIMITER ;. This is only when using the client.

Because stored procedures can be quite complicated, if you decide to use them, read the "CREATE PROCEDURE and CREATE FUNCTION Syntax" section of the online MySQL reference manual before trying to develop your own. There is more to creating stored procedures than described in this section.

Now suppose you want to execute a compound statement and return a result—you want to use it as a function. You can use functions to fill in data by performing calculations, data transformation, or simple translations. Functions therefore can be used to provide values to populate column values, provide aggregation, provide date operations, and more.

You have already seen a couple of functions (COUNT, AVG). These are considered built-in functions, and there is an entire section devoted to them in the online MySQL reference manual. However, you also can create your own functions. For example, you may want to create a function to perform data normalization on your data. More specific, suppose you have a sensor that produces a value in a specific range, but depending on that value and another value from a different sensor or lookup table, you want to add, subtract, average, and so on the value to correct it. You could write a function to do this and call it a trigger to populate the value for a calculation column.

Tip   Use a new column for calculated values so that you preserve the original value.

```
WHAT ABOUT CHANGING OBJECTS?
```

You may wonder what you to do when you need to modify a table, procedure, trigger, and so on. Rest easy, you do not have to start over from scratch! MySQL provides an ALTER command for each object. That is, there is an ALTER TABLE, ALTER PROCEDURE, and so on. See the online MySQL reference manual section, "Data Definition Statements" for more information about each ALTER command.

Summary

The MySQL database server is a powerful tool. Given its unique placement in the market as the database server for the Internet, it is not surprising that web developers (as well as many startup and similar Internet properties) have chosen MySQL for their solutions. Not only is the server robust and easy to use, it is also available as a free community license that you can use to keep your initial investment within budget.

In this chapter, you discovered some of the power of using the MySQL database server in its traditional role using the SQL interface; how to issue commands for creating databases and tables for storing data as well as commands for retrieving that data. Although this chapter presents only a small primer on MySQL, you learned how to get started with your own installation of MySQL.

In Chapter 3, we look at the NoSQL interface for MySQL. In particular, we look at using MySQL as a document store.

CHAPTER 3

JSON Documents

Now that we have the MySQL server installed, we can begin to learn more about what the document store is and how we can begin to work with it. The core concept is JavaScript Object Notation (JSON) documents. What we discover is that MySQL has two ways to work with JSON documents: a pure NoSQL document store mechanism complete with a full developer application programming interface and a very cool integration of JSON with relational databases.

The origins of the MySQL document store lie in several technologies that are leveraged together to form the document store. In particular, Oracle has combined a key, value mechanism with a new data type, a new programming library, and a new access mechanism to create what is now the document store. As we learned in Chapter 1, not only does this allow us to use MySQL with a NoSQL interface, it also allows us to build hybrid solutions that leverage the stability and structure of relational data while adding the flexibility of JSON documents.

In this chapter, we learn how MySQL supports JSON documents including how to add, find, update, and remove data (commonly referred to as create, read, update, and delete, respectfully). We begin with more information about the concepts and technologies you will encounter throughout this book. We then move on to learning more about the JSON data type and the JSON functions in the MySQL server. Although this chapter focuses on using JSON with relational data, a firm foundation on how to use JSON is required to master the MySQL document store NoSQL interface—the X Developer API (X DevAPI).

Let's begin with a review of the concepts and technologies we will encounter when working with the document store and JSON in MySQL.

© Charles Bell 2018
C. Bell, *Introducing the MySQL 8 Document Store*, https://doi.org/10.1007/978-1-4842-2725-1_3

Concepts and Technologies: Jargon Explained

As we learned in Chapter 1, there are several new concepts and technologies and associated jargon to navigate to learn how to use the document store in MySQL. We encountered some of these terms in Chapter 1, but we explore them in a little more detail here in the context of MySQL. That is, we see how these concepts and technologies explain what comprises the JSON data type and document store interface. Let's begin with most basic concept that JSON uses: key, value mechanisms.

Origins: Key, Value Mechanisms

As with most things in this world, nothing is truly new in the sense that it is completely original without some form of existence that came before and is typically built from existing technologies applied in novel ways. Key, value mechanisms are a prime example of a base technology. I use the term, *mechanism*, because the use of the key allows you to access the value.

When we say *key, value* we mean there exists some tag (normally a string) that forms the key and each key is associated with a value. For example, `"name":"George"` is an example where key (`name`) has a value (`George`). Although the values in a key, value store are normally short strings, values can be complex: numeric; alphanumeric; lists; or even nested key, value sets.

Key, value mechanisms are best known for being easy to use programmatically while still retaining readability. That is, with diligent use of whitespace, a complex nested key, value data structure can be read by humans. The following shows one example formatted in a manner how developers would format code. As you can see, it is very easy to see what this set of key, values are storing: name, address, and phone numbers.

```
{ "name": {
    "first":"George",
    "last":"Folger"
  },
  "phones": [
    {
      "work":"555-1212"
    },
```

```json
    {
      "cell":"555-2121"
    }
  ],
  "address": {
    "street":"123 Main Street",
    "city":"melborne",
    "state":"California",
    "zip":"90125"
  }
}
```

Recall from Chapter 1, we saw some examples of these constructs. Now we know how and why they are constructed.

One example of a key, value mechanism (or storage) is Extensible Markup Language (XML), which has been around for some time. The following is a simple example of XML using the data above. It is the result of a SQL SELECT query with the output (rows) shown in XML format.[1] Note how XML uses tags like HTML (because it is derived from HTML) along with the key, value storage of the data. Here, the keys are <row>, <field> and the values the contents between the start and end tag symbols ().

```xml
<?xml version="1.0"?>
<resultset statement="select * from thermostat_model limit 1;"
xmlns:xsi="http://www.w3.org/2001/XMLSchema-instance">
  <row>
    <field name="model_id">acme123</field>
    <field name="brand">Lennox</field>
  </row>
</resultset>
```

There are systems designed around key, value mechanisms (called key, value or relational stores) such as the Semantic Web.[2] In short, the Semantic Web is an attempt to leverage associations of data to describe things, events, and so forth. Sometimes the terms *relation store* or *triple store* are used to describe the types of storage systems

---

[1]The old MySQL client can do this using the --xml command line option.
[2]See https://www.w3.org/RDF/Metalog/docs/sw-easy.

employed. There are several forms of key, value mechanisms used in the Sematic Web including Resource Description Framework (RDF), Web Ontology Language (OWL), and XML.

There are other examples of key, value mechanisms but the one most pertinent to the document store is JSON.

JSON

I gave a brief description of JSON in Chapter 1. Recall that JSON is a human and machine readable data exchange format. It is also platform independent, which means that there are no concepts of the format that prohibit it from being used in almost any programming language. In addition, JSON is a widely popular format that is used on the Internet.

JSON allows you to describe data in any way you want to without forcing any structure. In fact, you can format (lay out) your data any way you want to. The only real restriction is the proper use of the descriptors (curly braces, square brackets, quotes, commas, etc.) that must be aligned and in some cases paired correctly. When supported in programming languages, developers can easily read the data by accessing it via the keys. Better still, developers don't need to know what the keys are (but it helps!) because they can use the language support mechanisms to get the keys and iterate over them. In this way, like XML, the data is self-describing.

Now let's look at another key component of the document store—the NoSQL interface starting with the programming library.

Application Programming Interface

An application programming interface (API), sometimes simply called a library or programming library, is a set of classes and methods that support operations for one or more capability. These capabilities, through the classes and methods, allow a programmer to use the classes and methods to perform various tasks.

For example, when we use any application with a graphical user interface on our phone, tablet, or computer, the application was built using one of several APIs. The graphical user interface itself was built using one or more APIs that encapsulated a set of classes and methods for drawing windows, creating buttons, and so forth—all of the things that the graphical user interface was engineered to provide for developers.

In the case of the MySQL document store, we use the X DevAPI to access the server through a set of classes and methods that provide connectivity to the server, abstractions of concepts (such as collections, tables, SQL operations), and more. As we learned earlier, the X DevAPI is also built on several other technologies including the X Protocol enabled through the X Plugin. These technologies are combined for a NoSQL interface to the MySQL server.

NoSQL Interface

There are several sometimes conflicting definitions (if not examples) of NoSQL. For the purpose of this book and MySQL in general, a NoSQL interface is an API that does not require the use of SQL statements to access data. The API itself provides the connection to the server as well as classes and methods for creating, retrieving, updating, and deleting data.

For example, if you want to fetch all the data that meets a specific criterion, you must first create a connection to the server, request access to the object containing the data, and then fetch the data. Each of these steps requires creating object instances and calling the methods for those object instances to manipulate the API.

In contrast, the normal mechanism used to interact with MySQL is through a SQL interface in which you must form all your interactions with objects and data with strictly formatted SQL commands. You issue the command and read the results. If you want to write an application that uses the SQL interface, say for getting data, you must use commands to search for the data then convert results into internal programming structures making the data seem like an auxiliary component rather than an integral part of the solution.

NoSQL interfaces break this mold by allowing you to use APIs to work with the data. More specific, you use programming interfaces rather than command-based interfaces.

It is at this point that you're wondering about how MySQL handles the hybrid option of using JSON documents with relational data. In basic terms, MySQL has been designed to permit storing and retrieving JSON documents in the relational data (via the SQL interface). That is, the server has been modified to handle the JSON document. There is also a set of functions that allows you to do all manner of things with the JSON data making it easy to use JSON via the SQL interface.

However, you also can use JSON documents via the NoSQL X DevAPI either through an SQL command or as a pure document store using the special classes and methods of the X DevAPI. We will learn more about the X DevAPI in Chapter 5.

Document Store

A document store (also known as a document-oriented database) is a storage and retrieval system for managing semistructured data (hence documents). Modern document store systems support a key, value construct such as those found in XML and JSON. Document store systems are therefore sometimes considered a subclass of key, value storage systems.

Document store systems also are commonly accessed by a NoSQL interface implemented as a programming interface (API) that permits developers to incorporate the storage and retrieval of documents in their programs without need of a third-party access mechanism (the API implements the access mechanism). Indeed, the metadata that describes the data is embedded with the data itself. Roughly, this means the keys and the layout (arrangement or nesting) of the keys form the metadata and the metadata becomes opaque to the storage mechanism. More specific, how the data is arranged (how the document is formed or describes the data) is not reflected in or managed by the storage mechanism. Access to the semistructured data requires accessing the mechanism designed to process the document itself using the NoSQL interface.

These two qualities: semistructured data and NoSQL interfaces are what separate document stores from relational data. Relational data requires structure that is not flexible forcing all data to conform to a specific structure. Data is also grouped together with the same structure and there is often little allowance for data that can vary in content. Thus, we don't normally see document store accessible via traditional relational data mechanism. That is, until now.

One thing that is interesting about working with the document store is you don't need to be an expert on JavaScript or Python to learn how to work with the document store. Indeed, most of what you will do doesn't require mastery of any programming language.[3] That is, there are plenty of examples of how to do things so you need not learn all that there is to know about the language to get started. In fact, you can pick up what you need very quickly and then learn more about the language as your needs mature.

Now, let's dive into what JSON documents are and how we can use them with MySQL.

---

[3]But it would help, of course.

Introducing JSON Documents

In MySQL 5.7.8 and beyond, we can use the JSON data type to store a JSON document in a column in a table. Recall from Chapter 1 that although it is possible to embed JSON in a TEXT or BLOB field, there are several very good reasons not to but the most compelling reason is because you would have to add the parsing of the data to your program thereby making it more complex and potentially error prone. The JSON data type overcomes this problem in two big ways.

- *Validation*: The JSON data type provides document validation. That is, only valid JSON can be stored in a JSON column.

- *Efficient access*: When a JSON document is stored in a table, the storage engine packs the data into a special optimized binary format allowing the server fast access to the data elements rather than parsing the data each time it is accessed.

This opens a whole new avenue for storing unstructured data in a structured form (relational data). However, Oracle didn't stop with simply adding a JSON data type to MySQL. Oracle also added a sophisticated programming interface as well as the concept of storing documents as collections in the database. We'll see more about these aspects later in the book. For now, let's see how to use JSON with relational data.

JSON Format Rules

JSON data is formed using strings bracketed with certain symbols. Although we have been discussing key, value mechanisms as they relate to JSON, there are two types of JSON attributes: arrays formed by a comma separated list and objects formed from a set of key, value pairs. You also can nest JSON attributes. For example, an array can contain objects and values in object keys can contain arrays or other objects. The combination of JSON arrays and objects is called a JSON document.

A JSON array contains a list of values separated by commas and enclosed within square brackets ([ ]). For example, the following are valid JSON arrays.

```
["red", "green", "yellow", "blue"]
[1,2,3,4,5,6]
[true, false, false]
```

Note that we started and ended the array with square brackets and used a comma to separate the values. Although I did not use whitespace, you can use whitespace and, depending on your programming language, you may be able to also use newlines, tabs, and carriage returns. For example, the following is still a valid JSON array.

```
["red", 27, "yellow", 4.75, "blue", false]
```

A JSON object is a set of key, value pairs where each key, value pair is enclosed within open and close curly braces ({ }) and separated by commas. For example, the following are valid JSON objects. Note that the key address has a JSON object as its value.

```
{"address": {
    "street": "123 First Street",
    "city": "Oxnard",
    "state": "CA",
    "zip": "90122"
}}
```

```
{"address": {
    "street":"4 Main Street",
    "city":"Melborne",
    "state":"California",
    "zip":"90125"
}}
```

```
{"address": {
    "street":"173 Caroline Ave",
    "city":"Montrose",
    "state":"Georgia",
    "zip":"31505"
}}
```

JSON arrays are typically used to contain lists of related (well, sometimes) things, and JSON objects are used to describe complex data. JSON arrays and objects can contain scalar values such as strings or numbers, the null literal (just like in relational data), or Boolean literals true and false. Keys must always be strings and are commonly enclosed in quotes. Finally, JSON values can also contain time information (date, time, or datetime). For example, the following shows a JSON array with time values.

```
["03:22:19.012000", "2016-02-03", "2016-02-03 03:22:19.012000"]
```

The following section describes how we can use JSON in MySQL. In this case, we are referring to relational data but the formatting of JSON documents is the same in the document store.

Using JSON in MySQL

When used in MySQL, JSON documents are written as strings. MySQL parses any string used in a JSON data type validating the document. If the document is not valid—it's not a properly formed JSON document—the server will produce an error. You can use JSON documents in any SQL statement where it is appropriate. For example, you can use it in INSERT and UPDATE statements as well as in clauses like the WHERE clause.

Properly formatting JSON documents can be a bit of a challenge for some, especially those not used to formatting data structures in programming or scripting languages. The things to remember most is to balance your quotes, use commas correctly, and balance all curly braces and square brackets. Easy, right? There's just one thing that can stymie some people: quotes!

When you specify keys and values as strings, you must use the double quote character ("), not the single quote ('). Because MySQL expects JSON documents as strings, you can use the single quote around the entire JSON document, but not within the document itself. Fortunately, MySQL provides a host of special functions that you can use with JSON documents, one of which is the JSON_VALID() function that permits you to check a JSON document for validity. It returns a 1 if the document is valid and a 0 if it is not. The following shows the results of an attempt to validate a JSON document with single quotes for the keys and values versus a properly formatted JSON document with double quotes.

Tip   If you want to use the MySQL Shell for SQL commands, be sure to start in SQL mode (--sql) or you can switch to SQL mode with \sql command once the shell is started.

```
MySQL  localhost:33060+ ssl  JS > \sql
Switching to SQL mode... Commands end with ;
MySQL  localhost:33060+ ssl  SQL > SELECT JSON_VALID("{'address':
{'street': '123 First Street','city': 'Oxnard','state': 'CA','zip': '90122'}}");
```

```
+------------------------------------------------------------------+
| JSON_VALID("{'address': {'street': '123 First Street','city':
'Oxnard','state': 'CA','zip': '90122'}}") |
+------------------------------------------------------------------+
|                                                              0 |
+------------------------------------------------------------------+
1 row in set (0.00 sec)

MySQL  localhost:33060+ ssl  SQL > SELECT JSON_VALID('{"address":
{"street": "123 First Street","city": "Oxnard","state":
"CA","zip": "90122"}}');
+------------------------------------------------------------------+
| JSON_VALID('{"address": {"street": "123 First Street","city":
"Oxnard","state": "CA","zip": "90122"}}') |
+------------------------------------------------------------------+
|                                                              1 |
+------------------------------------------------------------------+
1 row in set (0.00 sec)
```

Note that the string with the double quotes inside is valid but not the one with single quotes. This is what most people stumble over first when working with JSON.

Let's look at how to use the JSON document in SQL statements. Suppose we wanted to store the addresses listed previously in a table. For this example, we keep it simple and insert the data in a very simple table. Listing 3-1 shows a transcript of the exercise starting with creating a test table then inserting the first two addresses.

Tip   You can use the \G command that is appended to an SQL command to display the result in a vertical format to make it easier to read.

Listing 3-1. Using JSON with SQL Statements

```
MySQL  localhost:33060+ ssl  Py > \sql
Switching to SQL mode... Commands end with ;
 MySQL  localhost:33060+ ssl  SQL > CREATE DATABASE `test`;
```

```
Query OK, 1 row affected (0.00 sec)
 MySQL  localhost:33060+ ssl  SQL > USE `test`;
Query OK, 0 rows affected (0.00 sec)
 MySQL  localhost:33060+ ssl  SQL > CREATE TABLE `test`.`addresses`
 (`id` int(11) NOT NULL AUTO_INCREMENT, `address` json DEFAULT NULL,
 PRIMARY KEY (`id`)) ENGINE=InnoDB DEFAULT CHARSET=latin1;
Query OK, 0 rows affected (0.00 sec)
 MySQL  localhost:33060+ ssl  SQL > INSERT INTO `test`.`addresses`
 VALUES (NULL, '{"address": {"street": "123 First Street","city":
 "Oxnard","state": "CA","zip": "90122"}}');
Query OK, 1 row affected (0.00 sec)
 MySQL  localhost:33060+ ssl  SQL > INSERT INTO `test`.`addresses` VALUES
 (NULL, '{"address": {"street":"4 Main Street","city":"Melborne","state":
 "California","zip":"90125"}}');
Query OK, 1 row affected (0.00 sec)
 MySQL  localhost:33060+ ssl  SQL > SELECT * FROM `test`.`addresses` \G
*************************** 1. row ***************************
     id: 1
address: {"address": {"zip": "90122", "city": "Oxnard", "state":
"CA", "street": "123 First Street"}}
*************************** 2. row ***************************
     id: 2
address: {"address": {"zip": "90125", "city": "Melborne", "state":
"California", "street": "4 Main Street"}}
2 rows in set (0.00 sec)
```

Note that in the CREATE statement we used the data type JSON. This signals MySQL to allocate special storage mechanisms in the storage engine for handling JSON. Contrary to some reports, the JSON data type is not simply direct storage of a string. On the contrary, it is organized internally to optimize retrieval of the elements. Thus, it is very important that the JSON be formatted correctly. You can have multiple JSON columns in a table. However, the sum of the JSON documents in a table row is limited to the value of the variable max_allowed_packet.

Note   JSON columns cannot have a default value like other columns (data types) in a table.

Now, let's see what happens if we use an invalid JSON document (string) in the SQL statement. The following shows an attempt to insert the last address from the previous example only without the correct quotes around the keys. Note the error thrown.

```
MySQL  localhost:33060+ ssl  SQL > INSERT INTO test.addresses VALUES (NULL,
'{"address": {street:"173 Caroline Ave",city:"Monstrose",state:"Georgia",
zip:31505}}');
ERROR: 3140: Invalid JSON text: "Missing a name for object member." at
position 13 in value for column 'addresses.address'.
```

You can expect to see errors like this and others for any JSON document that isn't formatted correctly. If you want to test your JSON first, use the JSON_VALID() function. However, there are two other functions that may also be helpful when building JSON documents: JSON_ARRAY() and JSON_OBJECT().

The JSON_ARRAY() function takes a list of values and returns a valid formatted JSON array. The following shows an example. Note that it returned a correctly formatted JSON array complete with correct quotes (double instead of single) and the square brackets.

```
MySQL  localhost:33060+ ssl  SQL > SELECT JSON_ARRAY(1, true, 'test', 2.4);
+---------------------------------+
| JSON_ARRAY(1, true, 'test', 2.4) |
+---------------------------------+
| [1, true, "test", 2.4]          |
+---------------------------------+
1 row in set (0.00 sec)
```

The JSON_OBJECT() function takes a list of key, value pairs and returns a valid JSON object. The following shows an example. Note that here I used single quotes in calling the function. This is just one example in which it is confusing which quotes to use. In this case, the parameters for the function are not JSON documents; they're normal SQL strings, which can use single or double quotes.

```
MySQL  localhost:33060+ ssl  SQL > SELECT JSON_OBJECT("street","
4 Main Street","city","Melborne",'state','California','zip',90125);
+----------------------------------------------------------------------+
| JSON_OBJECT("street","4 Main Street","city","Melborne",'state','California',
'zip',90125) |
+----------------------------------------------------------------------+
| {"zip": 90125, "city": "Melborne", "state": "California", "street": "4
Main Street"}       |
+----------------------------------------------------------------------+
1 row in set (0.00 sec)
```

Note once again that the automatic conversion of the quotes in the function result. This can be helpful if you need to build JSON on the fly (dynamically).

There is one other useful function for constructing JSON documents: the JSON_ TYPE() function. This function takes a JSON document and parses it into a JSON value. It returns the value's JSON type if it is valid or throws an error if it is not valid. The following shows use of this function with the above statements.

```
MySQL  localhost:33060+ ssl  SQL > SELECT JSON_TYPE('[1, true, "test", 2.4]');
+------------------------------------+
| JSON_TYPE('[1, true, "test", 2.4]') |
+------------------------------------+
| ARRAY                              |
+------------------------------------+
1 row in set (0.00 sec)
```

```
MySQL  localhost:33060+ ssl  SQL > SELECT JSON_TYPE('{"zip": 90125, "city":
"Melborne", "state": "California", "street": "4 Main Street"}') \G
*************************** 1. row ***************************
JSON_TYPE('{"zip": 90125, "city": "Melborne", "state": "California",
"street": "4 Main Street"}'): OBJECT
1 row in set (0.00 sec)
```

There are more functions that MySQL provides to work with the JSON data type. We will see more about these in a later section.

This section described only the basics for using JSON with MySQL in SQL statements. In fact, the formatting of the JSON document also applies to the document store. However, there is one item we haven't talked about yet—how to access the elements in a JSON document.

To access an element—via its key—we use special notation called path expressions. The following shows a simple example. Note the WHERE clause. This shows a path expression in which I check to see if the address column includes the JSON key 'city' referenced with the special notation address->'$.address.city'. We see more details about path expressions in the "Path Expressions" section.

```
MySQL  localhost:33060+ ssl  SQL > SELECT id, address->'$.address.city'
FROM test.addresses WHERE address->'$.address.zip' = '90125';
+----+---------------------------+
| id | address->'$.address.city' |
+----+---------------------------+
|  2 | "Melborne"                |
+----+---------------------------+
1 row in set (0.00 sec)
```

Path Expressions

If you consider that a JSON document can be a complex set of semistructured data and that at some point you will need to access certain elements in the document, you also may be wondering how to go about getting what you want from the JSON document. Fortunately, there is a mechanism to do this and it is called a path expression. More specific, it is shortcut notation that you can use in your SQL commands (or in the X DevAPI) to get an element without additional programming or scripting.

As you will see, it is a very specific syntax that, although not very expressive (it doesn't read well in English), the notation can get you what you need without a lot of extra typing. Path expressions are initiated with the dollar sign symbol ($) enclosed in a string. But this notation must have a context. When using path expressions in SQL statements, you must use the JSON_EXTRACT() function, which allows you to use a path expression to extract data from a JSON document. This is because, unlike the X DevAPI classes and methods, path expressions are not directly supported in all SQL statements (but are for some, as we will see). For example, if you wanted the third item in an array, you would use the function as follows.

```
MySQL  localhost:33060+ ssl  SQL > SELECT JSON_EXTRACT('[1,2,3,4,5,6]', '$[2]');
+-----------------------------------------+
| JSON_EXTRACT('[1,2,3,4,5,6]', '$[2]') |
+-----------------------------------------+
| 3                                       |
+-----------------------------------------+
1 row in set (0.00 sec)
```

Note that this accesses data in a JSON array. Here we use an array subscript with square brackets around the index (elements start at 0) as you would for an array in many programming languages.

Tip   The use of path expressions in the SQL interface is limited to either one of the JSON functions or used only in specific clauses that have been modified to accept path expressions such as SELECT column lists or WHERE, HAVING, ORDER BY, or GROUP BY clauses.

Now suppose you wanted to access an element by key. You can do that too. In this case, we use the dollar sign followed by a period then the key name. The following shows how to retrieve the last name for a JSON object containing the name and address of an individual.

```
MySQL  localhost:33060+ ssl  SQL > SELECT JSON_EXTRACT('{"name":
{"first":"Billy-bob","last":"Throckmutton"},"address": {"street":"4 Main
Street","city":"Melborne","state":"California","zip":"90125"}}', '$.name.
first') AS Name;
+-------------+
| Name        |
+-------------+
| "Billy-bob" |
+-------------+
1 row in set (0.00 sec)
```

Note that I had to use two levels of access. That is, I wanted the value for the key named first from the object named name. Hence, I used `'$.name.first'`. This demonstrates how to use path expressions to drill down into the JSON document. This also is why we call this a path expression because the way we form the expression gives us the "path" to the element.

Now that we've seen a few examples, let's review the entire syntax for path expressions; both for use in SQL and the NoSQL interfaces. Unless otherwise stated, the syntax aspects apply to both interfaces.

Once again, a path expression starts with the dollar sign and can optionally be followed by several forms of syntax called selectors that allow us to request a part of the document. These selectors include the following:

- A period followed by the name of a key name references the value for that key. The key name must be specified within double quotation marks if the name without quotes is not valid (it requires quotes to be a valid identifier such as a key name with a space).

- Use square brackets with an integer index (`[n]`) to select an element in an array. Indexes start at 0.

- Paths can contain the wildcards * or ** as follows.

  - `.[*]` evaluates to the values of all members in a JSON object.

  - `[*]` evaluates to the values of all elements in a JSON array.

  - A sequence such as prefix**suffix evaluates to all paths that begin with the named prefix and end with the named suffix.

- Paths can be nested using a period as the separator. In this case, the path after the period is evaluated within the context of the parent path context. For example, `$.name.first` limits the search for a key named first to the name JSON object.

If a path expression is evaluated as false or fails to locate a data item, the server will return `null`. For example, the following returns `null` because there are only 6 items in the array. Can you see why? Remember, counting starts at 0. This is a common mistake for those new to using path expressions (or arrays in programming languages).

```
MySQL  localhost:33060+ ssl  SQL > SELECT JSON_EXTRACT('[1,2,3,4,5,6]', '$[6]');
+---------------------------------------+
| JSON_EXTRACT('[1,2,3,4,5,6]', '$[6]') |
+---------------------------------------+
| NULL                                  |
+---------------------------------------+
1 row in set (0.00 sec)
```

But wait, there's one more nifty option for path expressions. We can use a shortcut! That is, the dash and greater than symbol (->) can be used in place of the JSON_EXTRACT() function when accessing data in SQL statements by column. How cool is that? The use of the -> operation is sometimes called an *inline path expression*. For example, we could have written the example above to find the third item in a JSON array from a table as follows.

```
MySQL  localhost:33060+ ssl  SQL > USE test;
Query OK, 0 rows affected (0.00 sec)
MySQL  localhost:33060+ ssl  SQL > CREATE TABLE ex1 (id int AUTO_INCREMENT
PRIMARY KEY, recorded_data JSON);
Query OK, 0 rows affected (0.00 sec)
MySQL  localhost:33060+ ssl  SQL > INSERT INTO test.ex1 VALUES (NULL,
JSON_ARRAY(1,2,3,4,5,6));
Query OK, 1 row affected (0.00 sec)
MySQL  localhost:33060+ ssl  SQL > INSERT INTO test.ex1 VALUES (NULL,
JSON_ARRAY(7,8,9));
Query OK, 1 row affected (0.00 sec)
MySQL  localhost:33060+ ssl  SQL > SELECT * FROM test.ex1 WHERE recorded_
data->'$[2]' = 3;
+----+--------------------+
| id | recorded_data      |
+----+--------------------+
|  1 | [1, 2, 3, 4, 5, 6] |
+----+--------------------+
1 row in set (0.00 sec)
```

Note that I simply used the column name, recorded_data, and appended the -> to the end then listed the path expression. Brilliant!

There is one other form of this shortcut. If the result of the -> operation (JSON_EXTRACT) evaluates to a quoted string, we can use the ->> symbol (called the inline path operator) to retrieve the value without quotes. This is helpful when dealing with values that are numbers. The following shows two examples. One example is with the -> operation and the same with the ->> operation.

```
 MySQL  localhost:33060+ ssl  SQL > INSERT INTO test.ex1 VALUES (NULL,
'{"name":"will","age":"43"}');
Query OK, 1 row affected (0.00 sec)
 MySQL  localhost:33060+ ssl  SQL > INSERT INTO test.ex1 VALUES (NULL,
'{"name":"joseph","age":"11"}');
Query OK, 1 row affected (0.00 sec)
 MySQL  localhost:33060+ ssl  SQL > SELECT * FROM test.ex1 WHERE recorded_
data->>'$.age' = 43;
+----+-------------------------------+
| id | recorded_data                 |
+----+-------------------------------+
|  3 | {"age": "43", "name": "will"} |
+----+-------------------------------+
1 row in set (0.00 sec)

MySQL  localhost:33060+ ssl  SQL > SELECT * FROM test.ex1 WHERE recorded_
data->'$.age' = 43;
Empty set (0.00 sec)
```

Note that the recorded_data values (age and name) were stored as a string. But what if the data were stored as an integer? Observe.

```
 MySQL  localhost:33060+ ssl  SQL > INSERT INTO test.ex1 VALUES (NULL,
'{"name":"amy","age":22}');
Query OK, 1 row affected (0.00 sec)
 MySQL  localhost:33060+ ssl  SQL > SELECT * FROM test.ex1 WHERE recorded_
data->'$.age' = 22;
```

```
+----+------------------------------+
| id | recorded_data                |
+----+------------------------------+
|  5 | {"age": 22, "name": "amy"}   |
+----+------------------------------+
1 row in set (0.00 sec)
 MySQL  localhost:33060+ ssl  SQL > SELECT * FROM test.ex1 WHERE recorded_
data->>'$.age' = 22;
+----+------------------------------+
| id | recorded_data                |
+----+------------------------------+
|  5 | {"age": 22, "name": "amy"}   |
+----+------------------------------+
1 row in set (0.00 sec)
```

Aha! So, the ->> operation is most useful when values must be unquoted. If they were already unquoted (such as an integer), the ->> operation returns the same as the -> operation.

Now, let's see a few more examples of path expressions. Listing 3-2 shows several examples without explanation. Take a few minutes to look through these and examine the data it is operating on so you can see how each works. With a little imagination, you can drill down to a single data element!

Listing 3-2. Examples of Path Expressions

```
 MySQL  localhost:33060+ ssl  SQL > INSERT INTO test.ex1 VALUES (NULL,
'{"name": {"last": "Throckmutton", "first": "Billy-bob"}, "address":
{"zip": "90125", "city": "Melborne", "state": "California", "street":
"4 Main Street"}}');
Query OK, 1 row affected (0.00 sec)
 MySQL  localhost:33060+ ssl  SQL > SELECT recorded_data FROM test.ex1
WHERE recorded_data->'$.name' IS NOT NULL \G
*************************** 1. row ***************************
recorded_data: {"age": "43", "name": "will"}
*************************** 2. row ***************************
recorded_data: {"age": "11", "name": "joseph"}
```

```
*************************** 3. row ***************************
recorded_data: {"age": 22, "name": "amy"}
*************************** 4. row ***************************
recorded_data: {"name": {"last": "Throckmutton", "first": "Billy-bob"},
"address": {"zip": "90125", "city": "Melborne", "state": "California",
"street": "4 Main Street"}}
4 rows in set (0.00 sec)
 MySQL  localhost:33060+ ssl  SQL > SELECT recorded_data->'$.name' FROM
test.ex1 WHERE recorded_data->'$.name' IS NOT NULL;
+--------------------------------------------------+
| recorded_data->'$.name'                          |
+--------------------------------------------------+
| "will"                                           |
| "joseph"                                         |
| "amy"                                            |
| {"last": "Throckmutton", "first": "Billy-bob"}   |
+--------------------------------------------------+
4 rows in set (0.00 sec)
 MySQL  localhost:33060+ ssl  SQL > SELECT recorded_data->'$.name.first' as
first, recorded_data->'$.name.last' as last FROM test.ex1 WHERE recorded_
data->'$.name.first' IS NOT NULL;
+-------------+----------------+
| first       | last           |
+-------------+----------------+
| "Billy-bob" | "Throckmutton" |
+-------------+----------------+
1 row in set (0.00 sec)
 MySQL  localhost:33060+ ssl  SQL > INSERT INTO test.ex1 VALUES (NULL,
'{"phones": [{"work": "555-1212"}, {"cell": "555-2121"}]}');
Query OK, 1 row affected (0.00 sec)
 MySQL  localhost:33060+ ssl  SQL > SELECT recorded_data->>'$.phones' FROM
test.ex1 WHERE recorded_data->>'$.phones' IS NOT NULL;
+--------------------------------------------------+
| recorded_data->>'$.phones'                       |
+--------------------------------------------------+
```

```
| [{"work": "555-1212"}, {"cell": "555-2121"}] |
+--------------------------------------------------+
1 row in set (0.00 sec)
 MySQL  localhost:33060+ ssl  SQL > SELECT recorded_data->'$.phones[1]'
FROM test.ex1 WHERE recorded_data->>'$.phones' IS NOT NULL;
+------------------------------+
| recorded_data->'$.phones[1]' |
+------------------------------+
| {"cell": "555-2121"}         |
+------------------------------+
1 row in set (0.00 sec)
 MySQL  localhost:33060+ ssl  SQL > SELECT recorded_data->'$.phones[1].
cell' FROM test.ex1 WHERE recorded_data->>'$.phones' IS NOT NULL;
+-----------------------------------+
| recorded_data->'$.phones[1].cell' |
+-----------------------------------+
| "555-2121"                        |
+-----------------------------------+
1 row in set (0.00 sec)
```

Note that I use the path expression in the WHERE clause checking to see if the result is not NULL. This is a good trick on selecting rows in a table that have the elements you're looking for in the document. That is, you want only the rows that contain a specific data element (via the path expression).

However, the use of the shortcuts (inline path expressions) is not a direct replacement for the JSON_EXTRACT() function. The following summarizes the limitations.

- *Data source*: When used in a SQL statement, the inline path expression uses the field (column) specified only. The function can use any JSON typed value.

- *Path expression string*: An inline path expression must use a plain string; the function can use any string typed value.

- *Number of expressions*: An inline path expression can use only one path expression against a single field (column). The function can use multiple path expressions against a JSON document.

Tip For more information about path expressions, see the section, "The JSON Data Type" in the online MySQL reference manual.

Now let's look at the various JSON functions that we can use to work with JSON documents.

JSON Functions

There are several functions for working with JSON in MySQL. I describe many of the functions available in this section. Although we won't explore the nuance of every function, we will see the more commonly used functions for working with JSON documents. Let's begin with an overview in the form of a list of the available functions. Table 3-1 lists the JSON functions available in MySQL 8.0.11.

Table 3-1. *JSON Functions in MySQL*

Function	Description and Use
JSON_ARRAY()	Evaluates a list of values and returns a JSON array containing those values
JSON_ARRAYAGG()	Aggregates a result set as a single JSON array whose elements consist of the rows
JSON_ARRAY_APPEND()	Appends values to the end of the indicated arrays within a JSON document and returns the result
JSON_ARRAY_INSERT()	Updates a JSON document, inserting an array within the document and returning the modified document
JSON_CONTAINS()	Returns 0 or 1 to indicate whether a specific value is contained in a target JSON document, or, if a path argument is given, at a specific path within the target document
JSON_CONTAINS_PATH()	Returns 0 or 1 to indicate whether a JSON document contains data at a given path or paths
JSON_DEPTH()	Returns the maximum depth of a JSON document

(continued)

Table 3-1. (*continued*)

Function	Description and Use
JSON_EXTRACT()	Returns data from a JSON document, selected from the parts of the document matched by the path arguments
JSON_INSERT()	Inserts data into a JSON document and returns the result
JSON_KEYS()	Returns the keys from the top-level value of a JSON object as a JSON array, or, if a path argument is given, the top-level keys from the selected path
JSON_LENGTH()	Returns the length of JSON document, or, if a path argument is given, the length of the value within the document identified by the path
JSON_MERGE()	Merges two or more JSON documents and returns the merged result
JSON_MERGE_PATCH()	Merges two or more JSON documents replacing values where keys are duplicated
JSON_MERGE_PRESERVE()	Merges two or more JSON documents saving values where keys are duplicated
JSON_OBJECT()	Evaluates a list of key/value pairs and returns a JSON object containing those pairs
JSON_OBJECTAGG()	Takes two column names or expressions as arguments, the first of these being used as a key and the second as a value, and returns a JSON object that contains key/value pairs
JSON_PRETTY()	Prints a nicer looking layout of the JSON document
JSON_QUOTE()	Quotes a string as a JSON value by wrapping it with double quote characters and escaping interior quote and other characters, then returned the result as a utf8mb4 string
JSON_REMOVE()	Removes data from a JSON document and returns the result
JSON_REPLACE()	Replaces existing values in a JSON document and returns the result
JSON_SEARCH()	Returns the path to the given string within a JSON document
JSON_SET()	Inserts or updates data in a JSON document and returns the result

(*continued*)

Table 3-1. (*continued*)

Function	Description and Use
JSON_STORAGE_FREE()	Displays amount of space remaining in a JSON column following a partial update
JSON_STORAGE_SIZE()	Displays the storage used by a JSON value
JSON_TABLE()	Extracts data from a JSON document and returns it as a relational table
JSON_TYPE()	Returns a utf8mb4 string indicating the type of a JSON value
JSON_UNQUOTE()	Removes quotes from the JSON value and returns the result as a utf8mb4 string
JSON_VALID()	Returns 0 or 1 to indicate whether a value is a valid JSON document

Note   The JSON_MERGE() function was deprecated in version 8.0.3 (and also in 5.7.22).

Mastery of these functions is not essential to working with the document store, but can help greatly when developing hybrid solutions in which you use JSON in SQL statements.

These functions can be grouped into categories based on how they are used. We will see functions useful for adding data, those for retrieving (searching) data, and more. The following show how to use the functions using brief examples.

Most functions take a JSON document as the first parameter and a path expression and value as the second and third parameters. Path expressions must be valid for the document and must not contain the wildcards * or **. The functions also return the result so you can use them in SQL statements.

Creating JSON Data

There are several useful functions for creating JSON data. We have already seen two important functions; JSON_ARRAY() that builds a JSON array type and JSON_OBJECT() that builds a JSON object type. This section discusses some of the other functions that you can use to help create JSON documents including functions for aggregating, appending, and inserting data in JSON arrays.

The JSON_ARRAYAGG() function is used to create an array of JSON documents from several rows. It can be helpful when you want to summarize data or combine data from several rows. The function takes a column name and combines the JSON data from the rows into a new array. Listing 3-3 shows examples of using the function. This example takes the rows in the table and combines them to form a new array of JSON objects.

Listing 3-3. Using the JSON_ARRAYARG Function

```
MySQL  localhost:33060+ ssl  SQL > CREATE TABLE test.favorites (id int
AUTO_INCREMENT PRIMARY KEY, preferences JSON);
Query OK, 0 rows affected (0.00 sec)
 MySQL  localhost:33060+ ssl  SQL > INSERT INTO test.favorites VALUES
(NULL, '{"color": "red"}');
Query OK, 1 row affected (0.00 sec)
 MySQL  localhost:33060+ ssl  SQL > INSERT INTO test.favorites VALUES
(NULL, '{"color": "blue"}');
Query OK, 1 row affected (0.00 sec)
 MySQL  localhost:33060+ ssl  SQL > INSERT INTO test.favorites VALUES
(NULL, '{"color": "purple"}');
Query OK, 1 row affected (0.00 sec)
 MySQL  localhost:33060+ ssl  SQL > SELECT * FROM test.favorites;
+----+---------------------+
| id | preferences         |
+----+---------------------+
|  1 | {"color": "red"}    |
|  2 | {"color": "blue"}   |
|  3 | {"color": "purple"} |
+----+---------------------+
3 rows in set (0.00 sec)
 MySQL  localhost:33060+ ssl  SQL > SELECT JSON_ARRAYAGG(preferences) FROM
test.favorites;
```

```
+-----------------------------------------------------------------+
| JSON_ARRAYAGG(preferences)                                      |
+-----------------------------------------------------------------+
| [{"color": "red"}, {"color": "blue"}, {"color": "purple"}]      |
+-----------------------------------------------------------------+
1 row in set (0.00 sec)
```

The JSON_ARRAY_APPEND() is an interesting function that allows you to append data to a JSON array either at the end or immediately after a given path expression. The function takes as parameters a JSON array, a path expression, and the value (including a JSON document) to be inserted. Listing 3-4 shows several examples.

Listing 3-4. Using the JSON_ARRAY_APPEND Function

```
MySQL  localhost:33060+ ssl  SQL > SET @base = '["apple","pear",{"grape":"
red"},"strawberry"]';
Query OK, 0 rows affected (0.00 sec)
MySQL  localhost:33060+ ssl  SQL > SELECT JSON_ARRAY_APPEND(@base, '$',
"banana");
+----------------------------------------------------------------+
| JSON_ARRAY_APPEND(@base, '$', "banana")                        |
+----------------------------------------------------------------+
| ["apple", "pear", {"grape": "red"}, "strawberry", "banana"]    |
+----------------------------------------------------------------+
1 row in set (0.00 sec)
MySQL  localhost:33060+ ssl  SQL > SELECT JSON_ARRAY_APPEND(@base,
'$[2].grape', "green");
+----------------------------------------------------------------+
| JSON_ARRAY_APPEND(@base, '$[2].grape', "green")                |
+----------------------------------------------------------------+
| ["apple", "pear", {"grape": ["red", "green"]}, "strawberry"]   |
+----------------------------------------------------------------+
1 row in set (0.00 sec)
MySQL  localhost:33060+ ssl  SQL > SET @base = '{"grape":"red"}';
Query OK, 0 rows affected (0.00 sec)
MySQL  localhost:33060+ ssl  SQL > SELECT JSON_ARRAY_APPEND(@base,
'$', '{"grape":"red"}');
```

```
+---------------------------------------------------+
| JSON_ARRAY_APPEND(@base, '$', '{"grape":"red"}') |
+---------------------------------------------------+
| [{"grape": "red"}, "{\"grape\":\"red\"}"]         |
+---------------------------------------------------+
1 row in set (0.00 sec)
```

Note that the first example simply adds a new value to the end of the array. The second example changes the value of the key in the JSON object in the third index to an array and adds a new value. This is an interesting by-product of this function. We see this again in the third example where we change a basic JSON object to a JSON array of JSON objects.

The JSON_ARRAY_INSERT() function is similar except it inserts the value before the path expression. The function takes as parameters a JSON array, a path expression, and the value (including a JSON document) to be inserted. When including multiple path expression and value pairs, the effect is cumulative where the function evaluates the first path expression and value applying the next pair to the result, and so on. Listing 3-5 shows some examples using the new function, which are similar to the previous examples. Note that the positions of the data inserted is before the path expression.

Listing 3-5. Using the JSON_ARRAY_INSERT Function

```
 MySQL  localhost:33060+ ssl  SQL > SET @base = '["apple","pear",
{"grape":["red","green"]},"strawberry"]';
Query OK, 0 rows affected (0.00 sec)
 MySQL  localhost:33060+ ssl  SQL > SELECT JSON_ARRAY_INSERT(@base, '$[0]',
"banana");
+--------------------------------------------------------------------------+
| JSON_ARRAY_INSERT(@base, '$[0]', "banana")                               |
+--------------------------------------------------------------------------+
| ["banana", "apple", "pear", {"grape": ["red", "green"]}, "strawberry"] |
+--------------------------------------------------------------------------+
1 row in set (0.00 sec)
 MySQL  localhost:33060+ ssl  SQL > SELECT JSON_ARRAY_INSERT(@base,
'$[2].grape[0]', "white");
```

```
+------------------------------------------------------------------+
| JSON_ARRAY_INSERT(@base, '$[2].grape[0]', "white")               |
+------------------------------------------------------------------+
| ["apple", "pear", {"grape": ["white", "red", "green"]}, "strawberry"] |
+------------------------------------------------------------------+
1 row in set (0.00 sec)
 MySQL  localhost:33060+ ssl  SQL > SET @base = '[{"grape":"red"}]';
Query OK, 0 rows affected (0.00 sec)
 MySQL  localhost:33060+ ssl  SQL > SELECT JSON_ARRAY_INSERT(@base, '$[0]',
'{"grape":"red"}');
+------------------------------------------------+
| JSON_ARRAY_INSERT(@base, '$[0]', '{"grape":"red"}') |
+------------------------------------------------+
| ["{\"grape\":\"red\"}", {"grape": "red"}]      |
+------------------------------------------------+
1 row in set (0.00 sec)
```

The JSON_INSERT() function is designed to take a JSON document and inserts one or more values at a specified path expression. That is, you can pass pairs of path expression and value at one time. But there is a catch. The path expression in this case must not evaluate to an element in the document. As with the last function, when including multiple path expressions, the effect is cumulative where the function evaluates the first path expression applying the next path expression to the result, and so on. Listing 3-6 shows an example. Note that the third path expression and value is not inserted because the path expression, $[0], evaluates to the first element, apple.

Listing 3-6. Using the JSON_INSERT Function

```
 MySQL  localhost:33060+ ssl  SQL > SET @base = '["apple","pear",{"grape":[
"red","green"]},"strawberry"]';
Query OK, 0 rows affected (0.00 sec)
 MySQL  localhost:33060+ ssl  SQL > SELECT JSON_INSERT(@base, '$[9]',
"banana", '$[2].grape[3]', "white", '$[0]', "orange");
```

```
+----------------------------------------------------------------------+
| JSON_INSERT(@base, '$[9]', "banana", '$[2].grape[3]', "white", '$[0]', "orange") |
+----------------------------------------------------------------------+
| ["apple", "pear", {"grape": ["red", "green", "white"]}, "strawberry", "banana"]  |
+----------------------------------------------------------------------+
1 row in set (0.00 sec)
```

The JSON_MERGE_PATCH() and JSON_MERGE_PRESERVE() functions are designed to take two or more JSON documents and combine them. The JSON_MERGE_PATH() function replaces values for duplicate keys whereas the JSON_MERGE_PRESERVE() preserves the values for duplicate keys. As with the previous function, you can include as many JSON documents as you want. Note how I used this function to build the example JSON document from the earlier examples. Listing 3-7 shows an example using the methods.

Listing 3-7. Using the JSON_MERGE_PATCH and JSON_MERGE_PRESERVE Functions

```
 MySQL  localhost:33060+ ssl  SQL > SELECT JSON_MERGE_
PATCH('["apple","pear"]', '{"grape":["red","green"]}', '["strawberry"]');
+-------------------------------------------------------------------+
| JSON_MERGE_PATCH('["apple","pear"]', '{"grape":["red","green"]}',
'["strawberry"]') |
+-------------------------------------------------------------------+
| ["strawberry"]                                                    |
+-------------------------------------------------------------------+
1 row in set (0.00 sec)
 MySQL  localhost:33060+ ssl  SQL > SELECT JSON_MERGE_PRESERVE('{"grape":["
 red","green"]}', '{"grape":["white"]}');
+-------------------------------------------------------------------+
| JSON_MERGE_PRESERVE('{"grape":["red","green"]}', '{"grape":["white"]}') |
+-------------------------------------------------------------------+
| {"grape": ["red", "green", "white"]}                              |
+-------------------------------------------------------------------+
1 row in set (0.00 sec)
```

If any JSON function is passed an invalid parameter, invalid JSON document, or the path expression does not find an element, some functions return null whereas others may return the original JSON document. Listing 3-8 shows an example. In this case, there is no element at position 8 because the array only has 4 elements.

Listing 3-8. Using the JSON_ARRAY_APPEND Function

```
 MySQL  localhost:33060+ ssl  SQL > SET @base = '["apple","pear",
{"grape":"red"},"strawberry"]';
Query OK, 0 rows affected (0.00 sec)
 MySQL  localhost:33060+ ssl  SQL > SELECT JSON_ARRAY_APPEND(@base, '$[7]',
"flesh");
+-------------------------------------------------------+
| JSON_ARRAY_APPEND(@base, '$[7]', "flesh")             |
+-------------------------------------------------------+
| ["apple", "pear", {"grape": "red"}, "strawberry"]     |
+-------------------------------------------------------+
1 row in set (0.00 sec)
```

Now let's see functions that we can use to modify JSON data.

Modifying JSON Data

There are several useful functions for modifying JSON data. This section discusses functions that you can use to help modify JSON documents by removing, replacing, and updating elements in the JSON document.

The JSON_REMOVE() function is used to remove elements that match a path expression. You must provide the JSON document to operate on and one or more path expressions and the result will be the JSON document with the elements removed. When including multiple path expressions, the effect is cumulative where the function evaluates the first path expression applying the next path expression to the result, and so on. Listing 3-9 shows an example. Note that I had to imagine what the intermediate results would be—that is, I used $[0] three times because the function removed the first element twice leaving the JSON object as the first element.

Listing 3-9. Using the JSON_REMOVE Function (Single)

```
 MySQL  localhost:33060+ ssl  SQL > SET @base = '["apple","pear",{"grape":
["red","white"]},"strawberry"]';
Query OK, 0 rows affected (0.00 sec)
 MySQL  localhost:33060+ ssl  SQL > SELECT JSON_REMOVE(@base, '$[0]',
'$[0]', '$[0].grape[1]');
```

```
+------------------------------------------------------------+
| JSON_REMOVE(@base, '$[0]', '$[0]', '$[0].grape[1]') |
+------------------------------------------------------------+
| [{"grape": ["red"]}, "strawberry"]                         |
+------------------------------------------------------------+
1 row in set (0.00 sec)
```

This may take a little getting used to but you can use the function multiple times or nested as shown in the examples in Listing 3-10.

Listing 3-10. Using the JSON_REMOVE Function (Nested)

```
 MySQL  localhost:33060+ ssl  SQL > SET @base = '["apple","pear",{"grape":
["red","white"]},"strawberry"]';
Query OK, 0 rows affected (0.00 sec)
 MySQL  localhost:33060+ ssl  SQL > SET @base = JSON_REMOVE(@base, '$[0]');
Query OK, 0 rows affected (0.00 sec)
 MySQL  localhost:33060+ ssl  SQL > SET @base = JSON_REMOVE(@base, '$[0]');
Query OK, 0 rows affected (0.00 sec)
 MySQL  localhost:33060+ ssl  SQL > SELECT JSON_REMOVE(@base, '$[0].grape[1]');
+-----------------------------------+
| JSON_REMOVE(@base, '$[0].grape[1]') |
+-----------------------------------+
| [{"grape": ["red"]}, "strawberry"] |
+-----------------------------------+
1 row in set (0.00 sec)
 MySQL  localhost:33060+ ssl  SQL > SET @base = '["apple","pear",{"grape":
["red","white"]},"strawberry"]';
Query OK, 0 rows affected (0.00 sec)
 MySQL  localhost:33060+ ssl  SQL > SELECT JSON_REMOVE(JSON_REMOVE(JSON_
REMOVE(@base, '$[0]'), '$[0]'), '$[0].grape[1]');
+-------------------------------------------------------------------+
| JSON_REMOVE(JSON_REMOVE(JSON_REMOVE(@base, '$[0]'), '$[0]'), '$[0].grape[1]') |
+-------------------------------------------------------------------+
| [{"grape": ["red"]}, "strawberry"]                                |
+-------------------------------------------------------------------+
1 row in set (0.00 sec)
```

The JSON_REPLACE() function takes a JSON document and pairs of path expression and value replacing the element that matches the path expression with the new value. Once again, the results are cumulative and work in order left to right. There is a catch with this function too. It ignores any new values or path expressions that evaluate to new values. Listing 3-11 shows an example. Note that the third pair was not removed because there is no tenth element.

Listing 3-11. Using the JSON_REPLACE Function

```
MySQL  localhost:33060+ ssl  SQL > SET @base = '["apple","pear",{"grape":
["red","white"]},"strawberry"]';
Query OK, 0 rows affected (0.00 sec)
 MySQL  localhost:33060+ ssl  SQL > SELECT JSON_REPLACE(@base, '$[0]',
"orange", '$[2].grape[0]', "green", '$[9]', "waffles");
+---------------------------------------------------------------------+
| JSON_REPLACE(@base, '$[0]', "orange", '$[2].grape[0]', "green", '$[9]',
"waffles") |
+---------------------------------------------------------------------+
| ["orange", "pear", {"grape": ["green", "white"]}, "strawberry"]     |
+---------------------------------------------------------------------+
1 row in set (0.00 sec)
```

The JSON_SET() function is designed to modify JSON document elements. As with the other functions, you pass a JSON document as the first parameter and then one or more pairs of path expression and value to replace. However, this function also inserts any elements that are not in the document (the path expression is not found). Listing 3-12 shows an example. Note that the last element did not exist so it adds it to the documents.

Listing 3-12. Using the JSON_SET Function

```
MySQL  localhost:33060+ ssl  SQL > SET @base = '["apple","pear",{"grape":
["red","white"]},"strawberry"]';
Query OK, 0 rows affected (0.00 sec)
 MySQL  localhost:33060+ ssl  SQL > SELECT JSON_SET(@base, '$[0]',
"orange", '$[2].grape[1]', "green", '$[9]', "123");
```

```
+-----------------------------------------------------------------------+
| JSON_SET(@base, '$[0]', "orange", '$[2].grape[1]', "green", '$[9]', "123") |
+-----------------------------------------------------------------------+
| ["orange", "pear", {"grape": ["red", "green"]}, "strawberry", "123"]    |
+-----------------------------------------------------------------------+
1 row in set (0.00 sec)
```

IGNORE OR NOT IGNORE, WHICH DOES WHAT?

One issue with the JSON functions is that some will operate on values that exist, others ignore values that exist, some add values that do not already exist, and so forth. It can become confusing if you aren't familiar with all the functions. The following summarizes the differences for those functions that can be the most confusing.

- JSON_INSERT(): adds new values but does not replace existing values

- JSON_REMOVE(): removes elements that exist in the document and ignores those that do not exist

- JSON_REPLACE(): replaces existing values and ignores new values

- JSON_SET(): replaces values for paths that exist and adds values for paths that do not exist

If you want to use these functions, be sure to check them with sample data until you understand the conditions.

Now let's look at the JSON functions you can use to find elements in the document.

Searching JSON Data

Another important operation for working with SQL and JSON data is searching for data in the JSON document. We discovered previously in the chapter how to reference data in the document with the special notation (path expressions), and we learned there are JSON functions that we can use to search for the data. In fact, we saw these two concepts used together in the previous section. In this section, we review the JSON data searching mechanism because you are likely to use these functions more than any other, especially in your queries.

There are four JSON functions that allow you to search JSON documents. As with the previous functions, these operate on a JSON document with one or more parameters. I call them searching functions not because they allow you to search a database or table for JSON data, but rather they allow you to find things in JSON documents. The functions include those for checking to see if a value or element exists in the document, whether a path expression is valid (something can be found using it), and retrieving information from the document.

The JSON_CONTAINS() function has two options: you can use it to return whether a value exists anywhere in the document or if a value exists using a path expression (the path expression is an optional parameter). The function returns a 0 or 1 where a 0 means the value was not found. An error occurs if either document argument is not a valid JSON document, the path argument is not a valid path expression, or contains a * or ** wildcard. There is another catch. The value you pass in must be a valid JSON string or document. Listing 3-13 shows several examples of using the function to search a JSON document.

Listing 3-13. Using the JSON_CONTAINS Function

```
MySQL  localhost:33060+ ssl  SQL > SET @base = '{"grapes":["red","white",
"green"],"berries":["strawberry","raspberry","boysenberry","blackberry"]}';
Query OK, 0 rows affected (0.00 sec)
MySQL  localhost:33060+ ssl  SQL > SELECT JSON_CONTAINS(@base,'["red",
"white","green"]');
+-------------------------------------------------+
| JSON_CONTAINS(@base,'["red","white","green"]')  |
+-------------------------------------------------+
|                                              0  |
+-------------------------------------------------+
1 row in set (0.00 sec)
MySQL  localhost:33060+ ssl  SQL > SELECT JSON_CONTAINS(@base,'{"grapes":
["red","white","green"]}');
+-----------------------------------------------------------+
| JSON_CONTAINS(@base,'{"grapes":["red","white","green"]}')  |
+-----------------------------------------------------------+
|                                                        1  |
+-----------------------------------------------------------+
1 row in set (0.00 sec)
```

```
 MySQL  localhost:33060+ ssl  SQL > SELECT JSON_CONTAINS(@base,'["red",
"white","green"]','$.grapes');
+---------------------------------------------------------------+
| JSON_CONTAINS(@base,'["red","white","green"]','$.grapes') |
+---------------------------------------------------------------+
|                                                         1 |
+---------------------------------------------------------------+
1 row in set (0.00 sec)
 MySQL  localhost:33060+ ssl  SQL > SELECT JSON_CONTAINS(@base,'
"blackberry"','$.berries');
+-----------------------------------------------+
| JSON_CONTAINS(@base,'"blackberry"','$.berries') |
+-----------------------------------------------+
|                                             0 |
+-----------------------------------------------+
1 row in set (0.00 sec)
 MySQL  localhost:33060+ ssl  SQL > SELECT JSON_CONTAINS(@base,
 'blackberry','$.berries');
ERROR: 3141: Invalid JSON text in argument 2 to function json_contains:
"Invalid value." at position 0.
 MySQL  localhost:33060+ ssl  SQL > SELECT JSON_CONTAINS(@base,'"red"',
'$.grapes');
+---------------------------------------+
| JSON_CONTAINS(@base,'"red"','$.grapes') |
+---------------------------------------+
|                                     1 |
+---------------------------------------+
1 row in set (0.00 sec)
```

As you can see, this is a very useful function but it requires a bit of care to use properly. That is, you must make sure the value is a valid string. In all examples save one, I am searching the JSON document for either a JSON document (that makes searching for nested data easier), or a single value using a path expression. Remember, the function searches for values, not keys.

Note the second to last example: this returns an error because the value is not a valid JSON string. You must use double quotes around it to correct it as shown in the following example.

The JSON_CONTAINS_PATH() function uses a parameter strategy that is a little different. The function searches a JSON document to see if a path expression exists but it also allows you to find the first occurrence or all occurrences. It also can take multiple paths and evaluate them either as an "or" or "and" condition depending on what value you pass as the second parameter as in the following:

- If you pass one, the function will return 1 if at least one path expression is found (OR).

- If you pass all, the function will return 1 only if all path expressions are found (AND).

The function returns 0 or 1 to indicate whether a JSON document contains data at a given path or paths. Note that it can return null if any of the path expressions or the document is null. An error occurs if the JSON document, or any path expression is not valid, or the second parameter is not one or all. Listing 3-14 shows several examples of using the function.

Listing 3-14. Using the JSON_CONTAINS_PATH Function

```
MySQL  localhost:33060+ ssl  SQL > SET @base = '{"grapes":["red","white",
"green"],"berries":["strawberry","raspberry","boysenberry","blackberrry"],"
numbers":["1","2","3","4","5"]}';
Query OK, 0 rows affected (0.00 sec)
 MySQL  localhost:33060+ ssl  SQL > SELECT JSON_CONTAINS_PATH(@base,'one','$');
+----------------------------------------+
| JSON_CONTAINS_PATH(@base,'one','$') |
+----------------------------------------+
|                                      1 |
+----------------------------------------+
1 row in set (0.00 sec)
 MySQL  localhost:33060+ ssl  SQL > SELECT JSON_CONTAINS_PATH(@base,'all','$');
+----------------------------------------+
| JSON_CONTAINS_PATH(@base,'all','$') |
+----------------------------------------+
|                                      1 |
+----------------------------------------+
```

```
1 row in set (0.00 sec)
 MySQL  localhost:33060+ ssl  SQL > SELECT JSON_CONTAINS_PATH(@base,
'all','$.grapes','$.berries');
+----------------------------------------------------------+
| JSON_CONTAINS_PATH(@base,'all','$.grapes','$.berries') |
+----------------------------------------------------------+
|                                                     1 |
+----------------------------------------------------------+
1 row in set (0.00 sec)
 MySQL  localhost:33060+ ssl  SQL > SELECT JSON_CONTAINS_PATH(@base,
'all','$.grapes','$.berries','$.numbers');
+----------------------------------------------------------------------+
| JSON_CONTAINS_PATH(@base,'all','$.grapes','$.berries','$.numbers') |
+----------------------------------------------------------------------+
|                                                                 1 |
+----------------------------------------------------------------------+
1 row in set (0.00 sec)
 MySQL  localhost:33060+ ssl  SQL > SELECT JSON_CONTAINS_PATH(@base,
'all','$.grapes','$.berries','$.num');
+--------------------------------------------------------------------+
| JSON_CONTAINS_PATH(@base,'all','$.grapes','$.berries','$.num') |
+--------------------------------------------------------------------+
|                                                              0 |
+--------------------------------------------------------------------+
1 row in set (0.00 sec)
 MySQL  localhost:33060+ ssl  SQL > SELECT JSON_CONTAINS_PATH(@base,
'one','$.grapes','$.berries','$.num');
+--------------------------------------------------------------------+
| JSON_CONTAINS_PATH(@base,'one','$.grapes','$.berries','$.num') |
+--------------------------------------------------------------------+
|                                                              1 |
+--------------------------------------------------------------------+
1 row in set (0.00 sec)
```

```
MySQL  localhost:33060+ ssl  SQL > SELECT JSON_CONTAINS_PATH(@base,
'one','$.grapes');
+-------------------------------------------+
| JSON_CONTAINS_PATH(@base,'one','$.grapes') |
+-------------------------------------------+
|                                         1 |
+-------------------------------------------+
1 row in set (0.00 sec)
MySQL  localhost:33060+ ssl  SQL > SELECT JSON_CONTAINS_PATH(@base,
'all','$.grape');
+------------------------------------------+
| JSON_CONTAINS_PATH(@base,'all','$.grape') |
+------------------------------------------+
|                                        0 |
+------------------------------------------+
1 row in set (0.00 sec)
MySQL  localhost:33060+ ssl  SQL > SELECT JSON_CONTAINS_PATH(@base,
'one','$.berries');
+--------------------------------------------+
| JSON_CONTAINS_PATH(@base,'one','$.berries') |
+--------------------------------------------+
|                                          1 |
+--------------------------------------------+
1 row in set (0.00 sec)
MySQL  localhost:33060+ ssl  SQL > SELECT JSON_CONTAINS_PATH(@base,
'all','$.berries');
+--------------------------------------------+
| JSON_CONTAINS_PATH(@base,'all','$.berries') |
+--------------------------------------------+
|                                          1 |
+--------------------------------------------+
1 row in set (0.00 sec)
```

Take some time to look through these examples so you can see how they work. Note that in the first two commands I used a path expression of a single dollar sign. This is simply the path expression to the entire document so naturally, it exists. Note also the differences in the use of one or all for the last two examples.

The JSON_EXTRACT() function is one of the most used functions. It allows you to extract a value, JSON array, JSON object, and so forth from a JSON document using one or more path expressions. We have already seen a couple of examples. Recall the function returns the portion of the JSON document that matches the path expression. Listing 3-15 shows a few more examples using complex path expressions.

Listing 3-15. Using the JSON_EXTRACT Function

```
MySQL  localhost:33060+ ssl  SQL > SET@base = '{"grapes":["red","white",
"green"],"berries":["strawberry","raspberry","boysenberry","blackberry"],
"numbers":["1","2","3","4","5"]}';
Query OK, 0 rows affected (0.00 sec)
MySQL  localhost:33060+ ssl  SQL > SELECT JSON_EXTRACT(@base,'$');
+---------------------------------------------------------------------+
| JSON_EXTRACT(@base,'$')                                             |
+---------------------------------------------------------------------+
| {"grapes": ["red", "white", "green"], "berries": ["strawberry",
"raspberry", "boysenberry", "blackberry"], "numbers": ["1", "2", "3", "4",
"5"]} |
+---------------------------------------------------------------------+
1 row in set (0.00 sec)
MySQL  localhost:33060+ ssl  SQL > SELECT JSON_EXTRACT(@base,'$.grapes');
+-------------------------------+
| JSON_EXTRACT(@base,'$.grapes') |
+-------------------------------+
| ["red", "white", "green"]     |
+-------------------------------+
1 row in set (0.00 sec)
MySQL  localhost:33060+ ssl  SQL > SELECT JSON_EXTRACT(@base,'$.grapes[*]');
```

```
+-----------------------------------+
| JSON_EXTRACT(@base,'$.grapes[*]') |
+-----------------------------------+
| ["red", "white", "green"]         |
+-----------------------------------+
1 row in set (0.00 sec)
 MySQL  localhost:33060+ ssl  SQL > SELECT JSON_EXTRACT(@base,'$.grapes[1]');
+-----------------------------------+
| JSON_EXTRACT(@base,'$.grapes[1]') |
+-----------------------------------+
| "white"                           |
+-----------------------------------+
1 row in set (0.00 sec)
 MySQL  localhost:33060+ ssl  SQL > SELECT JSON_EXTRACT(@base,'$.grapes[4]');
+-----------------------------------+
| JSON_EXTRACT(@base,'$.grapes[4]') |
+-----------------------------------+
| NULL                              |
+-----------------------------------+
1 row in set (0.00 sec)
 MySQL  localhost:33060+ ssl  SQL > SELECT JSON_EXTRACT(@base,'$.berries');
+-------------------------------------------------------------+
| JSON_EXTRACT(@base,'$.berries')                             |
+-------------------------------------------------------------+
| ["strawberry", "raspberry", "boysenberry", "blackberry"]   |
+-------------------------------------------------------------+
1 row in set (0.00 sec)
 MySQL  localhost:33060+ ssl  SQL > SELECT JSON_EXTRACT(@base,'$.berries[2]');
+------------------------------------+
| JSON_EXTRACT(@base,'$.berries[2]') |
+------------------------------------+
| "boysenberry"                      |
+------------------------------------+
1 row in set (0.00 sec)
 MySQL  localhost:33060+ ssl  SQL > SELECT JSON_EXTRACT(@base,
 '$.berries[2]','$.berries[3]');
```

```
+-----------------------------------------------------+
| JSON_EXTRACT(@base,'$.berries[2]','$.berries[3]') |
+-----------------------------------------------------+
| ["boysenberry", "blackberry"]                       |
+-----------------------------------------------------+
1 row in set (0.00 sec)
```

Note what happens when we use the single dollar sign. The function returns the entire document. Also, note what happens when we use a path expression, although its syntax is valid it does not evaluate to an element in the document (see the fifth command).

Note the last example where we pass in two path expressions. Then notice how it returns a JSON array whereas the example before it with only one path expression returns a JSON string value. This is one of the trickier aspects of the function. So long as you remember it returns a valid JSON string, array, or object, you will be able to use the function without issue.

The JSON_SEARCH() function is interesting because it is the opposite of the JSON_EXTRACT() function. More specific, it takes one or more values and returns path expressions to the values if they are found in the document. This makes it easier to validate your path expressions or to build path expressions on the fly.

As with the JSON_CONTAINS_PATH() function, the JSON_SEARCH() function also allows you to find the first occurrence or all occurrences returning the path expressions depending on what value you pass as the second parameter as in the following:

- If you pass one, the function will return the first match.

- If you pass all, the function will return all matches.

But there is a trick here too. The function takes a third parameter that forms a special search string that works as the LIKE operator in SQL statements. That is, search string argument can use the % and _ characters the same way as the LIKE operator. Note that to use a % or _ as a literal, you must precede it with the \ (escape) character.

The function returns 0 or 1 to indicate whether a JSON document contains the values. Note that it can return null if any of the path expressions or the document is null. An error occurs if the JSON document, or any path expression is not valid, or the second parameter is not one or all. Listing 3-16 shows several examples of using the function.

Listing 3-16. Using the JSON_SEARCH Function

```
 MySQL  localhost:33060+ ssl  SQL > SET @base = '{"grapes":["red","white",
"green"],"berries":["strawberry","raspberry","boysenberry","blackberrry"],
"numbers":["1","2","3","4","5"]}';
Query OK, 0 rows affected (0.00 sec)
 MySQL  localhost:33060+ ssl  SQL > SELECT JSON_SEARCH(@base,'all','red');
+-------------------------------+
| JSON_SEARCH(@base,'all','red') |
+-------------------------------+
| "$.grapes[0]"                 |
+-------------------------------+
1 row in set (0.00 sec)
 MySQL  localhost:33060+ ssl  SQL > SELECT JSON_SEARCH(@base,'all','gr___');
+----------------------------------+
| JSON_SEARCH(@base,'all','gr___') |
+----------------------------------+
| NULL                             |
+----------------------------------+
1 row in set (0.00 sec)
 MySQL  localhost:33060+ ssl  SQL > SELECT JSON_SEARCH(@base,'one','%berry');
+----------------------------------+
| JSON_SEARCH(@base,'one','%berry') |
+----------------------------------+
| "$.berries[0]"                   |
+----------------------------------+
1 row in set (0.00 sec)
 MySQL  localhost:33060+ ssl  SQL > SELECT JSON_SEARCH(@base,'all','%berry');
+----------------------------------------------------+
| JSON_SEARCH(@base,'all','%berry')                  |
+----------------------------------------------------+
| ["$.berries[0]", "$.berries[1]", "$.berries[2]"]   |
+----------------------------------------------------+
1 row in set (0.00 sec)
```

Now let's look at the last group of JSON functions; those that are utilitarian in nature allowing you to get information about the JSON document and perform simple operations to help work with JSON documents.

Utility Functions

Last, there are several functions that can return information about the JSON document, help add or remove quotes, and even find the keys in a document. We have already seen several of the utility JSON_TYPE() and JSON_VALID() functions. The following are additional utility functions you may find useful when working with JSON documents.

The JSON_DEPTH() function returns the maximum depth of a JSON document. If the document is an empty array, object, or a scalar value; the function returns a depth of 1. An array containing only elements of depth 1 or nonempty objects containing only member values of depth 1 returns a depth of 2. Listing 3-17 shows several examples.

Listing 3-17. Using the JSON_DEPTH Function

```
MySQL  localhost:33060+ ssl  SQL > SELECT JSON_DEPTH('8');
+-----------------+
| JSON_DEPTH('8') |
+-----------------+
|               1 |
+-----------------+
1 row in set (0.00 sec)
MySQL  localhost:33060+ ssl  SQL > SELECT JSON_DEPTH('[]');
+------------------+
| JSON_DEPTH('[]') |
+------------------+
|                1 |
+------------------+
1 row in set (0.00 sec)
MySQL  localhost:33060+ ssl  SQL > SELECT JSON_DEPTH('{}');
+------------------+
| JSON_DEPTH('{}') |
+------------------+
|                1 |
+------------------+
```

```
1 row in set (0.00 sec)
 MySQL  localhost:33060+ ssl  SQL > SELECT JSON_DEPTH('[12,3,4,5,6]');
+----------------------------+
| JSON_DEPTH('[12,3,4,5,6]') |
+----------------------------+
|                          2 |
+----------------------------+
1 row in set (0.00 sec)
 MySQL  localhost:33060+ ssl  SQL > SELECT JSON_DEPTH('[[], {}]');
+------------------------+
| JSON_DEPTH('[[], {}]') |
+------------------------+
|                      2 |
+------------------------+
1 row in set (0.00 sec)
 MySQL  localhost:33060+ ssl  SQL > SET @base = '{"grapes":["red","white",
"green"],"berries":["strawberry","raspberry","boysenberry","blackberrry"],
"numbers":["1","2","3","4","5"]}';
Query OK, 0 rows affected (0.00 sec)
 MySQL  localhost:33060+ ssl  SQL > SELECT JSON_DEPTH(@base);
+-------------------+
| JSON_DEPTH(@base) |
+-------------------+
|                 3 |
+-------------------+
1 row in set (0.00 sec)
 MySQL  localhost:33060+ ssl  SQL > SELECT JSON_DEPTH(JSON_EXTRACT(@base,
'$.grapes'));
+---------------------------------------------+
| JSON_DEPTH(JSON_EXTRACT(@base, '$.grapes')) |
+---------------------------------------------+
|                                           2 |
+---------------------------------------------+
1 row in set (0.00 sec)
```

The JSON_KEYS() function is used to return a list of keys from the top-level value of a JSON object as a JSON array. The function also allows you to pass a path expression, which results in a list of the top-level keys from the selected path expression value. An error occurs if the json_doc argument is not a valid JSON document or the path argument is not a valid path expression or contains a * or ** wildcard. The resulting array is empty if the selected object is empty.

There is one limitation. If the top-level value has nested JSON objects, the array returned does not include keys from those nested objects. Listing 3-18 shows several examples of using this function.

Listing 3-18. Using the JSON_KEYS Function

```
MySQL  localhost:33060+ ssl  SQL > SET @base = '{"grapes":["red","white",
"green"],"berries":["strawberry","raspberry","boysenberry","blackberrry"],
"numbers":["1","2","3","4","5"]}';
Query OK, 0 rows affected (0.00 sec)
MySQL  localhost:33060+ ssl  SQL > SELECT JSON_KEYS(@base);
+---------------------------------+
| JSON_KEYS(@base)                |
+---------------------------------+
| ["grapes", "berries", "numbers"] |
+---------------------------------+
1 row in set (0.00 sec)
MySQL  localhost:33060+ ssl  SQL > SELECT JSON_KEYS(@base,'$');
+---------------------------------+
| JSON_KEYS(@base,'$')            |
+---------------------------------+
| ["grapes", "berries", "numbers"] |
+---------------------------------+
1 row in set (0.00 sec)
MySQL  localhost:33060+ ssl  SQL > SELECT JSON_KEYS('{"z":123,"x":
{"albedo":50}}');
```

117

```
+-----------------------------------------+
| JSON_KEYS('{"z":123,"x":{"albedo":50}}') |
+-----------------------------------------+
| ["x", "z"]                              |
+-----------------------------------------+
```
```
1 row in set (0.00 sec)
 MySQL  localhost:33060+ ssl  SQL > SELECT JSON_KEYS('{"z":123,"x":
{"albedo":50}}', '$.x');
+-----------------------------------------------+
| JSON_KEYS('{"z":123,"x":{"albedo":50}}', '$.x') |
+-----------------------------------------------+
| ["albedo"]                                    |
+-----------------------------------------------+
```
```
1 row in set (0.00 sec)
```

The JSON_LENGTH() function returns the length of the JSON document passed. It also allows you to pass in a path expression and if provided, will return the length of the value that matches the path expression. An error occurs if the json_doc argument is not a valid JSON document or the path argument is not a valid path expression or contains a * or ** wildcard. However, the value returned has several constraints as in the following:

- A scalar has length 1.

- An array has a length equal to the number of array elements.

- An object has a length equal to the number of object members.

However, there is one surprising limitation: the length returned does not count the length of nested arrays or objects. Thus, you must use this function carefully using the path expression for nested documents.

Listing 3-19 shows several examples of using the function.

Listing 3-19. Using the JSON_LENGTH Function

```
 MySQL  localhost:33060+ ssl  SQL > SET @base = '{"grapes":["red","white",
"green"],"berries":["strawberry","raspberry","boysenberry","blackberrry"],
"numbers":["1","2","3","4","5"]}';
Query OK, 0 rows affected (0.00 sec)
```

```
 MySQL  localhost:33060+ ssl  SQL > SELECT JSON_LENGTH(@base,'$');
+----------------------+
| JSON_LENGTH(@base,'$') |
+----------------------+
|                    3 |
+----------------------+
1 row in set (0.00 sec)
 MySQL  localhost:33060+ ssl  SQL > SELECT JSON_LENGTH(@base,'$.grapes');
+-----------------------------+
| JSON_LENGTH(@base,'$.grapes') |
+-----------------------------+
|                           3 |
+-----------------------------+
1 row in set (0.00 sec)
 MySQL  localhost:33060+ ssl  SQL > SELECT JSON_LENGTH(@base,'$.grapes[1]');
+--------------------------------+
| JSON_LENGTH(@base,'$.grapes[1]') |
+--------------------------------+
|                              1 |
+--------------------------------+
1 row in set (0.00 sec)
 MySQL  localhost:33060+ ssl  SQL > SELECT JSON_LENGTH(@base,'$.grapes[4]');
+--------------------------------+
| JSON_LENGTH(@base,'$.grapes[4]') |
+--------------------------------+
|                           NULL |
+--------------------------------+
1 row in set (0.00 sec)
 MySQL  localhost:33060+ ssl  SQL > SELECT JSON_LENGTH(@base,'$.berries');
+------------------------------+
| JSON_LENGTH(@base,'$.berries') |
+------------------------------+
|                            4 |
+------------------------------+
1 row in set (0.00 sec)
```

```
MySQL  localhost:33060+ ssl  SQL > SELECT JSON_LENGTH(@base,'$.numbers');
+------------------------------+
| JSON_LENGTH(@base,'$.numbers') |
+------------------------------+
|                            5 |
+------------------------------+
1 row in set (0.00 sec)
```

Note the fourth command returns null because the path expression, although valid syntax, does not evaluate to a value or nested JSON array or object.

The JSON_QUOTE() function is a handy function to use that will help you add quotes where they are appropriate. That is, the function quotes a string as a JSON string by wrapping it with double quote characters and escaping interior quote and other characters and returns the result. Note that this function does not operate on a JSON document, rather, only a string.

You can use this function to produce a valid JSON string literal for inclusion within a JSON document. Listing 3-20 shows a few short examples of using the function to quote JSON strings.

Listing 3-20. Using the JSON_QUOTE Function

```
MySQL  localhost:33060+ ssl  SQL > SELECT JSON_QUOTE("test");
+--------------------+
| JSON_QUOTE("test") |
+--------------------+
| "test"             |
+--------------------+
1 row in set (0.00 sec)
MySQL  localhost:33060+ ssl  SQL > SELECT JSON_QUOTE('[true]');
+----------------------+
| JSON_QUOTE('[true]') |
+----------------------+
| "[true]"             |
+----------------------+
1 row in set (0.00 sec)
```

```
MySQL  localhost:33060+ ssl  SQL > SELECT JSON_QUOTE('90125');
+---------------------+
| JSON_QUOTE('90125') |
+---------------------+
| "90125"             |
+---------------------+
1 row in set (0.00 sec)
 MySQL  localhost:33060+ ssl SQL > SELECT JSON_QUOTE('["red","white","green"]');
+----------------------------------------+
| JSON_QUOTE('["red","white","green"]')  |
+----------------------------------------+
| "[\"red\",\"white\",\"green\"]"        |
+----------------------------------------+
1 row in set (0.00 sec)
```

Note that in the last example the function adds the escape character (\) because the string passed contains quotes. Why is this happening? Remember, this function takes a string, not a JSON array as the parameter.

The JSON_UNQUOTE() function is the opposite of the JSON_QUOTE() function. The JSON_UNQUOTE() function removes quotes JSON value and returns the result as a utf8mb4 string. The function is designed to recognize and not alter markup sequences as in the following:

- \": A double quote (") character
- \b: A backspace character
- \f: A formfeed character
- \n: A newline (linefeed) character
- \r: A carriage return character
- \t: A tab character
- \\: A backslash (\) character

Listing 3-21 shows examples of using the function.

121

Listing 3-21. Using the `JSON_UNQUOTE` Function

```
MySQL  localhost:33060+ ssl  SQL > SELECT JSON_UNQUOTE("test 123");
+-------------------------+
| JSON_UNQUOTE("test 123") |
+-------------------------+
| test 123                |
+-------------------------+
1 row in set (0.00 sec)
MySQL  localhost:33060+ ssl  SQL > SELECT JSON_UNQUOTE('"true"');
+-----------------------+
| JSON_UNQUOTE('"true"') |
+-----------------------+
| true                  |
+-----------------------+
1 row in set (0.00 sec)
MySQL  localhost:33060+ ssl  SQL > SELECT JSON_UNQUOTE('\"true\"');
+-------------------------+
| JSON_UNQUOTE('\"true\"') |
+-------------------------+
| true                    |
+-------------------------+
1 row in set (0.00 sec)
MySQL  localhost:33060+ ssl  SQL > SELECT JSON_UNQUOTE('9\t0\t125\\');
+---------------------------+
| JSON_UNQUOTE('9\t0\t125\\') |
+---------------------------+
| 9 0 125\                  |
+---------------------------+
1 row in set (0.00 sec)
```

The JSON_PRETTY() function formats a JSON document for easier viewing. You can use this to produce an output to send to users or to make the JSON look a bit nicer in the shell. Listing 3-22 shows an example without the function and the same with the function. Note how much easier it is to read when using JSON_PRETTY().

Listing 3-22. Using the JSON_PRETTY Function

```
 MySQL  localhost:33060+ ssl  SQL > SET @base = '{"name": {"last":
"Throckmutton", "first": "Billy-bob"}, "address": {"zip": "90125", "city":
"Melborne", "state": "California", "street": "4 Main Street"}}';
Query OK, 0 rows affected (0.00 sec)
 MySQL  localhost:33060+ ssl  SQL > SELECT @base \G
*************************** 1. row ***************************
@base: {"name": {"last": "Throckmutton", "first": "Billy-bob"}, "address":
{"zip": "90125", "city": "Melborne", "state": "California", "street":
"4 Main Street"}}
1 row in set (0.00 sec)
 MySQL  localhost:33060+ ssl  SQL > SELECT JSON_PRETTY(@base) \G
*************************** 1. row ***************************
JSON_PRETTY(@base): {
  "name": {
    "last": "Throckmutton",
    "first": "Billy-bob"
  },
  "address": {
    "zip": "90125",
    "city": "Melborne",
    "state": "California",
    "street": "4 Main Street"
  }
}
1 row in set (0.00 sec)
```

There are also functions for checking size; JSON_STORAGE_FREE() and JSON_STORAGE_SIZE(). The first is used after a partial update and the second is used to get the size of the binary representation of the JSON document. See the online MySQL reference manual for more details on these functions as they are new and not commonly used except for very special circumstances in which size is a concern.

Finally, there is a new function released in version 8.0.4 intriguingly named JSON_TABLE(). This function takes a JSON document and returns a tabular data list. In basic terms, rather than returning output as JSON, this function returns rows as a result set. Thus, you can use this function where you need more traditional rows to work within your applications.

The function has some peculiar syntax. It takes as parameters a JSON document (array), and an expression path and column definition. The last two are not separated by a comma (strangely). This arrangement makes the function a bit harder to use but once you see a working example it is easier to understand. So, let's do that. Listing 3-23 demonstrates how to use the function.

Listing 3-23. Using the JSON_TABLE Function

```
MySQL  localhost:33060+  SQL > set @phones = '[{"name":"Bill Smith","phone":
"8013321033"},{"name":"Folley Finn","phone":"9991112222"},{"name":"Carrie
Tonnesth","phone":"6498881212"}]';
Query OK, 0 rows affected (0.00 sec)

MySQL  localhost:33060+  SQL > SELECT * FROM JSON_TABLE(@phones, "$[*]"
COLUMNS(name char(20) PATH '$.name', phone char(16) PATH '$.phone')) as
phone_list;
+------------------+------------+
| name             | phone      |
+------------------+------------+
| Bill Smith       | 8013321033 |
| Folley Finn      | 9991112222 |
| Carrie Tonnesth  | 6498881212 |
+------------------+------------+
3 rows in set (0.00 sec)
```

Note that we are using a JSON array of names and phone numbers to keep it simple. The function is used as if it were a table so we add it to the FROM clause on a SELECT statement. The parameters are the JSON document, then the path and column definition. The expression path used is simply retrieving the entire element from the array. You can use a variety of path expression here if you wanted to select only part of the document to operate on. Next is the column definition and this should look familiar to you—it's like column definitions for tables. The difference is we append a path expression on the end with the keyword PATH. This simply locates the value in the JSON document.

As you can imagine, you can form complex definitions drilling down to precisely the elements you want. The demand and use cases for this function will likely grow given that it is a recent addition, but if you need to turn a JSON document into a result set, this function can achieve those results albeit with some creativity and path expressions.

For more information about the JSON_TABLE() function, see the section entitled "JSON Table Functions" in the online MySQL reference manual.

Tip   For more information about JSON functions, see the online MySQL reference manual. The JSON functions are listed with the other functions based on use. I recommend searching the document for the function you want to learn more about or use the index entitled, "Function Index," which lists all the functions in alphabetical order.

Now that we know more about JSON, the "Combining SQL and JSON—Indexing JSON DATA" section presents some advanced topics for working with JSON in SQL statements.

Combining SQL and JSON - Indexing JSON Data

One of the definitions of NoSQL is "not only SQL" and that moniker applies to MySQL when you consider that you can use JSON documents with your relational data. As we have seen in the examples describing the JSON functions, you can add JSON columns to your tables and store JSON data in the fields.

However, instead of storing the JSON document as a string, MySQL stores the JSON document using a special internal structure that permits MySQL to access, find, and extract the JSON document elements quickly from the row data. Note that this does not mean that MySQL can index the JSON data. In fact, JSON data columns cannot be indexed. At least, not directly. In this section, we will see how to index JSON data to help optimize searching on data elements for rows that contain JSON documents.

WHAT ABOUT CONVERTING TEXT TO JSON?

If you have a database in which you have stored semistructured data in a TEXT or BLOB field, you may want to consider converting the data to JSON documents. The JSON functions we've seen in this chapter are your key to successfully converting the data such as JSON_ARRAY(), JSON_OBJECT(), and JSON_VALID(). I will discuss more about this topic in Chapter 9, including suggestions and examples on how to convert existing data. You may also want to check out various blogs on converting data to JSON—just google phrases similar to, "convert to JSON." Although most blogs are Java-based, you can use them to get ideas for how to convert your own data.

Some may think the restriction prohibiting indexing of JSON columns an oversight, but it isn't. Consider the fact that JSON documents are semistructured data that is not required to conform to any specific layout. That is, one row could contain a JSON document that not only has different keys but also may arrange the document in a different order.

Although this isn't necessarily a show stopper for indexing and despite the special, internal mechanism used to access data in the document, indexing JSON documents directly would be cumbersome and likely to perform poorly. However, all is not lost. MySQL 5.7 introduced a new feature called *generated columns* (sometimes called *virtual columns*).

Generated columns are dynamically resolved columns that are defined by the CREATE or ALTER TABLE statements. There are two types of virtual columns: those that are generated on demand (called *virtual generated columns*), which do not use any additional storage; and those generated columns that can be stored in the rows. Virtual generated columns use the VIRTUAL option and stored generated columns use the STORED option in the CREATE or ALTER TABLE statement.

So how does this work? We create the generated column to extract data from the JSON document then use that column to create an index. Thus, the index can be used to find rows more quickly. That is if you want to perform grouping, ordering, or want to search for a subset of rows that predicate on the JSON data, you can create and index for the optimizer to use to retrieve the data more quickly.

Let's see an example. The following shows a table I created to store information in a JSON column.

```
CREATE TABLE `test`.`thermostats` (
  `model_number` char(20) NOT NULL,
  `manufacturer` char(30) DEFAULT NULL,
  `capabilities` json DEFAULT NULL,
  PRIMARY KEY (`model_number`)
) ENGINE=InnoDB DEFAULT CHARSET=latin1;
INSERT INTO `test`.`thermostats` VALUES ('AB-90125-C1', 'Jasper', '{"rpm":
1500, "color": "beige", "modes": ["ac"], "voltage": 110, "capability":
"auto fan"}');
INSERT INTO `test`.`thermostats` VALUES ('ODX-123','Genie','{"rpm": 3000,
"color": "white", "modes": ["ac", "furnace"], "voltage": 220, "capability":
"fan"}');
```

Note that this table has a single JSON field and a single character field for the model number that is also the primary key. Suppose the rows contain JSON data such as the following in the capabilities column.

```
MySQL  localhost:33060+ ssl  SQL > SELECT * FROM `test`.`thermostats` LIMIT 2 \G
*************************** 1. row ***************************
model_number: AB-90125-C1
manufacturer: Jasper
capabilities: {"rpm": 1500, "color": "beige", "modes": ["ac"], "voltage":
110, "capability": "auto fan"}
*************************** 2. row ***************************
model_number: ODX-123
manufacturer: Genie
capabilities: {"rpm": 3000, "color": "white", "modes": ["ac", "furnace"],
"voltage": 220, "capability": "fan"}
2 rows in set (0.00 sec)
```

Now suppose we wanted to execute queries to select rows by one or more of the data elements in the JSON document. For example, suppose we wanted to run queries that locate rows that have fans that operate at 110 volts. If the table contains hundreds of thousands or even tens of millions of rows and there is not index, the optimizer must read all the rows (a table scan). However, if there is an index on the data, the optimizer merely needs to generate the virtual generated column, which is potentially more efficient.

To mitigate the potential performance issue, we can add a virtual generated column on the table using the voltage element. The following shows the ALTER TABLE statements we can use to add the virtual generated column.

```
ALTER TABLE `test`.`thermostats` ADD COLUMN voltage INT GENERATED ALWAYS AS
(capabilities->'$.voltage') VIRTUAL;
ALTER TABLE `test`.`thermostats` ADD INDEX volts (voltage);
```

Note   If you leave off the option, the generated column generated is a virtual generated column.

You also can recreate the table if you want, but that will require reloading the data. However, I show the new CREATE TABLE statement below so you can see how to create a virtual generated column on the table at the time that it is created.

```
CREATE TABLE `test`.`thermostats` (
  `model_number` char(20) NOT NULL,
  `manufacturer` char(30) DEFAULT NULL,
  `capabilities` json DEFAULT NULL,
  `voltage` int(11) GENERATED ALWAYS AS (json_extract(`capabilities`,
  '$.voltage')) VIRTUAL,
  PRIMARY KEY (`model_number`),
  KEY `volts` (`voltage`)
) ENGINE=InnoDB DEFAULT CHARSET=latin1;
```

Note that I used the shortcut -> in the ALTER TABLE statement but the CREATE TABLE statement has the JSON_EXTRACT() function instead.

If you're curious if adding the virtual generated column and index makes a difference, Listing 3-24 shows how the optimizer would run the query before adding the column and after adding the column.

Listing 3-24. Optimizer EXPLAIN Results for Query

```
 MySQL  localhost:33060+ ssl  SQL > DROP TABLE IF EXISTS
`test`.`thermostats`;
Query OK, 0 rows affected (0.00 sec)
 MySQL  localhost:33060+ ssl  SQL > CREATE TABLE `test`.`thermostats`
(`model_number` char(20) NOT NULL,`manufacturer` char(30) DEFAULT
NULL,`capabilities` json DEFAULT NULL,PRIMARY KEY (`model_number`))
ENGINE=InnoDB DEFAULT CHARSET=latin1;
Query OK, 0 rows affected (0.00 sec)
 MySQL  localhost:33060+ ssl  SQL > INSERT INTO `test`.`thermostats`
VALUES ('ODX-123','Genie','{"rpm": 3000, "color": "white", "modes": ["ac",
"furnace"], "voltage": 220, "capability": "fan"}');
Query OK, 1 row affected (0.00 sec)
 MySQL  localhost:33060+ ssl  SQL > INSERT INTO `test`.`thermostats` VALUES
('AB-90125-C1', 'Jasper', '{"rpm": 1500, "color": "beige", "modes": ["ac"],
"voltage": 110, "capability": "auto fan"}');
Query OK, 1 row affected (0.00 sec)
```

 # Query without virtual generated column.

```
 MySQL  localhost:33060+ ssl  SQL > EXPLAIN SELECT * FROM thermostats WHERE
capabilities->'$.voltage' = 110 \G
*************************** 1. row ***************************
           id: 1
  select_type: SIMPLE
        table: thermostats
   partitions: NULL
         type: ALL
possible_keys: NULL
          key: NULL
      key_len: NULL
          ref: NULL
         rows: 23302
```

```
      filtered: 100.00
         Extra: Using where
1 row in set, 1 warning (0.00 sec)
Note (code 1003): /* select#1 */ select `test`.`thermostats`.`model_
number` AS `model_number`,`test`.`thermostats`.`manufacturer` AS `man
ufacturer`,`test`.`thermostats`.`capabilities` AS `capabilities` from
`test`.`thermostats` where (json_extract(`test`.`thermostats`.`capabilities`,
'$.voltage') = 110)
 MySQL  localhost:33060+ ssl  SQL > ALTER TABLE `test`.`thermostats`
ADD COLUMN color char(20) GENERATED ALWAYS AS (capabilities->'$.color')
VIRTUAL;
Query OK, 0 rows affected (0.00 sec)
```

Query with virtual generated column.

```
 MySQL  localhost:33060+ ssl  SQL > DROP TABLE `test`.`thermostats`;
Query OK, 0 rows affected (0.00 sec)

 MySQL  localhost:33060+ ssl  SQL > CREATE TABLE `thermostats` (`model_
number` char(20) NOT NULL, `manufacturer` char(30) DEFAULT NULL,
`capabilities` json DEFAULT NULL, `voltage` int(11) GENERATED ALWAYS AS
(json_extract(`capabilities`,'$.voltage')) VIRTUAL, PRIMARY KEY (`model_
number`), KEY `volts` (`voltage`)) ENGINE=InnoDB DEFAULT CHARSET=latin1;
Query OK, 0 rows affected (0.00 sec)

 MySQL  localhost:33060+ ssl  SQL > EXPLAIN SELECT * FROM thermostats WHERE
capabilities->'$.voltage' = 110 \G
*************************** 1. row ***************************
           id: 1
  select_type: SIMPLE
        table: thermostats
   partitions: NULL
         type: ALL
possible_keys: NULL
          key: NULL
      key_len: NULL
          ref: NULL
```

```
      rows: 1102
   filtered: 100.00
      Extra: Using where
1 row in set, 1 warning (0.00 sec)
Note (code 1003): /* select#1 */ select `test`.`thermostats`.`model_number`
AS `model_number`,`test`.`thermostats`.`manufacturer` AS `manufacturer`,
`test`.`thermostats`.`capabilities` AS `capabilities`,`test`.`thermostats`.
`color` AS `color` from `test`.`thermostats` where (json_extract(`test`.
`thermostats`.`capabilities`,'$.voltage') = 110)
```

Note that the first EXPLAIN shows no use of an index (no key, key_len) whereas the second does show the use of an index. The rows result shows how many rows (estimated) will be read to make the comparison. It is clear that adding a generated column and an index can help us optimize our queries of JSON data in relational tables. Cool.

However, there is one thing the example did not cover. If the JSON data element is a string, you must use the JSON_UNQUOTE() function to remove the quotes from the string. Let's suppose we wanted to add a generated column for the color data element. If we add the column and index with the ALTER TABLE statements without removing the quotes, we will get some unusual results as shown in Listing 3-25.

Listing 3-25. Removing Quotes for Generated Columns on JSON Strings

```
MySQL  localhost:33060+ ssl  SQL > DROP TABLE IF EXISTS `test`.`thermostats`;
Query OK, 0 rows affected (0.00 sec)
 MySQL  localhost:33060+ ssl  SQL > CREATE TABLE `test`.`thermostats`
(`model_number` char(20) NOT NULL,`manufacturer` char(30) DEFAULT
NULL,`capabilities` json DEFAULT NULL,PRIMARY KEY (`model_number`))
ENGINE=InnoDB DEFAULT CHARSET=latin1;
Query OK, 0 rows affected (0.00 sec)
 MySQL  localhost:33060+ ssl  SQL > INSERT INTO `test`.`thermostats`
VALUES ('ODX-123','Genie','{"rpm": 3000, "color": "white", "modes": ["ac",
"furnace"], "voltage": 220, "capability": "fan"}');
Query OK, 1 row affected (0.00 sec)
 MySQL  localhost:33060+ ssl  SQL > INSERT INTO `test`.`thermostats` VALUES
('AB-90125-C1', 'Jasper', '{"rpm": 1500, "color": "beige", "modes": ["ac"],
"voltage": 110, "capability": "auto fan"}');
Query OK, 1 row affected (0.00 sec)
```

```
 MySQL  localhost:33060+ ssl  SQL > ALTER TABLE `test`.`thermostats`
ADD COLUMN color char(20) GENERATED ALWAYS AS (capabilities->'$.color')
VIRTUAL;
Query OK, 0 rows affected (0.00 sec)
 MySQL  localhost:33060+ ssl  SQL > SELECT model_number, color FROM
thermostats WHERE color = "beige";
Empty set (0.00 sec)
 MySQL  localhost:33060+ ssl  SQL > SELECT model_number, color FROM
thermostats LIMIT 2;
+--------------+---------+
| model_number | color   |
+--------------+---------+
| AB-90125-C1  | "beige" |
| ODX-123      | "white" |
+--------------+---------+
2 rows in set (0.00 sec)
 MySQL  localhost:33060+ ssl  SQL > ALTER TABLE thermostats DROP COLUMN color;
Query OK, 0 rows affected (0.00 sec)
 MySQL  localhost:33060+ ssl  SQL > ALTER TABLE thermostats ADD COLUMN color
char(20) GENERATED ALWAYS AS (JSON_UNQUOTE(capabilities->'$.color')) VIRTUAL;
Query OK, 0 rows affected (0.00 sec)
 MySQL  localhost:33060+ ssl  SQL > SELECT model_number, color FROM
thermostats WHERE color = 'beige' LIMIT 1;
+--------------+-------+
| model_number | color |
+--------------+-------+
| AB-90125-C1  | beige |
+--------------+-------+
1 row in set (0.00 sec)
```

Note that in the first SELECT statement, there is nothing returned. This is because the virtual generated column used the JSON string with the quotes. This is often a source of confusion when mixing SQL and JSON data. Note that in the second SELECT statement, we see there should have been several rows returned. Note also that after I dropped the column and added it again with the JSON_UNQUOTE() function, the SELECT returns the correct data.

We normally use a virtual generated column so that we don't store anything extra in the row. This is partly because we may not use the index on the JSON data very often and may not need it maintained, but more important because there are restrictions on how you can use/define a stored generated column. The following summarize the restrictions.

- The table must have a primary key defined.

- You must use either a FULLTEXT or RTREE index (instead of the default BTREE).

However, if you have a lot of rows or are using the index on the JSON data frequently or have more than one index on the JSON data, you may want to consider using the stored generated column because virtual generated columns can be computationally taxing when accessing complex or deeply nested data frequently.

Tip   For more information about virtual columns, see the section, "CREATE TABLE and Generated Columns" or "ALTER TABLE and Generated Columns" in the online MySQL reference manual (`https://dev.mysql.com/doc/refman/8.0/en/`).

Summary

The addition of the JSON data type to MySQL has ushered a paradigm shift for how we use MySQL. For the first time, we can store semistructured data inside our relational data (tables). Not only does this give us far more flexibility that we ever had before, it also means we can leverage modern programming techniques to access the data in our applications without major efforts and complexity. JSON is a well-known format and used widely in many applications.

Understanding the JSON data type is key to understanding the document store. This is because the JSON data type, while designed to work with relational data, forms the pattern for how we store data in the document store—in JSON documents! We will see more about the document store in later chapters.

In this chapter, we explored the JSON data type in more detail. We saw examples of how to work with the JSON data in relational tables via the numerous built-in JSON functions provided in MySQL. The JSON data type is key to allowing users to develop hybrid solutions that span the gulf of SQL and NoSQL applications.

In Chapter 4, I explore the MySQL Shell in more detail including an introduction on how to use the MySQL Shell to develop your applications.

CHAPTER 4

The MySQL Shell

One of the largest missing features in the old MySQL client (mysql) was the absence of any form of scripting capability. However, it is possible to use the old client to process a batch of SQL commands and there is limited support in the client for writing stored routines (procedures and functions). For those who wanted to create and use scripts for managing their databases (and server), to date there have been external tool options including the MySQL Workbench and MySQL Utilities but nothing dedicated to incorporating multiple scripting languages.

MySQL Workbench is a fantastically popular product from Oracle. MySQL Workbench is a GUI tool designed as a workstation-based administration tool. It provides a host of features including tools for database design and modeling, SQL development, database administration, database migration, and scripting support with Python. For more information about MySQL Workbench, see `http://dev.mysql.com/doc/workbench/en/`.

MySQL Utilities on the other hand, is a set of Python tools that are used to assist in maintaining and administering MySQL servers, achieving with a single command what would otherwise involve many steps or complex scripting. There are tools for administering the server, working with replication, and more. A library of Python classes is included for those who want to write their own Python scripts. For more information about MySQL Utilities, see `https://dev.mysql.com/doc/mysql-utilities/1.6/en/`.

Note MySQL Utilities is currently limited for use with MySQL 5.7. There is no release available that works with MySQL 8.0 or the document store.

Aside from these products, there has been no answer to requests to add scripting languages to the MySQL client. That is, until now. However, rather than retool the existing (and quite long lived) MySQL client tool, Oracle has released a new client called the MySQL Shell, which supports scripting languages, the X DevAPI, as well as SQL commands and more. But there is far more to the new shell than that.

© Charles Bell 2018

C. Bell, *Introducing the MySQL 8 Document Store*, https://doi.org/10.1007/978-1-4842-2725-1_4

In this chapter, we explore the MySQL Shell in more detail. We saw the shell in action in Chapter 3, but in this chapter we learn more about its major features and options as well as see how to use the new shell to execute scripts interactively. As you will see, the MySQL Shell is another critical element of the future of MySQL.

I recommend reading through the sections in this chapter leading up to the examples at least once before trying out the MySQL Shell yourself. The information presented will help you adjust to using the new commands and connections, which can sometimes be a bit confusing until you understand the concepts.

Note   I use the term, *shell* to refer to features or objects supported by the MySQL Shell. I use *MySQL Shell* to refer to the product itself.

Getting Started

MySQL Shell is a new and exciting addition to the MySQL portfolio. MySQL Shell represents the first modern and advanced client for connecting to and interacting with MySQL. The shell can be used as a scripting environment for developing new tools and applications for working with data. Although it does support an SQL mode, its main purpose is to permit access to data with the JavaScript and Python languages. That's right; you can write Python scripts and execute them within the shell interactively or as a batch. Cool!

Recall from Chapter 1, that the MySQL Shell is designed to use the new X Protocol for communicating with the server via the X Plugin. However, the shell can also connect to the server using the older protocol albeit with limited features in the scripting modes. What this means is, the shell allows you to work with both relational (SQL), JSON documents (NoSQL), or both.

The addition of the SQL mode provides an excellent stepping-stone to learn how to manage your data with scripts. That is, you can continue to use your SQL commands (or batches) until you convert them to JavaScript or Python. Furthermore, you can use both to ensure your migration is complete. Figure 4-1 shows an example of launching MySQL Shell. Note the nifty prompt that displays the MySQL logo, connection information, and mode. Nice!

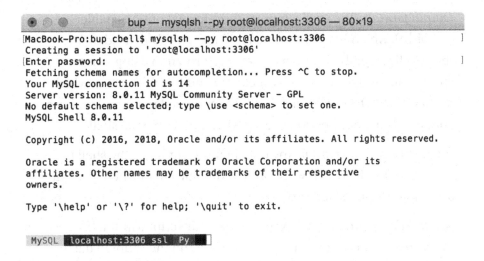

```
●  ●  ●              bup — mysqlsh --py root@localhost:3306 — 80×19
[MacBook-Pro:bup cbell$ mysqlsh --py root@localhost:3306                        ]
Creating a session to 'root@localhost:3306'
[Enter password:                                                               ]
Fetching schema names for autocompletion... Press ^C to stop.
Your MySQL connection id is 14
Server version: 8.0.11 MySQL Community Server - GPL
No default schema selected; type \use <schema> to set one.
MySQL Shell 8.0.11

Copyright (c) 2016, 2018, Oracle and/or its affiliates. All rights reserved.

Oracle is a registered trademark of Oracle Corporation and/or its
affiliates. Other names may be trademarks of their respective
owners.

Type '\help' or '\?' for help; '\quit' to exit.


MySQL   localhost:3306 ssl   Py
```

Figure 4-1. *The MySQL Shell*

The following sections present the major features of the shell at a high level. We will not explore every detail of every feature or option, rather, this chapter provides a broad overview so that you can get started quickly and, more important, learn enough about the shell so that you can follow along with the examples in this book.

For more information about the MySQL Shell, see the section entitled, "MySQL Shell User Guide" in the online MySQL reference manual.

Features

The MySQL Shell has many features including support for traditional SQL command processing, script prototyping, and even support for customizing the shell. In the following I list some of the major features of the shell. Most of the features can be controlled via command line options or with special shell commands. I take a deeper look at some of the more critical features in later sections.

- *Logging*: You can create a log of your session for later analysis or to keep a record of messages. You can set the level of detail with the --log-level option ranging from 1 (nothing logged) to 8 (max debug).

- *Output formats*: The shell supports three format options: table (`--table`), which is the traditional grid format you're used to from the old client; tabbed, which presents information using tabs for spacing and is used for batch execution; and JSON (`--json`), which formats the JSON documents in an easier to read manner. These are command-line options you specify when launching the shell.

- *Interactive code execution*: The default mode for using the shell is interactive mode, which works as a traditional client where you enter a command and get a response.

- *Batch code execution*: If you want to run your script without the interactive session, you can use the shell to run the script in batch mode. However, the output is limited to nonformatted output (but can be overridden with the `--interactive` option).

- *Scripting languages*: The shell supports both JavaScript and Python although you can use only one at a time.

- *Sessions*: Sessions are essentially connections to servers. The shell allows you to store and remove sessions. We will see more about sessions in a later section.

- *Startup scripts*: you can define a script to execute when the shell starts. You can write the script in either JavaScript or Python.

- *Command history and command completion*: The shell saves the commands you enter allowing you to recalling them using the up and down arrow keys. The shell also provides code completion for known keywords, API functions, and SQL keywords.

- *Global variables*: The shell provides a few global variables you can access when in interactive mode. These include the following:

  - `session`: global session object if established

  - `db`: schema if established via a connection

  - `dba`: the AdminAPI object for working with the InnoDB Cluster

  - `shell`: general purpose functions for using the shell

  - `util`: utility functions for working with servers

- *Customize the prompt*: You also can change the default prompt by updating a configuration file named ~/.mysqlsh/prompt.json using a special format or by defining an environment variable named MYSQLSH_PROMPT_THEME. See the MySQL Shell reference manual for more details about changing the prompt.

- *Auto completion*: Starting in 8.0.4, the shell permits users to press the TAB key to auto complete keywords in SQL mode and the major classes and methods in JavaScript and Python modes.

Shell Commands

As with the original MySQL client, there are some special commands that control the application itself rather than interact with data (via SQL or the X DevAPI). To execute a shell command, issue the command with a slash (\). For example, \help prints the help for all of the shell commands. Table 4-1 lists some of the more frequently used shell commands.

Table 4-1. *Shell Commands*

Command	Shortcut	Description
\		Start multiline input (SQL mode only)
\connect	(\c)	Connect to a server
\help	(\?,\h)	Print the help text
\js		Switch to JavaScript mode
\nowarnings	(\w)	Don't show warnings
\py		Switch to Python mode
\quit	(\q,\exit)	Quit
\source	(\.)	Executes the script file specified
\sql		Switch to SQL mode
\status	(\s)	Print information about the connection
\use	(\u)	Set the schema for the session
\warnings	(\W)	Show warnings after each statement

Note that you can use the \sql, \js, and \py shell commands to switch the mode on the fly. This makes working with SQL and NoSQL data much easier because you don't have to exit the application to switch modes. Furthermore, you can use these shell commands even if you used the startup option to set the mode.

Tip   To get help with any shell command, use the \help command. For example, to learn more about the \connect command, enter \help connect.

Finally, note the way you exit the shell (\q or \quit). If you type quit as you used to in the old client, the shell will respond differently depending on the mode you're in. The following presents an example of what happens in each mode.

```
MySQL   SQL > quit;
ERROR: You have an error in your SQL syntax; check the manual that
corresponds to your MySQL server version for the right syntax to use near
'quit' at line 1
 MySQL   SQL > \js
Switching to JavaScript mode...
 MySQL   JS > quit
ReferenceError: quit is not defined
 MySQL   JS > \py
Switching to Python mode...
 MySQL   Py > quit
Use quit() or Ctrl-D (i.e. EOF) to exit
 MySQL   Py > \q
Bye!
```

You may see similar oddities if you are used to the old MySQL client and accidentally use an old client command, but it only takes a bit of regular use to remind you of the correct commands to use. Now, let's look at the startup options for the shell.

Note   Unlike the old client, which requires a server connection to launch, when you launch the shell without specifying a server connection, the shell will run but it is not connected to a server. You must use the \connect shell command to connect to a server.

Options

The shell can be launched using several startup options that control the mode, connection, behavior, and more. This section introduces some of the more common options that you may want to use. We will see more about connection options in a later section. Table 4-2 shows a list of common shell options.

Table 4-2. *Common MySQL Shell Options*

Option	Description
-f, --file=file	Processes file for execution
-e, --execute=<cmd>	Executes command and quit
--uri	Connects via a Uniform Resource Identifier (URI)
-h, --host=name	Hostname to use for connection
-P, --port=#	Port number to use for connection
-S, --socket=sock	Socket name to use for connection in UNIX or a named pipe name in Windows (only classic sessions)
-u, --dbuser=name	User to use for the connection
--user=name	An alias for dbuser
--dbpassword=name	Password to use when connecting to server
--password=name	An alias for dbpassword
-p	Requests password prompt to set the password
-D --schema=name	Schema to use
--database=name	An alias for --schema
--sql	Starts in SQL mode
--sqlc	Starts in SQL mode using a classic session
--sqlx	Starts in SQL mode using Creating an X protocol session
--js	Starts in JavaScript mode
--py	Starts in Python mode
--json	Produces output in JSON format
--table	Produces output in table format (default for interactive mode)

(*continued*)

Table 4-2. (*continued*)

Option	Description
`-i,` `--interactive[=full]`	To use in batch mode, it forces emulation of interactive mode processing. Each line on the batch is processed as if it were in interactive mode.
`--log-level=value`	The log level; value must be an integer between 1 and 8 or any of [none, `internal`, `error`, `warning`, `info`, `debug`, debug2, debug3]
`--mx --mysqlx`	Creates an X protocol session (simply called *Session*)
`--mc --mysql`	Creates a classic (old protocol) session
`--ma`	Creates session with automatic protocol selection
`--nw, --no-wizard`	Disables wizard mode (noninteractive) for executing scripts.
`--ssl-mode`	Enables SSL for connection (automatically enabled with other flags)
`--ssl-key=name`	X509 keys in PEM format
`--ssl-cert=name`	X509 certs in PEM format
`--ssl-ca=name`	CA file in PEM format (check OpenSSL docs)
`--ssl-capath=dir`	CA directory.
`--ssl-cipher=name`	SSL Cipher to use.
`--ssl-crl=name`	Certificate revocation list.
`--ssl-crlpath=dir`	Certificate revocation list path.
`--tls-version=version`	TLS version to use, permitted values are: TLSv1, TLSv1.1.
`--auth-method=method`	Authentication method to use.
`--dba=enableXProtocol`	Enables the X Protocol in the server connected to. Must be used with `--mysql`.

Note that there are aliases for some of the options that have the same purpose as the original client. This makes switching to the shell a bit easier if you have scripts for launching the client to perform operations. Note that there is also a set of options for using a secure socket layer (SSL) connection.

Most of these are self-explanatory and we've seen several of these previously. Let's now look at the sessions and connections available and how to use them.

142

For a complete list of options, execute the shell with the --help option as shown in the following.

```
$ mysqlsh --help
MySQL Shell 8.0.11

Copyright (c) 2016, 2018, Oracle and/or its affiliates. All rights reserved.

Oracle is a registered trademark of Oracle Corporation and/or its
affiliates. Other names may be trademarks of their respective owners.

Usage: mysqlsh [OPTIONS] [URI]
       mysqlsh [OPTIONS] [URI] -f <path> [script args...]
       mysqlsh [OPTIONS] [URI] --dba [command]
       mysqlsh [OPTIONS] [URI] --cluster
  -?, --help                  Display this help and exit.
  -e, --execute=<cmd>         Execute command and quit.
  -f, --file=file             Process file.
  --uri=value                 Connect to Uniform Resource Identifier. Format:
                              [user[:pass]@]host[:port][/db]
  -h, --host=name             Connect to host.
  -P, --port=#                Port number to use for connection.
  -S, --socket=sock           Socket name to use in UNIX, pipe name to use in
                              Windows (only classic sessions).
  -u, --dbuser=name           User for the connection to the server.
  --user=name                 see above
  -p, --password[=name]       Password to use when connecting to server.
  --dbpassword[=name]         see above
  -p                          Request password prompt to set the password
  -D, --schema=name           Schema to use.
  --database=name             see above
  --recreate-schema           Drop and recreate the specified schema.Schema
                              will be deleted if it exists!
  -mx, --mysqlx               Uses connection data to create Creating an X
                              protocol session.
  -mc, --mysql                Uses connection data to create a Classic Session.
  -ma                         Uses the connection data to create the session
                              withautomatic protocol detection.
...
```

Sessions and Modes

As with the original client and indeed most MySQL client applications, you will need to connect to a MySQL server so that you can run commands. The MySQL Shell supports several ways to connect to a MySQL server and a variety of options for interacting with the server (called a session). Within a session, you can change the way the shell accepts commands (called modes) to include SQL, JavaScript, or Python commands.

Given all the different and new concepts of working with servers, those new to using the shell may find the difference subtle and even at times confusing. Indeed, the online MySQL Shell reference manual and various blogs and other reports sometimes use mode and session interchangeably, but as you will see, they are different (however subtle). The following sections clarify each of the major concepts including sessions, modes, and connections so that you can get accustomed to the new methods faster. I introduce the concepts first with some simple examples then discuss making connections in detail with examples. Let's begin by looking at the session objects available.

Session Objects

The first thing to understand about sessions is that a session is a connection to a single server. The second thing to understand is that each session can be started using one of two session objects that exposes a specific object for use in working with the MySQL server using a specific communication protocol. That is, sessions are connections to servers (with all parameters defined), and a session object is what the shell uses to interact with a server in one of several ways. More specific, a MySQL Shell session object simply defines how you interact with the server including what modes are supported and even how the shell communicates with the server. The shell supports two session objects as in the following:

- *Session*: An X Protocol session is used for application development and supports the JavaScript, Python, and SQL modes. Typically used to develop scripts or execute scripts. To start the shell with this option, use the `--mx` (`--mysqlx`) option.

- *Classic session*: Uses the older server communication protocol with very limited support for the DevAPI. Use this mode with older servers that do not have the X Plugin or do not support the X Protocol. Typically used for SQL mode with older servers. To start the shell with this option, use the `--mc` (`--mysqlc`) option.

Note   A classic session is only available in the MySQL Shell. It is not part of the X DevAPI. Only the session connection via the X Protocol is available via the X DevAPI.

You can specify the session object (protocol) to use when you use the \connect shell command by specifying -mc for classic session, -mx for X Protocol session, or -ma for automatic protocol selection. The following shows each of these in turn. Note that <URI> specifies a uniform resource identifier.

- \connect -mx <URI>: Use the X Protocol (session)

- \connect -mc <URI>: Use the classic protocol (classic session)

- \connect -ma <URI>: Use automatic protocol selection

Recall sessions are loosely synonymous with a connection. However, a session is a bit more than just a connection because all the settings used to establish the connection including the session object are included as well as the communication protocol used with the server. Thus, we sometimes encounter the term, "protocol" for describing a session. We will see more examples of using sessions in later sections.

WAIT, WHAT SESSION WAS THAT???

It is likely you will see the sessions described using several names. In particular, the normal, default session is called *Session*, *X Protocol Session*, or more rarely, *X Session*. These refer to a session object (connection) that communicates with MySQL via the X Protocol. The older server communication protocol is supported in a session called *Classic Session*, *Classic*, or more rarely, *Old Protocol*. These refer to a session object (connection) that communicates with a MySQL server via the old protocol. Sadly, these multiple names can make reading different texts a challenge. You should strive to read *Session* and *Classic Session* whenever these alternative terms are used.

For more information about using sessions programmatically, see the online MySQL Shell reference manual.

Modes Supported

The shell supports three modes (also called language support or simply the active language); SQL, JavaScript, and Python. Recall that we can initiate any one of these modes by using a shell command. You can switch modes (languages) as often as you want without disconnection each time. The following lists the three modes and how to switch to each.

- `\sql`: Switch to the SQL language

- `\js`: Switch to the JavaScript language (default mode)

- `\py`: Switch to the Python language

Now that we understand sessions, session objects, modes, we can look at how to make connections to MySQL servers.

Connections

Making connections in the shell is one area that may take some getting used to doing differently than the original MySQL client.[1] You can use a specially formatted URI string or connect to a server using individual options by name (like the old client). SSL connections are also supported. Connections can be made via startup options, shell commands, and in scripts. However, all connections are expected to use a password. Thus, unless you state otherwise, the shell will prompt for a password if one is not given.

Note   If you want to use a connection without a password (not recommended), you must use the `--password` option or, if using an URI, include an extra colon to take the place of the password.

Rather than discuss all the available ways to connect and all the options to do so, the following presents one example of each method of making a connection in the following sections.

---

[1]However, if you've used MySQL Fabric or Utilities, using an URI for a connection will look very familiar.

Using a URI

A URI in the case of a MySQL Shell connection is a special string coded using the following format: `<dbuser>[:<dbpassword>]@host[:port][/schema/]` where `<>` indicates string values for the various parameters. Note that the password, port, and schema are optional but the user and host are required. Schema in this case is the default schema (database) that you want to use when connecting.

Note   The default port for the X Protocol is 33060.

To connect to a server using a URI on the command line when starting the shell, specify it with the `--uri` option as follows.

```
$ mysqlsh --uri root:secret@localhost:33060
```

The shell assumes all connections require a password and will prompt for a password if one is not provided.[2] Listing 4-1 shows the same connection earlier made without the password. Note how the shell prompts for the password.

Tip   The world_x database is a sample database you can download from `https://dev.mysql.com/doc/index-other.html`.

Listing 4-1. Connecting with a URI

```
$ mysqlsh --uri root@localhost:33060/world_x
Creating a session to 'root@localhost:33060/world_x'
Enter password:
Fetching schema names for autocompletion... Press ^C to stop.
Your MySQL connection id is 13 (X protocol)
Server version: 8.0.11 MySQL Community Server (GPL)
Default schema `world_x` accessible through db.
MySQL Shell 8.0.11
```

---

[2]Although you can specify passwords in a URI, it is a poor security practice.

```
Type '\help' or '\?' for help; '\quit' to exit.
 MySQL  localhost:33060+  world_x  JS >
```

Note that I also specified the default schema (world_x) with the /schema option in the URI.

Using Individual Options

You also can specify connections on the shell command line using individual options. The available connection options available are those shown in Table 4-1. For backward compatibility (and to make the transition to the MySQL Shell easier, the shell also supports --user in place of --dbuser, --password in place of --dbpassword, and --database in place of --schema. Listing 4-2 shows how to connect to a MySQL server using individual options.

Listing 4-2. Connecting Using Individual Options

```
$ mysqlsh --dbuser root --host localhost --port 33060 --schema world_x --py -mx
Creating an X protocol session to 'root@localhost:33060/world_x'
Enter password:
Fetching schema names for autocompletion... Press ^C to stop.
Your MySQL connection id is 14 (X protocol)
Server version: 8.0.11 MySQL Community Server (GPL)
Default schema `world_x` accessible through db.
MySQL Shell 8.0.11
```

```
Type '\help' or '\?' for help; '\quit' to exit.

MySQL  localhost:33060+  world_x  Py >
```

Note that I changed the mode (language) to Python with the --py option.

Using Connections in Scripts

If you plan to use the shell to create scripts or simply as a prototyping tool, you also will want to use sessions in your scripts. In this case, we will create a variable to contain the session once it is fetched. A session created in this manner is called a global session because once it is created, it is available to any of the modes.

However, depending on the session object we're using (recall this is classic or X Protocol), we will use a different method of the mysqlx object to create an X or classic session. We use the getSession() method for an X Protocol session object, and the getClassicSession() method for a classic session object.

Tip   If you want to know more about the internals of the MySQL Shell including more about the mysql and mysqlx modules, see http://dev.mysql.com/doc/dev/mysqlsh-devapi/.

The following demonstrates getting an X Protocol session object in JavaScript. Note that I specify the password in an URI as the method parameter.

```
MySQL  JS > var js_session = mysqlx.getSession('root@localhost:33060', 'secret')
MySQL  JS > print(js_session)
<Session:root@localhost:33060>
```

The following demonstrates getting a Classic session object in JavaScript.

```
MySQL  JS > var js_session = mysql.getClassicSession('root@
localhost:3306', 'secret')
MySQL  JS > print(js_session)
<ClassicSession:root@localhost:3306>
```

WHAT HAPPENED TO PORT 3306?

If you've been following along with the examples in this section, you may have noticed that the port we are using is 33060. That is not a typographical error. The X Plugin listens on port 33060 by default rather than port 3306 as the original default port of the server. In fact, port 3306 is still the default for the old protocol and you can connect to the server using port 3306, but you must use the classic session (mysqlsh --classic -uroot -hlocalhost --port=3306). Although this shows that you can connect to a server using the old protocol, recall that it does limit what you can do because the DevAPI is not fully supported in the classic session object.

Using SSL Connections

You also can create SSL connections for secure connections to your servers. To use SSL, you must configure your server to use SSL. To use SSL on the same machine where MySQL is running, you can use the `--ssl-mode=REQUIRED` option. You also can specify the SSL options as shown in Table 4-1. You can specify them on the command line using the command line options or as an extension to the `\connect` shell command. The following shows how to connect to a server using SSL and command line options.

```
$ mysqlsh -uroot -h127.0.0.1 --port=33060 --ssl-mode=REQUIRED
```

Tip See the section, "Using Encrypted Connections" in the online MySQL Shell reference manual for more details about encrypted connections.

Now that we know how to connect to our servers, let's review how to set up and install the shell and, more important, ensure the X Plugin is set up correctly.

Set Up and Install

Recall from Chapter 2, we need to install the MySQL Shell as a separate product from the server. We also must enable the X Plugin in the server. The following sections demonstrate the steps needed to install the MySQL Shell and how to configure the X Plugin for use. Although we saw a short example of how to install the X Plugin in Chapter 2, this section goes into greater detail including how to automatically install the X Plugin using the MySQL Shell.

Caution   If you are installing the MySQL Shell version 8.0.4 or later to be used with MySQL Server version 8.0.4 or later, you will be using the new `caching_sha2_password` authentication plugin to use SSL connections. This is normally done during setup by default, but if you installed the server without the automatic installation, or you are using an older version of the server, you may need to configure the server to use SSL connections. See the online MySQL reference manual for more information or for more information about the change to the authentication default, read the engineering blog at `https://mysqlserverteam.com/mysql-8-0-4-new-default-authentication-plugin-caching_sha2_password`.

Install the MySQL Shell

Installing the MySQL Shell follows the same pattern as installing the MySQL server. That is, you can simply download the installer for your platform and install it by clicking through the dialog panels. There is one exception, however. At the time of this writing, the latest release of the MySQL Shell is not part of the MySQL Windows Installer.

You can find the installation package on `http://dev.mysql.com/downloads/shell/`. Just select the latest version and package for your platform (in this case, macOS) and install the shell.

When you launch the `installer` (`.pkg` or `.dmg`), you will be presented with a welcome dialog that contains the name and version of the product you are going to install. Figure 4-2 shows the welcome panel for the MySQL Shell installer.

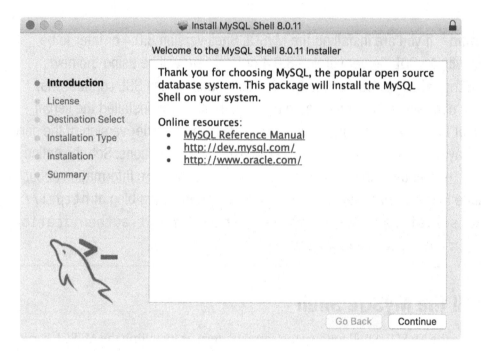

Figure 4-2. *Installer welcome panel*

Note that in Figure 4-2 I am installing a release candidate version of the MySQL Shell, namely, version 8.0.11. You should install the latest version of the shell available for your platform to ensure you have the latest features.

Once you are ready, click *Continue*. You will then be presented with the end-user license agreement as shown in Figure 4-3.

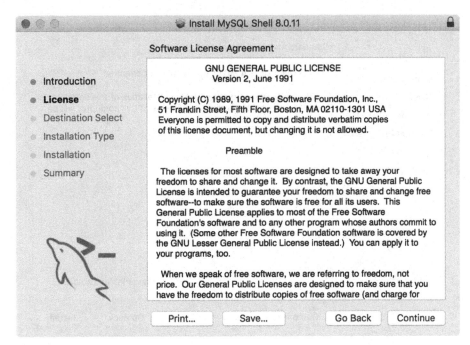

Figure 4-3. *License panel*

Once you have read the license,[3] click *Continue*. You will be asked to accept the license as shown in Figure 4-4. Click *Agree* to continue.

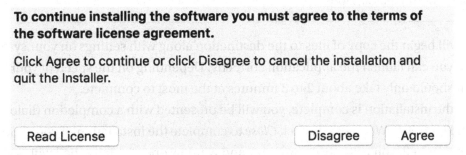

Figure 4-4. *Destination folder panel*

Once you've accepted the license, and are okay with installing in the default location (for macOS that's always a good idea), click *Continue*. You will be asked to approve the installation as shown in Figure 4-5. Click *Install* when ready to begin the installation.

---

[3]No, really. You should read it.

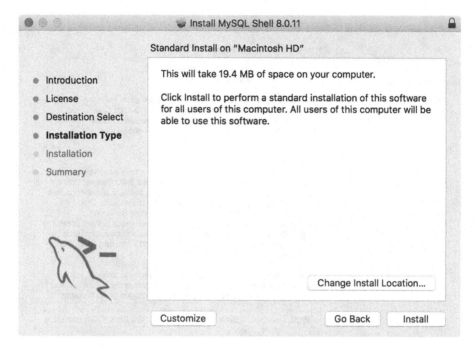

Figure 4-5. *Installation panel*

Tip   When installing on Windows, you may be asked by Windows to approve the escalation of the installation.

This will begin the copy of files to the destination along with settings on your system to ensure you can launch the application correctly. Depending on the speed of your system, it should only take about 2 to 3 minutes at the most to complete.

Once the installation is complete, you will be presented with a completion dialog as shown in Figure 4-6. When ready, click *Close* to complete the installation. If you choose to launch the shell, you will see a new command window open and the shell will start.

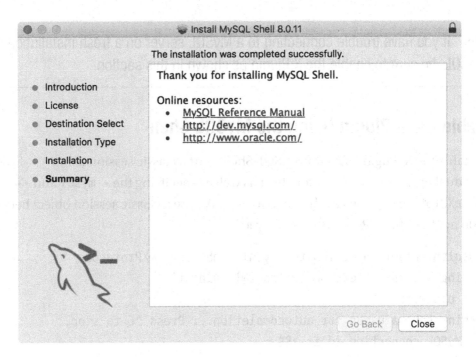

Figure 4-6. *Installation complete*

Recall you can launch the shell without specifying a server and the shell will run but it is not connected to any MySQL server. You must use the \connect shell command to connect to a server if you do not specify a server connection (URI or individual options) on the command line.

Now that the MySQL Shell is installed, we need to configure the X Plugin.

Setup the X Plugin

If you installed MySQL 8.0.11 or later on your system, you already have the X Plugin installed and enabled. However, some of the older installations do not setup or enable the X Plugin by default. Thus, you may need to enable the plugin to connect to your server with the shell. Although you can still use the shell to connect using a classic session object, you won't be able to use the X Protocol session object until the X Plugin is enabled.

Furthermore, if you installed the server on Windows using the Windows Installer, you can enable the X Plugin during installation by checking the *Enable X Protocol/MySQL as a Document Store* checkbox. If you did not do that or are installing on a different platform, there are at least two other methods for enabling the X Plugin; you can use the new MySQL Shell or you can use the old client. The following demonstrates each option.

Tip   If you have trouble connecting to a MySQL server on a fresh installation of MySQL, be sure to enable the X Plugin as shown in this section.

Enable the X Plugin Using the MySQL Shell

To enable the X Plugin using the MySQL Shell, start a classic session using individual options for the user and host as well as specifying the --mysql and --dba enableXProtocol options as shown following. We use a classic session object because we do not have the X Protocol enabled yet.

```
$ mysqlsh -uroot -hlocalhost --mysql --dba enableXProtocol
Creating a Classic session to 'root@localhost'
Enter password:
Fetching schema names for autocompletion... Press ^C to stop.
Your MySQL connection id is 285
Server version: 8.0.11 MySQL Community Server (GPL)
No default schema selected; type \use <schema> to set one.
enableXProtocol: Installing plugin mysqlx...
enableXProtocol: done
```

Enable the X Plugin Using the MySQL Client

To enable the X Plugin using the old MySQL client, you must connect to the server and install the plugin manually. That is, there is no new magical command option to turn it on for you. This involves using the INSTALL PLUGIN SQL command as shown in Listing 4-3.

Listing 4-3. Enabling the X Plugin Using the MySQL Client

```
$ mysql -uroot -p
Enter password:
Welcome to the MySQL monitor.  Commands end with ; or \g.
Your MySQL connection id is 343
Server version: 8.0.11 MySQL Community Server (GPL)

Copyright (c) 2000, 2018, Oracle and/or its affiliates. All rights reserved.
```

Oracle is a registered trademark of Oracle Corporation and/or its affiliates. Other names may be trademarks of their respective owners.

Type 'help;' or '\h' for help. Type '\c' to clear the current input statement.

```
mysql> INSTALL PLUGIN mysqlx SONAME 'mysqlx.so';
Query OK, 0 rows affected (0.00 sec)

mysql> SHOW PLUGINS \G
*************************** 1. row ***************************
   Name: keyring_file
 Status: ACTIVE
   Type: KEYRING
Library: keyring_file.so
License: GPL
...
*************************** 43. row ***************************
   Name: mysqlx
 Status: ACTIVE
   Type: DAEMON
Library: mysqlx.so
License: GPL
43 rows in set (0.00 sec)
```

Note that I used the SHOW PLUGINS SQL command to list the plugins installed before and after the command. I omit some of the lengthy output for clarity.

Tip   You can perform these operations in the shell using a classic session object. I show the commands using the old client for readers accustomed to using the old client.

It is interesting that you also can uninstall a plugin using the UNINSTALL PLUGIN SQL command as follows. This may be helpful if you need to diagnose connections using the X Protocol or want to test scripts with the MySQL Shell using only the classic session object.

```
mysql> UNINSTALL PLUGIN mysqlx;
Query OK, 0 rows affected (0.80 sec)
```

Now, let's see the MySQL Shell in action by way of a demonstration of executing a simple task in each of the three modes (SQL, JavaScript, and Python).

Tutorial: MySQL Shell by Example

The following sections demonstrate how to use the MySQL shell in each of the three modes. The example is inserting new data in the world_x database. A brief overview of the built-in X DevAPI objects via the shell will be presented along with how to get started installing the sample database.

This tutorial is designed to present a complete example of how to use the MySQL Shell to solve a task in all the modes (languages) supported. Thus, we will see the same tasks performed using SQL, JavaScript, and Python commands.

The task is to insert new data in the database then conduct a search to retrieve rows that meet criteria that contains the new data. I use a relational table to illustrate the concepts because that is easier for those of us familiar with "normal" database operations. However, we will see in later chapters how to work with pure documents (collections) in the document store.

Each session presented begins with an example of how to connect to the server, learn about what the server supports (what databases exist), how to insert new data, and how to query for data. As you will see, some of the commands are quite different but they all produce the same results. Although the SQL commands shown will be familiar to most readers, I include them here to show how to equate those commands with your scripting language of choice.

Note   Recall from Chapter 3, it is not a requirement to be a JavaScript master or even a Pythonista[4] to get started writing scripts in the shell. Indeed, most of what you need to do can be found by way of examples in this book and the online MySQL Shell reference manual.

---

[4]Python masters often refer to themselves in this manner. Not to be confused with the Knights who say "Ni!".—https://en.wikipedia.org/wiki/Knights_who_say_Ni

The operations we will see for JavaScript and Python work with CRUD operations on relational tables. As such, we aren't using collections; rather, we're using a relational table that has a JSON data type column. We will see examples of inserting data (create), select data (read), updating data (updated), and deleting data (delete).

Before we begin our journey, let's take a moment to install the sample database we will need, the world_x sample MySQL database from Oracle.

Installing the Sample Database

Oracle provides several sample databases for you to use in testing and developing your applications. Sample databases can be downloaded from http://dev.mysql.com/doc/index-other.html. The sample database we want to use is named world_x to indicate it contains JSON documents and is intended for testing with the X DevAPI, the shell, and so forth. Go ahead and navigate to that page and download the database.

The sample database contains several relational tables (country, city, and countrylanguage) as well as a collection (countryinfo). We will only use the relational tables in this chapter, but will see more examples working with collections in later chapters.

Once you've downloaded the file, uncompress it and note the location of the files. You will need that when we import it. Next, start the MySQL Shell and make a connection to your server. Use the \sql shell command to switch to SQL mode then the \source shell command to read the world_x.sql file and process all its statements.

Listing 4-4 shows an excerpt of the commands and the responses you should see. I highlight the commands and a row in the output to show that this world database does indeed permit storing of JSON documents in a table.

Listing 4-4. Installing the world_x Database in SQL Mode

```
 MySQL  JS > \connect root@localhost:33060
Creating a session to 'root@localhost:33060'
Enter password:
Your MySQL connection id is 9 (X protocol)
Server version: 8.0.11 MySQL Community Server (GPL)
No default schema selected; type \use <schema> to set one.
 MySQL  localhost:33060+ ssl  JS > \sql
Switching to SQL mode... Commands end with ;
 MySQL  localhost:33060+ ssl  SQL > \source /Users/cbell/Downloads/world_x-
 db/world_x.sql
```

```
...
Query OK, 0 rows affected (0.00 sec)

MySQL  localhost:33060+ ssl  SQL > SHOW DATABASES;
+--------------------+
| Database           |
+--------------------+
| animals            |
| contact_list1      |
| contact_list2      |
| contact_list3      |
| greenhouse         |
| information_schema |
| library_v1         |
| library_v2         |
| library_v3         |
| mysql              |
| performance_schema |
| rolodex            |
| sys                |
| test               |
| world_x            |
+--------------------+
15 rows in set (0.00 sec)
 MySQL  localhost:33060+ ssl  SQL > USE world_x;
Query OK, 0 rows affected (0.00 sec)
 MySQL  localhost:33060+ ssl  SQL > SHOW TABLES;
+------------------+
| Tables_in_world_x |
+------------------+
| city             |
| country          |
| countryinfo      |
| countrylanguage  |
+------------------+
4 rows in set (0.00 sec)
```

```
MySQL  localhost:33060+ ssl  SQL > EXPLAIN city;
+--------------+-----------+------+-----+---------+----------------+
| Field        | Type      | Null | Key | Default | Extra          |
+--------------+-----------+------+-----+---------+----------------+
| ID           | int(11)   | NO   | PRI | NULL    | auto_increment |
| Name         | char(35)  | NO   |     |         |                |
| CountryCode  | char(3)   | NO   |     |         |                |
| District     | char(20)  | NO   |     |         |                |
| Info         | json      | YES  |     | NULL    |                |
+--------------+-----------+------+-----+---------+----------------+
5 rows in set (0.00 sec)
```

Note that the \source shell command is a way to load a file and execute the commands in a batch. This is a very popular method of replaying frequently used command sequences and it does work for JavaScript and Python commands too.

Tip   If the path to the file has spaces in it, you should include the path within double quotes.

You can also install the sample database using the --recreate-schema option on the command line as follows. Note that this will delete and recreate the database if it already exists. This is another example of running the SQL commands as a batch.

```
$ mysqlsh -uroot -hlocalhost --sql --recreate-schema --schema=world_x
< ~/Downloads/world_x-db/world_x.sql
Enter password:
Recreating schema world_x...
```

Of course, you could install the sample database with the old client by using the similar source command, but where's the fun in that?

Now, let's see our example task in SQL mode.

SQL

The task we want to do is to insert two rows into the city table adding a JSON document in each and then read data from the table only those rows that have the extra data. More specific, we are going to be adding a list of places of interest to the table so that we can ask questions later about which cities have places of interest. Think of it as a way to add your own comments about places you've visited in those cities that you found interesting and would recommend to others.

Because this exercise is an example, we will also see how to delete the data we added so that we return the database to its original state. It also helps to do this if you plan to follow along with these examples so that completing one doesn't affect trying out the next.

Let's begin with listing the databases on the server then listing the tables in the world_x database. Listing 4-5 shows a transcript of the familiar SQL commands to accomplish these steps. I omit some of the messages for brevity. Note that I started the shell in the SQL mode using the command option.

Listing 4-5. Listing and Using Databases—SQL Mode

```
$ mysqlsh -uroot -hlocalhost --sql
Creating a session to 'root@localhost'
Enter password:
Your MySQL connection id is 13 (X protocol)
Server version: 8.0.11 MySQL Community Server (GPL)
No default schema selected; type \use <schema> to set one.
MySQL Shell 8.0.11

Copyright (c) 2016, 2018, Oracle and/or its affiliates. All rights reserved.

Oracle is a registered trademark of Oracle Corporation and/or its
affiliates. Other names may be trademarks of their respective
owners.

Type '\help' or '\?' for help; '\quit' to exit.
```

```
MySQL  localhost:33060+ ssl  SQL > SHOW DATABASES;
+--------------------+
| Database           |
+--------------------+
| animals            |
| contact_list1      |
| contact_list2      |
| contact_list3      |
| greenhouse         |
| information_schema |
| library_v1         |
| library_v2         |
| library_v3         |
| mysql              |
| performance_schema |
| rolodex            |
| sys                |
| test               |
| world_x            |
+--------------------+
15 rows in set (0.00 sec)
 MySQL  localhost:33060+ ssl  SQL > USE world_x;
Query OK, 0 rows affected (0.00 sec)

 MySQL  localhost:33060+ ssl  SQL > SHOW TABLES;
+-----------------+
| Tables_in_world_x |
+-----------------+
| city            |
| country         |
| countryinfo     |
| countrylanguage |
+-----------------+
4 rows in set (0.00 sec)                              ... ;
Query OK, 0 rows affected (0.00 sec)
```

```
MySQL  localhost:33060+ ssl  SQL > SHOW TABLES;
+--------------------+
| Tables_in_rolodex |
+--------------------+
| contacts           |
+--------------------+
1 row in set (0.00 sec)
```

Next, let's insert some data. We will insert two rows into the table; one for each city I've visited recently (Charlotte, North Carolina and Daytona, Florida). In this step, we will use the INSERT SQL command to insert data. Recall from earlier, we need to format our JSON document carefully so that we don't encounter errors. In particular, we want to add structured data including the name, country code, and district but we also want to add a JSON document that contains the population and a list (array) of places of interest. Recall from Chapter 1, we can do this in the INSERT statement by creating the JSON document inline. The following shows each of the commands we would use to insert the rows.

```
INSERT INTO world_x.city (Name, CountryCode, District, Info) VALUES
('Charlotte', 'USA', 'North Carolina', '{"Population": 792862, "Places_
of_interest": [{"name": "NASCAR Hall of Fame"}, {"name": "Charlotte Motor
Speedway"}]}');
```

```
INSERT INTO world_x.city (Name, CountryCode, District, Info) VALUES
('Daytona', 'USA', 'Florida', '{"Population": 590280, "Places_of_interest":
[{"name": "Daytona Beach"}, {"name": "Motorsports Hall of Fame of
America"}, {"name": "Daytona Motor Speedway"}]}');
```

Caution   Do not use spaces in key names in JSON documents. The SQL functions cannot correctly identify keys with spaces in them.

Although that seems a bit messy (and it is), if you read the statements carefully, you will see the JSON document is encoded as a string. For example, a well-formatted version of the JSON document for the first insert is shown following. Clearly, that's a lot easier to read. You could enter the statement using formatting like this, but the results will be shown without the extra formatting.

Note that we retain the population key per the other rows in the table (select some and see) and we also add an array named `Places_of_interest` to list those places we may want to visit.

```
{
  "Population": 792862,
  "Places_of_interest": [
    {
      "name": "NASCAR Hall of Fame"
    },
    {
      "name": "Charlotte Motor Speedway"
    }
  ]
}
```

Note   I truncated the table formatting rows (the dashed lines) from the examples for brevity.

Now, let's see how the data looks if we use a SELECT SQL statement. In this case, we'll just select the two rows by city name because they are unique in the table. The following is an excerpt of the results.

```
MySQL  localhost:33060+ ssl  SQL > SELECT * FROM city WHERE Name in
('Charlotte', 'Daytona') \G
*************************** 1. row ***************************
         ID: 3818
       Name: Charlotte
CountryCode: USA
   District: North Carolina
       Info: {"Population": 540828}
*************************** 2. row ***************************
         ID: 4080
       Name: Charlotte
CountryCode: USA
   District: North Carolina
```

```
        Info: {"Population": 792862, "Places_of_interest": [{"name": "NASCAR
Hall of Fame"}, {"name": "Charlotte Motor Speedway"}]}
************************** 3. row **************************
          ID: 4081
        Name: Daytona
CountryCode: USA
    District: Florida
        Info: {"Population": 590280, "Places_of_interest": [{"name":
"Daytona Beach"}, {"name": "Motorsports Hall of Fame of America"}, {"name":
"Daytona Motor Speedway"}]}
```

That's interesting, but it doesn't answer the question we want to ask. That is, which cities have places of interest? To do that, we need to use a number of special functions designed for the JSON data type. All of the functions begin with the name JSON_*. Let's see each of these in turn starting with a way to search for rows that have a specific key in the JSON document. In this case, we select all of the data for rows that have places of interest.

To determine if a JSON document has a specific key, we use the JSON_CONTAINS_ PATH() function. Recall a path is simply a resolution of the keys in the document. In this case, we want to know if the JSON document contains a path for Places_of_interest. Because the function returns a 0 for no match and 1 for at least one match, we check to see if it is equal to 1. You can omit the equality, but it is best to be pedantic when experimenting with new features and commands. We also use the 'all' option to tell the function to return all of the matches (values) as opposed to 'one', which returns only the first occurrence. You can also use the slightly more correct IS NOT NULL comparison.

```
MySQL  localhost:33060+ ssl  SQL > SELECT * FROM city WHERE JSON_CONTAINS_
PATH(info, 'all', '$.Places_of_interest') = 1 \G
************************** 1. row **************************
          ID: 4080
        Name: Charlotte
CountryCode: USA
    District: North Carolina
        Info: {"Population": 792862, "Places_of_interest": [{"name": "NASCAR
Hall of Fame"}, {"name": "Charlotte Motor Speedway"}]}
```

```
*************************** 2. row ***************************
        ID: 4081
      Name: Daytona
CountryCode: USA
  District: Florida
      Info: {"Population": 590280, "Places_of_interest": [{"name":
"Daytona Beach"}, {"name": "Motorsports Hall of Fame of America"}, {"name":
"Daytona Motor Speedway"}]}
2 rows in set (0.00 sec)
```

Now, let's say we only want to see those places of interest and not the entire JSON document. In this case, we need to use the JSON_EXTRACT() function to extract the values from the document. In particular, we want to search the info column for all values in the array Places_of_interest. Although that seems complicated, it isn't too bad as you can see in the following.

```
MySQL  localhost:33060+ ssl  SQL > SELECT Name, District, JSON_
EXTRACT(info, '$.Places_of_interest') as Sights FROM city WHERE JSON_
EXTRACT(info, '$.Places_of_interest') IS NOT NULL \G
*************************** 1. row ***************************
    Name: Charlotte
District: North Carolina
  Sights: [{"name": "NASCAR Hall of Fame"}, {"name": "Charlotte Motor
Speedway"}]
*************************** 2. row ***************************
    Name: Daytona
District: Florida
  Sights: [{"name": "Daytona Beach"}, {"name": "Motorsports Hall of Fame of
America"}, {"name": "Daytona Motor Speedway"}]
2 rows in set (0.00 sec)
```

Now, what if we wanted to only retrieve the values for the Places_of_interest array? In this case, we can use a special format of the JSON access to get these values from the array. The following demonstrates the technique. Note the portion highlighted in bold.

```
MySQL  localhost:33060+ ssl  SQL > SELECT Name, District, JSON_
EXTRACT(info, '$.Places_of_interest[*].name') as Sights FROM city WHERE
JSON_EXTRACT(info, '$.Places_of_interest') IS NOT NULL \G
*************************** 1. row ***************************
     Name: Charlotte
District: North Carolina
   Sights: ["NASCAR Hall of Fame", "Charlotte Motor Speedway"]
*************************** 2. row ***************************
     Name: Daytona
District: Florida
   Sights: ["Daytona Beach", "Motorsports Hall of Fame of America", "Daytona
Motor Speedway"]
2 rows in set (0.00 sec)
```

Okay, now that's a lot easier to read, isn't it? It's also a bit messy SQL command. And if all of that seemed a bit painful, you're right, it was. Working with JSON data in SQL works with the help of the JSON functions, but it is an extra step and can be a bit confusing in syntax. See the online MySQL reference manual for full explanations of each of the JSON_* functions.

If you've used the old MySQL client much to query data with wide rows, chances are you've used the \G option to display the results in a vertical format, which makes reading the data easier. With the shell, we don't have that option but we can display data using the --json option. Although the option is easier to read, it tends to be a bit verbose. We will see this in action in the Python section.

Finally, we can remove the rows with the DELETE SQL command as shown in the following.

```
MySQL  localhost:33060+ ssl  SQL > DELETE FROM city WHERE Name in
('Charlotte', 'Daytona');
Query OK, 3 rows affected (0.00 sec)
```

Now, let's see the same operations performed using JavaScript.

JavaScript

To execute the example task in JavaScript, we're going to start the shell with the X Protocol session object and pass in the world_x schema to demonstrate how you can save a step. We will then use the getTables() method of the global db object (sometimes called a variable) to get the list of tables the world_x database. Listing 4-6 demonstrates these commands.

Listing 4-6. Listing and Using Databases—JavaScript Mode

```
$ mysqlsh -uroot -hlocalhost -mx --schema=world_x
Creating an X protocol session to 'root@localhost/world_x'
Enter password:
Your MySQL connection id is 15 (X protocol)
Server version: 8.0.11 MySQL Community Server (GPL)
Default schema `world_x` accessible through db.
MySQL Shell 8.0.11

Copyright (c) 2016, 2018, Oracle and/or its affiliates. All rights reserved.

Oracle is a registered trademark of Oracle Corporation and/or its
affiliates. Other names may be trademarks of their respective
owners.

Type '\help' or '\?' for help; '\quit' to exit.

 MySQL  localhost:33060+ ssl  world_x  JS > db
<Schema:world_x>
 MySQL  localhost:33060+ ssl  world_x  JS > db.getTables();
[
    <Table:city>,
    <Table:country>,
    <Table:countrylanguage>
]
```

Now, let's insert the data. Note that in Listing 4-6, the result of the db.getTables() method shows three tables. We can use the table name to reference a table object by name. For example, to access the city table, we use db.city. To insert data, we will use the db.city.insert() method as shown in the following.

169

```
MySQL  localhost:33060+ ssl  world_x  JS > db.city.insert("Name",
"CountryCode", "District", "Info").values('Charlotte', 'USA', 'North
Carolina', '{"Population": 792862, "Places_of_interest": [{"name": "NASCAR
Hall of Fame"}, {"name": "Charlotte Motor Speedway"}]}');
Query OK, 1 item affected (0.00 sec)

MySQL  localhost:33060+ ssl  world_x  JS > db.city.insert("Name",
"CountryCode", "District", "Info").values('Daytona', 'USA', 'Florida',
'{"Population": 590280, "Places_of_interest": [{"name": "Daytona Beach"},
{"name": "Motorsports Hall of Fame of America"}, {"name": "Daytona Motor
Speedway"}]}');
Query OK, 1 item affected (0.00 sec)
```

Note   When running code interactively, you can omit the execute() function
call for most create, read, update, and delete operations because the MySQL Shell
explicitly executes the statements in interactive mode. For example, the insert()
function would normally require chaining the execute() function to complete the
operation, but you can omit it in interactive mode.

Now that we have the data, let's select the rows with the following code. Here we
use the db.city.select() method along with the where() method for the TableSelect
object (the object returned from db.city.select). Note that we specify the list of
columns quoted and listed inside square brackets. Within that list, we can specify data
in a JSON document using the column name and the special -> operator to extract a key.
In this case, we want the Places_of_interest key (path) in the document stored in the
Info column.

```
MySQL  localhost:33060+ ssl  world_x  JS > db.city.select(["Name",
"District", "Info->'$.Places_of_interest'"]).where("Info->'$.Places_of_
interest' IS NOT NULL");
+-----------+---------------+---------------------------------------------------+
| Name      | District      | JSON_EXTRACT(`Info`,'$.Places_of_interest')|
+-----------+---------------+---------------------------------------------------+
| Charlotte | North Carolina | [{"name": "NASCAR Hall of Fame"}, {"name":
                              "Charlotte Motor Speedway"}]                       |
```

Daytona	Florida	[{"name": "Daytona Beach"}, {"name": "Motorsports Hall of Fame of America"}, {"name": "Daytona Motor Speedway"}]

2 rows in set (0.00 sec)

Note the column type in the result. It's a JSON function! That means we can use a JSON function in our code to narrow the resulting column data to only the values for the Places_of_interest array as we did in the SQL example as shown in the following. How cool is that?

```
MySQL  localhost:33060+ ssl  world_x  JS > db.city.select(["Name",
"District", "JSON_EXTRACT(info, '$.Places_of_interest[*].name')"]).
where("Info->'$.Places_of_interest' IS NOT NULL");
```

Name	District	JSON_EXTRACT(`info`,'$.Places_of_interest[*].name')
Charlotte	North Carolina	["NASCAR Hall of Fame", "Charlotte Motor Speedway"]
Daytona	Florida	["Daytona Beach", "Motorsports Hall of Fame of America", "Daytona Motor Speedway"]

2 rows in set (0.00 sec)

Now, let's remove the rows we added to restore the data.

```
MySQL  localhost:33060+ ssl  world_x  JS > db.city.delete().where("Name in
('Charlotte', 'Daytona')");
Query OK, 2 items affected (0.00 sec)
```

Okay, that wasn't so bad. If you're thinking it seems more programmatic than SQL and perhaps even a bit more intuitive, they you're on the right track. Don't worry if it seems a bit strange. The more you use scripting in the shell, the easier and more natural it will become. It is also good practice because the future of working with MySQL is the MySQL Shell and scripting languages!

Now, let's see the same script executed as Python.

Python

Because we've already seen the task demonstrated twice, I skip the details of the execution of each step and show you the transcript of my Python session.

One thing you will notice right away is that once we get the tables from the db object, the code is the same as the JavaScript example except the names of the functions are spelled a bit different. This is by design. Because the db object is actually a special variable in the shell, it has the same syntax in both languages. You only see differences when you start using the X DevAPI objects, which we will see in more detail in Chapter 5.

Note   The general rule is that JavaScript uses camelCase and Python uses underscore_separated names when the function is composed by multiple names. For example, `createCluster()` and `create_cluster()`, respectively. In cases where the functions are a single word, the names are the same, that is, "`select`", "`insert`", "`delete`".

Listing 4-7 shows the complete transcript of running the task using Python. Note that the only difference is the call for getting tables. In this case, we use `db.get_tables()` method in Python. It's the same method with the same functionality only it is named differently in accordance with typical Python naming conventions.

Listing 4-7. Listing, Inserting, Selecting, and Deleting in Databases—Python Mode

```
$ mysqlsh -uroot -hlocalhost -mx --py --schema=world_x
Creating an X protocol session to 'root@localhost/world_x'
Enter password:
Your MySQL connection id is 19 (X protocol)
Server version: 8.0.11 MySQL Community Server (GPL)
Default schema `world_x` accessible through db.
MySQL Shell 8.0.11

Copyright (c) 2016, 2018, Oracle and/or its affiliates. All rights reserved.

Oracle is a registered trademark of Oracle Corporation and/or its
affiliates. Other names may be trademarks of their respective
owners.
```

```
Type '\help' or '\?' for help; '\quit' to exit.

 MySQL  localhost:33060+ ssl  world_x  Py > db
<Schema:world_x>
 MySQL  localhost:33060+ ssl  world_x  Py > db.get_tables()
[
    <Table:city>,
    <Table:country>,
    <Table:countrylanguage>
]
 MySQL  localhost:33060+ ssl  world_x  Py > db.city.insert("Name",
"CountryCode", "District", "Info").values ('Charlotte', 'USA', 'North
Carolina', '{"Population": 792862, "Places_of_interest": [{"name": "NASCAR
Hall of Fame"}, {"name": "Charlotte Motor Speedway"}]}')
Query OK, 1 item affected (0.00 sec)
 MySQL  localhost:33060+ ssl  world_x  Py > db.city.insert("Name", "CountryCode",
"District", "Info").values('Daytona', 'USA', 'Florida', '{"Population": 590280,
"Places_of_interest": [{"name": "Daytona Beach"}, {"name": "Motorsports Hall of
Fame of America"}, {"name": "Daytona Motor Speedway"}]}')
Query OK, 1 item affected (0.00 sec)
 MySQL  localhost:33060+ ssl  world_x  Py > db.city.select(["Name",
"District", "JSON_EXTRACT(info, '$.Places_of_interest[*].name')"]).
where("Info->'$.Places_of_interest' IS NOT NULL")
+-----------+----------------+------------------------------------------------+
| Name      | District       | JSON_EXTRACT(`info`,'$.Places_of_              |
|           |                | interest[*].name')                             |
+-----------+----------------+------------------------------------------------+
| Charlotte | North Carolina | ["NASCAR Hall of Fame", "Charlotte Motor       |
|           |                | Speedway"]                                     |
| Daytona   | Florida        | ["Daytona Beach", "Motorsports Hall of Fame    |
|           |                | of America", "Daytona Motor Speedway"]         |
+-----------+----------------+------------------------------------------------+
2 rows in set (0.00 sec)
 MySQL  localhost:33060+ ssl  world_x  Py > db.city.delete().where("Name in
('Charlotte', 'Daytona')")
Query OK, 2 items affected (0.00 sec)
```

Note how the code is similar to the JavaScript version. This makes learning the X DevAPI easier because you can use your favorite language and even when you must use another language, everything is familiar. Cool.

WHAT ABOUT OTHER LANGUAGES?

Although the shell currently only supports JavaScript and Python, the X DevAPI is not limited to these languages. In fact, you can also use Java, .Net, and also C++ via the appropriate connector to work with the X DevAPI. See the links under the X DevAPI heading on `http://dev.mysql.com/doc/` for more information about writing applications with the X DevAPI using the respective connector.

Summary

The MySQL Shell is a huge leap forward in technology for MySQL clients. Not only is it designed to work with SQL in MySQL in a smarter way; it is also designed to enable prototyping of JavaScript and Python. You can work with any language you want and switch between them easily without having to restart the application or drop the connection. How cool is that?

If that wasn't enough, the added benefit of the X DevAPI and built-in objects make using the shell as a front end to the document store means you don't have to write separate applications to manage your data. You simply choose the mode (language) that fits your needs, switch to that language, and perform the tasks. As we learned in Chapter 1, the shell also forms the front end to the newest features including the InnoDB Cluster giving you a one-stop client for all your MySQL administrative, programming, and high availability needs.

In this chapter, we learned how to use the MySQL Shell including a look at the start-up options, shell commands, connections, sessions, and we even learned how to do a bit of interactive scripting in JavaScript and Python. This chapter therefore is the key chapter for learning how to get started with the MySQL Shell and working with JSON and relational data. Although this chapter is not an exhaustive coverage of all the features of the MySQL Shell, it provides a broad tutorial for how to use it for the most common tasks.

In Chapter 5, I explore X DevAPI in more detail including a closer look at the objects and facilities available for writing applications and scripts. I discuss full scripts in both JavaScript and Python to access the document store.

CHAPTER 5

X Developer API

The X Developer Application Programming Interface, or X DevAPI, is a library of classes and methods that implement a new NoSQL interface for MySQL. To be specific, the X DevAPI is designed to allow easy interaction with JSON documents and relational data. The X DevAPI has classes devoted to supporting both concepts allowing developers to use either (or both) in their applications. The X DevAPI together with the X Protocol, X Plugin, and clients written to expose the X DevAPI, forms the new MySQL 8 Document Store feature.

As we will see, there are many aspects to working with the X DevAPI. However, once you master the basics of connecting and requesting object instances, forming expressions, and working with the JSON documents, the X DevAPI is very easy to learn and is efficient for writing document store or relational data applications.

We have already seen several examples of the X DevAPI in action throughout this book for relational data as most database administrators are familiar with that form of database interaction. However, we have not seen a comprehensive list of the classes and methods provided for the document store. This chapter contains nearly all the public classes and methods available in the X DevAPI (some lesser used classes are omitted for brevity).

Although all the X DevAPI client connectors support all the classes, there are some minor differences in how each of the clients implements the X DevAPI. In particular, the names of classes and methods vary slightly to match the development practices for the language. For example, the accepted style guide for a language may discourage camelCase names whereas the style guide for another may suggest the use of underscores and no capitalization.

When learning to use the X DevAPI, it can be helpful to review examples from other languages. Although the naming schemes may differ and the syntax may be quite different, the basic classes and methods are similar enough that you can still learn what methods to use. This is the major reason I use Python examples. You can use the Python examples to see how to use the classes and although the methods may have

175

© Charles Bell 2018
C. Bell, *Introducing the MySQL 8 Document Store*, https://doi.org/10.1007/978-1-4842-2725-1_5

slightly different naming schemes, the methods and practices are the same from one language to another. Plus, Python is easy to read and you do not need large, complicated development tools (e.g., a C++ or .Net compiler). All you need is a Python interpreter and it is available for almost all platforms.

Although this chapter contains some similar information from other chapters, it uses a stepwise approach to demonstrate the X DevAPI via a series of code examples. A set of tables describing the major classes and their methods is included as a reference to use as a guide when writing your own code for a document store application.

I begin with a comprehensive overview of the characteristics of the X DevAPI and then I move on to a detailed reference of the major classes and methods. Along the way I give many examples using the X DevAPI. We will not see every possible class or method that is part of the X DevAPI, but we will see the major components (classes and methods) that you will need to master to write document store applications. If you need additional information for the less frequently used classes and methods, see the "For More Information" section for references to developer documentation.

Overview

There are several powerful features in the X DevAPI. We have seen most of these in action in previous chapters but now we will see the features that the X DevAPI provides. Recall that these features are realized through the clients that support the X Protocol as well as the X DevAPI. The features included in the X DevAPI include the following. We will see these features and how they are realized later in this chapter.

- *MySQLX*: A module used to get a session object resulting from an X Protocol connection to a MySQL server.

- *Sessions*: A connection to a MySQL server.

- *Collections*: An organizational abstraction for storing JSON documents.

- *Documents*: JSON documents are the primary storage mechanism for data in collections.

- *CRUD operations*: Simple methods for create, read, update, and delete operations. Read operations are simple and easy to understand.

- *Relational data*: Implements CRUD operations for traditional relational data including SQL statement execution and results processing.

- *Expressions*: Use modern practices and syntax styles are used to get away from traditional SQL-String-Building for finding things in your collections and documents.

- *Parallel execution*: Nonblocking, asynchronous calls follow common host language patterns.

- *Method chaining*: The API is built so that methods that create or retrieve (get) an object return an instance of that object. This allows us to combine several methods together (called method chaining). Although method chaining is neither a new concept nor unique to the X DevAPI, it is a very powerful mechanism for making our code more expressive and easier to read.

Note   The X DevAPI is only available when using the X Plugin. You cannot use the X DevAPI without the X Plugin installed and then only through an X Protocol enabled client or database connector.

Clients

The X DevAPI is only available through one of the clients that implement the X Protocol. Furthermore, to use any of these clients, you also must have the X Plugin installed and configured for use on your server. In particular with any of the following:

- *MySQL Shell*: version 8.0.4 and later (`https://dev.mysql.com/downloads/shell/`)

- *Connector/J*: version 8.0.8 and later (`https://dev.mysql.com/downloads/connector/j/`)

- *Connector/Net*: version 8.0.8 and later (`https://dev.mysql.com/downloads/connector/net/`)

- *Connector/Node.js*: version 8.0.8 and later (`https://dev.mysql.com/downloads/connector/nodejs/`)

- *Connector/Python*: version 8.0.5 and later (`https://dev.mysql.com/downloads/connector/python/`)

- *Connector/C++*: version 8.0.6 and later (`https://dev.mysql.com/downloads/connector/cpp/`)

Note   Some of the database connector versions are not yet generally available (GA) releases. In those cases, you can find the correct version by clicking on the `Development Releases` tab on the download page. As long as you're not using them in production, using a DMR release should be fine. Be sure to contact your MySQL sales representative for assistance if you do not see a GA release of a component you want to use.

Target Language Conformity

When you encounter a new API such as the X DevAPI, it is often the case that you would expect the names of classes and methods to be the same from one language to another. That is, a class with a method named getSomething() would be spelled the same from one language to another. However, it is a common (and some would say preferred) practice to obey platform- and language-specific naming conventions sacrifice commonality in the API to ensure continued compliance for the language naming standard. If you work with different programming languages as I do, you will find this is common place and thus one knows to expect some variations from one language to another for the same API.

The X DevAPI subscribes to this practice and the clients that implement the API conform to their platform and language standards. In most cases, this may be only a change in the use of capital letters in the name but may also result in the addition (or omission) of underscores. We have already discovered that Connector/Python (C/Py) uses underscores in the names and does not use capital letters. Connector/Java (C/J), Connector/Node.js (C/Node.js), Connector/.Net (C/Net), and Connector/C++ (C/C++) use slightly different capitalization.

It is not just the method names that have different spellings. There also may be subtle differences in how you work with the results from methods or interact with objects. That is, the clients conform to the normal practices for the language for common constructs and concepts such as iteration. For example, if the language has a concept of a list for returning multiple items (say versus an array), the methods will return a list. Although this may seem strange as you read more about the X DevAPI, it does pay benefits. That is, the resulting code you write is compliant with your choice of language standards.

To demonstrate the differences, Table 5-1 shows an example of the minor differences in languages for the MySQL X package method names. Note that even the package name is spelled differently from one language to another. A Python developer would see the Python naming scheme and not think it unusual but the Java example may seem strange.

Table 5-1. *MySQL X Module*

Returns	Name	Method	Language	Parameters
Session Object	`MysqlxSessionFactory`	`getSession()`	Java	Connection URI or connection properties
	`mysqlx`	`getSession()`	Node.js	Connection URI or connection properties
	`MySQLX`	`GetSession()`	DotNet	Connection URI or connection data object
	`mysqlx`	`get_session()`	Python	Connection dictionary

There is one other difference you may notice when exploring the X DevAPI. The clients that implement the API have some very different mechanisms for how to work with data. In some cases, such as C/Net, everything is a class and it is common to use a class to contain data but in C/Py, the use of lists and dictionaries are preferred. Thus, the clients (specifically the database connectors) may implement some of the mechanisms for iteration, retrieval, and encapsulation differently. However, as with the naming conventions, the differences are for the benefit of the developer so that the X DevAPI "works" the way it should in the target language.

Let's look at one more example of the differences. Table 5-2 shows the method available for working with schemas. I've included the four languages for the four database connectors (but group Java and JavaScript) as well as a short description of the task, parameter, and return type for each method.

Table 5-2. *Session—Create Schema Method*

Description	Returns	Language	Method	Parameters
Create a new schema	Schema object	Java/Node.js	`createSchema()`	String—schema name
		DotNet	`CreateSchema()`	String—schema name
		Python	`create_schema()`	String—schema name

In the next section, we examine the major code module, named `mysqlx`, for the X DevAPI.

Note   The code examples in this chapter are written in Python as scripts that use the Connector/Python database connector. Thus, you will need the connector installed to use these examples. Finally, to run the examples, you execute them with the python command like this: `python ./script1.py`.

The `mysqlx` module (sometimes called a package) works with a Session (X Protocol). There is also a module for working with InnoDB Cluster (named dba), and several common classes including those for columns, rows, and so forth.

Note   This chapter contains a lot of information about objects and classes. Objects are an instance of a code class (at execution) and a class is simply the code construct.

MySQL X Module

The `mysqlx` module is the entry point for writing your document store applications and communicating with the X DevAPI. We use this module to pass connection information to the server in the form of a connection string or a language-specific construct (e.g., a dictionary in Python) to pass the connection parameters either as a URI or a connection dictionary as the parameter (not both). Recall that a uniform resource identifier (URI) a special string coded uses the following format:

```
ConnectURI ::= ' 'user_id' ':' 'user_password' '@' 'hostname' ':' 'port_
number' '/' 'default_schema_name' '
```

Note that the password, port, and schema are optional but the user and host are required. Schema in this case is the default schema (database) that you want to use when connecting. The method to get a session object is shown in the following.

```
get_session(<URI or connection dictionary>)
```

The following shows examples of getting a session object instance using a dictionary of connection options and getting a session object instance using a connection string (URI) .

```
import mysqlx
mysqlx_session1 = mysqlx.get_session({'host': 'localhost', 'port': 33060,
'user': 'root', 'password': 'secret'})
mysqlx_session2 = mysqlx.get_session('root:secret@localhost:33060')
```

The resulting variable will point to an object instance should the connection succeed. If it fails, you could get an error or an uninitialized connection as the result. We will see more about checking errors in a later section.

In the next section, we begin our exploration of the classes and methods (components) in the X DevAPI.

Classes and Methods

The following sections examine each of the major classes and their methods (features) for the mysqlx module. These classes are only accessible from a Session object—the same returned from the get_session( ) method. Because this book is about the document store, we focus on those classes for the mysqlx module.

We will discover the methods including classes and for working with schemas (databases), managing transactions, and checking or closing the connection. The material presented includes the most frequently used classes and methods grouped by use or application rather than a strict hierarchy. This allows for a shorter overview that follows a more logical path exploring the API. If you want to see all the details of the modules and classes as well as the raw Doxygen documentation for the code, see the "For More Information" section at the end of the chapter for links to the API documentation for each database connector. I include examples in this chapter that illustrates many of the methods presented.

Let's begin with a brief overview of the mysqlx module. Table 5-3 shows the objects available in the module. Use this table as a quick reference guide to the X DevAPI.

Table 5-3. *Objects in the mysqlx Module*

Area	Method	Description
Connection	Session	Enables interaction with an X Protocol enabled MySQL Product
CRUD	Schema	A client-side representation of a database schema; provides access to the schema contents
	Collection	Represents a collection of documents on a schema
	Table	Represents a database table on a schema
	View	Represents a database view on a schema
Result	ColumnMetaData	Returns metadata on the columns
	Row	Represents a row element returned from a SELECT query
	Result	Allows retrieving information about nonquery operations performed on the database
	BufferingResult	Provides base functionality for buffering result objects
	RowResult	Allows traversing the Row objects returned by a Table.select operation
	SqlResult	Represents a result from a SQL statement

Table 5-3. (*continued*)

Area	Method	Description
Statement	DbDoc	Represents a generic document in JSON format
	Statement	Provides base functionality for statement objects
	FilterableStatement	A statement to be used with filterable statements
	SqlStatement	A statement for SQL execution
	FindStatement	A statement document selection on a collection
	AddStatement	A statement for document addition on a collection
	RemoveStatement	A statement for document removal from a collection
	ModifyStatement	A statement for document update operations on a collection
	SelectStatement	A statement for record retrieval operations on a table
	InsertStatement	A statement for insert operations on table
	DeleteStatement	A statement that drops a table
	UpdateStatement	A statement for record update operations on a table
	CreateCollectionIndexStatement	A statement that creates an index on a collection
	ReadStatement	Provide base functionality for read operations
	WriteStatement	Provide common write operation attributes

(continued)

Table 5-3. (*continued*)

Area	Method	Description
Errors	DataError	Exception for errors reporting problems with processed data
	DatabaseError	Exception for errors related to the database
	Error	Exception that is base class for all other error exceptions
	IntegrityError	Exception for errors regarding relational integrity
	InterfaceError	Exception for errors related with the interface
	InternalError	Exception for internal database errors
	NotSupportedError	Exception for errors when an unsupported database feature was used
	OperationalError	Exception for errors related to a database operation
	PoolError	Exception for errors relating to connection pooling
	ProgrammingError	Exception for errors programming errors

Let's begin our tour of the X DevAPI with the Session class.

Session Class

The Session class is the major class we will use to begin working with a document store. Once we have a connection, the next step is to get the session object. From there, we can begin working with the document store. The following is a tour of the classes and methods grouped by area and application. We start with the schema methods.

Schema Methods

The X DevAPI uses the term *schema* to refer to a set of collections; the collections are a collection of documents. However, when working with relational data, we use "database" to refer to a collection of tables and similar objects. One may be tempted to conclude "schema" is synonymous with "database" and for older versions of MySQL that is true. However, when working with the document store and the X DevAPI, you should use "schema" and when you refer to relational data, you should use "database."

SCHEMA OR DATABASE: DOES IT MATTER?

Since MySQL 5.0.2, the two terms have been synonyms via the CREATE DATABASE and CREATE SCHEMA SQL commands. However, other database systems make a distinction. That is, some state a schema is a collection of tables and a database is a collection of schemas. Others state a schema is what defines the structure of data. If you use other database systems, be sure to check the definitions so that you use the terms correctly.

When starting work with a document store, the first item you will need to do is either select (get) an existing schema, delete an existing schema, or create a new one. You also may want to list the schemas on the server. The Session class provides several methods for performing these operations. Table 5-4 lists the methods, parameters, and return values for the methods concerning schemas.

Table 5-4. *Session Class—Schema Methods*

Method	Returns	Description
create_schema(str name)	Schema	Creates a schema on the database and returns the corresponding object
get_schema(str name)	Schema	Retrieves a schema object from the current session through its name
get_default_schema()	Schema	Retrieves the schema configured as default for the session
drop_schema(str name)	None	Drops the schema with the specified name

Listing 5-1 shows an example of how you can work with session objects to create a schema object. Once again, we will expand on this example as we examine more classes and methods. In this case, we use the session object to work with a schema.

Listing 5-1. Working with Schemas

```
# Import the MySQL X module
import mysqlx
# Get a session with a URI
mysqlx_session = mysqlx.get_session("root:secret@localhost:33060")
# Get an unknown schema
schema1 = mysqlx_session.get_schema("not_there!")
# Does it exist?
print("Does not_there! exist? {0}".format(schema1.exists_in_database()))
# Create the schema
schema = mysqlx_session.create_schema("test_schema")
# Does it exist?
print("Does test_schema exist? {0}".format(schema.exists_in_database()))
mysqlx_session.close()
```

Note the code to retrieve a schema that doesn't exist. I use a method of the schema object to check to see if it exists then print out the result. Assuming the schema not_there! doesn't exist, the code will print "False." Finally, I create the schema test_schema at the end of the code. We will see the schema class in more detail in a later section as well as a better way to check to see if a schema exists. If you save this code to a file named listing5-1.py and execute it, you will see output like the following.

```
$ python ./listing5-1.py
Does not_there! exist? False
Does test_schema exist? True
```

Let us now look at the transactional methods for performing ACID compliant transactions.

Transaction Methods

Transactions provide a mechanism that permits a set of operations to execute as a single atomic operation. For example, if a database were built for a banking institution, the macro operations of transferring money from one account to another would preferably be executed completely (money removed from one account and placed in another) without interruption.

Transactions permit these operations to be encased in an atomic operation that will back out any changes should an error occur before all operations are complete, thus avoiding data being removed from one table and never making it to the next table. A sample set of operations in the form of SQL statements encased in transactional commands is the following:

```
START TRANSACTION;
UPDATE SavingsAccount SET Balance = Balance - 100
WHERE AccountNum = 123;
UPDATE CheckingAccount SET Balance = Balance + 100
WHERE AccountNum = 345;
COMMIT;
```

MySQL's InnoDB storage engine (the default storage engine) supports ACID transactions that ensure data integrity with the ability to only commit (save) the resulting changes if all operations succeed or rollback (undo) the changes if any one of the operations fail.

WHAT IS ACID?

ACID stands for atomicity, consistency, isolation, and durability. Perhaps one of the most important concepts in database theory, it defines the behavior that database systems must exhibit to be considered reliable for transaction processing.

Atomicity means that the database must allow modifications of data on an "all or nothing" basis for transactions that contain multiple commands. That is, each transaction is atomic. If a command fails, the entire transaction fails, and all changes up to that point in the transaction are discarded. This is especially important for systems that operate in highly transactional environments, such as the financial market. Consider for a moment the ramifications of a money transfer. Typically, multiple steps are involved in debiting one account and crediting another. If the transaction fails after the debit step and doesn't credit the money back to the first account, the owner of that account will be very angry. In this case, the entire transaction from debit to credit must succeed, or none of it does.

Consistency means that only valid data will be stored in the database. That is, if a command in a transaction violates one of the consistency rules, the entire transaction is discarded, and the data is returned to the state they were in before the transaction began. On the other hand, if a transaction completes successfully, it will alter the data in a manner that obeys the database consistency rules.

Isolation means that multiple transactions executing at the same time will not interfere with one another. This is where the true challenge of concurrency is most evident. Database systems must handle situations in which transactions cannot violate the data (alter, delete, etc.) being used in another transaction. There are many ways to handle this. Most systems use a mechanism called locking that keeps the data from being used by another transaction until the first one is done. Although the isolation property does not dictate which transaction is executed first, it does ensure they will not interfere with one another.

Durability means that no transaction will result in lost data nor will any data created or altered during the transaction be lost. Durability is usually provided by robust backup-and-restore maintenance functions. Some database systems use logging to ensure that any uncommitted data can be recovered on restart.

The Session classes implement methods for transaction processing that mirror the SQL commands shown previously. Table 5-5 lists the transaction methods.

Table 5-5. *Transaction Methods*

Method	Returns	Description
`start_transaction()`	None	Starts a transaction context on the server
`commit()`	None	Commits all the operations executed after a call to `startTransaction()`
`rollback()`	None	Discards all the operations executed after a call to `startTransaction()`
`set_savepoint(str name="")`	str	Creates or replaces a transaction savepoint with the given name
`release_savepoint(str name)`	None	Removes a savepoint defined on a transaction
`rollback_to(str name)`	None	Rolls back the transaction to the named savepoint without terminating the transaction

Note that the last three methods allow you to create a named transaction savepoint, which is an advanced form of transaction processing. See the online MySQL reference manual for more information about savepoints and transactions.

We will see an example of transactions later in this chapter. Now, let's look at the methods that concern the connection to the server.

Connection Methods

There are two methods for the underlining connection. One to check to see if the connection is open and another to close the connection. Table 5-6 shows the remaining utility methods available in the Session class.

Table 5-6. *Connection Methods*

Method	Returns	Description
`close()`	None	Closes the session
`is_open()`	Bool	Returns true if session is known to be open

The following shows how to use these methods if you want to check the connection as an extra step in your application.

Listing 5-2. Working with Sessions

```
# Import the MySQL X module
import mysqlx
# Get a session with a URI
mysqlx_session = mysqlx.get_session("root:secret@localhost:33060")
# Check the connection
if not mysqlx_session.is_open():
    print("Connection failed!")
else:
    print("Connection succeeded.")
# Close the connection
mysqlx_session.close()
```

If you save this code to a file named listing5-2.py and execute it, you will see output like the following.

```
$ python ./listing5-2.py
Connection succeeded.
```

Miscellaneous Methods

There are also several utility methods in the Session class. Table 5-7 lists the additional functions. See the online X DevAPI reference for more information about these methods.

Table 5-7. *Miscellaneous Methods*

Method	Returns	Description
Is_open()	Bool	True if the connection is open and active
sql(str sql)	SqlStatement	Creates a SqlStatement object to allow running the received SQL statement on the target MySQL server

CRUD Operations

The X DevAPI implements a create, read, update, and delete (CRUD) model for working with the objects that are contained in a schema. A schema can contain any number of collections, documents, tables, views, and other relational data objects (i.e., triggers). In this section, we see an overview of the schema, collection, tables (relational data), and data sets. The CRUD model is implemented for all objects in the schema that can contain data for both document store and relational data.

Most of the examples in the book up to this point have used relational data for demonstration because most readers are familiar with working with SQL. This chapter continues the discussion from Chapter 3 to complete the introduction to working with the X DevAPI to build document store applications.

Document store data CRUD operations use the verbs add, find, modify, and remove whereas relational data uses terms that match the equivalent SQL command. Table 5-8 provides a quick look at how the methods are named as well as a brief description of each. Furthermore, we use the Collection class for document store data and the `Table` class for relational data.

Table 5-8. *CRUD Operations for Document Store and Relational Data*

CRUD Operation	Description	Document Store	Relational Data
Create	Add a new item/object	`collection.add()`	`table.insert()`
Read	Retrieve/search for data	`collection.find()`	`table.select()`
Update	Modify data	`collection.modify()`	`table.update()`
Delete	Remove item/object	`collection.remove()`	`table.delete()`

We will see the methods specific to each class (Schema, Collection, Table, and View) in the following sections. Let's begin with a look at the details of the Schema class.

Schema Class

The schema is a container for the objects that store your data. Recall that this can be a collection for document store data or a table or view for relational data. Much like the old days working with relational data, you must select (or use) a schema for storing data in either a collection, table, or view.

Although you can mix the use of document store data (collections) and relational data (tables, views), to keep things easy to remember, we will examine the Schema class methods as they pertain to each in turn starting with the document store methods.

The document store methods of the Schema class include methods for creating collections, using, and finding collections. Table 5-9 shows the document store methods for working with collections and tables. Note the create and get methods return an instance of an object. For example, the get_collection() method returns a Collection object. This is another example of how you can use the X DevAPI to combine several operations into a single statement.

Table 5-9. *Schema Class—Document Store and Table Methods*

Method	Returns	Description
get_tables()	List	Returns a list of tables for this schema
get_collections()	List	Returns a list of collections for this schema
get_table(str name)	Table	Returns the table of the given name for this schema
get_collection(str name)	Collection	Returns the collection of the given name for this schema
get_collection_as_table(str name)	Table	Returns a Table object representing a collection on the database
create_collection(str name)	Collection	Creates in the current schema a new collection with the specified name and retrieves an object representing the new collection created

Now, let's continue our example and show some of the Schema methods for working with collections in action. Listing 5-3 shows how to create a schema and create several collections then list the collections in the schema. Note that I use the name property of the collection object.

Listing 5-3. Collection Methods

```
# Import the MySQL X module
import mysqlx
# Get a session with a URI
mysqlx_session = mysqlx.get_session("root:secret@localhost:33060")
# Check the connection
if not mysqlx_session.is_open():
    print("Connection failed!")
    exit(-1)
# Get the schema
schema = mysqlx_session.create_schema("test_schema")
# Create a new collection
testCol = schema.create_collection('test_collection1', True)
# Create a new collection
testCol = schema.create_collection('test_collection2', True)
# Show the collections.
collections = schema.get_collections()
for col in collections:
    print(col.name)
mysqlx_session.close()
```

If you save this code to a file named listing5-3.py and execute it, you will see output like the following.

```
$ python ./listing5-3.py
test_collection1
test_collection2
```

Note that in the table there is a method to retrieve a document as a relational table. This method, get_collection_as_table() allows developers who want to store standard SQL columns with documents can convert (cast) a collection to a table. That is, the collection can be fetched as a table object, which then behaves as a normal relational table. Accessing data in the table object using CRUD operations use the following syntax.

```
doc->'$.field_name'
```

This syntax is supported by most connectors.[1] You can form complex document paths (like those we saw in Chapter 3) as well.

```
doc->'$.something_else.field_name.like[1].other_thing'
```

The reason we need this syntax is because a collection returned as a table results in a table with only two fields: doc and _id, where doc is where the document is store and _id is the document id. Listing 5-4 shows how to use this syntax.

Listing 5-4. Collection as Table Example

```
# Import the MySQL X module
import mysqlx
# Get a session with a URI
mysqlx_session = mysqlx.get_session("root:secret@localhost:33060")
# Get the schema
schema = mysqlx_session.create_schema("test_schema")
# Create a new collection
pets = schema.create_collection("pets_json")
# Insert some documents
pets.add({'name': 'Violet', 'age': 6, 'breed':'dachshund', 'type':'dog'}).
execute()
pets.add({'name': 'JonJon', 'age': 15, 'breed':'poodle', 'type':'dog'}).
execute()
pets.add({'name': 'Mister', 'age': 4, 'breed':'siberian khatru',
'type':'cat'}).execute()
pets.add({'name': 'Spot', 'age': 7, 'breed':'koi', 'type':'fish'}).
execute()
pets.add({'name': 'Charlie', 'age': 6, 'breed':'dachshund', 'type':'dog'}).
execute()
# Fetch collection as Table
pets_tbl = schema.get_collection_as_table('pets_json')
# Now do a find operation to retrieve the inserted document
result = pets_tbl.select(["doc->'$.name'", "doc->'$.age'"]).execute()
```

[1]The current release of Connector/Python does not support the syntax.

```
record = result.fetch_one()
# Print the first row
print("Name : {0}, Age: {1}".format(record[0], record[1]))
# Drop the collection
schema.drop_collection("pets_json")
# Close the session
mysqlx_session.close()
```

If you save this code to a file named listing5-4.py and execute it, you will see output like the following.

```
$ python ./listing5-4.py
Name : "Violet", Age: 6
```

Collection Class

The Collection class is used to store documents (data). You can consider it the same organizational concept as a table in relational data. The Collection class therefore implements the CRUD operations for documents as well as a few utility methods such as those for creating an index or counting the documents in the collection. Table 5-10 shows the methods for the collection class.

Table 5-10. *Collection Class*

Method	Returns	Description
add(*values)	AddStatement	Inserts one or more documents into a collection
find(str search_condition)	FindStatement	Retrieves documents from a collection, matching a specified criterion
remove(str search_condition)	RemoveStatement	Creates a document deletion handler
modify(str search_condition)	ModifyStatement	Modifies documents matching a specified criterion
drop_index(str name)	None	Drops an index from a collection
replace_one(str id, document doc)	Result	Replaces an existing document with a new document

(continued)

Table 5-10. (*continued*)

Method	Returns	Description
add_or_replace_one(str id, document doc)	Result	Replaces or adds a document in a collection
remove_one(str id)	Result	Removes document with the given _id value
get_one(str id)	Document	Fetches the document with the given _id from the collection

Note one thing about this table that each of the CRUD operations returns an object instance for the operation. For example, the find() method returns a FindStatement object. As you may surmise, this means that the resulting object instance has methods we can use to do more with the statement. We will see those classes and methods next. For now, let's see an example using the base CRUD operations.

Now that we have enough knowledge about the X DevAPI, we can start reviewing examples that are more complete. That is, examples that do something with data. Listing 5-5 shows a complete Python script that demonstrates how to work with a collection. I include the session code and connection error handling as we've seen previously. The example is a simple document store for recoding information about pets.

Listing 5-5. CRUD Example Using a Collection

```
# Import the MySQL X module
import mysqlx
# Get a session with a URI
mysqlx_session = mysqlx.get_session("root:secret@localhost:33060")
# Check the connection
if not mysqlx_session.is_open():
    print("Connection failed!")
    exit(1)
# Create a schema.
schema = mysqlx_session.create_schema("animals")
# Create a new collection
pets = schema.create_collection("pets_json", True)
```

```
# Insert some documents
pets.add({'name': 'Violet', 'age': 6, 'breed':'dachshund', 'type':'dog'}).
execute()
pets.add({'name': 'JonJon', 'age': 15, 'breed':'poodle', 'type':'dog'}).
execute()
pets.add({'name': 'Mister', 'age': 4, 'breed':'siberian khatru',
'type':'cat'}).execute()
pets.add({'name': 'Spot', 'age': 7, 'breed':'koi', 'type':'fish'}).execute()
pets.add({'name': 'Charlie', 'age': 6, 'breed':'dachshund', 'type':'dog'}).
execute()
# Do a find on the collection - find the fish
mydoc = pets.find("type = 'fish'").execute()
print(mydoc.fetch_one())
# Drop the collection
mysqlx_session.drop_schema("animals")
# Close the connection
mysqlx_session.close()
```

The script creates a new schema then creates a new collection named animals and within the schema a collection named pets_json. The script then adds several documents (pets) to the collection. To demonstrate the find operation, the script calls the find() method on the pets collection looking for all of the fish. That is, a document that has a type equal to 'fish'. We will see more about expressions you can use in the find() method in a later section.

If you save this code to a file named listing5-5.py and execute it, you will see output like the following. We found the fish!

```
$ python ./listing5-5.py
{"breed": "koi", "age": 7, "_id": "7c3c0201f5e24bd99f586e772aad0369",
"type": "fish", "name": "Spot"}
```

Rather than issue a separate add() method for each document, you can add more than one document at the same time by combining the data in a list (array). This is like using a bulk insert option for relational data. The following code is equivalent to the five add() method calls above.

```
# Insert some documents
pets.add([{'name': 'Violet', 'age': 6, 'breed':'dachshund', 'type':'dog'},
  {'name': 'JonJon', 'age': 15, 'breed':'poodle', 'type':'dog'},
  {'name': 'Mister', 'age': 4, 'breed':'siberian khatru', 'type':'cat'},
  {'name': 'Spot', 'age': 7, 'breed':'koi', 'type':'fish'},
  {'name': 'Charlie', 'age': 6, 'breed':'dachshund', 'type':'dog'}]).
  execute()
```

Note the syntax used inside the add() method. This is a special notation that all document store class methods use for specifying JSON documents and listing expressions. In this example, the syntax is optional syntax and is normally used to specify multiple documents. That is, you enclose the documents inside [ ] comma-separated as in the following. In this case, I am adding two documents with one method call. Thus, for one document, the [ ] are optional.

```
pets.add([
    {'name': 'whizzy', 'age': 2, 'breed':'carp', 'type':'fish'},
    {'name': 'blobby', 'age': 3, 'breed': 'carp', 'type': 'fish'},
]).execute()
```

Although this streamlines the code a bit, there may be a reason you would want to add a document at a time. For example, if you need to use the resulting object returned from the add() method to get more information or check warnings, you may want to add one document at a time.

Recall from Table 5-10 that the CRUD methods each return an object instance for a class. These classes have several methods that you can use to work with the statements appropriate for the operation. Table 5-11 shows the classes and their methods.

Table 5-11. *Classes for CRUD Operations for Document Store Data*

Class	Method	Returns	Description
AddStatement	A statement for document addition on a collection		
	add(*values)	AddStatement	Adds a list of documents into a collection
	execute()	Result	Executes the statement
	get_values()	list	Returns the list of values
	is_doc_based()	bool	Checks if it is document based
	is_upsert()	bool	Returns true if it's an upsert
	schema	Schema	The Schema object
	target	object	The database object target
	upsert(val=True)		Sets the upset flag to the boolean of the value provided

(*continued*)

Table 5-11. (*continued*)

Class	Method	Returns	Description
FindStatement	Find documents in a collection		
	bind(*args)	FilterableStatement	Binds a value to a specific placeholder
	execute()	Result	Executes the statement
	fields(*fields)	FindStatement	Sets a document field filter
	get_binding_map()	dict	Returns the binding map dictionary
	get_bindings()	list	Returns the bindings list
	get_grouping()	list	Returns the grouping expression list
	get_having()	object	Returns the having expression
	get_limit_offset()	int	Returns the limit offset
	get_limit_row_count()	int	Returns the limit row count
	get_projection_expr()	object	Returns the projection expression
	get_sort_expr()	object	Returns the sort expression
	get_where_expr()	object	Returns the where expression
	group_by(*fields)	ReadStatement	Sets a grouping criterion for the resultset
	having(condition)	ReadStatement	Sets a condition for records to be considered in aggregate function operations

Table 5-11. (*continued*)

Class	Method	Returns	Description
	is_doc_based()	bool	Checks if it is document based
	is_lock_exclusive()	bool	Returns true if is EXCLUSIVE LOCK
	is_lock_shared()	bool	Returns true if is SHARED LOCK
	limit(row_count, offset=0)	FilterableStatement	Sets the maximum number of records or documents to be returned
	lock_exclusive()	ReadStatement	Executes a read operation with EXCLUSIVE LOCK; only one lock can be active at a time
	lock_shared()	ReadStatement	Executes a read operation with SHARED LOCK; only one lock can be active at a time
	schema	Schema	The Schema object
	sort(*sort_clauses)	FilterableStatement	Sets the sorting criteria
	target	object	The database object target
	where(condition)	FilterableStatement	Sets the search condition to filter

(*continued*)

Table 5-11. (*continued*)

Class	Method	Returns	Description
ModifyStatement	Modify documents in a collection		
	array_append(doc_path, value)	ModifyStatement	Inserts a value into a specific position in an array attribute in documents of a collection
	array_insert(field, value)	ModifyStatement	Inserts a value into the specified array in documents of a collection
	bind(*args)	FilterableStatement	Binds a value to a specific placeholder
	change(doc_path, value)	ModifyStatement	Adds an update to the statement setting the field, if it exists at the document path, to the given value
	execute()	Result	Executes the statement.
	get_binding_map()	dict	Returns the binding map dictionary
	get_bindings()	list	Returns the bindings list
	get_grouping()	list	Returns the grouping expression list
	get_having()	object	Returns the having expression
	get_limit_offset()	int	Returns the limit offset
	get_limit_row_count()	int	Returns the limit row count
	get_projection_expr()	object	Returns the projection expression
	get_sort_expr()	object	Returns the sort expression

Table 5-11. (*continued*)

Class	Method	Returns	Description
	get_update_ops()	list	Returns the list of update operations
	get_where_expr()	object	Returns the where expression
	is_doc_based()	bool	Checks if it is document based
	limit(row_count, offset=0)	FilterableStatement	Sets the maximum number of records or documents to be returned
	patch(doc)	ModifyStatement	Inserts a value into a specific position in an array attribute in documents of a collection
	schema	Schema	The Schema object
	set(doc_path, value)	ModifyStatement	Sets or updates attributes on documents in a collection.
	sort(*sort_clauses)	FilterableStatement	Sets the sorting criteria.
	target	object	The database object target
	unset(*doc_paths)	ModifyStatement	Removes attributes from documents in a collection
	where(condition)	FilterableStatement	Sets the search condition to filter

(*continued*)

Table 5-11. (*continued*)

Class	Method	Returns	Description
RemoveStatement	Remove documents from a collection		
	bind(*args)	FilterableStatement	Binds a value to a specific placeholder
	execute()	Result	Executes the statement
	get_binding_map()	dict	Returns the binding map dictionary
	get_bindings()	list	Returns the bindings list
	get_grouping()	list	Returns the grouping expression list
	get_having()	object	Returns the having expression
	get_limit_offset()	int	Returns the limit offset
	get_limit_row_count()	int	Returns the limit row count
	get_projection_expr()	object	Returns the projection expression
	get_sort_expr()	object	Returns the sort expression
	get_where_expr()	object	Returns the where expression
	is_doc_based()	bool	Checks if it is document based
	limit(row_count, offset=0)	FilterableStatement	Sets the maximum number of records or documents to be returned
	schema	Schema	The Schema object
	sort(*sort_clauses)	FilterableStatement	Sets the sorting criteria
	target	object	The database object target
	where(condition)	FilterableStatement	Sets the search condition to filter

Note that we now see there is more you can do than simply call the add(), find(), modify(), and remove() methods. Because each of these returns an object instance of another class, we can either use a variable to store the object instance and then if you need to specify additional information for the operation, we can call the appropriate method of the new object.

In fact, many of the objects returned have the capability to chain other methods to help filter or modify the search. Table 5-12 lists some of the common methods available for searching documents. Optional methods are shown in [ ]. Also shown are those methods where they can be used.

Table 5-12. *Common Methods for Searching Documents*

Method	Description	Used By
[.fields(...)]	This function sets the fields to be retrieved from each document matching the criteria on this find operation.	find(),
[.group_by(...) [.having(searchCondition)]]	Sets a grouping criteria for the result set. The having clause sets a condition for records to be considered in aggregate function operations.	find(),
[.sort(...)]	If used, the operation will return the records sorted with the defined criteria.	find(), remove(), modify()
[.limit(numberOfRows)	If used, the operation will return at most numberOfRows documents.	find(), remove(), modify()
[.bind(placeHolder, value) [.bind(...)]]	Binds a value to a specific placeholder used on this object	find(), remove(), modify()
execute()	Executes the operation with all the configured options	add(), find(), remove(), modify()

(continued)

Table 5-12. (*continued*)

Method	Description	Used By
[.set(...)]	Adds an operation into the modify handler to set an attribute on the documents that were included on the selection filter and limit	modify()
[.unset(String attribute)]	Removes attributes from documents in a collection	modify()
[.patch(...)]	Performs modifications on a document based on a patch JSON object	modify()
[.array_insert(...)]	Adds an operation into the modify handler to insert a value into an array attribute on the documents that were included on the selection filter and limit	modify()
[.array_append(...)]	Adds an operation into the modify handler to append a value into an array attribute on the documents that were included on the selection filter and limit	modify()

For example, suppose we want to limit the fields for the find() call in the example code used in Listing 5-5. That is, we only want the name and breed of the pet that meets the criteria. We can use the fields() method of the FindStatement class to project the correct fields. Listing 5-6 shows the code to do this.

Listing 5-6. Demonstration of the FindStatement Class

```
# Import the MySQL X module
import mysqlx
# Get a session with a URI
```

```
mysqlx_session = mysqlx.get_session("root:secret@localhost:33060")
# Check the connection
if not mysqlx_session.is_open():
    print("Connection failed!")
    exit(1)
# Create a schema.
schema = mysqlx_session.create_schema("animals")
# Create a new collection
pets = schema.create_collection("pets_json", True)
# Insert some documents
pets.add({'name': 'Violet', 'age': 6, 'breed':'dachshund', 'type':'dog'}).
execute()
pets.add({'name': 'JonJon', 'age': 15, 'breed':'poodle', 'type':'dog'}).
execute()
pets.add({'name': 'Mister', 'age': 4, 'breed':'siberian khatru',
'type':'cat'}).execute()
pets.add({'name': 'Spot', 'age': 7, 'breed':'koi', 'type':'fish'}).execute()
pets.add({'name': 'Charlie', 'age': 6, 'breed':'dachshund', 'type':'dog'}).
execute()
# Do a find on the collection - find the fish
find = pets.find("type = 'fish'")
filterable = find.fields(['name','type'])
mydoc = filterable.execute()
print(mydoc.fetch_one())
```

Note the find() method, here we see once again the use of [ ] to specify a list. In this case, it is a list of fields for the operations. This is a common syntax that you will see in many of the CRUD methods.

If you save this code to a file named listing5-6.py and execute it, you will see output like the following.

```
$ python ./listing5-6.py
{"type": "fish", "name": "Spot"}
```

Note also that we have set a variable to receive the object instance from each method. However, we can chain these methods into a single line of code as follows. Just replace the three lines in Listing 5-6 with the one chained method call.

```
# Do a find on the collection - find the fish
mydoc = pets.find("type = 'fish'").fields(['name','type']).execute()
print(mydoc.fetch_one())
```

Although these new classes may seem a lot of extra work, as you become more accustomed to using them, they will become more intuitive. Indeed, if you are used to working with relational data, some of the methods may seem familiar in concept.

Note also that some of the methods allow you to pass in conditions, which are expressions that you can build to form criteria for the operation. We will discuss expressions in a later section. Now, let's look at the Table class.

Table Class

The table is the major organizational mechanism for relational data. In the X DevAPI, a table is the same relational data construct with which we are all familiar. The X DevAPI has a Table (you can use them with views too) class complete with CRUD operations (select, insert, update, and delete) as well as additional methods for counting the rows or whether the base object is a view. Table 5-13 shows the methods for the Table class.

Table 5-13. *Table Class*

Method	Returns	Description
am_i_real()	bool	Verifies if this object exists in the database
count()	int	Counts the rows in the table.
delete(condition=None)	DeleteStatement	Creates a new mysqlx.DeleteStatement object
exists_in_database()	bool	Verifies if this object exists in the database
get_connection()	Connection	Returns the underlying connection
get_name()	String	Returns the name of this database object
get_schema()	Schema	Returns the schema object of this database object
insert(*fields)	InsertStatement	Creates a new mysqlx.InsertStatement object

(continued)

Table 5-13. (*continued*)

Method	Returns	Description
is_view()	bool	Determines if the underlying object is a view or not
name	str	The name of this database object
schema	Schema	The Schema object
select(*fields)	SelectStatement	Creates a new mysqlx.SelectStatement object
update()	UpdateStatement	Creates a new mysqlx.UpdateStatement object
who_am_i()	String	Returns the name of this database object

Note that there aren't methods for creating the table. We must use the CREATE TABLE SQL command to do this or the sql() method to execute the SQL statement. In fact, there are no methods to create any relational data objects. You must use SQL to issue the appropriate create statement to create the objects. For example, to create a table for our pets data in the previous example, we can use the following CREATE TABLE statement.

```
CREATE TABLE `animals`.`pets_sql` (
  `id` int(11) NOT NULL AUTO_INCREMENT,
  `name` char(20) DEFAULT NULL,
  `age` int(11) DEFAULT NULL,
  `breed` char(20) DEFAULT NULL,
  `type` char(12) DEFAULT NULL,
  PRIMARY KEY (`id`)
) ENGINE=InnoDB DEFAULT CHARSET=latin1;
```

Tip   There are no create methods to create table or views. You must pass the SQL command to the sql() method to create these (and other relational data) objects.

Let's take the script from the previous document store example and rewrite it to use relational data. In this case, I create a new table named pets_sql in the schema named animals and insert a few rows then select one of them. Listing 5-7 shows the code for this example.

Listing 5-7. CRUD Example Using a Table

```python
# Import the MySQL X module
import mysqlx
# Get a session with a URI
mysqlx_session = mysqlx.get_session("root:secret@localhost:33060")
# Check the connection
if not mysqlx_session.is_open():
    print("Connection failed!")
    exit(1)
# Create a schema.
schema = mysqlx_session.create_schema("animals")
# Create a new table
mysqlx_session.sql("CREATE TABLE animals.pets_sql ("
            "`id` int auto_increment primary key, "
            "`name` char(20), "
            "`age` int, "
            "`breed` char(20), "
            "`type` char(12))").execute()
pets = schema.get_table("pets_sql", True)
# Insert some documents
pets.insert().values([None, 'Violet', 6, 'dachshund', 'dog']).execute()
pets.insert().values([None, 'JonJon', 15,'poodle', 'dog']).execute()
pets.insert().values([None, 'Mister', 4,'siberian khatru', 'cat']).execute()
pets.insert().values([None, 'Spot', 7,'koi', 'fish']).execute()
pets.insert().values([None, 'Charlie', 6,'dachshund', 'dog']).execute()
# Do a select (find) on the table - find el gato
mydoc = pets.select().where("type = 'cat'").execute()
print(", ".join("{0}".format(c.get_column_name()) for c in mydoc.columns))
print(", ".join("{0}".format(r) for r in mydoc.fetch_one()))
# Drop the collection
mysqlx_session.drop_schema("animals")
# Close the connection
mysqlx_session.close()
```

If you save this code to a file named listing5-7.py and execute it, you will see output like the following.

```
$ python ./listing5-7.py
id, name, age, breed, type
3, Mister, 4, siberian khatru, cat
```

Although I put the CREATE TABLE statement in the example code, it is not normal practice to do so. In fact, most developers will create the table separately from the application. That is, they would execute the CREATE SQL statements manually (or possibly through a DevOps[2] tool) and not include them in the application. However, there are some arguments for using temporary tables in which case you would likely include those in the application, but in general, permanent database objects are created separately from the application. The next example shows how to get the table from an existing schema.

Note that there are some interesting new method calls. First, unlike the add() method for collections, the insert() method uses additional chained methods. In this case, we needed the values() method to add the values. This is because the insert() method returns an instance of the InsertStatement class.

This may seem strange until you consider the syntax for the SQL INSERT statement. In particular, the equivalent statements in SQL for these operations are as follows. As you can see, we have a VALUES clause.

```
INSERT INTO animals.pets VALUES (Null, 'Violet', 6, 'dachshund', 'dog');
INSERT INTO animals.pets VALUES (Null, 'JonJon', 15,'poodle', 'dog');
INSERT INTO animals.pets VALUES (Null, 'Mister', 4,'siberian khatru', 'cat');
INSERT INTO animals.pets VALUES (Null, 'Spot', 7,'koi', 'fish');
INSERT INTO animals.pets VALUES (Null, 'Charlie', 6,'dachshund', 'dog');
```

The same is true for the select() method, which returns a SelectStatement object where we chained the where() clause. As you may have surmised, the same thing happens for the update() and delete() methods. This is natural for those used to using the SQL statements. Table 5-14 lists the methods for each of the classes related to the CRUD operations for relational data.

---

[2]https://en.wikipedia.org/wiki/DevOps

Table 5-14. Classes for CRUD Operations for Relational Data

Class	Method	Returns	Description
SelectStatement	A statement for record retrieval operations on a table.		
	bind(*args)	FilterableStatement	Binds a value to a specific placeholder
	execute()	Result	Executes the statement
	get_binding_map()	dict	Returns the binding map dictionary
	get_bindings()	list	Returns the bindings list
	get_grouping()	list	Returns the grouping expression list
	get_having()	object	Returns the having expression
	get_limit_offset()	int	Returns the limit offset
	get_limit_row_count()	int	Returns the limit row count
	get_projection_expr()	object	Returns the projection expression
	get_sort_expr()	object	Returns the sort expression
	get_sql()	String	Returns the generated SQL
	get_where_expr()	object	Returns the where expression
	group_by(*fields)	ReadStatement	Sets a grouping criterion for the resultset
	having(condition)	ReadStatement	Sets a condition for records to be considered in aggregate function operations

Table 5-14. (*continued*)

Class	Method	Returns	Description
	is_doc_based()	bool	Checks if it is document based
	is_lock_exclusive()	bool	Returns true if is EXCLUSIVE LOCK
	is_lock_shared()	bool	Returns true if is SHARED LOCK
	limit(row_count, offset=0)	FilterableStatement	Sets the maximum number of records or documents to be returned
	lock_exclusive()	ReadStatement	Executes a read operation with EXCLUSIVE LOCK; only one lock can be active at a time
	lock_shared()	ReadStatement	Executes a read operation with SHARED LOCK; only one lock can be active at a time
	order_by(*clauses)	SelectStatement	Sets the order by criteria.
	schema	Schema	The Schema object
	sort(*sort_clauses)	FilterableStatement	Sets the sorting criteria
	target	object	The database object target
	where(condition)	FilterableStatement	Sets the search condition to filter

(*continued*)

Table 5-14. (*continued*)

Class	Method	Returns	Description
InsertStatement	A statement for insert operations on table		
	execute()	Result	Executes the statement
	get_values()	list	Returns the list of values
	is_doc_based()	bool	Checks if it is document based
	is_upsert()	bool	Returns true if it's an upsert
	schema	Schema	The Schema object
	target	object	The database object target
	upsert(val=True)		Sets the upsert flag to the boolean of the value provided; setting of this flag allows updating of the matched rows/documents with the provided value
	values(*values)	InsertStatement	Sets the values to be inserted

Table 5-14. (*continued*)

Class	Method	Returns	Description
UpdateStatement	A statement for record update operations on a table		
	bind(*args)	FilterableStatement	Binds a value to a specific placeholder
	execute()	Result	Executes the statement
	get_binding_map()	dict	Returns the binding map dictionary
	get_bindings()	list	Returns the bindings list
	get_grouping()	list	Returns the grouping expression list
	get_having()	object	Returns the having expression
	get_limit_offset()	int	Returns the limit offset
	get_limit_row_count()	int	Returns the limit row count
	get_projection_expr()	object	Returns the projection expression
	get_sort_expr()	object	Returns the sort expression
	get_update_ops()	list	Returns the list of update operations
	get_where_expr()	object	Returns the where expression
	is_doc_based()	bool	Checks if it is document based
	limit(row_count, offset=0)	FilterableStatement	Sets the maximum number of records or documents to be returned

(*continued*)

Table 5-14. (*continued*)

Class	Method	Returns	Description
	schema	Schema	The Schema object
	set(field, value)	UpdateStatement	Updates the column value on records in a table
	sort(*sort_clauses)	FilterableStatement	Sets the sorting criteria
	target	object	The database object target
	where(condition)	FilterableStatement	Sets the search condition to filter
DeleteStatement	A statement that drops a table		
	bind(*args)	FilterableStatement	Binds a value to a specific placeholder
	execute()	Result	Executes the statement
	get_binding_map()	dict	Returns the binding map dictionary
	get_bindings()	list	Returns the bindings list
	get_grouping()	list	Returns the grouping expression list
	get_having()	object	Returns the having expression
	get_limit_offset()	int	Returns the limit offset
	get_limit_row_count()	int	Returns the limit row count

Table 5-14. (*continued*)

Class	Method	Returns	Description
	get_projection_expr()	object	Returns the projection expression
	get_sort_expr()	object	Returns the sort expression
	get_where_expr()	object	Returns the where expression
	is_doc_based()	bool	Checks if it is document based
	limit(row_count, offset=0)	FilterableStatement	Sets the maximum number of records or documents to be returned
	schema	Schema	The Schema object
	sort(*sort_clauses)	FilterableStatement	Sets the sorting criteria
	target	object	The database object target
	where(condition)	FilterableStatement	Sets the search condition to filter

Before we proceed, let us review the sample data needed to execute the examples in the rest of this chapter.

WHAT ABOUT CLASSICSESSION?

If you've read the documentation for the MySQL Shell, you may have encountered a global object named mysqlx, which mirrors the mysqlx module. You also may have encountered a session object named ClassicSession that exists in the mysql global object. This object is only available via the MySQL Shell and is not to be confused with the module named mysql in the Connector/Python code—they are not the same. In fact, the X DevAPI does not have any objects named ClassicSession.

Because this book focuses on the MySQL Document Store and the X DevAPI we present a brief list of the methods in the ClassicSession class. The following lists the commonly used methods.

- close(): Closes the internal connection to the MySQL server held on this session object.

- start_transaction(): Starts a transaction context on the server.

- commit(): Commits all the operations executed after a call to startTransaction().

- rollback(): Discards all the operations executed after a call to startTransaction().

- get_uri(): Retrieves the URI string.

- run_sql(str query, list args=[]): Executes a query and returns the corresponding ClassicResult object.

- query(str query, list args=[]): Executes a query and returns the corresponding ClassicResult object.

- is_open(): Returns True if the session is open.

Once again, these methods are for the ClassicSession class, which is only available through the MySQL Shell. This brief sidebar was included for completeness and to clarify the origins of the class.

Example Data Used in this Chapter

The example code for the rest of this chapter uses data we created in the previous examples. I include it here for your convenience. More specific, I include the SQL statements for creating the relational data and a short script for creating the document store data. Listing 5-8 is the code needed for creating the sample document store.

Listing 5-8. Sample Document Store

```
# Create a schema.
# Import the MySQL X module
import mysqlx
# Get a session with a URI
mysqlx_session = mysqlx.get_session("root:secret@localhost:33060")
# Check the connection
if not mysqlx_session.is_open():
    print("Connection failed!")
    exit(1)
# Create a schema.
schema = mysqlx_session.create_schema("animals")
# Create a new collection
pets = schema.create_collection("pets_json", True)
# Insert some documents
pets.add({'name': 'Violet', 'age': 6, 'breed':'dachshund', 'type':'dog'}).
execute()
pets.add({'name': 'JonJon', 'age': 15, 'breed':'poodle', 'type':'dog'}).execute()
pets.add({'name': 'Mister', 'age': 4, 'breed':'siberian khatru',
'type':'cat'}).execute()
pets.add({'name': 'Spot', 'age': 7, 'breed':'koi', 'type':'fish'}).execute()
pets.add({'name': 'Charlie', 'age': 6, 'breed':'dachshund', 'type':'dog'}).
execute()
# Close the connection
mysqlx_session.close()
```

You may note that this resembles many of the previous listings. However, because from this point on we will be using the animals schema, we have omitted the drop_schema( ) call at the end.

Listing 5-9 includes the SQL statements for creating the sample relational data.

Listing 5-9. Sample Relational Data

```sql
CREATE TABLE `animals`.`pets_sql` (
  `id` int(11) NOT NULL AUTO_INCREMENT,
  `name` char(20) DEFAULT NULL,
  `age` int(11) DEFAULT NULL,
  `breed` char(20) DEFAULT NULL,
  `type` char(12) DEFAULT NULL,
  PRIMARY KEY (`id`)
) ENGINE=InnoDB DEFAULT CHARSET=latin1;

INSERT INTO animals.pets_sql VALUES (Null, 'Violet', 6, 'dachshund', 'dog');
INSERT INTO animals.pets_sql VALUES (Null, 'JonJon', 15,'poodle', 'dog');
INSERT INTO animals.pets_sql VALUES (Null, 'Mister', 4,'siberian khatru', 'cat');
INSERT INTO animals.pets_sql VALUES (Null, 'Spot', 7,'koi', 'fish');
INSERT INTO animals.pets_sql VALUES (Null, 'Charlie', 6,'dachshund', 'dog');

CREATE VIEW `animals`.`num_pets` AS
SELECT type as Type, COUNT(*) as Num
FROM animals.pets_sql
GROUP BY type;
```

Although the preceding examples create these objects, you may want to refer to this section when experimenting with the examples and when running the examples later in the chapter.

Now let's see the classes for working with results and data sets from the find(), select(), and other methods that return results.

Working with Data Sets

Until now we have seen a few simple examples of working with results and while it may appear all results are the same class, there are several result classes. The object instance for the Result class returned depends on the operation. Table 5-15 shows the type of object instance returned by the origin operation as well as the type of data returned.

Table 5-15. *Result Classes (Object Instances) Returned*

Object Instance	Origin	Description	Content Returned
Result	Create, update, delete	Returned by `add()`. `execute()`, `modify()`. `execute()`, `remove().execute()`	`affected_item_count`, `auto_increment_value`, `last_document_id`
SqlResult	Session	Returned by `session.sql()`	`auto_increment_value`, `affected_row_count`, fetched data – data set
RowResult	Relational Data select	Returned by `select()`. `execute()`	fetched data—data set

Note that the content column shows either a result or data set as the content returned. The X DevAPI uses the term *data set* to refer to the data returned from the read CRUD operation (`find()`, `select()`, and `sql()` methods) and *result*[3] to refer to the data returned from a create, update and delete CRUD operation.

Also, note that there are different objects returned for each of the class of operations. The classes `RowResult` and `SqlResult` inherit from a base class (`BaseResult`) and thus have a lot of the same methods. What sets these apart from the `Result` class returned from the create, update, and delete operations is the `Result` class does not support an iterator. This is because a Result object contains the data returned from the server pertaining to the create, update, and delete operations, which do not return any data but may return warnings and similar metadata and is equivalent to the results returned from traditional SQL `INSERT`, `UPDATE`, and `DELETE` statements in MySQL.

Table 5-16 shows all the classes and their methods that you will encounter when working with data sets and results.

---

[3]Sadly, this is sometimes called a *result set* in the documentation and blogs, which may be confusing because result set is a common term used in relational data to mean the same thing as data set. When working with the X DevAPI, it is best to think result set and data set as synonyms.

Table 5-16. *Classes and Methods for Working with Data Sets and Results*

Class	Method	Returns	Description
RowResult	Allows traversing the Row objects returned by a Table.select operation		
	columns	list	The list of columns
	count	int	The total of items
	fetch_all()	list	Fetches all items
	fetch_one()	mysqlx.Row or mysqlx.DbDoc	Fetches one item
	get_warnings()	list	Returns the warnings
	get_warnings_count()	int	Returns the number of warnings
	index_of(col_name)	int	Returns the index of the column
	set_closed(flag)		Sets if resultset fetch is done
	set_generated_id(generated_id)		Sets the generated ID
	set_has_more_results(flag)		Sets if has more resultsets
	set_rows_affected(total)		Sets the number of rows affected

Table 5-16. (*continued*)

Class	Method	Returns	Description
SqlResult	Represents a result from a SQL statement		
	columns	list	The list of columns
	count	int	The total of items
	fetch_all()	list	Fetches all items
	fetch_one()	mysqlx.Row or mysqlx.DbDoc	Fetches one item
	get_autoincrement_value()	string	Returns the identifier for the last record inserted
	get_warnings()	list	Returns the warnings
	get_warnings_count()	int	Returns the number of warnings
	index_of(col_name)	int	Returns the index of the column
	next_result()	bool	Processes the next result
	set_closed(flag)		Sets if resultset fetch is done
	set_generated_id(generated_id)		Sets the generated ID
	set_has_more_results(flag)		Sets if has more resultsets

(continued)

Table 5-16. (*continued*)

Class	Method	Returns	Description
BufferingResult	Provides base functionality for buffering result objects		
	count	int	The total of items
	fetch_all()	list	Fetches all items
	fetch_one()	mysqlx.Row or mysqlx.DbDoc	Fetches one item
	get_warnings()	list	Returns the warnings
	get_warnings_count()	int	Returns the number of warnings
	index_of(col_name)	int	Returns the index of the column
	set_closed(flag)		Sets if resultset fetch is done
	set_generated_id(generated_id)		Sets the generated ID
	set_has_more_results(flag)		Sets if has more resultsets
	set_rows_affected(total)		Sets the number of rows affected

Table 5-16. (*continued*)

Class	Method	Returns	Description
Result	Allows retrieving information about nonquery operations performed on the database		
	append_warning(level, code, msg)		Appends a warning
	get_affected_items_count()	int	Returns the number of affected items for the last operation
	get_autoincrement_value()	int	Returns the last insert id auto generated
	get_document_id()	String	Returns ID of the last document inserted into a collection
	get_document_ids()	list	Returns the list of generated documents IDs
	get_warnings()	list	Returns the warnings

The three classes that have iterators implement two methods: `fetch_one()` and `fetch_all()`. They work as you would imagine and return either a data set or a set of objects for a set of documents. The `fetch_one()` method returns the next data item in the data set or NULL if there are no more data items and `fetch_all()` returns all the data items. More specific, `fetch_one()` retrieves one data item at a time from the server whereas `fetch_all()` retrieves all the data from the server in one pass. Which one you would use depends on the size of the data set and how you would want to process the data.

Note   Once you fetch a data item, you cannot fetch it again. That is, the iterators are forward only.

Before we look at how to access data in the data set, let us review document identifiers and auto increment columns.

Tip   From this point on in the examples, you should have the JSON data loaded as described in Listing 5-8 and the relational data as described in Listing 5-9.

Document Identifiers

Recall each document you store in a document store collection has a document identifier (doc id or document id), which is a string of characters that uniquely identifies the document in a collection.[4] You do not need to create your own document ids—they are assigned for you automatically.

There are two methods available to retrieve the document id from the Result class (the content returned for create, update, and delete operations). In particular, you can use the get_document_id() method to retrieve the last document id assigned or the get_document_ids() to return a list of the document ids for the bulk add option for the add() method as described above. Listing 5-10 demonstrates retrieving the document ids when adding documents.

---

[4]Equivalent in principle to a primary key (such as an auto increment column).

Note   The listing from this point on assumes the `animals` collection does not exist. If you are planning to run the code examples one after another, you should add the `drop_schema()` call shown in Listing 5-5.

Listing 5-10. Getting Document Ids

```python
# Import the MySQL X module
import mysqlx
# Get a session with a URI
mysqlx_session = mysqlx.get_session("root:secret@localhost:33060")
# Check the connection
if not mysqlx_session.is_open():
    print("Connection failed!")
    exit(1)
# Drop the collection
mysqlx_session.drop_schema("animals")
# Create a schema.
schema = mysqlx_session.create_schema("animals")
# Create a new collection
pets = schema.create_collection("pets_json")
# Insert some documents and get the document ids.
res = pets.add({'name': 'Violet', 'age': 6, 'breed':'dachshund',
'type':'dog'}).execute()
print("New document id = '{0}'".format(res.get_document_id()))
res = pets.add({'name': 'JonJon', 'age': 15, 'breed':'poodle',
'type':'dog'}).execute()
print("New document id = '{0}'".format(res.get_document_id()))
res = pets.add({'name': 'Mister', 'age': 4, 'breed':'siberian khatru',
'type':'cat'}).execute()
print("New document id = '{0}'".format(res.get_document_id()))
res = pets.add({'name': 'Spot', 'age': 7, 'breed':'koi', 'type':'fish'}).
execute()
print("New document id = '{0}'".format(res.get_document_id()))
```

```
res = pets.add({'name': 'Charlie', 'age': 6, 'breed':'dachshund',
'type':'dog'}).execute()
print("New document id = '{0}'".format(res.get_document_id()))# Drop the
collection
mysqlx_session.drop_schema("animals")
# Close the connection
mysqlx_session.close()
```

If you run the code snippet, you will see the document ids as in the following.

```
New document id = '9801A79DE0939A8311E805FB3419B12B'
New document id = '9801A79DE093B93111E805FB341CC7B5'
New document id = '9801A79DE093AD4311E805FB341CF6D9'
New document id = '9801A79DE09397AD11E805FB341D1F87'
New document id = '9801A79DE09382E911E805FB341D4568'
```

Auto Increment

If you are working with relational data and have specified an auto increment field, you can retrieve the last auto increment value using the get_autoincrement_value() method of the SqlResult and Result classes. This method returns the auto increment value generated, which can be helpful if you need to retrieve the last row inserted by the surrogate primary key.

Accessing Data in Data Sets

Let us consider accessing data in data sets. In this case, we issue a find() method on a collection that returns several documents as represented by a specific result object. In this case, we have a set of DbDoc objects to fetch.

There are three ways we can access the data in the data item; we can simply get the data item as a string (naturally), we can access the data elements via a property with the name of the key for the data element, or we can use an array index to find the data element with its key. Listing 5-11 shows a complete script with an example of each mechanism. Note that you should have created the schema and collection populating it with the data using Listing 5-8.

Listing 5-11. Reading Data from a Data Set

```
# Import the MySQL X module
import mysqlx
# Get a session with a URI
mysqlx_session = mysqlx.get_session("root:secret@localhost:33060")
# Check the connection
if not mysqlx_session.is_open():
    print("Connection failed!")
    exit(1)
# Get the collection.
pets = mysqlx_session.get_schema("animals").get_collection("pets_json")
# Do a find on the collection - find the dog
find = pets.find("type = 'dog'").execute()
res = find.fetch_one()
while (res):
    print("Get the data item as a string: {0}".format(res))
    print("Get the data elements: {0}, {1}, {2}".format(res.name, res.age,
    res['breed']))
    res = find.fetch_one()
# Close the connection
mysqlx_session.close()
```

Note how I retrieved the data set with the find().execute() method, which returns an object that I can iterate over. In this case, I fetch the first data item then a while loop to loop through the items. Inside the while loop, I print the string returned from the fetch and demonstrate how to retrieve data elements by property (e.g., res.age, res.name) or by array index using the key name (e.g., res['breed']).

If you save this code to a file named listing5-11.py and execute it, you will see output like the following.

```
$ python ./listing5-11.py
Get the data item as a string: {"breed": "dachshund", "age": 6, "_id":
"9801A79DE093B2B011E805FBCB1FAC51", "type": "dog", "name": "Violet"}
Get the data elements: Violet, 6, dachshund
Get the data item as a string: {"breed": "poodle", "age": 15, "_id":
"9801A79DE093B43A11E805FBCB215AFA", "type": "dog", "name": "JonJon"}
```

```
Get the data elements: JonJon, 15, poodle
Get the data item as a string: {"breed": "dachshund", "age": 6, "_id":
"9801A79DE093BFD511E805FBCB21CF30", "type": "dog", "name": "Charlie"}
Get the data elements: Charlie, 6, dachshund
```

Now lets' see how to get rows from a relational data query.

Accessing Metadata in Results

When using relational data and the table or view select() method. This returns an
SQL data set that represents the rows you would expect to get from a typical SQL SELECT
query. We can then access the data in the row by column name as a property, column
index number as the array index, or by column name as the array index. Listing 5-12
demonstrates both methods of getting the data from the row.

Listing 5-12. Data Set Example—Relational Data

```python
# Import the MySQL X module
import mysqlx
# Get a session with a URI
mysqlx_session = mysqlx.get_session("root:secret@localhost:33060")
# Check the connection
if not mysqlx_session.is_open():
    print("Connection failed!")
    exit(1)
# Get the collection.
pets = mysqlx_session.get_schema("animals").get_table("pets_sql")
# Do a select (find) on the table - find the dogs
res = pets.select().where("type = 'dog'").execute()
# Working with column properties
print("Get the data using column names as properties:")
for row in res.fetch_all():
    for col in res.columns:
        print(row.get_string(col.get_column_name())),
    print("")
# Working with column indexes
print("Get the data using column index by integer:")
```

```
for row in res.fetch_all():
    for i in range(0,len(res.columns)):
        print(row[i]),
    print("")
# Working with column names
print("Get the data using column index by name:")
for row in res.fetch_all():
    for col in res.columns:
        print(row[col.get_column_name()]),
    print("")
# Close the connection
mysqlx_session.close()
```

If you save this code to a file named listing5-12.py and execute it, you will see output as the following.

```
$ python ./listing5-12.py
Get the data using column names as properties:
1 Violet 6 dachshund dog
2 JonJon 15 poodle dog
5 Charlie 6 dachshund dog
Get the data using column index by integer:
1 Violet 6 dachshund dog
2 JonJon 15 poodle dog
5 Charlie 6 dachshund dog
Get the data using column index by name:
1 Violet 6 dachshund dog
2 JonJon 15 poodle dog
5 Charlie 6 dachshund dog
```

Note how I retrieve the data set with the select().execute() method, which returns an object that I can iterate over. In this case, I fetch the items (rows) using a for loop. Inside the for loop, I use the Row object's get_string() method, which takes a key name for the column or in this case column name. I use a little trick with iterating over the columns inside a nested for loop. I discuss how to work with the column metadata in the next section.

Column Metadata

The two result classes for relational data (RowResult and SqlResult) support the concept of columns as you would expect from a typical SQL SELECT query. You can get the columns using the columns() method (columns property), which returns a list of Column objects. You can then use the properties in that object to discover more about the columns in the data set. Table 5-17 shows the ColumnMetaData class and its methods.

Table 5-17. *ColumnMetaData Class*

Method	Returns	Description
get_schema_name()	str	Retrieves the name of the schema where the column is defined
get_table_name()	str	Retrieves table name where the column is defined
get_table_label()	str	Retrieves table alias where the column is defined
get_column_name()	str	Retrieves column name
get_column_label()	str	Retrieves column alias
get_type()	Type	Retrieves column type
get_length()	int	Retrieves column length
get_fractional_digits()	int	Retrieves the fractional digits if applicable
is_number_signed()	bool	Indicates if a numeric column is signed
get_collation_name()	str	Retrieves the collation name
get_character_set_name()	str	Retrieves the character set name

Note that there are several interesting methods including those for discovering the type, character and collation, size, and more. Note also there are methods for getting the name or label of the column. The name is the name from the operation whereas the label is alias or alternative labeling specified in the operation. To see the difference, consider the following SQL statement.

```
SELECT pet_name as name, age as years_young FROM animals.pets_sql
```

When you call the get_column_name() and get_column_label() methods, you get the following values. Listing 5-13 demonstrates how to work with these methods.

Listing 5-13. Working with Column Names and Labels

```
# Import the MySQL X module
import mysqlx
# Get a session with a URI
mysqlx_session = mysqlx.get_session("root:secret@localhost:33060")
# Check the connection
if not mysqlx_session.is_open():
    print("Connection failed!")
    exit(1)
res = mysqlx_session.sql("SELECT name as pet_name, age as years_young FROM
animals.pets_sql").execute()
cols = res.columns
for col in cols:
    print "name =", col.get_column_name(), "label =", col.get_column_label()
mysqlx_session.close()
```

If you save this code to a file named listing5-13.py and execute it, you will see output like the following.

```
$ python ./listing5-13.py
name = name label = pet_name
name = age label = years_young
```

Now let's discuss the use of expressions to filter data.

Expressions

Expressions are another element in the X DevAPI that is a simple, yet powerful feature. Expressions are synonymous with the clauses we use in SQL statements for filtering data in CRUD statements. There are several forms of expressions. We can use strings, Boolean expressions, or embed actual expressions such as equality or inequality. Let's examine each of these.

Expression Strings

Expression strings are those strings that need to be evaluated at runtime. Typically, they use one or more variables "bound" (called *parameter binding*) to placeholders in the string. This permits you to assign values at runtime for dynamic filtering rather than static values as we will see in the next section. We will see more about parameter binding in a later section.

Listing 5-14 shows an example like one we used in a previous example looking for the fish in our pets_json collection. However, in this case, we use a parameter to contain the type, which could presumably be read at runtime and thus allow us to make our code dynamically filter the collection find results.

Listing 5-14. Expression Strings

```
# Import the MySQL X module
import mysqlx
# Get a session with a URI
mysqlx_session = mysqlx.get_session("root:secret@localhost:33060")
# Check the connection
if not mysqlx_session.is_open():
    print("Connection failed!")
    exit(1)
# Get the collection.
pets = mysqlx_session.get_schema("animals").get_collection("pets_json")
# Do a find on the collection - find the fish with an expression string and
parameter binding
fish_type = 'fish'
mydoc = pets.find("type = :mytype").bind('mytype', fish_type).execute()
print(mydoc.fetch_one())
# Close the connection
mysqlx_session.close()
```

If you save this code to a file named listing5-14.py and execute it, you will see output like the following.

```
$ python ./listing5-14.py
{"breed": "koi", "age": 7, "_id": "9801A79DE0938FBD11E805FBCB21AB35",
"type": "fish", "name": "Spot"}
```

Boolean Expression Strings

This form of expression uses a string much like we use in the WHERE clause for SQL statements. That is, we express the filter using natural language where the comparison is either true or false. Listing 5-15 are Boolean expression strings from previous examples. The first line is a relational data example in which we want the results to include only those items whose type column is equal to "dog." The second is a document store example in which we want the results to include only those items whose type element has the value "fish."

Listing 5-15. Boolean Expression Strings

```python
# Import the MySQL X module
import mysqlx
# Get a session with a URI
mysqlx_session = mysqlx.get_session("root:secret@localhost:33060")
# Check the connection
if not mysqlx_session.is_open():
    print("Connection failed!")
    exit(1)
# Get the collection.
pets_json = mysqlx_session.get_schema("animals").get_collection("pets_
json")
# Get the table.
pets_sql = mysqlx_session.get_schema("animals").get_table("pets_sql")
res = pets_sql.select().where("type = 'dog'").limit(1).execute()
print("SQL result ="),
for row in res.fetch_all():
    for i in range(0,len(res.columns)):
        print("{0}".format(row[i])),
print("")
mydoc = pets_json.find("type = 'fish'").execute()
print("JSON result = {0}".format(mydoc.fetch_one()))
# Close the connection
mysqlx_session.close()
```

If you save this code to a file named `listing5-15.py` and execute it, you will see output like the following.

```
$ python ./listing5-15.py
SQL result = 1 Violet 6 dachshund dog
JSON result = {"breed": "koi", "age": 7, "_id":
"9801A79DE0938FBD11E805FBCB21AB35", "type": "fish", "name": "Spot"}
```

Tip   You can find a complete set of extended Backus-Naar form[5] drawings for expressions and method chaining in the X DevAPI Users guide at `https://dev.mysql.com/doc/x-devapi-userguide/en/`.

Warnings and Errors

Another area in which we need to spend some time learning about is the report of warnings sent from the server and handling errors from the X DevAPI. Fortunately, the X DevAPI has facilities for getting the warnings. However, errors will take a bit more work. Let's look at warnings first.

Warnings from the Server

Handling warnings is easy because the X DevAPI has a mechanism built in to help you get the warnings information. The `Warning` class has three properties as shown in the following. We can use these to get the warnings should they occur.

- *Level*—level of the warning
- *Code*—warning code
- *Message*—warning message

---

[5]Extended Backus-Naar form is a style of diagraming used to document context-free grammars. See `https://en.wikipedia.org/wiki/Extended_Backus%E2%80%93Naur_form`.

Note By default, all warnings are sent from the server to the client. However, you can suppress warnings to save bandwidth. Use the set_fetch_warnings() in the Session class to control whether warnings are discarded at the server or sent to the client. Use the get_fetch_warnings() method to get the active setting.

In fact, we can use the get_warnings() method to check to see if there are warnings we need to process. However, the X DevAPI sends warnings to the client each time they occur so if you want to check for warnings, you must do so after each execution. Listing 5-16 shows one way you can write code to handle errors. It is by no means the only way, but does demonstrate the Warning class methods.

Note This example requires the animals database setup. See the "Example Data Used in this Chapter" section previously for how to setup the database.

Listing 5-16. Processing Warnings

```
#This method checks the result for warnings and prints them
# if any exist.
#
# result[in]      result object
def process_warnings(result):
    if result.get_warnings_count():
        for warning in result.get_warnings():
            print("WARNING: Type {0} (Code {1}): {2}".format(*warning))
    else:
        print "No warnings were returned."

# Import the MySQL X module
import mysqlx
# Get a session with a URI
mysqlx_session = mysqlx.get_session("root:secret@localhost:33060")
# Check the connection
if not mysqlx_session.is_open():
    print("Connection failed!")
    exit(1)
```

```
# Get the animals schema.
schema = mysqlx_session.get_schema("animals")
# Try to create the table using a SQL string. It should throw a warning.
res = mysqlx_session.sql("CREATE TABLE IF NOT EXISTS animals.pets_sql ("
                         "`id` int auto_increment primary key, "
                         "`name` char(20), "
                         "`age` int, "
                         "`breed` char(20), "
                         "`type` char(12))").execute()
process_warnings(res)
# Close the connection
mysqlx_session.close()
```

Note that I wrote a method named process_warnings() that takes a result object and checks to see if there are errors by calling the get_warnings_count() method. If this method returns a positive integer, it means there are warnings and if so, I get the type, code, and message from the warning object and print the data. If there are no warnings, I print a message stating there were no errors (but you probably don't want to know that).

If you save this code to a file named listing5-16.py and execute it, you will see the following results. Note that you may have to run it a second time if you deleted the animals collection.

```
$ python ./listing5-16.py
WARNING: Type 1 (Code 1050): Table 'pets_sql' already exists
```

Now let's see how we can handle errors from the X DevAPI.

Errors from the X DevAPI

As I mentioned, there is nothing implemented in the X DevAPI specifically for handling errors, but there are facilities that we can use. In this case, we're going to get some help from our database connectors. That is, the database connectors implement the language-specific error handling (exception handling) mechanisms making it natural to handle errors from the X DevAPI methods. In other words, they implement exception handling.[6]

---

[6]See https://en.wikipedia.org/wiki/Exception_handling.

Using Python as an example, the Python language implements a try...exception block (sometimes called a *try* or *exception block*). This construct allows code that "raises" an exception in the form of the raise() method to have the exception captured by the calling code (the code with the nearest try block). The syntax is as follows.

```
try:
    # some operation 1
    # some operation 2
    # some operation 3
    # some operation 4
    # some operation 5
except:
    # catch the exception
finally:
    # do this after the success or capture
```

What this allows us to do is "try" an operation (or more) and if they fail by raising an exception, the code will skip any remaining operations in the try segment and skip to the except segment.

Let's look at what happens when you do not use exception handling and the code fails. That is, the X DevAPI throws an exception. Listing 5-17 shows a simple script with errors. Can you spot them? Hint: check the password and what happens when you try to create a table that already exists?

Listing 5-17. Not Handling Errors

```
# Import the MySQL X module
import mysqlx
import getpass
# Get a session with a URI
mysqlx_session = mysqlx.get_session("root:wrongpassworddude!
@localhost:33060")
# Check the connection
if not mysqlx_session.is_open():
    print("Connection failed!")
    exit(1)
# Get the animals schema.
```

```
schema = mysqlx_session.get_schema("animals")
# Try to create the table using a SQL string. It should throw an
# error that it already exists.
res = mysqlx_session.sql("CREATE TABLE animals.pets_sql ("
                          "`id` int auto_increment primary key, "
                          "`name` char(20), "
                          "`age` int, "
                          "`breed` char(20), "
                          "`type` char(12))").execute()
# Close the connection
mysqlx_session.close()
```

If you save this code to a file named listing5-17.py and execute it, you will see the following results (extraneous data removed for brevity).

```
$ python ./listing5-17.py
Traceback (most recent call last):
  File "./listing5-17.py", line 6, in <module>
    mysqlx_session = mysqlx.get_session("root:wrongpassworddude!@
localhost:33060")
...
  File "/Library/Python/2.7/site-packages/mysqlx/protocol.py", line 129, in
read_auth_ok
    raise InterfaceError(msg.msg)
mysqlx.errors.InterfaceError: Invalid user or password
```

Oh, dear, that's terrible! What we've got here is a traceback dump, which is how Python communicates unhandled exceptions. The key message we should heed is the first line that shows us the line of code in the script that started a sequence of method calls that resulted in the exception thrown as shown in the last two lines. Here we see that the get_session() call resulted in a mysqlx.errors.InterfaceError thrown from the X Protocol code in the connector. This demonstrates how badly things can go if you do not use exception handling. But we can make it a lot better.

Let's look at an example with exception handling. Listing 5-18 shows a script with deliberate errors that will cause the X DevAPI to throw exceptions. In this case, it is the CREATE TABLE SQL statement that will fail. More specific, it will fail because the table already exists.

If you run this script and it does not fail, be sure to check that the table already exists. We are using the fact that the table already exists so when the CREATE is executed, we will get an exception. As you will see, the exception is not easily understood either.

Listing 5-18. Handling Errors—Global Exception

```
# Import the MySQL X module
import mysqlx
try:
    # Get a session with a URI
    mysqlx_session = mysqlx.get_session("root:secret@localhost:33060")
    # Check the connection
    if not mysqlx_session.is_open():
        print("Connection failed!")
        exit(1)
    # Get the animals schema.
    schema = mysqlx_session.get_schema("animals")
    # Try to create the table using a SQL string. It should throw an error
    # that it already exists.
    res = mysqlx_session.sql("CREATE TABLE animals.pets_sql ("
                             "`id` int auto_increment primary key, "
                             "`name` char(20), "
                             "`age` int, "
                             "`breed` char(20), "
                             "`type` char(12))").execute()
except Exception as ex:
    print("ERROR: {0}:{1}".format(*ex))
# Close the connection
mysqlx_session.close()
```

When we run this code, we get a much better result. If you save this code to a file named listing5-18.py and execute it, you will see the following results. Note that the output you can expect from this improved version. It is easier to read and more informative.

```
$ python ./listing5-18.py
ERROR: -1: Table 'pets_sql' already exists
```

Although there is no tried and true rule for how much you can place in an exception block, you should keep exception blocks small—say isolated to a single concept or process—to avoid cases where debugging the code makes it difficult to know which of the dozens of method calls triggered the exception. If you use a language like Python that throws a call stack trace, that may not be difficult but if your language doesn't have it or rerunning the code to create one is not possible, keeping the exception blocks small can help you isolate the code where the problem occurred.

Listing 5-19 shows an example that includes try blocks around each X DevAPI statement. It also demonstrates how to capture specific exceptions thrown. That is, the except: syntax allows you to specify a specific exception. In this case, I capture the exception thrown by the X DevAPI.

Listing 5-19. Handling Errors—Local Exceptions

```python
# Import the MySQL X module
import mysqlx
import getpass
# Get a session with a URI
mysqlx_session = None
try:
    mysqlx_session = mysqlx.get_session("root:wrongpassworddude!
@localhost:33060")
except mysqlx.errors.InterfaceError as ex:
    print("ERROR: {0} : {1}".format(*ex))
    passwd = getpass.getpass("Wrong password, try again: ")
finally:
    mysqlx_session = mysqlx.get_session("root:{0}@localhost:33060".
    format(passwd))
# Check the connection
if not mysqlx_session.is_open():
    print("Connection failed!")
    exit(1)
# Demostrate error from get_schema()
schema = mysqlx_session.get_schema("animal")
if (not schema.exists_in_database()):
    print("Schema 'animal' doesn't exist.")
```

```
# Get the animals schema.
schema = mysqlx_session.get_schema("animals")
try:
    # Try to create the table using a SQL string. It should throw an
    # error that it already exists.
    res = mysqlx_session.sql("CREATE TABLE animals.pets_sql ("
                      "`id` int auto_increment primary key, "
                      "`name` char(20), "
                      "`age` int, "
                      "`breed` char(20), "
                      "`type` char(12))").execute()
except mysqlx.errors.OperationalError as ex:
    print("ERROR: {0} : {1}".format(*ex))
# Close the connection
if mysqlx_session:
    mysqlx_session.close()
```

If you save this code to a file named listing5-19.py and execute it, you will see the following results. Be sure to enter the correct password when prompted. This is because there is only one test for a correct password. Your challenge is to determine a way to improve the code by allowing multiple retries. Hint: use a loop.

```
$ python ./listing5-19.py
ERROR: -1 : Invalid user or password
Wrong password, try again:
Schema 'animal' doesn't exist.
ERROR: -1 : Table 'pets_sql' already exists
```

The example also shows an interesting way you can handle exceptions—retrying the statement. Normally, you would place the statement you want to retry in a loop or similar structure with a time or attempt limit. Here I just retry the session method once prompting the user for the password.

> **Tip**   For best results, encapsulate your code using shorter exception blocks so that you can isolate the code that caused the error easily.

Now let's look at the additional features available when using the X DevAPI.

Additional Features

Now that we have seen all the major classes and methods available in the X DevAPI, let us now examine some of the features that are exposed by the X DevAPI; specifically, examples of parameter binding, chaining methods, prepared statements, and asynchronous execution.

> **Note**   This example uses the `world_x` database, which you can download from `https://dev.mysql.com/doc/index-other.html`. Simply download the compressed file, uncompress it, then include it in the MySQL Shell with the `\source` command or use the `mysql` client and the `source` command. For a walk-through of how to install the `world_x` database, see the "Installing the Sample Database" section in Chapter 4.

Parameter Binding

Parameter binding allows us to apply values to expressions at runtime. Parameter binding is typically used for filters and is done prior to executing the operation (hence you will see `.bind().execute()` often). Therefore, the benefits of parameter binding are that it allows you to separate values from your expressions. This is accomplished with the `bind()` method for all classes that support parameter binding.

Parameters can be "bound" using one of two methods: you can use anonymous parameters or you can use named parameters. However, there are restrictions on when you can use each. In particular, anonymous parameters can only be used in SQL strings (expression) whereas named parameters are used in CRUD operations. Let's see an example of each.

Listing 5-20 shows an example of using anonymous parameters. Anonymous parameters are signified by using a question mark. Note how we do this in the SQL statements in the following.

Listing 5-20. Parameter Binding Example (MySQL Shell)

```
$ mysqlsh root@localhost:33060 --sql
Creating a session to 'root@localhost:33060'
Enter password:
Your MySQL connection id is 74 (X protocol)
Server version: 8.0.11 MySQL Community Server (GPL)
No default schema selected; type \use <schema> to set one.
MySQL Shell 8.0.11

Copyright (c) 2016, 2018, Oracle and/or its affiliates. All rights
reserved.

Oracle is a registered trademark of Oracle Corporation and/or its
affiliates. Other names may be trademarks of their respective
owners.

Type '\help' or '\?' for help; '\quit' to exit.

 MySQL  localhost:33060+ ssl  SQL > PREPARE STMT FROM 'SELECT * FROM
world_x.city WHERE name like ? LIMIT ?';
Query OK, 0 rows affected (0.00 sec)
 MySQL  localhost:33060+ ssl  SQL > SET @name_wild = 'Ar%';
Query OK, 0 rows affected (0.00 sec)
 MySQL  localhost:33060+ ssl  SQL > SET @numrows = 1;
Query OK, 0 rows affected (0.00 sec)
 MySQL  localhost:33060+ ssl  SQL > EXECUTE STMT USING @name_wild, @numrows;
+----+--------+-------------+------------+------------------------+
| ID | Name   | CountryCode | District   | Info                   |
+----+--------+-------------+------------+------------------------+
| 18 | Arnhem | NLD         | Gelderland | {"Population": 138020} |
+----+--------+-------------+------------+------------------------+
```

```
1 row in set (0.00 sec)
 MySQL  localhost:33060+ ssl  SQL > \q
Bye!
```

We can take away a couple of things from this example. First, anonymous parameters are only used in SQL statements. Second, anonymous parameters are completed (values provided) in the order they appear in the SQL statement. Third, and finally anonymous parameters can be used with prepared statements.[7]

Listing 5-21 shows several examples of using named parameters. The key point to notice is how the parameter is given a name preceded by a colon. When the bind() method is called, we supply the named parameter (without the colon) and its value.

Listing 5-21. Parameter Binding Example

```
# Import the MySQL X module
import mysqlx
mysqlx_session = mysqlx.get_session("root:secret@localhost:33060")
schema = mysqlx_session.get_schema("world_x")

# Collection.find() function with hardcoded values
myColl = schema.get_collection('countryinfo')
myRes1 = myColl.find("GNP >= 828").execute()
print(myRes1.fetch_one())

# Using the .bind() function to bind parameters
myRes2 = myColl.find('Name = :param1 and GNP = :param2').
bind('param1','Aruba').bind('param2', '828').execute()
print(myRes2.fetch_one())

# Using named parameters
myColl.modify('Name = :param').set('GNP', '829').bind('param', 'Aruba').
execute()

# Binding works for all CRUD statements except add()
myRes3 = myColl.find('Name LIKE :param').bind('param', 'Ar%').execute()
print(myRes3.fetch_one())
```

---

[7]For more information about anonymous parameters, see the SELECT Syntax section in the MySQL online reference manual.

```
# Ok, now put the candle back...
myColl.modify('Name = :param').set('GNP', '828').bind('param', 'Aruba').
execute()

# Close the connection
mysqlx_session.close()
```

Note how we pass multiple parameters to be bound. In this case, we simply call bind() as many times as we have parameters to bind. This is possible due to the method chaining feature as described in the next section. That is, the bind() method returns an instance of itself and thus when we call the next bind() method, it is repeating the call but with a different parameter and its value.

Tip   Named parameters may not start with a number. For example, :1test is not a valid named parameter name.

If you save this code to a file named listing5-21.py and execute it, you will see the following results.

```
$ python ./listing5-21.py
{"GNP": "828", "Name": "Aruba", "government": {"GovernmentForm":
"Nonmetropolitan Territory of The Netherlands", "HeadOfState": "Beatrix"},
"demographics": {"LifeExpectancy": 78.4000015258789, "Population":
103000}, "_id": "ABW", "IndepYear": null, "geography": {"SurfaceArea": 193,
"Region": "Caribbean", "Continent": "North America"}}
{"GNP": "828", "Name": "Aruba", "government": {"GovernmentForm":
"Nonmetropolitan Territory of The Netherlands", "HeadOfState": "Beatrix"},
"demographics": {"LifeExpectancy": 78.4000015258789, "Population":
103000}, "_id": "ABW", "IndepYear": null, "geography": {"SurfaceArea": 193,
"Region": "Caribbean", "Continent": "North America"}}
{"GNP": "829", "Name": "Aruba", "government": {"GovernmentForm":
"Nonmetropolitan Territory of The Netherlands", "HeadOfState": "Beatrix"},
"demographics": {"LifeExpectancy": 78.4000015258789, "Population":
103000}, "_id": "ABW", "IndepYear": null, "geography": {"SurfaceArea": 193,
"Region": "Caribbean", "Continent": "North America"}}
```

Now let's look at method chaining and how it works.

Method Chaining

Method chaining (also known as *named parameter idiom*), is a design constraint in object-oriented programming where each method (that supports chaining) returns an instance of an object. Thus, one can access (call) any method on the returned object simply by adding the call to the end of the first method.

For example, if a class X has a method a() that returns object Y with a method b(), we can chain calls together as follows.

```
x = something.get_x()
res = x.a().b()
```

In this case, the x.a() method executes first, then when it returns with a Y object instance, it calls the b() method on the Y object instance.

Where method chaining shines in the X DevAPI is in the implementation of the relational data methods. In particular, those classes and methods that support the SQL CRUD commands. Listing 5-22 is an example of a complex SELECT operation for a table.

Listing 5-22. Method Chaining

```
# Import the MySQL X module
import mysqlx
mysqlx_session = mysqlx.get_session("root:secret@localhost:33060")
# Get the table
city = mysqlx_session.get_schema("world_x").get_table("city")
# Perform a complex select
res = city.select(['Name', 'District']).where("Name LIKE :param1").order_
by(["District", "Name"]).bind('param1', 'X%').limit(1).execute()
# Show results
print("SQL result ="),
for row in res.fetch_all():
    for i in range(0,len(res.columns)):
        print("{0}".format(row[i])),
print("")
# Close the connection
mysqlx_session.close()
```

If you save this code to a file named listing5-22.py and execute it, you will see the following results.

```
$ python ./listing5-22.py
SQL result = Xuangzhou Anhui
```

Here we see two lines of code and several object instances in use and a host of methods. On the second code line (ignoring comments), we use a mysqlx session object to get a schema object then chain that with a call to the Schema class method get_table(), which returns a table object instance.

On the third code line, we are using the table object instance calling the select() method, which returns a SelectStatement object instance that we chain by calling its where() method, which returns the same SelectStatement object and we call its order_by() method, which returns the same SelectStatement object then we bind the parameter with the bind() method that returns the same SelectStatement object, and finally we call the execute() method, which returns a SqlResult object. Wow!

If you're getting the idea that method chaining hides a lot of the details about objects and avoids repetitious code of storing object instances in variables, you're right! That's exactly what we're doing.

As you can see, method chaining allows us to express concepts in our code much more clearly that the older style of classes with methods do not return object instances (or even older styles that simply return 0 or 1 to indicate success or failure[8]). Mastering the X DevAPI means mastering how you can chain methods together to simplify and make your code easier to read and understand. Cool, eh?

For more information about the concepts of method chaining, see https://en.wikipedia.org/wiki/Method_chaining.

CRUD Prepared Statements

Prepared CRUD statements are cases in which we want to perform a number of operations on an object prior to calling the execute() method. In this way, we "prepare" the object instance (statement) for execution. That is, instead of directly binding and executing CRUD operations by chaining bind() and execute() or simply execute() it,

---

[8]One of the things I disliked about the older code in the server was most methods returned a 0 or 1 passing objects and variables by pointers for returning data. Method chaining is far more elegant and useful for writing applications quickly.

we can manipulate the CRUD operation to store such things as filters and other criteria in a variable for later execution.

The advantage of doing this means we can bind several parameters or sets of variables to the expressions. This gives us better performance because we can "prepare" variables ahead of time and execute them later. This can give us get better performance when executing many similar operations.

You may be thinking that CRUD prepared statements are similar in concept to SQL prepared statements. This is true, but unlike SQL prepared statements, CRUD prepared statements are implemented in class methods and thus can be incorporated in our code with very little effort.

Let's look at an example. Listing 5-23 shows an example of preparing a CRUD statement. In this case, we prepare a find() statement using a parameter and save the result (the FindStatement object) to a variable. When we want to execute this statement, we use the variable to call the bind() method providing a value then the execute() method to execute the FindStatement.

Listing 5-23. CRUD Prepared Statements

```
# Import the MySQL X module
import mysqlx
# Get a session with a URI
mysql_session = mysqlx.get_session("root:secret@localhost:33060")
# Check the connection
if not mysql_session.is_open():
    print("Connection failed!")
    exit(1)
# Create a schema.
schema = mysql_session.get_schema("animals")
# Create a new collection
pets = schema.get_collection("pets_json")
# Prepare a CRUD statement.
find_pet = pets.find("name = :param")
# Now execute the CRUD statement different ways.
mydoc = find_pet.bind('param', 'JonJon').execute()
print(mydoc.fetch_one())
mydoc = find_pet.bind('param', 'Charlie').execute()
```

```
print(mydoc.fetch_one())
mydoc = find_pet.bind('param', 'Spot').execute()
print(mydoc.fetch_one())
# Close the connection
mysql_session.close()
```

Note the three find_pet.bind() method calls. Here we execute the find statement three times; once for each pet's name we want to find. Clearly, this is only a small example but demonstrates the power of using CRUD prepared statements.

If you save this code to a file named listing5-23.py and execute it, you will see the following results.

```
$ python ./listing5-23.py
{"breed": "poodle", "age": 15, "_id": "9801A79DE093B43A11E805FBCB215AFA",
"type": "dog", "name": "JonJon"}
{"breed": "dachshund", "age": "6", "_id":
"9801A79DE093BFD511E805FBCB21CF30", "type": "dog", "name": "Charlie"}
{"breed": "koi", "age": 7, "_id": "9801A79DE0938FBD11E805FBCB21AB35",
"type": "fish", "name": "Spot"}
```

Asynchronous Execution

For those clients that support asynchronous programming such as C/J, C/Node.js, and C/Net, the X DevAPI permits the use of asynchronous mechanisms such as callbacks, async() calls, and so forth. These mechanisms make it possible to allow an operation to run in parallel with other operations. Let's see an example from Java.

Note   Currently, neither the C/Py nor C/C++ permit asynchronous execution but may in the future. Check new releases of these connectors for updates.

```
Table employees = db.getTable("employee");
// execute the query asynchronously, obtain a future
CompletableFuture<RowResult> rowsFuture = employees.select("name", "age").
where("name like :name").orderBy("name").bind("name", "m%").executeAsync();
```

Here we see the executeAsync() method, which is how the Java connector permits the asynchronous execution of the execute() method. That is, the select() runs asynchronously and when it returns (finishes), it triggers the future defined by the CompletableFuture template/class (or generic class in Java[9]).

> **Note**   Depending on which language you are using, the X DevAPI may implement a function such as executeAsync() in addition to or instead of execute(). Check the X DevAPI documentation for your chosen connector for the correct method names and uses.

For more information about asynchronous execution, see the X DevAPI guide for the connector that matches your choice of language.

For More Information

If you would like to know more detailed information about the implementations of the X DevAPI in the database connectors and MySQL Shell, visit the following links for descriptions and lists of all classes, methods, properties, and help functions. The sites are developer focused and may not include detailed explanations or examples.

- MySQL Shell: there are several resources available including the following

  - https://dev.mysql.com/doc/mysql-shell-excerpt/5.7/en/

  - https://dev.mysql.com/doc/mysql-shell-excerpt/8.0/en/

  - https://dev.mysql.com/doc/dev/mysqlsh-api-javascript/8.0/

  - https://dev.mysql.com/doc/dev/mysqlsh-api-python/8.0/

- MySQL Connector/J: http://dev.mysql.com/doc/dev/connector-j/

- MySQL Connector/Node.js: http://dev.mysql.com/doc/dev/connector-nodejs/

---

[9]See https://docs.oracle.com/javase/tutorial/java/generics/types.html

- MySQL Connector/Net: `http://dev.mysql.com/doc/dev/connector-net/`

- MySQL Connector/Python: `http://dev.mysql.com/doc/dev/connector-python`

- MySQL Connector/C++: `https://dev.mysql.com/doc/dev/connector-cpp/`

Note   Some of the documentation for these components may not match the version numbers listed at the beginning of the chapter. It is fine if the documentation is for a newer release and you should install the newest releases. However, at the time of this writing, the MySQL Shell Users Guide was in the process of being updated. Check back regularly to ensure you are using the latest documentation available.

Summary

The X DevAPI is a marvel of sophistication to the point of simplification for NoSQL interface with a MySQL server. The X DevAPI introduces a new, modern and easy-to-learn way to work with your data.

The X DevAPI is the primary mechanism you will use to build document store applications. Although the X DevAPI isn't a standalone library—you must use a client that exposes the X DevAPI through the X Protocol—the X DevAPI is still a major effort to change the way you interact with MySQL. For the first time, we now have both an SQL and a NoSQL interface for MySQL.

In this chapter, we explored the X DevAPI and examined the major classes and methods available for connecting to the MySQL server, creating collections, working with results, and even how to work with relational data. Finally, we also saw a set of quick references tables that you can use as the primary reference for developing document store applications.

In Chapter 6, we have a deep dive into the X Plugin, which will give you a better understanding of what the X Plugin does, how to configure it, and how best to manage it as part of your normal database administration tasks. Following that chapter, we will see the details of the X Protocol and later a working example of a document store application.

CHAPTER 6

X Plugin

The X Dev API is a great new way to interact with MySQL. As we learned, the new NoSQL mechanism is built on the X DevAPI, X Plugin, and the X Protocol. You may have the impression these technologies are just there and once enabled nothing more is needed. That is largely true, but as with all good features, there is more to the story than simply enabling the feature.

In this chapter, we take a closer look at the X Plugin. As you will see, there is more to it than simply turning it on. The fact that it just works with the defaults means it is very stable and is applicable in most cases. However, you can configure it in several ways including a very interesting option for securing connections. However, there is more about this and even how to monitor the X Plugin in following sections.

Note   I use the term, *plugin* in this chapter to refer to plugins in general and *X Plugin* to refer to specific features of the X Plugin.

Overview

Recall from Chapter 2 that the X Plugin is a separately compiled component of MySQL that can be loaded and unloaded at runtime. Oracle named the X Plugin mysqlx and it is listed with that name in the server. Once loaded (installed), the plugin will start automatically each time the server is restarted. Also, recall that the plugin feature in MySQL is the primary mechanism Oracle uses to extend the functionality of the server without having to rebuild the code from scratch. Although plugin technology has been in MySQL for some time and initially used for storage engines, it has become the default mechanism Oracle uses for expanding and adding new features to the server.

© Charles Bell 2018
C. Bell, *Introducing the MySQL 8 Document Store*, https://doi.org/10.1007/978-1-4842-2725-1_6

In that respect, the X Plugin is an excellent example of the power that a plugin can bring to the server. For example, by default, the server communicated with clients using a fixed protocol commonly referred to as *the MySQL client/server protocol* or simply, *the MySQL protocol* or *the old protocol*. This protocol was built into the server and except for some minor changes through the lifetime of MySQL; it hasn't changed much since the MySQL 4.X code base. Until the X Plugin came about, this was the only way clients could communicate with the server.[1] Now, once you load the X Plugin, it enables a new communication protocol for the client and server using the X Protocol.

HOW DO MYSQL PLUGINS WORK?

In the most general sense, when a plugin is installed or started on startup, the server and plugin communicate using a special plugin API that allows the plugin to register itself as part of the server. For instance, the plugin provides callback methods for processing status variables as well as methods for enabling its functionality. This negotiation process is how a plugin can extend the functionality of the server without having to force the server to restart and does not require a recompile of the server.

That said, it is important to note that plugins are compiled against the common server libraries and as such must match the server for specific versions as well as platform (e.g., you cannot use a plugin compiled for Linux on Windows). Detection of compatibility is provided using a special versioning mechanism that is checked during startup of the plugin. Most plugins are published clearly listing the versions of the server supported. When you decide to use a new plugin, be sure to check that it is compatible with your server version. For more information about plugins, see the section "The MySQL Plugin API" in the online MySQL reference manual.

Features

Once again, the X Plugins primary purpose is to support the X Protocol for communication with the server to enable the X DevAPI (NoSQL) interface. Although that is its primary focus, there are some interesting features that you can use to help make the experience better. These including configuring the plugin to use different secure socket layer (SSL) settings than the server and changing the behavior of the

---

[1]It should be noted that MySQL Replication uses extensions built into the original protocol.

plugin using system variables. We will see how to change the SSL settings and how to change the default port in the following sections. We will see more about the other system variables in a later section.

Note   Although the documentation and other text show variables for the X Plugin with initial capital letters, the variables are shown in the SQL results with lowercase names. For example, you may see a prefix of Mysqlx_, but the output from the server with display as mysqlx_. Fortunately, most SQL commands on most platforms will accept either version.

Secure Socket Layer (SSL) Connections

If you use SSL connections on your MySQL servers and want to use secure connections for the X Plugin (and your NoSQL applications), you can setup the X Plugin to use different values for the SSL options than the server. This means you can setup the X Plugin to use one SSL certificate and the server to use another. This can be very helpful in making your NoSQL applications secure without sharing the SSL data among client/ server and X Protocols.

You can place the system variables and their values in the my.cnf file or pass the system variables on the server startup command (command-line). When used in this manner, system variables are often referred to as startup options. Listing the system variables and their current values can be accomplished using the following command. Note that I used the MySQL Shell to get the information using batch mode.

```
$ mysqlsh -uroot -hlocalhost --sql -e "SHOW VARIABLES LIKE 'mysqlx_ssl%'"
Enter password:
+--------------------+-------+
| Variable_name      | Value |
+--------------------+-------+
| mysqlx_ssl_ca      |       |
| mysqlx_ssl_capath  |       |
| mysqlx_ssl_cert    |       |
| mysqlx_ssl_cipher  |       |
| mysqlx_ssl_crl     |       |
| mysqlx_ssl_crlpath |       |
| mysqlx_ssl_key     |       |
+--------------------+-------+
```

You can set these variables in your configuration file (my.cnf) by placing them in the section for the server named [msyqld] but you should omit the dashes. The following shows an excerpt demonstrating how to use a different SSL configuration for the server and X Plugin.

```
[mysqld]
...
ssl-ca=/my_ssl/certs/ca_server.pem
ssl-cert=/my_ssl/certs/server-cert.pem
ssl-key=/my_ssl/certs/server-key.pem
...
mysqlx-ssl-ca=/my_ssl/certs/ca_xplugin.pem
mysqlx-ssl-cert=/my_ssl/certs/xplugin-cert.pem
mysqlx-ssl-key=/my_ssl/certs/xplugin-key.pem
...
```

Note that I have included both sets of SSL options only the X Plugin options are named with the mysqlx_ prefix.

> **Note**   In general, most system variables have corresponding startup options and are used in the configuration file with the same name only the underscores are changed to dashes. For example, the startup option for the mysqlx_ssl_ca system variable is --mysqlx-ssl-ca. However, the --mysqlx_ssl_ca version also works for those who forget.

To change the values temporarily or as part of a shell or batch file, you can specify the system variables as options on the command line as shown in the following. Note that we used the same values as shown previously.

```
$ mysqld  ... --mysqlx-ssl-ca=/my_ssl/certs/ca_xplugin.pem
--mysqlx-ssl-cert=/my_ssl/certs/xplugin-cert.pem \
                --mysqlx-ssl-key=/my_ssl/certs/xplugin-key.pem
```

Although you can use the options on the command line like this, it is not the best method. This is because unless you record the new command line somewhere or use it in a shell or batch command (and even then), it is very easy to forget what value you used or even which system variables were used. Thus, for the best method, always place custom system variable changes in your MySQL configuration file.

Changing the Default Port

Recall the X Plugin uses a different port than the server. The default port is 33060. If you want to change the default port, you can do so using the mysqlx_port system variable. As with the SSL options, you can place this in the my.cnf file or pass it as a startup option on the server startup command (command-line). You can also check the default port with the following command. The valid range of values is 1-65535. For example, you can setup the X Plugin to use port 3307.

```
$ mysqlsh -uroot -hlocalhost --sql -e "SHOW VARIABLES LIKE 'mysqlx_port'"
Enter password:
+---------------+-------+
| Variable_name | Value |
+---------------+-------+
| mysqlx_port   | 3307  |
+---------------+-------+
```

Because the `mysqlx_port` system variable is only read at startup (for obvious reasons), changing the value requires a restart to use a different port.

As with the SSL options, you can set the port on the command line as shown in the following. In this case, we start the server on port 3307 and the X Plugin listens on port 3308.

```
$ mysqld  --port=3307 --datadir... --socket=...mysql.sock
--mysqlx-port=3308 --mysqlx-socket=...mysqlx.sock
```

Once again, this is not the recommended method because command-line options tend to be forgotten if not placed in a shell or batch file.

Going Deeper—Journey into the Source Code

If you want to see how the X Plugin works by examining the source code, you can do so by downloading the source code from `http://dev.mysql.com/downloads/mysql/`. To download the MySQL 8 source code, select Source Code from the platform dropdown box and download the file that matches your platform. If you do not see one that matches your platform, and you just want to explore the source code, choose the generic Linux option. Figure 6-1 shows an excerpt from the website highlighting the tab and drop down box.

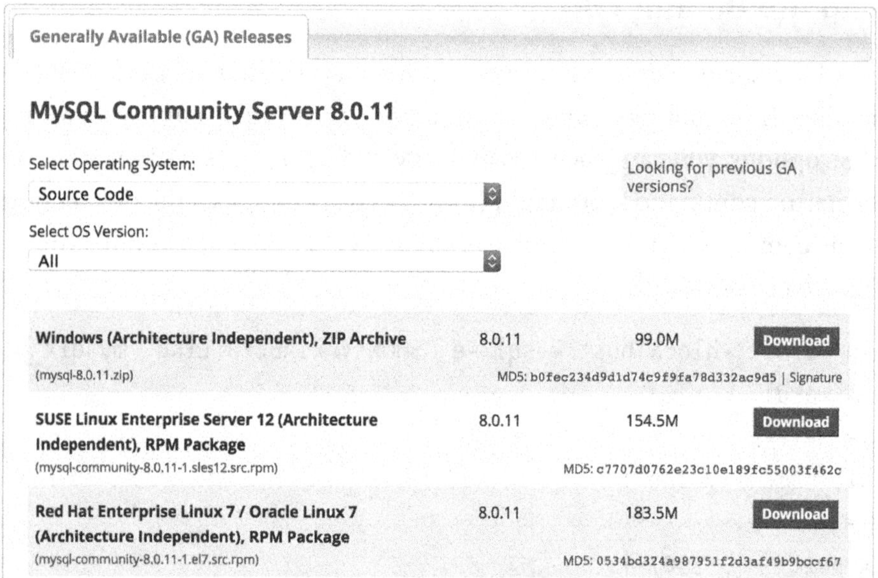

Figure 6-1. *Downloading the MySQL 8 source code*

Once downloaded, you can find the X Plugin source code in the rapid/plugin/x folder. You can browse the source code and see how it works and even how it negotiates with the server on startup. For example, to see the system variables, open the xpl_plugin.cc file in the rapid/plugin/x/src folder and scroll down to about line number 240 or so. You will find a structure like the example in Listing 6-1 that lists the variables supported by the plugin.

Listing 6-1. System Variable Definition (X Plugin)

```
...
static struct st_mysql_sys_var* xpl_plugin_system_variables[]= {
  MYSQL_SYSVAR(port),
  MYSQL_SYSVAR(max_connections),
  MYSQL_SYSVAR(min_worker_threads),
  MYSQL_SYSVAR(idle_worker_thread_timeout),
  MYSQL_SYSVAR(max_allowed_packet),
  MYSQL_SYSVAR(connect_timeout),
  MYSQL_SYSVAR(ssl_key),
  MYSQL_SYSVAR(ssl_ca),
  MYSQL_SYSVAR(ssl_capath),
  MYSQL_SYSVAR(ssl_cert),
  MYSQL_SYSVAR(ssl_cipher),
  MYSQL_SYSVAR(ssl_crl),
  MYSQL_SYSVAR(ssl_crlpath),
  MYSQL_SYSVAR(socket),
  MYSQL_SYSVAR(bind_address),
  MYSQL_SYSVAR(port_open_timeout),
  MYSQL_SYSVAR(wait_timeout),
  MYSQL_SYSVAR(interactive_timeout),
  MYSQL_SYSVAR(read_timeout),
  MYSQL_SYSVAR(write_timeout),
  NULL
};
...
```

Note that there is a macro definition, MYSQL_SYSVAR, that is used to define the system variables. There is also system variables listed by their names. Once the plugin is started, you can see system variables using the command in Listing 6-2. Note that the variables are named with the prefix mysqlx_ and all 14 are present (the host system was running macOS—your results may vary).

Listing 6-2. Listing the System Variables for the X Plugin

```
MySQL  localhost:33060+ ssl  SQL > SHOW VARIABLES LIKE 'mysqlx_%';
+------------------------------------+------------------+
| Variable_name                      | Value            |
+------------------------------------+------------------+
| mysqlx_bind_address                | *                |
| mysqlx_connect_timeout             | 30               |
| mysqlx_idle_worker_thread_timeout  | 60               |
| mysqlx_max_allowed_packet          | 1048576          |
| mysqlx_max_connections             | 100              |
| mysqlx_min_worker_threads          | 2                |
| mysqlx_port                        | 33060            |
| mysqlx_port_open_timeout           | 0                |
| mysqlx_socket                      | /tmp/mysqlx.sock |
| mysqlx_ssl_ca                      |                  |
| mysqlx_ssl_capath                  |                  |
| mysqlx_ssl_cert                    |                  |
| mysqlx_ssl_cipher                  |                  |
| mysqlx_ssl_crl                     |                  |
| mysqlx_ssl_crlpath                 |                  |
| mysqlx_ssl_key                     |                  |
+------------------------------------+------------------+
16 rows in set (0.00 sec)
```

We discover more about the system variables in the next section. If you're adventurous, keep reading the code in that file for more clues about status variables. Hint: look at the file named xpl_global_status_variables.h.

Options and Variables

As we saw in the previous section, the X Plugin has several system variables that can be set at startup either in the configuration file or on the server command line. The configuration items that can be controlled include such items as the default port, configure parameters for connections, and establish timeout limits. You also can see several status variables that the X Plugin reports concerning performance, statistics, and more. These status variables can be used to monitor the X Plugin to help you tune its options to match your environment. I explore the commonly used startup options, system variables, and status variables in the following sections.

Note   I use the term *variable* to apply to qualities and features that are common to startup options, system variables, and status variables.

Variables can have two scope levels: global that apply to all connections and session that apply only to the current connection (session), that is, the connection you are currently using. There is no provision to capture data from other sessions that you are not currently using.

Variables also can support dynamic values that can be set at runtime and values that can only be set at startup. Although you can view the values of any variable regardless of scope, you can only set values at runtime for dynamic variables. You must take care when setting global variables so that you do not adversely affect other connections.

How to View Values of Variables

There are several ways to see the values of variables. We saw in the last section that you can use the SQL commands `SHOW VARIABLES` to see system variables and `SHOW STATUS` command to see the values of status variables. Remember, startup options are associated with a system variable so using the `SHOW VARIABLES` command is all you need to see those.

You can also see the values of system variables by using a special form of the `SELECT` command using a special notation or shortcut in the form of @@GLOBAL for the value at the global scope and @@SESSION for the value at the session scope. Although there are currently no session level system variables for the X Plugin, the following shows the global system variable `mysqlx_connect_timeout`.

```
MySQL  localhost:33060+ ssl  SQL > SELECT @@GLOBAL.mysqlx_connect_timeout;
+----------------------------------+
| @@GLOBAL.mysqlx_connect_timeout |
+----------------------------------+
|                               30 |
+----------------------------------+
1 row in set (0.00 sec)
```

You also can see the values of variables using the PERFORMANCE_SCHEMA tables (views). In this case, you can see the status variables either by session or global scope. Or you can write a SQL query to combine the data with scope and shown in Listing 6-3 (your results may vary). I formatted the following SQL statement to make it easier to read.

```
SELECT *, 'SESSION' as SCOPE FROM PERFORMANCE_SCHEMA.session_status
WHERE variable_name LIKE 'mysqlx_%'
UNION SELECT *, 'GLOBAL' as SCOPE FROM PERFORMANCE_SCHEMA.global_status
WHERE variable_name LIKE 'mysqlx_%'
```

Listing 6-3. X Plugin Status Variables with Scope

```
MySQL  localhost:33060+ ssl  SQL > SELECT *, 'SESSION' as SCOPE FROM
PERFORMANCE_SCHEMA.session_status WHERE variable_name LIKE 'mysqlx_%' UNION
SELECT *, 'GLOBAL' as SCOPE FROM PERFORMANCE_SCHEMA.global_status WHERE
variable_name LIKE 'mysqlx_%' \G
*************************** 1. row ***************************
 VARIABLE_NAME: Mysqlx_address
VARIABLE_VALUE: ::
         SCOPE: SESSION
*************************** 2. row ***************************
 VARIABLE_NAME: Mysqlx_bytes_received
VARIABLE_VALUE: 1002
         SCOPE: SESSION
*************************** 3. row ***************************
 VARIABLE_NAME: Mysqlx_bytes_sent
VARIABLE_VALUE: 8851
         SCOPE: SESSION
```

```
************************* 4. row *************************
 VARIABLE_NAME: Mysqlx_connection_accept_errors
VARIABLE_VALUE: 0
         SCOPE: SESSION
************************* 5. row *************************
 VARIABLE_NAME: Mysqlx_connection_errors
VARIABLE_VALUE: 0
         SCOPE: SESSION
...
************************* 119. row *************************
 VARIABLE_NAME: Mysqlx_worker_threads
VARIABLE_VALUE: 2
         SCOPE: GLOBAL
************************* 120. row *************************
 VARIABLE_NAME: Mysqlx_worker_threads_active
VARIABLE_VALUE: 1
         SCOPE: GLOBAL
120 rows in set (0.00 sec)
```

Note that we see the same variables and their scope.

Note   A complete description and tutorial of using the Performance Schema
is beyond the scope of this book. For more information about the performance
schema, see the section "MySQL Performance Schema" in the online MySQL
reference manual.

You may have noticed in previous examples that I used the SHOW SQL command
to see the values of variables. There are two SHOW commands: one for system variables
(SHOW VARIABLES) and another for status variables (SHOW STATUS). You can use the LIKE
clause to find all the X Plugin variables. The LIKE clause allows you to specify part of a
name and use wildcards. For example, you can find all the system and status variables
for the X Plugin using the following two commands.

```
SHOW VARIABLES LIKE 'mysqlx_%';
SHOW STATUS LIKE 'mysqlx_%';
```

Note that I use the LIKE clause using mysqlx_%. This will show all the variables that start with mysqlx_. Because all X Plugin variables have this prefix, we see all the variables for the X Plugin.

Tip   The LIKE clause can be very handy in another way. You can use it to search for a variable that you may have forgotten its name simply by using a keyword. For example, if you wanted to see all the variables that have dir in the name, use LIKE '%dir%'.

By now you may be thinking that we're using a lot of SQL commands. You may be wondering if there is a way to see the values of variables using the NoSQL interface. As of this writing, there are no objects in the X DevAPI or part of the MySQL Shell that you can use to get information about variables and their values.[2] This is the reason I mentioned earlier in the book that the SQL interface is still needed for some routine maintenance tasks. Checking and setting variables is one of the maintenance and configuration tasks that require the use of SQL commands.

WHAT ABOUT INFORMATION_SCHEMA?

If you are familiar with the special INFORMATION_SCHEMA database, you may be wondering what happened to using the session_* and global_* tables (views) for showing values of variables. Starting with server version 5.7.6, these tables (views) were deprecated. This is because they were replaced with tables (views) in PERFORMANCE_SCHEMA. For more information about the changes and migrating to PERFORMANCE_SCHEMA, see the section "Migrating to Performance Schema System and Status Variable Tables" in the online MySQL reference manual.

How to Set Values of Variables

We have already discovered we can set system variables in the configuration file and we can use startup options to set the system variables. These methods are used for variables that can only be set at startup. However, for those variables that can be set dynamically,

---

[2]If we had such objects, it would make interacting with the server a lot easier.

you can change their values for session or global scope using the SET command and the @@SESSION and @@GLOBAL notation shown previously. However, because there are no session variables currently, we can only set the values for global variables as shown in Listing 6-4.

Listing 6-4. Setting Global System Variables

```
$ mysqlsh -uroot -hlocalhost --sql --json=pretty -e "SELECT @@GLOBAL.
mysqlx_connect_timeout"
{
    "password": "Enter password: "
}

{
    "executionTime": "0.00 sec",
    "warningCount": 0,
    "warnings": [],
    "rows": [
        {
            "@@GLOBAL.mysqlx_connect_timeout": 30
        }
    ],
    "hasData": true,
    "affectedRowCount": 0,
    "autoIncrementValue": 0
}
$ mysqlsh -uroot -hlocalhost --sql --json=pretty -e "SET
@@GLOBAL.mysqlx_connect_timeout = 90"
{
    "password": "Enter password: "
}

{
    "executionTime": "0.00 sec",
    "warningCount": 0,
    "warnings": [],
    "rows": [],
```

```
        "hasData": false,
        "affectedRowCount": 0,
        "autoIncrementValue": 0
}
$ mysqlsh -uroot -hlocalhost --sql --json=pretty -e "SELECT
@@GLOBAL.mysqlx_connect_timeout"
{
        "password": "Enter password: "
}

{
        "executionTime": "0.00 sec",
        "warningCount": 0,
        "warnings": [],
        "rows": [
            {
                    "@@GLOBAL.mysqlx_connect_timeout": 90
            }
        ],
        "hasData": true,
        "affectedRowCount": 0,
        "autoIncrementValue": 0
}
```

Should session dynamic system variables be introduced, you can set their values with the SET @@SESSION.<variable_name> command.

Tip   System variables that can be changed at runtime are known as dynamic variables. This only applies to those system variables that can be changed while the X Plugin is running.

Now that we know more about variables and how to see and set values, let's look at the specific variables for the X Plugin. Let's begin with those system variables that you can place in the configuration file.

System Variables and Startup Options

Recall that most system variables have a corresponding option that you can use to configure the system at startup. That is, we call system variables that can be set in this manner startup options. Other system variables can be changed at runtime and are often referred to as dynamic system variables. However, there are some variables that can only be used in the configuration file or the command line. As you can surmise, some variables can be used as startup options. Table 6-1 lists those system variables that can be used as startup options (as well as those are also system variables) for the X Plugin. I also include which variables can be set dynamically and a short description of each.

Table 6-1. *System Variables and Startup Options (X Plugin)*

Name	Default	SysVar	Dynamic	Description
mysqlx_bind_address	*	Yes	No	The network address that X Plugin uses for connections.
mysqlx_connect_ timeout	30	Yes	Yes	Number of seconds to wait for the first packet to be received from newly connected clients
mysqlx_idle_worker_ thread_timeout	60	No	No	Time in seconds after which an idle worker thread is terminated
mysqlx_max_allowed_ packet	1048576	No	Yes	The Maximum size of a network packet that X Plugin can process.
mysqlx_max_ connections	100	Yes	Yes	The Maximum number of concurrent client connections the X Plugin can accept.
mysqlx_min_worker_ threads	2	No	Yes	The minimum number of worker threads the X Plugin uses for handling client requests.
mysqlx_port	33060	Yes	No	Specifies the port where the X Plugin listens for connections

(*continued*)

Table 6-1. (*continued*)

Name	Default	SysVar	Dynamic	Description
mysqlx_port_open_timeout	0	Yes	No	The amount of time in seconds that X Plugin waits for a TCP/IP port to become free.
mysqlx_socket	Platform dependent	Yes	No	The socket where X Plugin listens for connections.
mysqlx_ssl_ca		Yes	No	The path to a file with a list of trusted SSL CAs.
mysqlx_ssl_capath		Yes	No	The path to a directory that contains trusted SSL CA certificates in PEM format.
mysqlx_ssl_cert		Yes	No	The name of the SSL certificate file to use for establishing a secure connection.
mysqlx_ssl_cipher		No	No	The list of permissible ciphers to use for SSL encryption.
mysqlx_ssl_crl		Yes	No	The path to a file containing certificate revocation lists in PEM format.
mysqlx_ssl_crl_path		Yes	No	The path to a directory that contains files containing certificate revocation lists in PEM format.
mysqlx_ssl_key		Yes	No	The name of the SSL key file to use for establishing a secure connection.

As you can see, there are a number things we can set for the X Plugin including setting up the SSL connection, tuning the X Plugin with maximum connections limit, minimum of worker threads, and even setting the size of the data packet (how much data can be sent over the network in a single packet). Of course, we also can change the port that the X Plugin uses.

Status Variables

Recall system variables are those variables that only report statistics and other data from the plugin. Status variables cannot be set at runtime. However, most are reset whenever the server restarts. That is, counters are reset at reboot.

There are quite a few status variables for the X Plugin that report on several areas in the X Plugin. Rather than look at the status variables individually (there are over 120 if you count session and global scope), we look at the groups or areas that the status variables report on. We will see more about specific status variables in the next section where we see how to monitor the X Plugin.

The following lists a few of the more common status variables and a brief description of why you may want to examine the values. The notation, `mysqlx_*` indicates the status variables for the area contain several variables. For example, `mysqlx_bytes_*` includes `mysqlx_bytes_sent` and `mysqlx_bytes_received`.

- `mysqlx_connections_*`: the number of connections accepted, rejected, and closed.

- `mysqlx_sessions_*`: statistics about sessions such as accepted, closed, killed, and rejected.

- `mysqlx_stmt_*`: statistics for execution, drop, list, and create for collections.

There are a few other discrete status variables that you may want to examine including errors on startup (`mysqlx_init_error`) and the number of rows sent to clients (`mysqlx_rows_sent`). For a complete list of the available status variables for the X Plugin, see the section "Status Variables for X Plugin" in the online MySQL reference manual.

Now let's briefly look at some ways you can monitor the X Plugin and why you would want to do so.

Monitoring the X Plugin

If you want to keep an eye on the X Plugin either to ensure all is working correctly, diagnose problems, verify configuration, or tune performance, you can monitor the X Plugin using the system variables for the X Plugin. This requires reading the values at a specific time or when an event has occurred. Recall that some status variables have both a session and global scope. Thus, you may want to use the @@ notation discussed previously to query the session or global scope values.

You can see the values of status variables in several ways including using the SHOW STATUS command as well as reading the tables (views) from the PERFORMANCE_SCHEMA database. Listing 6-5 shows the tables (views) that can be used to read the values of status variables.

Listing 6-5. Performance Schema Views for Status Variables

```
$ mysqlsh -uroot -hlocalhost --sql -e "SHOW TABLES FROM PERFORMANCE_SCHEMA
LIKE '%status%'"
Enter password:
+-------------------------------------------+
| Tables_in_performance_schema (%status%)   |
+-------------------------------------------+
| global_status                             |
| replication_applier_status                |
| replication_applier_status_by_coordinator |
| replication_applier_status_by_worker      |
| replication_connection_status             |
| session_status                            |
| status_by_account                         |
| status_by_host                            |
| status_by_thread                          |
| status_by_user                            |
+-------------------------------------------+
```

Note that there are a few tables (views) for status variables including those for replication and by scope. Just remember to use the LIKE clause when querying for status variables for the X Plugin. However, as I mentioned previously, a complete tutorial of using the performance schema is beyond the scope of this book. Fortunately, the SHOW STATUS and SELECT with @@ notation SQL commands work well enough for most uses.[3]

---

[3]Some may say the SQL commands are easier to use.

Although there are a lot of status variables for the X Plugin, the status variables can be organized in several areas. The following list summarizes the categories I have defined.

- *Communication*: Information about messages and data sent and received.

- *Connections*: Information about connections including accepted, rejected, and deleted.

- *CRUD operations*: Statistics on created, read, updated, and deleted operations.

- *Errors and warnings*: Information about errors or warnings at startup or sent to the client.

- *Sessions*: Information about sessions including accepted, rejected, and deleted.

- *SSL*: Information about secure connections.

- *Statements*: Statistics about execution, creation, and more for the document store.

- *Worker threads*: Information about the worker threads in the X Plugin.

The following sections describe the eight areas in more detail including suggestions for tasks that you may want to perform using the variables. Each section also includes a complete list of the associated status variables, their scope and a brief description. You can use the sections as a guide when exploring the X Plugin during your diagnostic procedures or simply for curiosity.

Communication

The communication category includes status variables that report information that is transmitted to or received from the clients. You can observe the amount of traffic over the network for both a session or globally, see the number of rows sent to the client both session and globally, and check the expectation blocks for the X Protocol.

Expectation blocks are a mechanism the X Protocol uses to manage situations when there are messages in the pipeline that may have failed. That is, other, dependent tasks that are executed prior to the end of block. Expectation blocks are a way to ensure safe, reliable failure of the entire block (think transaction). There are several facets to expectation blocks and it is unlikely that you will be required to monitor them. If you'd like to know more about expectation blocks, see `https://dev.mysql.com/doc/internals/en/x-protocol-expect-expectations.html`.

Table 6-2 lists all the status variables for the communication category.

Table 6-2. *Communication Status Variables (X Plugin)*

Variables	Scope	Description
mysqlx_bytes_received	Both	The number of bytes received through the network.
mysqlx_bytes_sent	Both	The number of bytes sent through the network.
mysqlx_expect_close	Both	The number of expectation blocks closed.
mysqlx_expect_open	Both	The number of expectation blocks opened.
mysqlx_rows_sent	Both	The number of rows sent back to clients.

The types of tasks where you may want to use these status variables include observing how much data is sent and received and how many rows are sent to the client (in a result set). You also can see the expectation blocks data, but that may be a more advanced than what most will need when monitoring the X Plugin.

Connections

The connections category includes status variables for checking the state of connections. There are connection errors variables that you can use to see how many connections have had errors. These variables have both session and global scope, which makes them interesting for diagnosing individual connection issues. You also can see statistics for the number of connections that have been accepted (open), closed, and rejected (due to login failures, insufficient privileges, wrong password, etc.). These status variables only have global scope so they only show aggregates from all connections. Table 6-3 lists all the status variables for the connection category.

Table 6-3. *Connection Status Variables (X Plugin)*

Variables	Scope	Description
mysqlx_connection_accept_errors	Both	The number of connections that have caused accept errors.
mysqlx_connection_errors	Both	The number of connections that have caused errors.
mysqlx_connections_accepted	Global	The number of connections that have been accepted.
mysqlx_connections_closed	Global	The number of connections that have been closed.
mysqlx_connections_rejected	Global	The number of connections that have been rejected.

The types of tasks where you may want to use these status variables include monitoring the connection errors status variables for cases when there are a lot of failures (errors). This could be as simple as an application that is using the wrong credentials or could be as nefarious as attempts to discover a login account and password.

You also can use the accepted, closed, and rejected system variables to keep an eye on the number of connections that are used. That is, if your application is used by less than 10 users, you would expect to see rather low values for these status variables. High numbers could indicate applications that connect and disconnect too often (not always a bad thing) or cases where you have more instances of the application(s) than you thought.

CRUD Operations

The CRUD operations category provides statistics for the create, read (find), update, and delete operations on the document store. Note that these are counters used for the X DevAPI and not specifically for the SQL statement execution. You can see values for each of the CRUD operations at either session or global scope. Table 6-4 lists all the status variables for the CRUD operations category.

Table 6-4. *CRUD Status Variables (X Plugin)*

Variables	Scope	Description
mysqlx_crud_create_view	Both	The number of create view requests received.
mysqlx_crud_delete	Both	The number of delete requests received.
mysqlx_crud_drop_view	Both	The number of drop view requests received.
mysqlx_crud_find	Both	The number of find requests received.
mysqlx_crud_insert	Both	The number of insert requests received.
mysqlx_crud_modify_view	Both	The number of modify view requests received.
mysqlx_crud_update	Both	The number of update requests received.

The types of tasks where you may want to use these status variables include monitoring a document store application for activity such as how many requests for deletes are issued, number of new data items added (inserted), and so on. Because the status variables have both a session and global scope, you can see the activity for a specific session and compare that to the values for the global scope (overall statistics).

Errors and Warnings

The errors and warning category provides a means to see the number of errors that have occurred at startup and notices or errors sent to the client. All the status variables in this category have both session and global scope and thus can be used to check statistics for an individual connection (session) or aggregate values from all sessions.

Notices are a way for the X Protocol to send additional information to the client at either session or global scope. When sent at the sessions level (referred to as local in the internal manual), these can include a list of committed transaction identifiers, transaction state changes, SQL warnings, and changes to variables. When sent at the global level, these can include server shutdown, disconnections in group replication, table drops, and so forth. Keep in mind that status variables are only counters so although you cannot see the messages (notices) themselves, you can see how many have been sent and whether they are informational (warning) or a response to an error or another serious event. For more information about notices in the X Protocol, see http://dev.mysql.com/doc/internals/en/x-protocol-notices-notices.html.

Table 6-5 lists all the status variables for the errors and warnings category.

Table 6-5. *Errors and Warnings Status Variables (X Plugin)*

Variables	Scope	Description
mysqlx_errors_sent	Both	The number of errors sent to clients.
mysqlx_init_error	Both	The number of errors during initialization.
mysqlx_notice_other_sent	Both	The number of other types of notices sent back to clients.
mysqlx_notice_warning_sent	Both	The number of warning notices sent back to clients.

The types of tasks where you may want to use these status variables include checking for excessive errors for a session, which may indicate something is wrong with the application (or users' use thereof). The notices status variables may be helpful to gather data for diagnosing errors and warnings sent to the clients. That is, it may indicate there is additional data that you may want to look for in the logs. For example, a high count for these variables at the session level could indicate the application is attempting to do something it should not do or is performing the operations too often.

However, the most important status variable in this category to watch when starting out with the X Plugin or when changing its configuration is the mysqlx_init_error status variable. Check this variable to ensure there are no errors at startup (initialization) and if there are issues, track them down to make sure you have everything configured correctly. Although sometimes an error might be okay, in general you should not see any errors registered for initialization.

Sessions

The session category provides a way to track how many sessions have been created (accepted), closed, resulted in being closed due to an error, were killed unceremoniously, or rejected due to login or other errors when establishing the session. All the available status variables have only global scope. Table 6-6 lists all the status variables for the session category.

Table 6-6. *Session Status Variables (X Plugin)*

Variables	Scope	Description
mysqlx_sessions	Global	The number of sessions that have been opened.
mysqlx_sessions_accepted	Global	The number of session attempts that have been accepted.
mysqlx_sessions_closed	Global	The number of sessions that have been closed.
mysqlx_sessions_fatal_ error	Global	The number of sessions that have closed with a fatal error.
mysqlx_sessions_killed	Global	The number of sessions that have been killed.
mysqlx_sessions_ rejected	Global	The number of session attempts that have been rejected.

The types of tasks where you may want to use these status variables include checking to see how many sessions failed (msyqlx_sessions_fatal_error), were killed by someone like an admin (mysqlx_sessions_killed), and how many were opened or closed successfully. As with connection attempts, you could use the status variables in this category to monitor how often and how many sessions are being created and used. Too many may indicate more sessions than you originally planned, widespread use has increased, and so forth. Check these status variables whenever you have or think there may be issues with creating sessions or when sessions begin to fail frequently.

SSL

The SSL category is one of the largest categories and includes a host of status variables for monitoring secure connections. This is very important due to the continued vigilance information technology specialists must maintain to protect systems and data from unintended use, misuse, or exploitation. If you decide to use SSL connections, you will want to check these status variables to ensure your SSL connection settings are working properly. You can check the certificate status for validity, see a list of ciphers, the version of SSL employed, and more. Table 6-7 lists all the status variables for the SSL category.

Table 6-7. *SSL Status Variables (X Plugin)*

Variables	Scope	Description
mysqlx_ssl_accepts	Global	The number of accepted SSL connections
mysqlx_ssl_active	Both	If SSL is active
mysqlx_ssl_cipher	Both	The current SSL cipher (empty for non-SSL connections)
mysqlx_ssl_cipher_list	Both	A list of possible SSL ciphers (empty for non-SSL connections)
mysqlx_ssl_ctx_verify_depth	Both	The certificate verification depth limit currently set in ctx
mysqlx_ssl_ctx_verify_mode	Both	The certificate verification mode currently set in ctx
mysqlx_ssl_finished_accepts	Global	The number of successful SSL connections to the server
mysqlx_ssl_server_not_after	Global	The last date for which the SSL certificate is valid
mysqlx_ssl_server_not_before	Global	The first date for which the SSL certificate is valid
mysqlx_ssl_verify_depth	Global	The certificate verification depth for SSL connection
mysqlx_ssl_verify_mode	Global	The certificate verification mode for SSL connection
mysqlx_ssl_version	Both	The name of the protocol used for the connection ssl

The types of tasks where you may want to use these status variables include checking to ensure SSL is turned on for a session or for all sessions (mysqlx_ssl_active), viewing the number of SSL connections accepted (mysqlx_ssl_finished_accepts), and the dates for valid SSL certificates. This last operation can save you from a host of rabbit hole diagnosis[4] chasing down strange error messages.

Note that some of the variables have both a session and global scope so you can use these to help diagnose SSL connection issues at the session level. For example, if a client cannot connect properly to the X Plugin with SSL, takes a long time to connect, or there are errors during the connection.

For more information about these status variables, you can see the section "Using Secure Connections" in the online MySQL reference manual. Because most of these status variables are the same as those used by the server, the same techniques and descriptions apply.

---

[4] I call this rabbit hole diagnosis because it is often frustrating and seldom results in a correct diagnosis. SSL certificate expiration is one such cause.

Statements

The statements category is a very interesting category and can be quite handy in diagnosing or observing operations related to the X DevAPI. In particular, there are status variables that count the number of collection creates and drops, collection indexing, number of execution events, listing clients, and more.

Recall that a statement in the X DevAPI parlance is an action that exercises one or more of the CRUD operations. Even though CRUD operations are the major focus for this category of status variables, we also use that term for SQL commands there are status variables for SQL statements. The available status variables have both a session and global scope so they can be used for monitoring activities for a session or for aggregate details. Table 6-8 lists all the status variables for the statement category.

Table 6-8. *Statement Status Variables (X Plugin)*

Variables	Scope	Description
mysqlx_stmt_create_collection	Both	The number of create collection statements received.
mysqlx_stmt_create_collection_index	Both	The number of create collection index statements received.
mysqlx_stmt_disable_notices	Both	The number of disable notice statements received.
mysqlx_stmt_drop_collection	Both	The number of drop collection statements received.
mysqlx_stmt_drop_collection_index	Both	The number of drop collection index statements received.
mysqlx_stmt_enable_notices	Both	The number of enable notice statements received.
mysqlx_stmt_ensure_collection	Both	The number of ensure collection statements received.
mysqlx_stmt_execute_mysqlx	Both	The number of StmtExecute messages received with namespace set to mysqlx.

(*continued*)

Table 6-8. (*continued*)

Variables	Scope	Description
mysqlx_stmt_execute_sql	Both	The number of StmtExecute requests received for the SQL namespace.
mysqlx_stmt_execute_xplugin	Both	The number of StmtExecute requests received for the X Plugin namespace.
mysqlx_stmt_kill_client	Both	The number of kill client statements received.
mysqlx_stmt_list_clients	Both	The number of list client statements received.
mysqlx_stmt_list_notices	Both	The number of list notice statements received.
mysqlx_stmt_list_objects	Both	The number of list object statements received.
mysqlx_stmt_ping	Both	The number of ping statements received.

The types of tasks where you may want to use these status variables include monitoring the document store for creation and drop of collections and related indexes. This could be helpful if you are monitoring a document store application for how it is using collections. That is, frequent collection creation may indicate that the data is not being saved often or is being generated on the fly. This may lead you to discover ways to improve how your applications use data.

Other tasks include monitoring the notices (messages), number of times client kill requests were sent (not necessarily successfully executed), and listing notices, clients, and objects. Most of these status variables are beyond the scope of normal monitoring that most will require. Indeed, some of these status variables are referenced only briefly in the documentation and rarely anywhere else other than the source code itself.

One last status variable that may be helpful is the mysqlx_stmt_ping status variable to see how many times clients checked the server to see if it is alive. High values here could indicate potential network connectivity issues.

Worker Threads

The worker threads are the threads used by the X Plugin to execute tasks. There are only two status variables in this category that allow you to see the total number of worker threads available (global only) and the number of threads currently active (also global only). You can increase the minimum number of worker threads using the `mysqlx_min_worker_threads` system variable. Table 6-9 lists all the status variables for the threads category.

Table 6-9. *Worker Threads Status Variables (X Plugin)*

Variables	Scope	Description
mysqlx_worker_threads	Global	The number of worker threads available
mysqlx_worker_threads_active	Global	The number of worker threads currently used.

The types of tasks where you may want to use these status variables include when there are performance problems regarding slower execution. This can happen if more worker threads are active than what the system can handle or if there are not enough worker threads available for all the connections and requests for execution of tasks.

As the X Plugin matures, there are likely to be more tasks that you may want to perform for diagnosing problems or tuning performance, or simply configuring the plugin. If you are interested in monitoring the X Plugin, be sure to check the online MySQL reference manual as each new release of MySQL 8 is announced for updates to the status variables as well as tasks for monitoring the X Plugin.

Summary

The X Plugin is an extension to the MySQL Server that can be loaded dynamically. This is very significant because the X Plugin enables the document store feature permitting the storing and retrieving of JSON documents. In particular, the X Plugin permits communication between the server and clients using the X Protocol and interact with the X DevAPI to permit ACID compliant storage. Further, using the X DevAPI you can use a NoSQL like syntax to execute CRUD operations against the document store. It is the X Plugin the ties all the functionality together to turn the MySQL server into a document store.

In this chapter, we learned more about the X Plugin and how it works. In particular, we saw how to configure the X Plugin such as changing the port and enabling secure connections via SSL that are separate from the server. We also discovered the other system variables as well as a lengthy list of status variables that you can use to monitor the X Plugin. Finally, we discovered some interesting internal facts about the X Plugin such as how it registers system variables.

If you are still curious about the X Plugin and how it works internally, there is no better document to examine than the source code itself. Although it may not be for the uninitiated,[5] studying the source code is akin to reading the Greek originals.

In the next chapter, I take a closer look at how the new X Protocol works including a look at how the server exchanges packets with clients. As you will see, it is quite different than the old protocol. This is mostly due to the building blocks used to design and implement the new protocol.

---

[5]The source code is written in C++ and in true C++ form (sadly) the code has very little inline documentation.

CHAPTER 7

X Protocol

The X Protocol represents the first major deviation from the existing client/server protocol in MySQL. The X Protocol is designed to be extensible, maximize security, and ensure good performance. All three of these categories were at the top of the list for must-have features and requirements when the X Protocol was designed.

Although the X Protocol is mainly hidden behind an abstraction layer by the clients that wrapper (implement it) such as the X Plugin and database connectors, it is important to learn how it works if you ever plan to implement your own application using the X Protocol. We will do so in Chapters 8 and 9. Even if you never intend to develop a MySQL client, a closer look at the X Protocol will reveal and further emphasize an example of the leap in technology under the hood in MySQL 8.

In this chapter, we explore the X Protocol and discover how it works. We also look at how to get started working with the X Protocol through a database connector. We see some examples of writing small scripts to interact with the X Protocol in Python via the Connector/Python library. Let's get started with a detailed overview of the X Protocol and its origins.

Note I present a lot of the concepts we discovered in the previous chapters with minimal explanation for brevity only duplicating information where clarity is needed.

Overview

If you have ever written a communication protocol either designed from scratch or if you have had to write code to implement a communication protocol, then you are aware of the complexities and strict need to handle data exchange with unwavering precision. There simply isn't a quality of "good enough" when it comes to exchanging messages

© Charles Bell 2018
C. Bell, *Introducing the MySQL 8 Document Store*, https://doi.org/10.1007/978-1-4842-2725-1_7

from one system to another. The arrangement of the data sent to or received from another system must be arranged in an agreed format—both data alignment (what goes first) and how it is represented (encoding). Failure to get it right can lead to disaster.

The older client/server MySQL protocol is an excellent example of a communication protocol designed from scratch. Although it has been used for decades with only relatively minor changes, for some time it limited the MySQL engineers. They have struggled repeatedly when trying to implement new features because the old client/server protocol is not extensible.

However, adding new features isn't the only issue one must deal with during the evolution of the protocol. In the case of the client/server protocol in MySQL, security is a major concern. Although SSL extensions were added to the protocol, security was not enforced by default. That is, except for the exchange of the login password, the client/server messages are not required to be encrypted. Thus, it is possible for someone to discover the data being sent to/from the server if SSL or other form of encryption is not enabled.

Performance is another area where existing protocols designed for a specific, limited set of commands and messages can suffer. That is, newer technologies have shown it is possible to achieve better performance if one were to design the protocol exchanges using techniques like pipelining.

Adding these qualities to the existing client/server protocol isn't feasible. More specific, the engineers knew that to extend the client/server protocol, every system (client, application, server, etc.) that uses the protocol must be updated or modified to work with the new extensions. This is serious because you simply cannot expect every user of MySQL to suddenly update every version of their MySQL tools, custom applications, scripts, and so forth to comply with a new extension of the protocol. For this reason and many similar reasons, changing the client/server protocol in the past had been forbidden and limited to only those changes that ensure existing clients can continue to work despite the changes.

Despite this mandate, there have been a few minor changes along the way to the client/server protocol. The most recent occurred during the version 5.7 development releases concerning the returning of the Ok message. But even this minor change was built to ensure backward compatibility. To date, the client/server protocol continues to support pre- and post-Ok message protocol changes. Such is the bane of long-lived communication protocols: always having to maintain some level of backward compatibility at the expense of progress.

When the engineers began designing what is now the document store in MySQL including the new MySQL Shell, X Plugin, and X DevAPI, it became very clear that it was time to implement a new protocol that could enhance the new features. More specific, it was clear that the existing client/server protocol wasn't going to be sufficient to meet all the goals for MySQL 8 features and products. Hence, we needed a new protocol, which was dubbed the X Protocol to follow the new naming conventions.[1]

The X Protocol has been integrated in most of the MySQL suite of products including the following. I include a link for downloading each of the products listed. Note that there are several database connectors included (language-specific libraries for interacting with the MySQL server using either the client/server protocol or the X Protocol). Look for more products to implement the X Protocol in the future.

- *X Plugin*: integrated in the MySQL server (https://dev.mysql.com/downloads/mysql/)

- *Shell*: version 8.0.4 or later (https://dev.mysql.com/downloads/shell/)

- *Connector/J*: version 8.0.8 and later (https://dev.mysql.com/downloads/connector/j/)

- *Connector/Net*: version 8.0.8 and later (https://dev.mysql.com/downloads/connector/net/)

- *Connector/Node.js*: version 8.0.8 and later (https://dev.mysql.com/downloads/connector/nodejs/)

- *Connector/Python*: version 8.0.5 and later (https://dev.mysql.com/downloads/connector/python/)

Note   Connector products are often abbreviated such as C/J, C/Net, C/Node.js, and C/Py.

---

[1]Then, why is it MySQL 8 and not MySQL X?

We will see an example of how the Connector/Python connector implements and exposes the X Protocol in a later section. Now let's look at the goals and their motivations for developing and implement the X Protocol.

Goals for the X Protocol

As mentioned, the three main areas (called *design constraints* or simply goals) that the X Protocol was designed to address include extensibility, security, and performance. The next few sections present some of the driving motivations for the three major design constraints for the X Protocol.

Tip   If you want to see some of the actual engineering documents used to design the X Protocol, see the worklog[2] for the project at `http://dev.mysql.com/worklog/task/?id=8639`.

WHAT ABOUT THE CLIENT/SERVER PROTOCOL?

You may be wondering if the X Protocol works only for all things X. That is, it doesn't work with the old protocol. The answer is the X Protocol also supports the client/server protocol. This is how the MySQL Shell can connect to older servers without the need for using an intermediate library. More specific, the X Protocol includes an option to communicate using the older client/server protocol.

---

[2]A worklog is an internal document used to capture design and requirements for implementing features in MySQL.

Extensibility

When software is said to have the goal of extensibility, it means the software must be capable of being modified to add new features without requiring major rework or retooling. Although organizations may have slightly different definitions or examples of what rework means, in the case of the client/server protocol, it is not extensible because there is very little room for extending the protocol to include new messages, commands, and data without major changes to the code and the potential incompatibility with older products.

The engineers wanted to ensure the new protocol would be built from the start with extensibility in mind. In this case, extensibility includes the ability to add capabilities and features without causing existing products to fail or be reworked to comply with the changes.

Some of the areas where the X Protocol needed extensibility includes being able to add new messages, add new features (e.g., ensuring the protocol supports things such as pipelining to reduce round trips), permit the addition of new authentication mechanisms, change or add new encryption and compression facilities, and more.

Security

In this modern world of the Internet of Things and the rapid escalation of the population of modern civilizations becoming continuously connected, it has never been more important for systems to be as secure as possible. That is, to provide the very best options to permit data and users to be protected against accidental or deliberate exploitation.

Tip For more information about the Internet of Things and MySQL, see my book, *MySQL for the Internet of Things*, Charles Bell (Apress 2016) `https://www.apress.com/us/book/9781484212943`.

The engineers at Oracle take security very seriously. Indeed, it is a key aspect in almost every design, review, and quality control mechanism. At Oracle, security is paramount. Thus, when it came time to develop a new protocol, the security mechanisms were vastly improved from the client/server protocol. In particular, security defaults in the X Protocol use only trusted, proven standards such as transport layer security (TLS)[3] and simple authentication and security layer (SASL).[4]

Performance

As with security, performance is another key area that Oracle uses to evaluate the quality of products. In this case, performance must be such that the system can perform its tasks appropriately without unnecessary wait times, lag, or long running tasks. Unlike security, performance is often evaluated subjectively and anecdotally. That is, newer releases must run no slower than the previous release.

In the case of the X Protocol, performance goals are ensured by using sound foundational technologies and by leveraging features such as pipelining, which allows more than one message to be passed at a time, reducing the number of round trips (to/from the server and back to the client), and not waiting for a response from the server when sending multiple commands thereby not tying up a client to wait for a response.

In the next section, we look at the underpinnings of the X Protocol by studying the foundation of the design.

X Protocol and Protocol Buffers

One of the biggest things that the MySQL engineers wanted to overcome is the lengthy time required to develop the various aspects of a protocol mechanism from scratch. In particular, the engineers wanted to take advantage of established, well-documented, and superior technologies. After all, the problems of creating an extensible, secure, and high performance communication protocol have been solved by a lot of people to varying degrees of success.

Although several options were evaluated and discussed, it was important that the technology be well established and open source. Furthermore, the technology must support rapid implementation with little or no third-party dependencies, be language and platform independent,[5] and not require retooling of the development tools and processes to use it.

---

[3]An evolution of SSL: `https://en.wikipedia.org/wiki/Transport_Layer_Security`.

[4]A framework for authentication and data security: `https://en.wikipedia.org/wiki/Simple_Authentication_and_Security_Layer`.

[5]Asymptotically successful at best; there's always a fly in the ointment somewhere.

The technology that was chosen is called Protocol Buffers from Google (`https://developers.google.com/protocol-buffers/`). Google Protocol Buffers, affectionately named *protobuf*, is an extensible, language and platform independent mechanism for serializing structured data. It is designed for speed, compactness, and simplicity. Protobuf permits you to define a message exchange protocol quickly and easily. In that respect, protobuf is loosely similar to XML and other variants. Protobuf is available for several languages including C++, C#, Go, Java, and Python. The latest version of protobuf (version 3) supports additional languages such as Ruby.

However, language support in this sense means there is a compiler option available to translate the protobuf definition files into language-specific code that can be used by that language. For example, to use protobuf in C++, you must compile the protobuf definition files from their native, protobuf definition to files that can be read and compiled by the C++ compiler.

Protobuf is essentially a way to organize data so that it can be defined in a structured manner (called a *message*). That is, we can define a precise assembly of how the data is to be represented. This allows you to transmit and receive the data in an agreed on structure. This may not sound like a big deal until you consider the extensibility aspect where older messages are still valid even though there are newer versions of the message. Structured data mechanisms are supported in most languages with various degrees of type strictness. However, these are rarely extensible and any change to the structure renders the format incompatible (well, mostly). Protobuf is designed to allow you to extend the data organization without having to rebuild.

To understand the power of protobuf, let's look at a short example. In this case, we will use a variation of the rolodex of contacts example from earlier chapters. We need two messages (data structures); a way to store contact name and phone numbers (there may be more than one for each contact), and a message to store all the contacts. As you will see, this allows us to write some very simple code to read and write data.

Note   Although a complete tutorial of protobuf is beyond the scope of this book, the following will give you a bird's eye view of protobuf. However, Google has provided ample documentation should you need to know more about protobuf.

Installing the Protobuf Compiler

There two things we need to install. We must have the protobuf compiler and the protobuf libraries installed.

You can download the protobuf compiler from `https://github.com/google/protobuf/releases/tag/v3.0.0`. Scroll down to the bottom of the page and download the file that matches your platform. Most are in the form of a compressed file that you can download and uncompress. For most platforms, no installation is required. You can run the protobuf compiler (named `protoc`) from the bin folder of the download. For example, I downloaded the file for macOS named `protoc-3.0.2-osx-x86_64.zip` and thus can run the protobuf compiler as `./protoc-3.0.2-osx-x86_64/bin/protoc`. Or, you can place the location of `protoc` in your path.

You can install the protobuf libraries in several ways. See the runtime installation instructions for your language at `https://github.com/google/protobuf/#protobuf-runtime-installation` for instructions on how to install protobuf. For Linux and macOS platforms, you can use PyPi (pip) to install protobuf libraries as shown in the following. Note that if you installed pip using elevated privileges (e.g. sudo), you may need to specify sudo to install protobuf.

```
$ pip install protobuf
Collecting protobuf
  Downloading protobuf-3.5.1-py2.py3-none-any.whl (388kB)
    100% |████████████████████████████████| 389kB 1.0MB/s
Requirement already satisfied: setuptools in /System/Library/Frameworks/
Python.framework/Versions/2.7/Extras/lib/python (from protobuf)
Requirement already satisfied: six>=1.9 in /Library/Frameworks/Python.
framework/Versions/2.7/lib/python2.7/site-packages/six-1.10.0-py2.7.egg
(from protobuf)
Installing collected packages: protobuf
Successfully installed protobuf-3.5.1
```

Note   You also must have Python installed on your system. See `https://www.python.org/` for downloading and installing Python on your system. The example scripts in this chapter were written for and execute correctly for Python version 2.7. If you are using Python 3.0 or later, you may need to make minor changes to the code.

Protobuf Example

Let's begin with a look at the protobuf definition file. Protobuf files are named with a .proto extension. We will name our protobuf definition file contacts.proto. Listing 7-1 shows the contents of the protobuf file contacts.proto. Place this file in a folder as we will be adding additional files to compile and test the protobuf definition. This is a standard example pattern that you will see in other documentation—a data item definition followed by an array (or list) containing the data items.

Listing 7-1. Contacts Protobuf Definition

```
syntax = "proto2";

message Contact {
  required string first = 1;
  required int32 id = 2;
  optional string last = 3;

  message PhoneNumber {
    required string number = 1;
  }

  repeated PhoneNumber phones = 5;
}

message Contacts {
  repeated Contact list = 1;
}
```

Here we see code that looks a lot like C++. That is no accident and was chosen because several languages use similar syntax making this familiar to most developers. The first line we see is a directive for the protobuf compiler to use version 2 of the language (version 3 is the current version). MySQL uses version 2 as well.

In the first message, named Contact, we define two required fields, an id and a first name. The Id is an integer and the first name is a string. We can also define an optional field for the last name. Within that message is another message, named PhoneNumber, that stores a required field for the phone number. However, because this is a message, we add another field named phones to store 0 or more phone numbers. That is, the repeated declaration indicates it can contain 0 or more messages. Note the = N for each data item.

This is a required tag that must be unique. Most people just use a number starting from 1. Finally, we see a message named `Contacts` that we store 0 or more contacts named `list`.

To use the new protobuf definition, we must compile it. For this example, I will compile it for use with Python. The command to use is as follows. This generates a file named `contacts_pb2.py`, which we can import in our Python script. We use the option `--python_out` to tell the compiler two things: 1) that we want to compile for Python; and 2) that we want the output of the compiler to appear in the current folder (.). You will not see any additional output from this command—it is all written to the file. Be sure you have the protoc executable location on your path or call it directly using the location (path) as shown in the following.

```
$ protoc-3.0.2-osx-x86_64/bin/protoc --python_out=. contacts.proto
```

Recall that protobuf supports several languages. The following lists the languages supported and the correct option to use when compiling (`<out dir>` is the output directory for the resulting source files). As you can see, there are several options that cover most of the programming languages in use today. If you want to implement this example in another programming language, use the option shown in the following for your programming language.

- *C++*: `--cpp_out=<out_dir>`
- *C#* `--csharp_out=<out_dir>`
- *Java*: `--java_out=<out_dir>`
- *Java Nano* `--javanano_out=<out_dir>`
- *JavaScript*: `--js_out=<out_dir>`
- *Objective C*: `--objc_out=<out_dir>`
- *Python*: `--python_out=<out_dir>`
- *Ruby*: `--ruby_out=<out_dir>`

The contents of the contacts_pb2.py file isn't very interesting. In fact, it's quite complex. What is more interesting is how we use the new protocol. Because this is a data structure for storing contacts, let's write a script that is to write a couple of contacts to a file using the new messages. Listing 7-2 shows a simple Python script to write two contacts to a binary file. Why binary? Because protobuf is designed to allow us to serialize data quickly and easily while preserving typed (binary) data. As with the previous examples in the book, don't worry too much if you don't know Python. It's a very easy scripting language (see the side bar later in the chapter for more details).

Listing 7-2. Writing Contacts to a File (Protobuf Example)

```
import contacts_pb2

# Open the file
f = open("my_contacts", "wb")

# Create a contacts class instance
contacts = contacts_pb2.Contacts()

# Create a new contact message
new_contact = contacts.list.add()
new_contact.id = 90125
new_contact.first = "Andrew"

# Add phone numbers
phone_number = new_contact.phones.add()
phone_number.number = '212-555-1212'
phone_number = new_contact.phones.add()
phone_number.number = '212-555-1213'

# Create a new contact message
new_contact = contacts.list.add()
new_contact.id = 90126
new_contact.first = "William"
new_contact.last = "Edwards"

# Add phone numbers
phone_number = new_contact.phones.add()
phone_number.number = '301-555-1111'
phone_number = new_contact.phones.add()
phone_number.number = '301-555-3333'

# Write the data
f.write(contacts.SerializeToString())

# Close the file
f.close()
```

I used an inline coding style here rather than a loop to show you how to add new messages using the add() method from protobuf. However, note first that we must import the file we created with the protobuf compiler (contacts_pbs2). Then we create an instance to the Contacts class generated by the protobuf compiler. Recall this is an array (list) of type Contact. When calling the add() method, we get an instance to a Contact structure, which we can assign values using the field names. Thus, I set the id, first name, and then add phone numbers by creating a new phone number structure by referencing the nested message named phones and then populating it. Note that you must call add() each time you want to add a new message. Finally, I use the SerializeToString() method to serialize all the messages I've built in memory and write that to a file named my_contacts. Take a few moments to read through the code until you understand how it works.

Tip   Don't worry too much about the minor details or ways you can improve the code. I include the example code to demonstrate protobuf rather than demonstrate using Python. We'll see more about Python in a later section.

If you're following along and want to run the code, create a file named write_contacts.py, enter the code, save it, and then execute it with a command as in the following. You won't see any output here either because it creates the file my_contacts.

```
$ python ./write_contacts.py
```

If you're wondering what this data looks like in the file, the following shows a hex dump of the file, my_contacts. Note that it is indeed a binary file.

```
$ hexdump -C my_contacts
00000000  0a 2c 0a 06 41 6e 64 72 65 77 10 8d c0 05 2a 0e  |.,..Andrew....*.|
00000010  0a 0c 32 31 32 2d 35 35 35 2d 31 32 31 32 2a 0e  |..212-555-1212*.|
00000020  0a 0c 32 31 32 2d 35 35 35 2d 31 32 31 33 0a 36  |..212-555-1213.6|
00000030  0a 07 57 69 6c 6c 69 61 6d 10 8e c0 05 1a 07 45  |..William......E|
00000040  64 77 61 72 64 73 2a 0e 0a 0c 33 30 31 2d 35 35  |dwards*...301-55|
00000050  35 2d 31 31 31 31 2a 0e 0a 0c 33 30 31 2d 35 35  |5-1111*...301-55|
00000060  35 2d 33 33 33 33                                 |5-3333|
00000066
```

Now, let's see how we can read the contacts from the file. This code is considerably shorter and easier to read. Once again, we import the `contacts_pb2` file and then open the file for reading. However, in this case, we create a new instance of the Contacts class and then read from the file using the `ParseFromString()` method. This creates the contact list in memory, which we can then iterate through and print the data. The following shows the complete code for reading the contact lists.

```
import contacts_pb2

contacts = contacts_pb2.Contacts()

# Read the existing contacts.
with open("my_contacts", "rb") as f:
    contacts.ParseFromString(f.read())

# Print out the contacts
for contact in contacts.list:
    print contact
f.close()
```

As in the write example, we can execute this code but in this case, we will see the contact list printed out. Listing 7-3 shows the output. Note that we see a nicely formatted output that resembles C++ (and JSON a bit).

Listing 7-3. Reading the Contact List (protobuf example)

```
$ python ./read_contacts.py
first: "Andrew"
id: 90125
phones {
  number: "212-555-1212"
}
phones {
  number: "212-555-1213"
}

first: "William"
id: 90126
last: "Edwards"
```

```
phones {
  number: "301-555-1111"
}
phones {
  number: "301-555-3333"
}
```

Of course, you could write the code to access individual fields with dotted syntax. For example, you could print out just the first and last name with the following sample code.

```
# Print out the contacts
for contact in contacts.list:
    print contact.first, contact.last,
    for phone in contact.phones:
        print phone.number,
    print
```

When you execute this file, you see output like the following.

```
$ python ./read_contacts.py
Andrew   212-555-1212 212-555-1213
William Edwards 301-555-1111 301-555-3333
```

As you can see, working with protobuf makes reading and writing structured data easier with far less complexity than if we wrote our own structures. If this example is intriguing, I encourage you to play around with it and embellish it to your whim. If you want to know more about protobuf including how to get started building your own messages and protocol, see the online documentation at https://developers.google.com/protocol-buffers/docs/overview.

So, what is the MySQL protobuf called X Protocol then? Shouldn't it have been named, "MySQL Protocol Buffer"? Recall protobuf is a technology that can be leveraged to design protocols. The X Protocol therefore is a product of using the protobuf to define the messages, commands, and so forth that make up the new protocol. Thus, the X Protocol is a definition of a communication protocol using the language of protobuf. Cool, eh?

Now that we know more about the X Protocol, how (and why) it was designed, let's take a closer look at how it works at the code and protobuf level.

X Protocol: Under the Hood

Although it is true that developers are unlikely to have a need to write such low-level code that interfaces directly with the X Protocol, it is helpful to take a tour of how the X Protocol is implemented. In the interest of brevity, we will only see a few parts of the X Protocol before embarking on a detailed look at how one of the database connectors implements the X Protocol. If you're a code junky, you can assume your best coding posture now.[6]

Let's begin with a look at the protobuf definition files that define the MySQL X Protocol.

Protobuf Implementation

The MySQL protobuf definition files can be found in the source code download of any product that implements the X Protocol. For example, you can find them in the source code for the MySQL server in the `rapid/plugin/x/protocol` folder named with a prefix of `mysqlx` and a file extension of `.proto`. You can also see and download the X Protocol protobuf definition files from GitHub at `https://github.com/mysql/mysql-server/blob/5.7/rapid/plugin/x/protocol`.

I show the Github repository rather than having you download the server code because you can use the Github repository to drill down and view files without having to download anything. Just use the previous URL and click on the *mysqlx.proto* file link. Figure 7-1 shows an example of viewing the file in Github.

---

[6]In other words, place your chair in a semireclined state, put on your favorite music, and make sure plenty of your favorite beverage is near at hand.

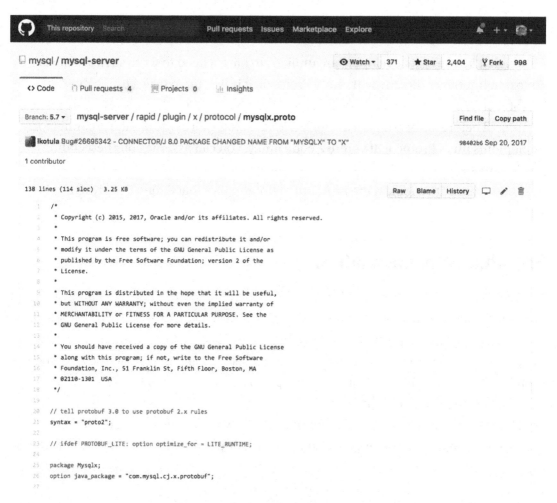

Figure 7-1. *The mysqlx.proto file (Github)*

However, if you prefer to download the server code, you can. Just visit `https://dev.mysql.com/downloads/mysql/`, choose the source code entry in the Select Operating System dropdown list, choose a file for your platform, and download it. Once you unzip (untar) the file, you can explore the server source code on your own PC.

These are the uncompiled, original protobuf definition files. Table 7-1 lists the protobuf definition files that comprise the X Protocol including the name of the file and a short description. Note that the file names are associated with the major concepts in the X DevAPI showing a clear mapping of the protobuf to the X Protocol.

Table 7-1. *Protobuf Definition Files (X Protocol)*

File	Description
mysqlx.proto	Defines messages for client, server, and general Ok and error messages; this is the main file that imports all the other files.
mysqlx_connection.proto	Defines messages for determining capabilities of the server during the connection negotiation process (see later)
mysqlx_crud.proto	Defines messages for handling the CRUD operations
mysqlx_datatypes.proto	Defines messages for working with scalar data types
mysqlx_expect.proto	Defines messages for working with pipelined messages
mysqlx_expr.proto	Defines messages for working with expressions
mysqlx_notice.proto	Defines messages for posting notices such as session and variable state changes
mysqlx_resultset.proto	Defines messages for result sets including rows and columns; this file is a key component of the X Protocol and demonstrates the power of protobuf.
mysqlx_sql.proto	Defines messages for executing statements
mysqlx_session.proto	Defines messages to manage sessions

To give you a glimpse at what the files contain, Listing 7-4 shows the error message from the mysqlx.proto file.

Listing 7-4. Generic Error Message (mysqlx.proto)

```
...
// generic Error message
//
// A ``severity`` of ``ERROR`` indicates the current message sequence is
// aborted for the given error and the session is ready for more.
//
// In case of a ``FATAL`` error message the client should not expect
// the server to continue handling any further messages and should
// close the connection.
//
```

```
// :param severity: severity of the error message
// :param code: error-code
// :param sql_state: SQL state
// :param msg: human readable error message
message Error {
  optional Severity severity = 1 [ default = ERROR ];
  required uint32 code = 2;
  required string sql_state = 4;
  required string msg = 3;

  enum Severity {
    ERROR = 0;
    FATAL = 1;
  };
}
...
```

Note that the message is very well defined and includes what you would expect to see if you've looked at the client/server protocol. In particular, we see an optional severity setting, error code, SQL state code (string), and an error message (string). Severity is an enumerated value and currently can be set to ERROR (0) or FAIL (1). Cool, eh?

You may be wondering what the protobuf compiler does to this code when compiled. Let's look at the resulting Python code. Listing 7-5 shows the compiled code for the generic error message. I omit some of the code for brevity.

Listing 7-5. Python Generic Error Message (mysqlx_pb2.proto)

```
...
_ERROR = _descriptor.Descriptor(
  name='Error',
  full_name='Mysqlx.Error',
  filename=None,
  file=DESCRIPTOR,
  containing_type=None,
```

```
  fields=[
    _descriptor.FieldDescriptor(
      name='severity', full_name='Mysqlx.Error.severity', index=0,
      number=1, type=14, cpp_type=8, label=1,
      has_default_value=False, default_value=0,
      message_type=None, enum_type=None, containing_type=None,
      is_extension=False, extension_scope=None,
      options=None),
    _descriptor.FieldDescriptor(
      name='code', full_name='Mysqlx.Error.code', index=1,
      number=2, type=13, cpp_type=3, label=1,
      has_default_value=False, default_value=0,
      message_type=None, enum_type=None, containing_type=None,
      is_extension=False, extension_scope=None,
      options=None),
...
  ],
  extensions=[
  ],
  nested_types=[],
  enum_types=[
    _ERROR_SEVERITY,
  ],
  options=None,
  is_extendable=False,
  syntax='proto3',
  extension_ranges=[],
  oneofs=[
  ],
  serialized_start=872,
  serialized_end=1001,
)
...
```

Gah! That's not even remotely as simple nor is easy to read. This is an excellent example to show how much protobuf can do for us. Clearly, defining the messages in protobuf is orders of magnitude (relatively speaking) than doing it in Python. In case you're curious, compiling the protobuf definition files in other languages creates equally as complex and seemingly incomprehensible code. But don't worry; we don't need to read the compiled files directly! That's good, isn't it?

To get a sense of the complexity (and completeness) of the X Protocol, let's look at how Connector/Python implements the X Protocol. In the next section, we will see how the X Protocol works using a few simple examples including the connection procedure.

Tip   I encourage you to explore the other `*.proto` files to see the messages they define.

X Protocol Examples

We explore two examples of the X Protocol in action: 1) an overview of how a connection is established starting with negotiation, authentication, and then commands; and 2) how SQL inserts are handled. These examples are easy to understand and, if you're curious, can be found easily in the protobuf definition files.

Example 1: Authentication

Let's assume we want to connect to a server using the older authentication for simplicity. This will give you a good idea of how a communication protocol works without the heavy lifting we see in the newer mechanisms. The goal is to understand how a typical communication protocol works by way of example. After all, it is not likely that you will build your own authentication protocol (but you can by building your own authentication plugin).

The life cycle of the procedure begins with a negotiation phase where the client requests from the server the authentication (and other) capabilities using the `CapabilitiesGet()` method. The server responds with the `CapabilitiesGet` message (defined in the `mysqlx_connection.proto` file). The client then sets the capabilities (such as setting the authentication extensions like TLS) sending the completed message back via the `CapabilitiesSet()` method. Assuming the data is correct, the server replies with the `Ok` message.

Authentication is then initiated by the client using the AuthenticateStart()
method. The server can then issue an AuthenticateContinue() method call to
request more data from the client. The client can then respond with the same
AuthenticateContinue() method call and once the authentication is complete, the
server responds with the AuthenticateOk() method call. From there, the client can
initiate commands. Figure 7-2 shows the life cycle example with the direction of the
message transports (the result of executing the associated methods).

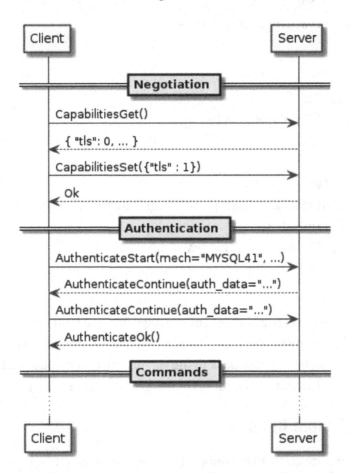

Figure 7-2. *X Protocol connection procedure (Courtesy of Oracle)*

Let's look at the CapabilitiesSet message. Listing 7-6 shows an excerpt from the
mysqlx_connection.proto file.

Listing 7-6. CapabilitiesSet Message (mysqlx_connection.proto)

```
...
// a Capability
//
// a tuple of a ``name`` and a :protobuf:msg:`Mysqlx.Datatypes::Any`
message Capability {
  required string name = 1;
  required Mysqlx.Datatypes.Any value = 2;
}

// Capabilities
message Capabilities {
  repeated Capability capabilities = 1;
}
...
// :precond: active sessions == 0
// :returns: :protobuf:msg:`Mysqlx::Ok` or :protobuf:msg:`Mysqlx::Error`
message CapabilitiesSet {
  required Capabilities capabilities = 1;
};
...
```

Note that we see the CapabilitiesSet message has one field named capabilities of the type Capabilities message. This is used as a placeholder for the client to complete the message with data and send it back to the server. The other values include SCALAR (1), OBJECT (2), or ARRAY (3) and can be found in the mysqlx_datatypes.proto file.

Example 2: Simple Inserts

In this example, we are going to examine what happens when an SQL statement is issued. In particular, two INSERT statements are executed against a simple table. At this point, we are working with an SQL object and the StmtExecute messages located in the however strangely named mysqlx_sql.proto file.

The procedure begins with the client sending the statement to the server using the Sql.StmtExecute() method. The server can then respond with the Sql.StmtExecuteOk() method. This process is repeated for the next INSERT statement as shown in Figure 7-3.

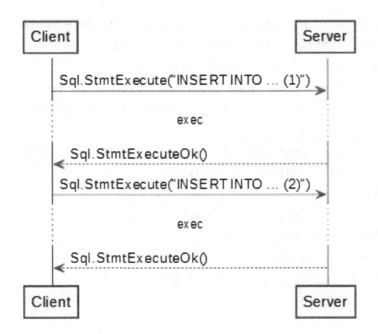

Figure 7-3. *X Protocol simple inserts (Courtesy of Oracle)*

Let's look at the Sql.StmtExecute message. Listing 7-7 shows an excerpt from the mysqlx_sql.proto file.

Listing 7-7. Sql.StmtExecute Message (mysqlx_sql.proto)

```
...
// execute a statement in the given namespace
//
// .. uml::
//
//    client -> server: StmtExecute
//    ... zero or more Resultsets ...
//    server --> client: StmtExecuteOk
//
// Notices:
//    This message may generate a notice containing WARNINGs generated by
     its execution.
//    This message may generate a notice containing INFO messages generated
     by its execution.
//
```

```
// :param namespace: namespace of the statement to be executed
// :param stmt: statement that shall be executed.
// :param args: values for wildcard replacements
// :param compact_metadata: send only type information for
:protobuf:msg:`Mysqlx.Resultset::ColumnMetadata`, skipping names and others
// :returns:
//     * zero or one :protobuf:msg:`Mysqlx.Resultset::` followed by
:protobuf:msg:`Mysqlx.Sql::StmtExecuteOk`
message StmtExecute {
  optional string namespace = 3 [ default = "sql" ];
  required bytes stmt = 1;
  repeated Mysqlx.Datatypes.Any args = 2;
  optional bool compact_metadata = 4 [ default = false ];
}
...
```

Note that we have fields for the namespace (set to SQL by default), the SQL statement stored in stmt. Note that it is of type byte so we can handle any character set including binary data. We then can have zero or more arguments (args) to allow for parameterized queries. Finally, we can have an optional compact_metadata setting to allow the server to only send the type information back to the client.

As you can see, the X Protocol has a lot going on under the hood. However, we don't have to know all there is to know about the X Protocol to use it. In fact, the best way to use the X Protocol is through the MySQL Shell, which we saw in detail in Chapter 4 or through the database connectors that support the X Protocol. Let's look at how one database connector implements the X Protocol.

WAIT! WHERE'S THE REST OF THE CODE?

If you take time to examine the protobuf definition files, you may notice two major things that are missing. Protobuf is a protocol definition language (API) but it does not include any support for direct transport of messages over the wire nor is there any direct support for encryption, compression, and other techniques for transmitting data.

The X Protocol therefore is where all this code exists. Now you can see why the X Protocol is more than just a protobuf implementation. There are other facilities that the X Protocol implements that isn't part of the protobuf message definitions. These include handshaking with the server, error message definitions, and much more.

X Protocol Walkthrough

To better understand the power and elegance of the X Protocol, we will examine how one of the database connectors implements the X Protocol. This presents an abstraction layer over the protobuf definition files, which given what we learned about how the protobuf, is a very good thing. As you will see, the connectors make working with the X Protocol very easy thus continuing the goals of protobuf to make communication protocols easy to create and use.

The database connector we use in this section and in the next is Connector/Python, C/Py. Once again, I chose C/Py for its simplicity and readability. If you want to follow along and see the code in context, you can download the source code for Connector/Python version 8.0.5 or later at `http://dev.mysql.com/downloads/connector/python/`. Note that you may need to click on the *Development Releases* tab then select the *Platform Independent* entry from the dropdown list.

We look at the C/Py code for each of the examples in the previous section. Thus, we will see the code for connecting to the server and executing an SQL INSERT statement.

Example 1: Authentication

We find the code for the authentication process in the C/Py source code file named `connection.py` found in the `/lib/mysqlx` folder. Listing 7-8 shows an excerpt of the source code (methods) that implements the procedure. I omit the specifics of collecting and passing connection information for brevity. The starting point to focus on is the `connect()` method in the Connection class.

Listing 7-8. Connection Methods for Authenticate Procedure (C/Py)

```
...
def connect(self):
    # Loop and check
    error = None
```

```
    while self._can_failover:
        try:
            self.stream.connect(self._connection_params())
            self.reader_writer = MessageReaderWriter(self.stream)
            self.protocol = Protocol(self.reader_writer)
            self._handle_capabilities()
            self._authenticate()
            return
        except socket.error as err:
            error = err

    if len(self._routers) <= 1:
        raise InterfaceError("Cannot connect to host: {0}".format(error))
    raise InterfaceError("Failed to connect to any of the routers.", 4001)

def _handle_capabilities(self):
    if self.settings.get("ssl-mode") == SSLMode.DISABLED:
        return
    if self.stream.is_socket:
        if self.settings.get("ssl-mode"):
            _LOGGER.warning("SSL not required when using Unix socket.")
        return

    data = self.protocol.get_capabilites().capabilities
    if not (get_item_or_attr(data[0], "name").lower() == "tls"
            if data else False):
        self.close_connection()
        raise OperationalError("SSL not enabled at server.")

    is_ol7 = False
    if platform.system() == "Linux":
        # pylint: disable=W1505
        distname, version, _ = platform.linux_distribution()
        try:
            is_ol7 = "Oracle Linux" in distname and version.split(".")[0]
            == "7"
        except IndexError:
```

```
        is_ol7 = False
    if sys.version_info < (2, 7, 9) and not is_ol7:
        self.close_connection()
        raise RuntimeError("The support for SSL is not available for "
            "this Python version.")

    self.protocol.set_capabilities(tls=True)
    self.stream.set_ssl(self.settings.get("ssl-mode", SSLMode.REQUIRED),
                        self.settings.get("ssl-ca"),
                        self.settings.get("ssl-crl"),
                        self.settings.get("ssl-cert"),
                        self.settings.get("ssl-key"))

def _authenticate(self):
    auth = self.settings.get("auth")
    if (not auth and self.stream.is_secure()) or auth == Auth.PLAIN:
        self._authenticate_plain()
    elif auth == Auth.EXTERNAL:
        self._authenticate_external()
    else:
        self._authenticate_mysql41()
...
```

Note that in the connect() method, we see a couple of things occur. First, we see the C/Py opens a stream connection to the server (via the _connection_params() method that returns the data set previously) then the code creates an instance to a reader/writer. This is how the connector transports the messages to/from the server.

Next, the code instantiates an instance of the Protocol class, which is the abstraction of the X Protocol. We'll see more details of that code later.

Now, focus on the last two statements in the connect() method. Here we see method calls for the CapabilitiesGet/Set methods in _handle_capabilities() and the authenticate phase in _authenticate(). Take a few moments to read through the code so you can see that all the steps from Figure 7-1 are shown.

The CapabilitiesGet/Set methods of the Protocol class can be found in the protocol. py file found in the /lib/mysqlx folder of the C/Py source code and are shown in Listing 7-9.

Listing 7-9. CapabilitiesGet/Set Methods for Authenticate Procedure (C/Py)

```
...
def get_capabilites(self):
    msg = Message("Mysqlx.Connection.CapabilitiesGet")
    self._writer.write_message(
        mysqlxpb_enum("Mysqlx.ClientMessages.Type.CON_CAPABILITIES_GET"),
        msg)
    return self._reader.read_message()

def set_capabilities(self, **kwargs):
    capabilities = Message("Mysqlx.Connection.Capabilities")
    for key, value in kwargs.items():
        capability = Message("Mysqlx.Connection.Capability")
        capability["name"] = key
        capability["value"] = self._create_any(value)
        capabilities["capabilities"].extend([capability.get_message()])
    msg = Message("Mysqlx.Connection.CapabilitiesSet")
    msg["capabilities"] = capabilities
    self._writer.write_message(
        mysqlxpb_enum("Mysqlx.ClientMessages.Type.CON_CAPABILITIES_SET"),
        msg)
    return self.read_ok()
)
...
```

It is at this point where we can see calls to the protobuf code by way of the MySQLx* classes that are generated by the protobuf compiler.

Example 2: Simple Inserts

This example is a bit easier to view so we'll go a bit deeper than the last example. We find the code for the authentication process in the C/Py source code file named statement. py in the /lib/mysqlx folder of the C/Py source code. Listing 7-10 shows an excerpt of the source code that implements a class for executing INSERT SQL statements.

Listing 7-10. SQL INSERT Class (C/Py)

```
...
class InsertStatement(WriteStatement):
    """A statement for insert operations on Table.

    Args:
        table (mysqlx.Table): The Table object.
        *fields: The fields to be inserted.
    """
    def __init__(self, table, *fields):
        super(InsertStatement, self).__init__(table, False)
        self._fields = flexible_params(*fields)

    def values(self, *values):
        """Set the values to be inserted.

        Args:
            *values: The values of the columns to be inserted.

        Returns:
            mysqlx.InsertStatement: InsertStatement object.
        """
        self._values.append(list(flexible_params(*values)))
        return self

    def execute(self):
        """Execute the statement.

        Returns:
            mysqlx.Result: Result object.
        """
        return self._connection.send_insert(self)
...
```

As you can see, the code is easy to read. The first thing to notice is the class is derived from a base class named WriteStatement (also in statement.py). That base class has an abstract (virtual) method named execute(), which this derived class implements. However, in this case, it calls the send_insert() method from the connection class (in connection.py). The following shows the send_insert() method.

```
@catch_network_exception
def send_insert(self, statement):
    self.protocol.send_insert(statement)
    ids = None
    if isinstance(statement, AddStatement):
        ids = statement._ids
    return Result(self, ids)
```

As you can see, this calls the Protocol class method send_insert() in the protocol.py file with the statement as shown in Listing 7-11.

Listing 7-11. The send_insert() Method in the Protocol Class (C/Py)

```
...
def send_insert(self, stmt):
    data_model = mysqlxpb_enum("Mysqlx.Crud.DataModel.DOCUMENT"
                               if stmt._doc_based else
                               "Mysqlx.Crud.DataModel.TABLE")
    collection = Message("Mysqlx.Crud.Collection",
                         name=stmt.target.name,
                         schema=stmt.schema.name)
    msg = Message("Mysqlx.Crud.Insert", data_model=data_model,
                  collection=collection)

    if hasattr(stmt, "_fields"):
        for field in stmt._fields:
            expr = ExprParser(field, not stmt._doc_based) \
                .parse_table_insert_field()
            msg["projection"].extend([expr.get_message()])

    for value in stmt._values:
        row = Message("Mysqlx.Crud.Insert.TypedRow")
        if isinstance(value, list):
            for val in value:
                row["field"].extend([build_expr(val).get_message()])
```

```
      else:
          row["field"].extend([build_expr(value).get_message()])
      msg["row"].extend([row.get_message()])

  msg["upsert"] = stmt._upsert
  self._writer.write_message(
      mysqlxpb_enum("Mysqlx.ClientMessages.Type.CRUD_INSERT"), msg)
...
```

As in the previous example, we can now see the protobuf interface and follow along in the code to see the steps outlined in Figure 7-2 in the code.

Tip   If you want to learn more about how the X Protocol works, see the MySQL Internals documentation at https://dev.mysql.com/doc/internals/en/x-protocol.html.

Now that we know a lot more about the X Protocol and can appreciate the abstraction provided by the X Plugin and Shell as well as the database connectors, let's look at how we can write client applications that take advantage of the X Protocol as provided by the MySQL connectors. In this case, we'll continue our quest to master the X Protocol by using the Connector/Python.

Creating X Clients

Creating MySQL client applications that use the X Protocol is best executed using either the MySQL Shell or ultimately one of the database connectors together with installing the X Plugin on the server. In this section, we will see two examples of standalone clients. One that was written using MySQL as a document store and another using only the relational data model.

The programming language we will use is a very easy scripting language called Python. As you will see, the commands are quite intuitive and very expressive. For the purposes of this demonstration, you do not need to be an expert with the language. I will provide all the code and commands you need as we go along.

PYTHON? ISN'T THAT A SNAKE?

The Python programming language is a high-level language designed to be as close to reading English as possible while being simple, easy to learn, and very powerful. Pythonistas will tell you the designers have indeed met these goals.

Python does not require a compilation step prior to being used. Rather, Python applications (whose file names end in .py) are interpreted on the fly. This is very powerful; but unless you use a Python development environment, some syntax errors (such as incorrect indentation) will not be discovered until the application is executed. Fortunately, Python provides a robust exception-handling mechanism.

If you have never used Python or you would like to know more about it, the following are a few good books that introduce the language. A host of resources are also available on the Internet, including the Python documentation pages at http://www.python.org/doc/:

- *Programming the Raspberry Pi*, by Simon Monk (McGraw-Hill, 2013).

- *Beginning Python from Novice to Professional*, 2nd Ed., by Magnus Lie Hetland (Apress, 2008).

- *Python Cookbook*, by David Beazley and Brian K. Jones (O'Reilly Media, 2013).

Interestingly, Python was named after the British comedy troupe Monty Python and not the reptile. As you learn Python, you may encounter campy references to Monty Python episodes. Having a fondness for Monty Python, I find these references entertaining. Of course, your mileage may vary.

To get started, you can either enter the code as shown in the examples or download the source code from the Apress site for this book. You can use any code editor you want when writing Python scripts. We begin with a short description of how to setup the environment to run the examples.

Tip   There are many available including a very powerful IDE from JetBrains named PyCharm (`http://www.jetbrains.com/pycharm/`). If you want a great open source for Python, check out PyCharm Community Edition.

Setup for the Examples

There are a couple of things you need to have installed to work with the examples in this section. You must download the Google Protocol Buffers Python library and install the programming language runtime. You must also have the source code for C/Py downloaded.

Recall, we need to have the protobuf compiler and protobuf libraries installed. If you have not already done this, please refer the previous section, "Installing the Protobuf Compiler."

The language-specific runtime libraries can be downloaded from `https://github.com/google/protobuf`. You should download the entire package by clicking on the *Clone or Download* button. Once the download is complete, you will see a file named `protobuf-master.zip` that you can uncompress. To install the library for your chosen language, navigate to the folder named for the language and read the README.md file for specific installation instructions. For example, we will be using Python in this chapter. The folder is named `/protobuf-master/python`. To install the Python on macOS, you run the following commands.

```
$ python ./setup.py build
$ sudo python ./setup.py install
```

Installing the Python libraries on other systems is similar. The only difference for installing it on Windows is you do not need to use sudo (super user). However, on my system there was an issue with locating the protobuf compiler. I received an error similar to the following.

```
protoc is not installed nor found in ../src.  Please compile it or install
the binary package.
```

Once I placed the protobuf compiler executable (`protoc`) in the specified directory (`../src`), I could install the Python protobuf libraries with the previous commands. You may encounter similar issues on other platforms.

> **Tip**   Scroll down to the bottom of the page on `https://github.com/google/protobuf` and click on the links in the table to see instructions for installing the protobuf libraries for other languages.

If you haven't already, you must download the source code for the C/Py version 8.0.5 or later from `http://dev.mysql.com/downloads/connector/python/`. Be sure to download the *Platform Independent* option from the dropdown list. We will be using some of the source files from the C/Py source tree in our example.

I chose to do it this way to help you see the details of how protobuf works with Python and how C/Py implements the X Protocol. Although the examples will show the X Protocol abstraction layer in C/Py, you can use your favorite debugger or Python IDE to drill down into the code and see how things work. Therefore, I have setup this example for the curious among us.[7] However, you need not go that far if you do not want to. Rather, you can concentrate on how the examples work to give you a better understanding of how to work with the new X Protocol via a database connector.

Perhaps more important, because the C/Py example we are using is a development milestone release (think beta), copying the source code will not affect any other installation of C/Py on your system thereby allowing you to run these examples and not have to install the development milestone release of the connector.

The files we need are in the `/lib/mysqlx` folder. But first, create a new folder on your system. Name it whatever you like such as `xclient`. Next, copy the `mysqlx` folder from the C/Py archive into the `xclient` folder. When you create the files for the following examples, save them in the `xclient` folder. For example, I named the document store example `xclient_json.py` and the relational data example `xclient_sql.py`.

> **Tip**   If you get an error that one or more libraries cannot be found, ensure you have copied the mysqlx folder into the same folder as the xclient_json.py and xclient_sql.py files.

---

[7]Or as I am sometimes accused of "not leaving things well enough alone." Guilty. I've been taking things apart since I was a child. And sometimes I'd put them back together!

Document Store Example

This example creates a simple client to demonstrate how to use the X Protocol abstraction available in C/Py. The example uses the concept of the rolodex of contacts we encountered in Chapter 1. In this case, the code will connect to the server, create a schema and collection in the schema and populate the collection with documents. The code will then retrieve all the documents and print them. But we don't just print the raw document. The code demonstrates how to do a find operation on the collection and iterate over the documents printing the phone numbers for each contact document found.

The following briefly describes the code portions. I highlight the pertinent code statements to draw your attention to the X Protocol abstraction methods. Most of the calls will be familiar to you because we encountered them in Chapter 5 and elsewhere in the book. Thus, I keep the explanations brief. Refer to Chapter 5 if you need more information about the classes and methods used in the example.

The first thing that we need to do is import the mysqlx library. Recall this is the set of files from the C/Py download. It contains the C/Py abstraction for the X Protocol files that we saw earlier. If you examine that folder, you will notice the .proto files are missing. This is because we only need the .py files that were generated when the protobuf compiler was run. Fortunately, all those files exist in the mysqlx folder.

Next, we ask the user to provide the logon credentials (user id, password, host, and port). We use this information to open a session (a connection) to the server. For this, we use the get_session() method and assign the resulting instance of the session object to a variable mysqlx_session. If something should happen that we cannot connect, we check the status of the session and if it is not open, exit. Note that we are using an X Session in this example because we are only going to execute CRUD operations and do not need any SQL support.

Next, we use the mysqlx_session object instance and attempt to get the schema with the get_schema() method.[8] This sets the default schema so that when we create a collection (or other objects perhaps); they will be contained in the schema. I use a constant to store the schema name and the collection name. If the schema is not on the server, we create it with the create_schema() method. Either way, we get a schema object instance, which we can use to create the collection with the create_collection()

---

[8]In SQL terms *use* it.

method, which gives us an object instance to the collection. Note that I use the remove()
method to empty the collection. This permits us to rerun the code without duplicating
data (I am not checking document Ids).

Let's look at the code before we continue. Listing 7-12 shows the completed code.
Take some time to read through the code so that you can see all the methods and actions
described thus far. All of the code up to the contacts.remove() call should be familiar to
you. If you want to execute this code to see what it does, you can place this code in a file
named xclient_json.py.

Listing 7-12. X Client Source Code (JSON)

```
#
# Introducing the MySQL 8 Document Store - xclient_json
#
# This file contains and example of how to read a collection from a MySQL
# server using the X Protocol via a Session object
#
# Dr. Charles Bell, 2018
#
import getpass
import mysqlx

# Declarations
TEST_SCHEMA = "rolodex"
TEST_COL = "contacts"

# Get user information
print("Please enter the connection information.")
user = raw_input("Username: ")
passwd = getpass.getpass("Password: ")
host = raw_input("Hostname [localhost]: ") or 'localhost'
port = raw_input("Port [33060]: ") or '33060'

# Get a session object using a dictionary of terms
mysqlx_session = mysqlx.get_session({'host': host, 'port': port, 'user':
user, 'password': passwd})
```

```python
# Check to see that the session is open. If not, quit.
if not mysqlx_session.is_open():
    exit(1)

# Get the schema and create it if it doesn't exist
schema = mysqlx_session.get_schema(TEST_SCHEMA)
if not schema.exists_in_database():
    schema = mysqlx_session.create_schema(TEST_SCHEMA)

# Create a collection or use it if it already exists
contacts = schema.create_collection(TEST_COL)

# Empty the collection
contacts.remove()

# Insert data with inline JSON
contacts.add({"name": {"first": "Allen"},
            "phones": [{"work": "212-555-1212"}]}).execute()
contacts.add({"name": {"first": "Joe", "last": "Wheelerton"},
            "phones": [{"work": "212-555-1213"}, {"home": "212-555-1253"}],
            "address": {"street": "123 main", "city": "oxnard",
            "state": "ca", "zip": "90125"},
            "notes": "Excellent car detailer. Referrals get $20 off next
            detail!"}).execute()

# Get all of the data
doc_results = contacts.find().execute()

# Show the results
print("\nList of Phone Numbers")
document = doc_results.fetch_one()
while document:
    print("{0}:\t".format(document.name['first'])),
    for phone in document.phones:
        for key, value in phone.iteritems():
            print("({0}) {1}".format(key, value)),
    print("")
    document = doc_results.fetch_one()
```

```
# Drop the collection
schema.drop_collection(TEST_COL)

# Drop the schema
mysqlx_session.drop_schema(TEST_SCHEMA)

# Close the session
mysqlx_session.close()
```

Tip   If you are using Python 3.0 or later, you will need to change the
`raw_input()` calls to `input()` and the `iteritems()` to `items()`. This is
because `raw_input()` and `iteritems()` are no longer supported in later
releases of Python.

Next, we can add some contacts. We do this using the `add()` method for the
collection object instance. In this case, we add a couple of documents; one for a person
that we only know their first name and a phone number, and another for someone that
we know their full name, several phone numbers, and some notes we've made about
them. This illustrates the power of using a document store: store what you need and
don't force the data to comply with a strict structure or the storage mechanism!

Once the documents are added, we use the `find()` method on the collection
without any expressions. We chain the find operation with the `execute()` method. This
simply returns all the documents in the collection in the form of a document result
object instance. We can then use that object to iterate over the documents with the
`fetch_one()` method. Note that this returns a document object instance, which we can
use to get the data elements directly using named attributes (a powerful expression).
Take a moment to read through the code for fetching the documents. Note that when the
collection is at the end, the `fetch_one()` returns None and the while loop terminates.

Finally, we drop the collection with the `drop_collection()` method and drop
the schema with the `drop_schema()` method so that we can rerun the code and avoid
duplication. However, you may notice I've added code to protect against accidental
execution. For example, if you use the debugger and terminate the code before the end,
the statements at the top of the code will use the schema if it already exists and empty
the collection.

Now let's see the script in action. In this case, we expect to see only the first name and a list of phone numbers for the people in our rolodex (in this case only two entries).

```
$ python ./xclient_json.py
Please enter the connection information.
Username: root
Password:
Hostname [localhost]:
Port [33060]:

List of Phone Numbers
Joe:      (work) 212-555-1213 (home) 212-555-1253
Allen:    (work) 212-555-1212
```

In case you're wondering if this is all an elaborate ruse and that the collection and documents we created are somehow stored elsewhere in MySQL, if you disable the drop_*() calls and run the program again, you can log into the server and see the construction of the underlying tables as shown in Listing 7-13.

Listing 7-13. Definition of the Contacts Collection

```
$ mysqlsh root@localhost:33060 --sql --json=pretty --schema=rolodex -e
"EXPLAIN contacts"
{
    "password": "Enter password: "
}
{
    "executionTime": "0.00 sec",
    "warningCount": 0,
    "warnings": [],
    "rows": [
        {
            "Field": "doc",
            "Type": "json",
            "Null": "YES",
            "Key": "",
```

```
                    "Default": null,
                    "Extra": ""
            },
            {
                    "Field": "_id",
                    "Type": "varchar(32)",
                    "Null": "NO",
                    "Key": "PRI",
                    "Default": null,
                    "Extra": "STORED GENERATED"
            }
    ],
    "hasData": true,
    "affectedRowCount": 0,
    "autoIncrementValue": 0
}
```

If you run a SELECT statement to get all the data from that table, you will see the
results similar to those shown in Listing 7-14. The order of the results may differ but you
should see the same data in the results. Note that the document ids are added to each of
the JSON documents.

Listing 7-14. Results of SELECT Statement for Contacts Collection

```
$ mysqlsh root@localhost:33060 --sql --json=pretty --schema=rolodex -e
"SELECT * FROM contacts"
{
    "password": "Enter password: "
}
{
    "executionTime": "0.00 sec",
    "warningCount": 0,
    "warnings": [],
```

```
  "rows": [
      {
          "doc": "{\"_id\": \"9801A79DE09382A811E806BFAD2FA2CF\",
          \"name\": {\"first\": \"Allen\"}, \"phones\": [{\"work\":
          \"212-555-1212\"}]}",
          "_id": "9801A79DE09382A811E806BFAD2FA2CF"
      },
      {
          "doc": "{\"_id\": \"9801A79DE0938DFD11E806BFAD314DE1\",
          \"name\": {\"last\": \"Wheelerton\", \"first\": \"Joe\"},
          \"notes\": \"Excellent car detailer. Referrals get $20 off
          next detail!\", \"phones\": [{\"work\": \"212-555-1213\"},
          {\"home\": \"212-555-1253\"}], \"address\": {\"zip\":
          \"90125\", \"city\": \"oxnard\", \"state\": \"ca\", \"street\":
          \"123 main\"}}",
          "_id": "9801A79DE0938DFD11E806BFAD314DE1"
      }
  ],
  "hasData": true,
  "affectedRowCount": 0,
  "autoIncrementValue": 0
}
```

That's cool, isn't it? We will see more code like this in Chapter 8 when we explore a full document store application example. But first, let's see an example of Connector/ Python using the X Protocol for executing SQL commands.

Relational Data Example

Now let's look at a relational data example using the X Protocol. We will use the same code from C/Py as the last example only this time we're going to execute an SQL statement rather than work with data. I chose this simple example because, if not at first, eventually your MySQL document store applications will use less and less SQL operations. Even so, you may need to execute an SQL statement now and again if you want to check variables, status, or similar operations with the server.

This example connects to the server using a Session and executes the SQL statement, SHOW VARIABLES LIKE, to retrieve all the system variables for the X Plugin. This is the same SQL statement we saw in Chapter 6. Although we aren't accessing any data, the result set returned from the SHOW VARIABLES statement is the same as would be returned if querying a table. So, we will see how to handle a result set from a SQL command without the need to create any sample data.

As in the last example, we begin by importing the mysqlx library and prompt the user for the logon credentials. Note that I demonstrate how to use defaults for user input. Next, we get a Session with the get_session() method. This returns a Session object instance. We then check to see if the connection is open and if it is not (e.g., the connection failed), we exit. Listing 7-15 shows the complete code for this example. Take a moment to read through it so that you can see all the concepts discussed thus far.

Listing 7-15. X Client Source Code (SQL)

```
#
# Introducing the MySQL 8 Document Store - xclient_sql
#
# This file contains an example of how to read a database (SQL) from a MySQL
# server using the X Protocol via a Session object
#
# Dr. Charles Bell, 2018
#
import getpass
import mysqlx

# Get user information
print("Please enter the connection information.")
user = raw_input("Username: ")
passwd = getpass.getpass("Password: ")
host =  raw_input("Hostname [localhost]: ") or 'localhost'
port = raw_input("Port [33060]: ") or '33060'

# Get a session object since we want to execute SQL statements
mysqlx_session = mysqlx.get_session({'host': host, 'port': port, 'user':
user, 'password': passwd})
```

```
# Check to see that the session is open. If not, quit.
if not mysqlx_session.is_open():
    exit(1)

# Get an SqlStatements object
sql_stmt = mysqlx_session.sql("SHOW VARIABLES LIKE 'mysqlx_%'")

# Execute and get a SqlResult object
sql_result = sql_stmt.execute()

print("\nVariables for the X Plugin:")
# Print the column labels (names)
for col in sql_result.columns:
    print("{0}\t".format(col.get_column_name())),
print("\n--------------------------------------------------")

# Print the rows
for row in sql_result.fetch_all():
    for col in row:
        print("{0}\t".format(col)),
    print("")

# Close the session
mysqlx_session.close()
```

Tip If you are using Python 3.0 or later, you may need to change the `raw_input()` calls to `input()`. This is because `raw_input()` is no longer supported in later releases of Python.

To execute a SQL statement, we need to ask the session for a SqlStatement object instance by passing in the SQL statement we want to execute. We do that by calling the sql() method for the session object instance. We can use that object to execute the statement and get a result object instance in return.

Next, we can iterate over the columns in the result set printing their names. This illustrates how to capture the column names in a result set.

Next, we use the `fetch_all()` method to get all the rows in a list, loop through them in a for loop and print the value for each column found. Note we use "row" and "column" here because this is not a document being returned—it's an old-fashioned SQL result set (well, via the X Protocol). Finally, we close the session. Listing 7-16 shows an example of the script running. You should be able to equate the output with the `print()` statements in the source code. Note that later versions of MySQL may have additional variables and some default values may differ.

Listing 7-16. X Client Results (SQL)

```
$ python ./xclient_sql.py
Please enter the connection information.
Username: root
Password:
Hostname [localhost]:
Port [33060]:

Variables for the X Plugin:
Variable_name     Value
--------------------------------------------
mysqlx_bind_address      *
mysqlx_connect_timeout   30
mysqlx_idle_worker_thread_timeout        60
mysqlx_max_allowed_packet        1048576
mysqlx_max_connections   100
mysqlx_min_worker_threads        2
mysqlx_port      33060
mysqlx_port_open_timeout         0
mysqlx_socket    /tmp/mysqlx.sock
mysqlx_ssl_ca
mysqlx_ssl_capath
mysqlx_ssl_cert
mysqlx_ssl_cipher
mysqlx_ssl_crl
mysqlx_ssl_crlpath
mysqlx_ssl_key
```

Note here that we see all the system variables for the X Plugin (those that start with `mysqlx_`). We also see the values for each system variable. The SSL entries do not have any values because the connection used in the example is not connecting via a secure connection.

As you can see, even with a language like Python, it is very easy to write clients that take advantage of the X Protocol and the X DevAPI. Of course, this is all possible with Connector/Python, which implements the X Protocol. For more information about the X Protocol, see the "X Protocol" section in the online MySQL internals reference manual at `https://dev.mysql.com/doc/internals/en/`. For specific information about writing clients with the connectors, see the individual connector online documentation at `https://dev.mysql.com/doc`. You can find information about using the X DevAPI with Connector/Python at `https://dev.mysql.com/doc/dev/connector-python/`.

Summary

The X Protocol is a revolutionary new feature in MySQL that overcomes a lot of the limitations of the older client/server protocol. The X Protocol is designed for extensibility so it can be extended without affecting the clients that rely on it. The X Protocol is also designed with a greater level of security and greater performance. For the first time in decades, MySQL clients can connect and interact with the server using modern, reliable technologies and promises to be the catalyst for many more new features in the future.

In this chapter, we examined the X Protocol starting with the motivations for why it was created, the chief tenets or goals of the design, and how it was implemented using protobuf as the foundation. We also saw a walkthrough of how portions of the X Protocol work for simple use cases. We then looked at how to use protobuf in our applications for moving data (messages) around in the code (on disk, over the wire, etc.), which illustrates the power of protobuf.

We also took a short tour of how C/Py implements the X Protocol by examining portions of the actual C/Py source code. We then used the X Protocol abstraction layer in C/Py in standalone Python scripts to demonstrate how well the X Protocol works—its ease of implementation as well as a concrete example of the technologies presented this far in the book.

As with the X Plugin, we also discovered that the X Protocol is much more than a feature, it's a carefully crafted and well abstracted mechanism that is one of the underpinnings for the future of MySQL. Even though we know we're using the X Protocol when using those connectors that support it, the X Protocol, it just works and works very well.

In Chapter 8, I provide a tutorial on writing applications using the X DevAPI, which we now know is enabled through the X Plugin and X Protocol. The project will use the MySQL document store to build a Python web-based solution for storing information about books.

CHAPTER 8

Library Application: User Interface

Now that we've learned what the MySQL Document Store is and how to use it via the MySQL Shell, we can explore a more complex example that demonstrates the three forms of data storage described: a pure relational database solution, a hybrid solution where we use one or more JSON fields using the SQL features of the X DevAPI, and a pure document store solution that uses the X DevAPI exclusively (a NoSQL solution). Therefore, we will see the application implemented in three separate implementations.

However, we must first understand how the sample application is designed and how it works. After all, the best examples should be something the reader can use in their own environment. Thus, the example must be complex enough and complete enough to be meaningful.

To continue the understandability of code in the previous chapters, we will be using Python for the application because Python is very easy to learn and the code reads with a level of clarity better than other languages. But don't worry if you prefer another language. You can easily rewrite the code in this chapter into any of the languages with connectors that support the X DevAPI.

The user interface on the other hand complicates things a bit. We can mitigate that by using a user interface design that is familiar. For this, we will use a web application. It is unfortunate that writing a web application in pure Python is tedious and requires more knowledge of how web application works than what one can expect in a work of this size.

To overcome that challenge, we will use one of the popular Python web application frameworks. In this case, we will use Flask complete with a primer, tutorial, and walk-through of the user interface code. As you will see, Flask is also easy to learn with only a moderate number of nuances and concepts to learn. Flask was originally developed by Armin Ronacher and has proven to be one of the easiest and most stable web platforms for Python.

© Charles Bell 2018
C. Bell, *Introducing the MySQL 8 Document Store*, https://doi.org/10.1007/978-1-4842-2725-1_8

In Chapter 9, we will complete the application adding the database access methods described previously.

Getting Started

If you want to follow along and implement the sample projects, you will need a few things installed on your computer to get going. This section will help you prepare your computer with the tools needed: what you need to install and how to configure your environment. We will also see a short primer on the user interface tools. Let's begin with a more detailed description of the application.

Library Application

The example application in this chapter is a rather simple application designed to demonstrate concepts. It is complete in that it supports the create, read, update, and delete (CRUD) operations on data. Error handling and the user interface components have less sophistication to keep the focus on the interaction with data. That said we will see how to implement a robust and nice looking web interface in Python using Flask.

The data for the application is a simple book database. We will be storing basic information about books such as the ISBN, title, publisher, and so forth. We also will have a notes section so we can keep notes on the books. I used something similar to this for many of my research papers and even some more advanced projects. The concept of operations was to record the bibliography information for each book along with notes about the content so that later it could be used to create a list of references. For example, if a book contained information pertinent to a topic in the paper, I would add a note indicating the subject and list page numbers and other important information. The information in the notes varied based on what I was recording, so all that was required was a search in a simple text field.

Unlike the application I used for research that permitted storing information about books, magazines, articles, blogs, and so forth, the application for this chapter has been simplified to store only books. This keeps the project small enough to be discussed without unnecessary detail. The focus for the chapter is to examine the benefits of migrating to a document store, not how best to implement a media reference application.

Thus, the basic operations will be to store and retrieve information about books, authors, and publishers. The user interface is designed to present a list of all the books in the database with the option to edit any book in the list. The default view is books but the first versions of the application (1 and 2) will allow you to view lists of authors and publishers. Users will also be permitted to create new books (authors, and publishers), edit, and delete books.

Each version of the application will behave slightly differently as we see how changing the way the data is stored and retrieved affects application design. A more detailed explanation of each project is included in later sections that discuss the project versions.

Now, let's look at how to setup our computers to run the sample application projects.

Setup Your Environment

The changes to your environment are not difficult nor are they lengthy. We will be installing Flask and a few extensions, which are needed for the application user interface. Flask is one of several web libraries you can use with Python. These web libraries make developing web applications with Python much easier than using raw HTML code and writing your own handlers and code for the requests. Plus, Flask is not difficult to learn.

The libraries we need to install are shown in Table 8-1. The table lists the name of the library/extension, a short description, and the URL for the product documentation.

Table 8-1. *List of Libraries Required*

Library	Description	Documentation
Flask	Python Web API	`http://flask.pocoo.org/docs/0.12/installation/`
Flask-Script	Scripting support for Flask	`https://flask-script.readthedocs.io/en/latest/`
Flask-Bootstrap	User interface improvements and enhancements	`https://pythonhosted.org/Flask-Bootstrap/`
Flask-WTF	WTForms integration	`https://flask-wtf.readthedocs.io/en/latest/`
WTForms	Forms validation and rendering	`https://wtforms.readthedocs.io/en/latest/`

Note   Depending on how your system is configured, you may see additional or fewer components installed for the components installed in this section.

Of course, you should already have Python installed on your system. If not, be sure to download and install the latest version of either the 2.X or 3.X editions. The example code in this chapter was tested with Python 2.7.10 and Python 3.6.0.

To install the libraries, we can use the Python package manager, `pip`, to install the libraries from the command line. The `pip` utility is included in most Python distributions, but if you need to install it, you can see the installation documentation at `https://pip.pypa.io/en/latest/installing/`.

If you need to install pip on Windows, you will need to download an installer, get-`pip.py` (`https://pip.pypa.io/en/stable/installing/#installing-with-get-pip-py`), and then add the path to the installed directory to the PATH environment variable. There are several articles that document this process in more detail. You can google for "installing pip on Windows 10" and find several including `https://matthewhorne.me/how-to-install-python-and-pip-on-windows-10/`, which is among the most accurate.

Note   If you have multiple versions of Python installed on your system, the `pip` command will install into whichever Python version environment is the default. To use `pip` to install to a specific version, use `pipN` where N is the version. For example, `pip3` installs packages in the Python 3 environment.

The `pip` command is very handy because it makes installing registered Python packages—those packages registered in the Python Package Index, abbreviated as PyPI[1] (`https://pypi.python.org/pypi`)—very easy. The `pip` command will download, unpack, and install using a single command. Let's discover how to install each of the packages we need.

---

[1]Also called the cheese shop, which is a reference to the Cheese Shop skit from Monty Python's Flying Circus (`https://en.wikipedia.org/wiki/Cheese_Shop_sketch`).

Caution   Some systems may require running pip with elevated privileges such as sudo (Linux, macOS), or in a command window run as an administrator user (Windows 10). You will know if you need elevated privileges if the install fails to copy files due to permission issues.

Installing Flask

Listing 8-1 demonstrates how to install Flask using the command, `pip install flask`. Note that the command downloads the necessary components, extracts them, and then runs the setup for each. In this case, we see Flask is composed of several components including Werkzeug, MarkupSafe, and Jinja2. We will learn more about some of these in the "Flask Primer" section.

Listing 8-1.   Installing Flask

```
$ pip3 install flask
Collecting flask
  Using cached Flask-0.12.2-py2.py3-none-any.whl
Collecting Werkzeug>=0.7 (from flask)
  Downloading Werkzeug-0.14.1-py2.py3-none-any.whl (322kB)
    100% |███████████████████████████████|
███████████| 327kB 442kB/s
Collecting Jinja2>=2.4 (from flask)
  Using cached Jinja2-2.10-py2.py3-none-any.whl
Collecting itsdangerous>=0.21 (from flask)
  Using cached itsdangerous-0.24.tar.gz
Collecting click>=2.0 (from flask)
  Downloading click-6.7-py2.py3-none-any.whl (71kB)
    100% |███████████████████████████████|
███████████| 71kB 9.4MB/s
Collecting MarkupSafe>=0.23 (from Jinja2>=2.4->flask)
  Using cached MarkupSafe-1.0.tar.gz
Installing collected packages: Werkzeug, MarkupSafe, Jinja2, itsdangerous,
click, flask
  Running setup.py install for MarkupSafe ... done
```

```
Running setup.py install for itsdangerous ... done
```
Successfully installed Jinja2-2.10 MarkupSafe-1.0 Werkzeug-0.14.1 click-6.7
flask-0.12.2 itsdangerous-0.24

Installing Flask-Script

Listing 8-2 demonstrates how to install Flask-Script using the command, pip install
flask-script. Note that in this case, we see the installation checking for prerequisites
and their versions.

Listing 8-2. Installing Flask-Script

```
$ pip3 install flask-script
Collecting flask-script
  Using cached Flask-Script-2.0.6.tar.gz
Requirement already satisfied: Flask in /Library/Frameworks/Python.
framework/Versions/3.6/lib/python3.6/site-packages (from flask-script)
Requirement already satisfied: click>=2.0 in /Library/Frameworks/Python.
framework/Versions/3.6/lib/python3.6/site-packages (from Flask->flask-
script)
Requirement already satisfied: Jinja2>=2.4 in /Library/Frameworks/Python.
framework/Versions/3.6/lib/python3.6/site-packages (from Flask->flask-
script)
Requirement already satisfied: Werkzeug>=0.7 in /Library/Frameworks/Python.
framework/Versions/3.6/lib/python3.6/site-packages (from Flask->flask-
script)
Requirement already satisfied: itsdangerous>=0.21 in /Library/Frameworks/
Python.framework/Versions/3.6/lib/python3.6/site-packages (from Flask-
>flask-script)
Requirement already satisfied: MarkupSafe>=0.23 in /Library/Frameworks/
Python.framework/Versions/3.6/lib/python3.6/site-packages (from
Jinja2>=2.4->Flask->flask-script)
Installing collected packages: flask-script
  Running setup.py install for flask-script ... done
Successfully installed flask-script-2.0.6
```

Installing Flask-Bootstrap

Listing 8-3 demonstrates how to install Flask-Bootstrap using the command, pip install flask-bootstrap. Once again, we see the installation checking for prerequisites and their versions as well as installation of dependent components.

Listing 8-3. Installing Flask-Bootstrap

```
$ pip3 install flask-bootstrap
Collecting flask-bootstrap
  Downloading Flask-Bootstrap-3.3.7.1.tar.gz (456kB)
    100% |████████████████████████████████|
  ███████████| 460kB 267kB/s
Requirement already satisfied: Flask>=0.8 in /Library/Frameworks/Python.
framework/Versions/3.6/lib/python3.6/site-packages (from flask-bootstrap)
Collecting dominate (from flask-bootstrap)
  Downloading dominate-2.3.1.tar.gz
Collecting visitor (from flask-bootstrap)
  Downloading visitor-0.1.3.tar.gz
Requirement already satisfied: click>=2.0 in /Library/Frameworks/Python.
framework/Versions/3.6/lib/python3.6/site-packages (from Flask>=0.8->flask-
bootstrap)
Requirement already satisfied: Jinja2>=2.4 in /Library/Frameworks/Python.
framework/Versions/3.6/lib/python3.6/site-packages (from Flask>=0.8->flask-
bootstrap)
Requirement already satisfied: Werkzeug>=0.7 in /Library/Frameworks/Python.
framework/Versions/3.6/lib/python3.6/site-packages (from Flask>=0.8->flask-
bootstrap)
Requirement already satisfied: itsdangerous>=0.21 in /Library/Frameworks/
Python.framework/Versions/3.6/lib/python3.6/site-packages (from Flask>=0.8-
>flask-bootstrap)
Requirement already satisfied: MarkupSafe>=0.23 in /Library/Frameworks/
Python.framework/Versions/3.6/lib/python3.6/site-packages (from
Jinja2>=2.4->Flask>=0.8->flask-bootstrap)
Installing collected packages: dominate, visitor, flask-bootstrap
  Running setup.py install for dominate ... done
```

```
  Running setup.py install for visitor ... done
  Running setup.py install for flask-bootstrap ... done
Successfully installed dominate-2.3.1 flask-bootstrap-3.3.7.1 visitor-0.1.3
```

Installing Flask-WTF

Listing 8-4 demonstrates how to install Flask-WTF using the command, `pip install flask-wtf`.

Listing 8-4. Installing Flask-WTF

```
$ pip3 install flask-wtf
Collecting flask-wtf
  Downloading Flask_WTF-0.14.2-py2.py3-none-any.whl
Requirement already satisfied: WTForms in /Library/Frameworks/Python.
framework/Versions/3.6/lib/python3.6/site-packages (from flask-wtf)
Requirement already satisfied: Flask in /Library/Frameworks/Python.
framework/Versions/3.6/lib/python3.6/site-packages (from flask-wtf)
Requirement already satisfied: Jinja2>=2.4 in /Library/Frameworks/Python.
framework/Versions/3.6/lib/python3.6/site-packages (from Flask->flask-wtf)
Requirement already satisfied: click>=2.0 in /Library/Frameworks/Python.
framework/Versions/3.6/lib/python3.6/site-packages (from Flask->flask-wtf)
Requirement already satisfied: Werkzeug>=0.7 in /Library/Frameworks/Python.
framework/Versions/3.6/lib/python3.6/site-packages (from Flask->flask-wtf)
Requirement already satisfied: itsdangerous>=0.21 in /Library/Frameworks/
Python.framework/Versions/3.6/lib/python3.6/site-packages (from Flask->
flask-wtf)
Requirement already satisfied: MarkupSafe>=0.23 in /Library/Frameworks/
Python.framework/Versions/3.6/lib/python3.6/site-packages (from
Jinja2>=2.4->Flask->flask-wtf)
Installing collected packages: flask-wtf
Successfully installed flask-wtf-0.14.2
```

Installing WTForms

The following demonstrates how to install WTForms using the command, `pip install WTforms`. In this case, the installation is simple because we only need the one package.

```
$ pip3 install wtforms
Collecting wtforms
  Using cached WTForms-2.1.zip
Installing collected packages: wtforms
  Running setup.py install for wtforms ... done
Successfully installed wtforms-2.1
```

USING PYTHON VIRTUAL ENVIRONMENTS

One of the nice things about working with Python is you can use a virtual environment to try things out. A virtual environment is a local (think private) installation of Python, which you can install packages and make changes to the Python environment without affecting the global Python installation on your system. So, for example, if you used a virtual environment to install Flask, it is only available to that virtual environment – it doesn't affect any other virtual environment or the global Python installation.

To use a virtual environment, you must have the virtualenv application installed. Not all systems have this and indeed it isn't supported on all platforms (but is on many). To install virtual environment on Linux, use the command, sudo apt-get install python-virtualenv. To install virtual environment on macOS, use the command, sudo easy_install virtualenv. To install virtual environment on Windows 10, you must download ez_setup.py (part of setuptools) from https://github.com/pypa/setuptools. Once downloaded, open a command window with administrative privileges then enter the command, python ez_setup.py to install easy_install then enter the command, easy_install virtualenv to install virtual environment.

To create and use a virtual environment, issue the command, virtualenv project1. This creates a folder name project1 with the virtual environment files that keep track of all the changes made when in that environment. To activate the environment, use the source ./project1/bin/activate command. Note that we are invoking a script in the new virtual environment folder. This will change your prompt to indicate you're using a virtual environment. To deactivate the environment, use the deactivate command while the virtual environment is active. This will return your Python environment back to the global defaults. The following demonstrates these commands on macOS.

```
$ mkdir virtual_environments
$ cd virtual_environments
$ virtualenv project1
New python executable in /virtual_environments/project1/bin/python
Installing setuptools, pip, wheel...done.
$ source ./project1/bin/activate
[Do something Python related here. Changes apply only to the active
virtual environment.]
(project1) $ deactivate
```

Removing a virtual environment is simply done by deleting the environment folder (after deactivating it):

```
$ deactivate
$ rm -r /virtual_environments/project1
```

Some recommend always using a virtual environment when experimenting with new things in Python, and for some things such as untrusted or untried libraries or libraries that conflict with existing installed libraries, which is a good practice. However, for mainstream items such as Flask and its supporting libraries, it isn't needed. If you want to use a virtual environment for the proceeding projects, feel free to do so. Just remember to activate it before issuing any Python commands and deactivate it when you're finished.

To learn more about virtual environments, see `https://virtualenv.pypa.io/en/stable/`.

You should also have the MySQL Connector/Python 8.0.5 or later database connector installed. If you do not, download it from `https://dev.mysql.com/downloads/connector/python/` and install it. If you have multiple versions of Python installed, be sure to install it in all Python environments you want to use. Otherwise, you may see an error like the following when starting the code.

```
$ python3 ./mylibrary_v1.py runserver -p 5001
Traceback (most recent call last):
  File "./mylibrary_v1.py", line 18, in <module>
    from database.library_v1 import Library, Author, Publisher, Book
  File ".../Ch08/version1/database/library_v1.py", line 15, in <module>
    import mysql.connector
ModuleNotFoundError: No module named 'mysql'
```

Pip also can be used to install MySQL Connector/Python. The following shows how to use PIP to install the connector.

```
$ pip3 install mysql-connector-python
Collecting mysql-connector-python
  Downloading mysql_connector_python-8.0.6-cp36-cp36m-macosx_10_12_x86_64.
whl (3.2MB)
    100% |███████████████████████████████
███████████| 3.2MB 16.9MB/s
Installing collected packages: mysql-connector-python
Successfully installed mysql-connector-python-8.0.6
```

If you installed MySQL Connector/Python manually or from source, you also may need to install Protobuf. You can use pip to install it as shown in the following.

```
$ pip3 install protobuf
Collecting protobuf
  Downloading protobuf-3.5.1-py2.py3-none-any.whl (388kB)
    100% |███████████████████████████████
███████████| 389kB 414kB/s
Requirement already satisfied: setuptools in /Library/Frameworks/Python.
framework/Versions/3.6/lib/python3.6/site-packages (from protobuf)
Requirement already satisfied: six>=1.9 in /Library/Frameworks/Python.
framework/Versions/3.6/lib/python3.6/site-packages/six-1.10.0-py3.6.egg
(from protobuf)
Installing collected packages: protobuf
Successfully installed protobuf-3.5.1
```

Now that our computer is setup, let's take a crash course on Flask and its associated extensions.

Flask Primer

Flask is one of several web application libraries (sometimes called *frameworks* or application programming interfaces—APIs) for use with Python. Flask is unique among the choices in that it is small and, once you are familiar with how it works, easy to use. That is, once you write the initialization code, most of your work with Flask will be limited to creating web pages, redirecting responses, and writing your feature code.

Flask is considered a micro framework because it is small and lightweight, and it doesn't force you into a box writing code specifically to interact with the framework. It provides everything you need leaving the choice of what to use in your code up to you.

Flask is made of two major components that provide the basic functionality: a Web Server Gateway Interface (WSGI) that handles all the work hosting web pages; and a template library for easier web page development that reduces the need to learn HTML, removes repetitive constructs, and provides a scripting capability for HTML code. The WSGI component is named *Werkzeug*, which loosely translated from German means, "work stuff" (http://werkzeug.pocoo.org/). The template component is named *Jinja2* and is modelled after Django (http://jinja.pocoo.org/docs/2.10/). Both were developed and maintained by the originators of Flask. Finally, both components are installed when you install Flask.

Flask is also an extensible library allowing other developers to create additions (extensions) to the basic library to add functionality. We saw how to install some of the extensions available for Flask in the previous section. We will be using the scripting, bootstrap, and WTForms extensions in this chapter. Having the ability to pick and choose the extensions you want means you can keep your application as small as necessary adding only what you need.

One of the components that you may consider "missing" from flask is the ability to interact with other services such as database systems. This was a purposeful design and functionality like this can be achieved through extensions. In fact, there are several database extensions available for Flask including those that allow you to work with MySQL. However, because we want to use the X DevAPI, we must use the Oracle-provided connector, MySQL Connector/Python. This is not only possible, it also illustrates the freedom you have when using Flask; we aren't limited to certain functionality as database server access, we can use any other Python library we want or require.[2]

Tip   If you're curious about the MySQL support for Flask, see http://flask-mysql.readthedocs.io/en/latest/.

---

[2]If you use enough frameworks, you will eventually encounter those that are not extensible and force you to use their database features, which are often too limited and may not meet your needs. How sad it is to discover a new framework only to find out you can't get to your data or you must refactor your database to use it in the framework.

Flask, together with the extensions described previously, provides all the wiring and plumbing you need to make a Web application in Python. It removes almost all the burdens required to write web applications such as interpreting client response packets, routing, HTML form handling, and more. If you've ever written a web application in Python, you will appreciate the ability to create robust web pages without the complexity of writing HTML and style sheets. Once you're familiar with how to use Flask, it will allow you to focus on the code for your application rather than spending a lot of time writing the user interface.

Now, let's get started learning Flask! If you take your time and try the sample application, your first Flask application will work on the first try. The hardest part of learning Flask is already past—installing Flask and its extensions. The rest is learning the concepts of writing applications in Flask. Before we do that, let's learn more about the terminology in Flask as well as how to setup the base code we will use to initialize the application instance that we will be using in this chapter.

Tip   If you want to explore Flask further, you should consider reading the online documentation, user guide, and examples at `http://flask.pocoo.org/docs/0.12/`.

Terminology

Flask is designed to make a lot of the tedium of writing web applications easier. In Flask parlance, a web page is rendered using two parts of your code: a view, which is defined in the HTML file(s) and a route, which processes the requests from a client. Recall, we can see one of two requests: a `GET` request that requests loading of a web page (read from the client's perspective), and a `POST` request that sends data from the client via the web page to the server (write from the client's perspective). Both requests are handled in Flask using functions you define.

These functions then render the web page to send back to the client to satisfy the request. Flask calls the functions view functions (or views for short). The way Flask knows which method to call is using decorators that identify the URL path (called a route in Flask). You can decorate a function with one or more routes making it possible to provide multiple ways to reach the view. The decorator used is `@app.route(<path>)`. The following shows an example of multiple routes for a view function.

```
@app.route('/book', methods=['GET', 'POST'])
@app.route('/book/<string:isbn_selected>', methods=['GET', 'POST'])
def book(isbn_selected=None):
    notes = None
    form = BookForm()
    form.publisher.choices = []
    form.authors.choices = []
    new_note = ""
    if request.method == 'POST':
        pass
    return render_template("book.html", form=form, notes=notes)
```

Note that there are multiple decorators. The first is book, which allows us to use a URL such as localhost:5000/book, which causes Flask to route execution to the book() function. The second is book/<isbn_selected>, which demonstrates how to use variables to pass information to the view. In this case, if the user (the application) uses the URL localhost:5000/book/978-1-4842-1294-3, which Flask places the value, 978-1-4842-1294-3, in the isbn_selected variable. In this way, we can pass information dynamically to our views.

Note also that the routes specify the methods allowed for each route. In this application, we can have a GET or POST for either route. If you leave these off the decorator, the default is GET only making the web page read only.

Finally, note that at the end of the function we return with a call to the render_template() function (imported from the flask module) that tells flask to return (refresh) the web page with data we've acquired or assigned. The web page, book.html, although part of the view is called a form in Flask. It is this concept that we will use to retrieve information from the database and send it to the user. We can return a simple HTML string (or an entire file) or what is called a form. Because we are using the Flask-WTF and WTForms extensions, we can return a template rendered as a form class. We will discuss forms, form classes, and other routes and views for the chapter project in a later section. As you will see, templates are another powerful feature making it easy to create web pages.

WHAT'S A DECORATOR?

In Python, we can specify special handling parameters by using decorators. Decorators are simply a way to change the behavior of functions. For example, you can use decorators to add stronger type checking, define macros, and invoke functions before and after execution. Decorators in Flask for routing are some of the best examples of using decorators correctly. To learn more about decorators, see `https://www.python.org/dev/peps/pep-0318`.

Flask builds a list of all the routes in the application making it easy for the application to route execution to the correct function when requested. But, what happens when a route is requested but it doesn't exist in the application? By default, you will get a generic error message like "Not Found. The requested URL was not found on the server." We will see how to add our own custom error handling routes in a later section.

Now that we know more about the terminology used in Flask and how it is structured to work with web pages, let's look at how a typical Flask application with the extensions we need is constructed.

Initialization and the Application Instance

Flask and its extensions provide the entry point for your web application. Instead of writing all that onerous code yourself, Flask does it for you! The Flask extensions we will be using in this chapter include Flask-Script, Flask-Bootstrap, Flask-WTF, and WTForms. The following sections briefly describe each.

Flask-Script

Flask-Script enables scripting in Flask applications by adding a command-line parser (manifested as manager) that you can use to link to functions you've written. This is enabled by decorating the function with @manager.command. The best way to understand what this does for us is through an example.

The following is a basic, raw Flask application that does nothing. It's not even a "hello, world" example because nothing is shown and there are no web pages hosted—it's just the raw Flask application.

```
from flask import Flask       # import the Flask framework
app = Flask(__name__)         # initialize the application
if __name__ == "__main__":    # guard for running the code
    app.run()                 # launch the application
```

Note the app.run() call. This is called the server startup and is executed when we load the script using the Python interpreter. When we run this code, all we see is the default message from Flask as shown in the following. Note that we don't have any way to see help as there are no such options. We also see that the code launches using defaults for the web server (which we can change in code if we desire). For example, we can change the port that the server is listening.

```
$ python ./flask-ex.py --help
 * Running on http://127.0.0.1:5000/ (Press CTRL+C to quit)
```

With Flask-Script, we add not only a help option but options to control the server. The following code shows how easy it is to add the statements to enable Flask-Script. The new statements are highlighted in bold.

```
from flask import Flask              # import the Flask framework
from flask_script import Manager # import the flask script manager class

app = Flask(__name__)                # initialize the application
manager = Manager(app)               # initialize the script manager class

# Sample method linked as a command-line option
@manager.command
def hello_world():
    """Print 'Hello, world!'"""
    print("Hello, world!")

if __name__ == "__main__":           # guard for running the code
    manager.run()                    # launch the application via manager class
```

When this code is run, we can see there are additional options available. Note that the documentation string (immediately following the method definition) is shown as the help text for the command added.

```
$ python ./flask-script-ex.py --help
usage: flask-script-ex.py [-?] {hello_world,shell,runserver} ...

positional arguments:
  {hello_world,shell,runserver}
    hello_world          Print 'Hello, world!'
    shell                Runs a Python shell inside Flask application context.
    runserver            Runs the Flask development server i.e. app.run()

optional arguments:
  -?, --help             show this help message and exit
```

Note that we see the command line arguments (commands) we added, hello_world, but we also see two new ones supplied by Flask-Script; shell and runserver. You must choose one of these commands when launching the server. The shell command allows you to use the code in a Python interpreter or similar tool and the runserver executes the code starting the web server.

Not only can we get help about the commands and options, Flask-Script also provides more control over the server from the command line. In fact, we can see all the options for each command by appending the --help option as shown in the following.

```
$ python ./flask-script-ex.py runserver --help
usage: flask-script-ex.py runserver [-?] [-h HOST] [-p PORT] [--threaded]
                                    [--processes PROCESSES]
                                    [--passthrough-errors] [-d] [-D] [-r] [-R]
                                    [--ssl-crt SSL_CRT] [--ssl-key SSL_KEY]

Runs the Flask development server i.e. app.run()

optional arguments:
  -?, --help             show this help message and exit
  -h HOST, --host HOST
  -p PORT, --port PORT
  --threaded
  --processes PROCESSES
```

```
--passthrough-errors
-d, --debug              enable the Werkzeug debugger (DO NOT use in production
                         code)
-D, --no-debug           disable the Werkzeug debugger
-r, --reload             monitor Python files for changes (not 100% safe for
                         production use)
-R, --no-reload          do not monitor Python files for changes
--ssl-crt SSL_CRT        Path to ssl certificate
--ssl-key SSL_KEY        Path to ssl key
```

Note here that we can control all manner of things about the server including the port, host, and even how it executes.

Finally, we can execute the method we've decorated as a command-line option as shown in the following.

```
$ python ./flask-script-ex.py hello_world
Hello, world!
```

Thus, Flask-Script provides some very powerful features with only a few lines of code. You've got to love that!

Flask-Bootstrap

Flask-Bootstrap was originally developed by Twitter for making uniform, nice-looking web clients. It is fortunate that they've made it a Flask extension so that everyone can take advantage of its features. Flask-Bootstrap is a framework on its own and provides even more command-line control as well as user interface components for clean, attractive web pages. It also is compatible with the newest web browsers.

The framework does its magic behind the scenes as a client library of cascading style sheets (CSS) and scripts that are invoked from the HTML templates (commonly referred to as either *HTML files* or *template files*) in Flask. We will learn more about templates in a later section. Because it is client-side, we won't see much by initializing it in the main application. Regardless, the following shows how to add Flask-bootstrap to our application code. Here, we see we have a skeleton with Flask-Script and Flask-Bootstrap initialized and configured.

```
from flask import Flask          # import the Flask framework
from flask_script import Manager # import the flask script manager class
```

```
from flask_bootstrap import Bootstrap  # import the flask bootstrap
extension

app = Flask(__name__)            # initialize the application
manager = Manager(app)           # initialize the script manager class
bootstrap = Bootstrap(app)       # initialize the bootstrap extension

if __name__ == "__main__":       # guard for running the code
    manager.run()                # launch the application via manager class
```

WTForms

WTForms is a component we need to support the Flask-WTF extension. It provides much of the functionality that the Flask-WTF component provides (because the Flask-WTF component is a Flask-specific wrapper for WTForms). Therefore, we need only install it as a prerequisite for Flask-WTF and we will discuss it in the context of Flask-WTF.

Note   Some package installations of Flask-WTF may include WTForms.

Flask-WTF

The Flask-WTF extension is an interesting component providing several very useful additions: most notable for our purposes integration with WTForms (a framework agnostic component) that permits the creation of form classes, and additional web security in the form of cross-site request forgery (CSRF) protection. These two features allow you to take your web application to a higher level of sophistication.

Form Classes

Form classes provide a hierarchy of classes that make defining web pages more logical. With Flask-WTF, you can define your form using two pieces of code; a special class derived from FormForm class (imported from the Flask framework) that you use to define fields using one or more additional classes that provide programmatic access to data, and an HTML file (or template) for rendering the web page. In this way, we see an abstraction layer (form classes) over the HTML files. We will see more about the HTML files in the next section.

Using form classes, you can define one or more fields such as TextField for text, StringField for a string, and more. Better still, you can define validators that allow you to programmatically describe the data. For example, you can define a minimum and maximum number of characters for a text field. If the number of characters submitted is outside of the range, an error message is generated. And, yes, you can define an error message! The following lists some of the validators available. See http://wtforms. readthedocs.io/en/latest/validators.html for a complete list of validators.

- DataRequired: Determines if input field is empty

- Email: Ensures the field follows email ID conventions

- IPAddress: Validates IP addresses

- Length: Ensures length of text is in given range

- NumberRange: Ensures text is numeric and within given range

- URL: Validates URLs

To form classes, we must import the class and any field classes we want to use in the preamble of the application. The following shows an example of importing the form class and form field classes. In this example, we also import some validators that we will use for validating the data automatically.

```
from flask_wtf import FlaskForm
from wtforms import (HiddenField, TextField, TextAreaField, SelectField,
                     SelectMultipleField, IntegerField, SubmitField)
from wtforms.validators import Required, Length
```

To define a form class, we must derive a new class from FlaskForm. From there, we can construct the class however we want but it is intended to allow you to define the fields. The FlaskForm parent class includes all the necessary code that Flask needs to instantiate and use the form class.

Let's look at a simple example. The following shows the form class for the author web page. The author table, which we will link to this code via the view function, contains three fields; an auto increment field (authorid), the first name of the author (firstname), and the last name of the author (lastname). Because the author id field is not something users need to see, we make that field a hidden field and the other fields derivatives of the TextField() class. Note how these were defined in the listing with names (labels) as the first parameter.

```
class AuthorForm(FlaskForm):
    authorid = HiddenField('AuthorId')
    firstname = TextField('First name', validators=[
            Required(message=REQUIRED.format("Firstname")),
            Length(min=1, max=64, message=RANGE.format("Firstname", 1, 64))
        ])
    lastname = TextField( 'Last name', validators=[
            Required(message=REQUIRED.format("Lastname")),
            Length(min=1, max=64, message=RANGE.format("Lastname", 1, 64))
        ])
    create_button = SubmitField('Add')
    del_button = SubmitField('Delete')
```

Note also that we defined an array of validators in the form of function calls imported from the WTForms component for the fields. In each case, we used strings for the messages to make the code easier to read and more uniform. These strings include the following.

```
REQUIRED = "{0} field is required."
RANGE = "{0} range is {1} to {2} characters."
```

We use the Required() validator that indicates the field must have a value. We augment the default error message with the name of the field to make it easier for the user to understand. We also use a Length() validator function that defines the minimal and maximum length of the field data. Once again, we augment the default error message. Validators are applied only on POST operations (when a submit event has occurred).

Next, we see there are two SubmitField() instances: one for a create (add) button, and another for a delete button. As you may surmise, in HTML parlance, these fields are rendered as <input> fields with a type of "submit".

Finally, to use a form class we instantiate the class in a view function. The following shows a stub for the author view function. Note that we instantiate the form class named AuthorForm() and assign it to a variable named form, which is passed to the render_template() function.

```
@app.route('/author', methods=['GET', 'POST'])
@app.route('/author/<int:author_id>', methods=['GET', 'POST'])
def author(author_id=None):
    form = AuthorForm()
```

```
if request.method == 'POST':
    pass
return render_template("author.html", form=form)
```

There are several field classes available for use. Table 8-2 shows a sample of the most commonly used field classes (also called HTML fields). You also can derive from these fields to create custom field classes and provide text for the label that you can display next to the field (or as the button text for example). We will see an example of this in a later section.

Table 8-2. *WTForms Field Classes*

Field Class	Description
BooleanField	A checkbox with True and False values
DateField	Accepts date values
DateTimeField	Accepts datetime values
DecimalField	Accepts decimal values
FileField	File upload field
FloatField	Accepts a floating-point value
HiddenField	Hidden text field
IntegerField	Accepts integer values
PasswordField	A password (masked) text field
RadioField	A list of radio buttons
SelectField	A dropdown list (choose one)
SelectMultipleField	A dropdown list of choices (choose one or more)
StringField	Accepts simple text
SubmitField	Form submit button
TextAreaField	Multiline text field

CSRF Protection

CSRF Protection is a technique that permits developers to sign web pages with an encrypted key that makes it more difficult for hackers to spoof a GET or POST request. This is accomplished by first placing a special key in the application code and then referencing the key in each of our HTML files. The following shows an example of the preamble of an application. Note that all we need to do is assign the SECRET_KEY index of the app.config array with a phrase. This should be a phrase that is not easily guessed.

```
from flask import Flask           # import the Flask framework
from flask_script import Manager  # import the flask script manager class
from flask_bootstrap import Bootstrap  # import the flask bootstrap
extension

app = Flask(__name__)             # initialize the application
app.config['SECRET_KEY'] = "He says, he's already got one!"
manager = Manager(app)            # initialize the script manager class
bootstrap = Bootstrap(app)        # initialize the bootstrap extension

if __name__ == "__main__":        # guard for running the code
    manager.run()                 # launch the application via manager class
```

To activate the CSRF in our web pages, we merely add the form.csrf_token to the HTML file. This is a special hidden field that Flask uses to validate the requests. We will see more about where to place this in a later section. But first, let's see a cool feature of Flask called flash.

Message Flashing

There are many cool features in Flask. The creators and the creators of the Flask extensions seem to have thought of everything—even error messaging. Consider a typical web application. How do you communicate errors to the user? Do you redirect to a new page,[3] issue a popup,[4] or perhaps display the error on the page? Flask has a solution for this called message flashing.

---

[3]Which I find particularly annoying when entering data as it is often lost when you return to the page. Please, don't use this method.

[4]If you have locked down your browser for better security, allowing popups can be problematic.

Message flashing is accomplished using the flash() method from the Flask framework. We simply import it in the preamble of our code then when we want to display a message, we call the flash() function passing in the error message we want to see. Flask will present the error in a nicely formatted box presented at the top of the form. It doesn't replace the form and isn't a popup but it does allow the user to dismiss the message. You can use flash messaging to communicate errors, warnings, and even state changes to the user. Figure 8-1 shows an example of a flash message. In this example, we see two flash messages that demonstrate you can display multiple messages at the same time. Note the small X to the right of the message used to dismiss the image.

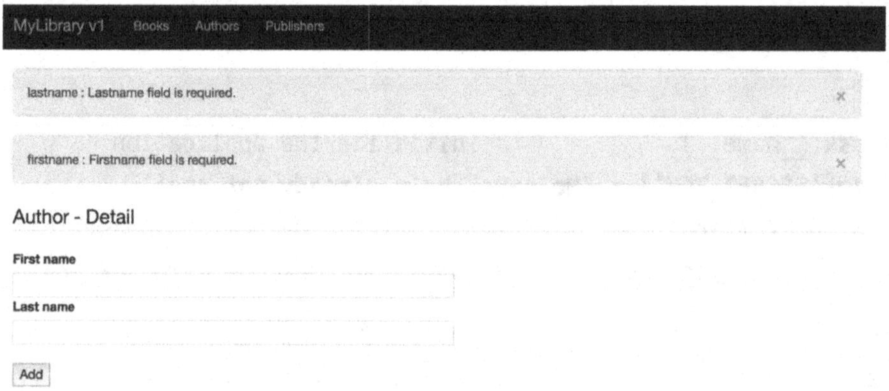

Figure 8-1. *Example flash message*

We will see a mechanism to build flash messaging into all our web pages in the next section.

HTML Files and Templates

Let's review our tour so far. We have discovered how to initialize an application with the various components, learned how Flask uses routes via the decorators to create a set of URLs for the application, these routes are directed to a view function, which instantiates the form class. The next piece of the puzzle is how to link the HTML web page to the form class.

Recall, this is done via the render_template() function where we pass in the name of a HTML file for processing. The reason template is in the name is because we can use the Jinja2 template component to make writing web pages easier. More specific, the HTML file contains both HTML tags and Jinja2 template constructs.

354

Note   All HTML files (templates) must be stored in the `templates` folder in the same location as the main application code. For example, if your code is in a file named `my-flask-app.py`, there should be a `templates` folder in the same folder as `my-flask-app.py`. If you place them anywhere else, Flask won't be able to find the HTML files.

Templates together with form classes are where the user interface is designed. In short, templates are used to contain presentation logic and HTML files are used to contain the presentation data. These topics are likely to be the areas where some may need to spend some time experimenting with how to use them. The following sections give you a brief overview of Jinja2 templates and how to use them in our HTML files through demonstration of working examples. See the online Flask documentation noted for more details.

Jinja2 Templates Overview

Jinja2 templates, (or *templates*), are used to contain any presentation logic like looping through data arrays, making decisions on what to display, and even formatting and presentation settings. If you are familiar with other web development environments, you may have seen this encapsulated in scripts or enabled through embedded scripting such as JavaScript.

Recall we rendered our web pages in our main code. This function tells Flask to read the file specified and convert the template constructs (render them) into HTML. That is, Flask will expand and compile the template constructs into HTML that the web server can present to the client.

There are several template constructs you can use to control the flow of execution, loops, and even comments. Whenever you want to use a template construct (think scripting language), you enclose it with {% %} prefix and suffix. This enables the Flask framework to recognize the construct as a template operation rather than HTML.

However, it is not unusual and quite normal to see the template constructs intermixed with HTML tags. In fact, that is exactly how you should do it. After all, the files you will create are named .html. They just happen to contain template constructs. Does that mean you can only use templates when working with Flask? No, certainly not. If you want, you can render a pure HTML file!

At first, looking at templates can be quite daunting. But it isn't that difficult. Just look at all the lines with the {% and %} as the "code" portions.[5] You also may see comments in the form of {# #} prefix and suffix.

Caution   All template constructs require a space after the {% and before the %}.

If you look at the template, you will see the constructs and tags and formatted using indentation of two spaces. Indentation and whitespace in general doesn't matter outside the tags and constructs. However, most developers will use some form of indentation to make the file easier to read. In fact, most coding guidelines require indentation.

One of the cool features of templates beyond the constructs (think code) is the ability to create a hierarchy of templates. This allows you to create a "base" template that your other templates can use. For example, you can create a boilerplate of template constructs and HTML tags so that all your web pages look the same.

Recall from our look at Flask-Bootstrap, bootstrap provides several nice formatting features. One of those features is creating a pleasant looking navigation bar. Naturally, we would want this to appear on all our web pages. We can do this by defining it in the base template and extending it in our other template (HTML) files. Let's look at a base template for the library application. Listing 8-5 shows the base template for the library application. Line numbers have been added for ease of discussion.

Listing 8-5. Sample Base Template

```
01 {% extends "bootstrap/base.html" %}
02 {% block title %}MyLibrary{% endblock %}
03 {% block navbar %}
04 <div class="navbar navbar-inverse" role="navigation">
05     <div class="container">
06         <div class="navbar-header">
07             <button type="button" class="navbar-toggle" data-
                toggle="collapse" data-target=".navbar-collapse">
08                 <span class="sr-only">Toggle navigation</span>
09                 <span class="icon-bar"></span>
```

---

[5]Few will use this word to describe the template constructs and although not accurate, it is okay to consider it a code-like component if it helps to learn how to use Jinja2 templates.

```
10                    <span class="icon-bar"></span>
11                    <span class="icon-bar"></span>
12                </button>
13                <a class="navbar-brand" href="/">MyLibrary Base</a>
14            </div>
15            <div class="navbar-collapse collapse">
16                <ul class="nav navbar-nav">
17                    <li><a href="/list/book">Books</a></li>
18                </ul>
19                <ul class="nav navbar-nav">
20                    <li><a href="/list/author">Authors</a></li>
21                </ul>
22                <ul class="nav navbar-nav">
23                    <li><a href="/list/publisher">Publishers</a></li>
24                </ul>
25            </div>
26        </div>
27 </div>
28 {% endblock %}
29
30 {% block content %}
31 <div class="container">
32     {% for message in get_flashed_messages() %}
33     <div class="alert alert-warning">
34         <button type="button" class="close" data-dismiss="alert">&times;
           </button>
35         {{ message }}
36     </div>
37     {% endfor %}
38     {% block page_content %}{% endblock %}
39 </div>
40 {% endblock %}
```

Wow, there is a lot going on here! Note the first line. This tells us that we're inheriting (extending) another template named bootstrap/base.html template. This is provided for you free when you install Flask-Bootstrap and it is this template that contains support

357

for the bootstrap navigation bar feature. This is a very common method of building a set of HTML files for a Flask application as we will see later in this section.

Let's start our tour with a bird's eye view. Note that there are two "blocks" designated with {% block <> %} and {% endblock %} (lines 2, 3, 28, 30, 38, and 40). These are logical sections where we can apply formatting to the tags and constructs inside the block. In coding terms, this would be like a code block. The first block defines the title for the page. In this case, MyLibrary, which is the executable name for the library application.

The second block defines the navigation bar (think menu) for the application. Note in that section lines 5–27 define simple HTML <div> tags forming the items on the navigation bar. Of note are line 13, which specifies text to be used as the name of the application, which appears to the left of the navigation bar and acts like a "home" link. Lines 15–24 define the navigation bar items (submit buttons) for three web pages (forms). Note also the collapse keyword. This indicates it is possible to collapse the navigation bar. So, what does the navigation bar look like? Figure 8-2 shows the navigation bar for the library application in normal, collapsed, and expanded mode. The normal and collapsed mode operates based on the size of the browser window collapsing when the navigation item labels cannot be displayed. The expanded mode operates when users click on the button to the right when in collapsed mode. Cool, eh?

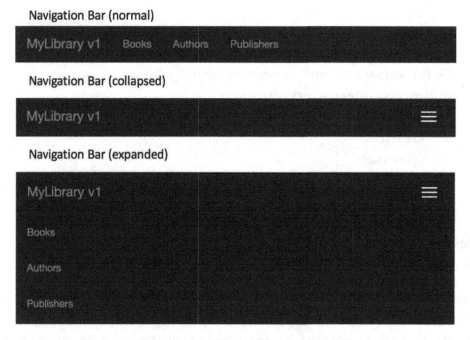

Figure 8-2. *Bootstrap navigation bar demonstration*

The last block in lines 30–39 defines the template construct and HTML tags for the flash messages. Let's take a deeper look at this code (repeated here for convenience).

```
30 {% block content %}
31 <div class="container">
32     {% for message in get_flashed_messages() %}
33     <div class="alert alert-warning">
34         <button type="button" class="close" data-dismiss="alert">&times;
           </button>
35         {{ message }}
36     </div>
37     {% endfor %}
38     {% block page_content %}{% endblock %}
39 </div>
40 {% endblock %}
```

Here, we see another <div> tag that contains a button. This is the button we use to dismiss the flash message. Note that this tag is placed inside a for loop as designated with {% for ... %} and ended with {% endfor %}. In this case, we are looping over the messages returned from the get_flashed_messages() function, which is collected by the flash() function in our application code. This tells us several things: we can use loops in our templates, the template allows the display of multiple images (which we saw earlier), and templates can call functions! This is an example of the power of templates.

Note   Templates are not required to be formatted in any manner. That is, whitespace doesn't do anything outside the HTML tags or template constructs.

Finally, note the variable we defined in the for loop in line 32. This variable, message, is defined local to the block in which it appears (in this case, the for loop), and can be referenced at any point by enclosing it in {{ }}. For example, we see in line 35 we use {{ message }} inside the <div> tag, which means this text will appear on the client rendered in place by Flask. The use of variables will become more important when we discuss how to build user interfaces with templates.

Template Language Constructs

The Jinja2 template features are many and a complete discussion of all features is beyond the scope of this book. However, it is handy to have a quick reference for the major constructs of Jinja2. The following present some of the commonly used constructs including some that we discovered in the last section (for completeness). Each is presented with a short example of how the construct would appear in a template. Feel free to refer to this section when exploring the library application later in the chapter or when writing your own Flask applications.

Comments

You can embed your own comments in your templates. You may want to do this to ensure you sufficient explain what you are doing and as a reminder in case you reuse the code later.[6] The following is an example of using comments in templates. Recall, comments begin with {# and end with #} and can span multiple lines.

```
{# This is a line comment written by Dr. Charles Bell on Dec. 12, 2017. #}

{#
   Introducing the MySQL 8 Document Store

   This template defines the base template used for all of the HTML forms
and
   responses in the MyLibrary application. It also defines the menu for the
   basic operations.

   Dr. Charles Bell, 2017
#}
```

Include

If your template files grow and you find there are portions that are reusable such as a <div> tag, you can save the tag and template constructs in a separate file and include it in other templates using the {% include %} construct. The {% include %} construct

---

[6]The older you get, the more often you read code and say, "who wrote this?" Sadly, it's often your own code! A few comments here and there will go a long ways toward remembering what you were doing (and why).

takes as a parameter the name of the file you want to include. As with templates, these must reside in the templates folder. In this way, we avoid repetition and the hassle and error-prone task of maintaining repetitive code.

```
{# Include the utilities common tags for a list. #}
{% include 'utilities.html' %}
```

Macros

Another form of reducing repetitive code is to create a macro for use in your templates (think functions). In this case, we use the {% macro … %} and {% endmacro %} constructs to define a macro that we can call (use) later in our code. The following shows an example of defining a simple macro and later using it inside a loop. Note how we pass variables to the macro for operating on the data.

```
{# Macro definition #}
{% macro bold_me(data) %}
    <b>{{ data }}</b>
{% endmacro %}

{# Invoke the macro #}
{% for value in data %}
    {{ bold_me(value) }}
{% endfor %}
```

Import

One of the best ways to use macros is to place them in a separate code file therefore further enhancing reusability. To use a macro from a separate file, we use the {% import … %} construct supplying the name of the file from which to import. The following shows an example of importing the macro defined previously in a separate file. As with the include, this file must be in the templates folder. Note we can use an alias and refer to the macros using dot notation.

```
{% import 'utilities.html' as utils %}
...
{{ utils.bold_me(value) }}
```

Extend (Inherit)

We can use a hierarchy of templates by inheriting (extending) them. We saw this earlier when we examined a base template. In this case, we use the {% extend ... %} construct supplying the name of the template we want to extend. The following shows an example from the base template previously.

```
{% extends "base.html" %}
```

Blocks

Blocks are used to isolate execution and scope (for variables). We use blocks whenever we want to isolate a set of template constructs (think a code block). The {% block ... %} construct is used with the {% endblock %} construct to define the block. The constructs allow you to name the block. The following shows an example.

```
{% block if_true %}
...
{% endblock if_true %}
```

Loops

Loops are a way to execute the same block multiple times. We do this with the {% for <variable> in <data_array> %} construct. In this case, the loop will iterate over the array replacing the value in <variable> with the value in each index of the array. This construct is great for looping through an array to create a table, show a list of data, and similar presentation activities. The following shows a for loop using in constructing a table. Note that we use two for loops: one to loop over the columns in an array named *columns*, and another to loop over the rows in an array named *rows*.

```
<table border="1" cellpadding="1" cellspacing="1">
  <tr>
    <td style="width:80px"><b>Action</b></td>
    {% for col in columns %}
      {{ col|safe }}
    {% endfor %}
  </tr>
  {% for row in rows %}
    <tr>
```

```
    <td><a href="{{ '/%s/%s'%(kind,row[0]) }}">Modify</a></td>
    {% for col in row[1:] %}
      <td> {{ col }} </td>
    {% endfor %}
  </tr>
  {% endfor %}
</table>
```

You may be wondering at this point how the data in columns and rows gets to the template. Recall the render_template() function. If you want to pass data to the template, you simply list it in the parameters when you render the template. In this case, we would pass the columns and rows as follows. In this case, row_data and col_data are variables defined in the view function and passed to the rows and columns variables in the template through assignment. Cool, eh?

```
render_template("list.html", form=form, rows=row_data, columns=col_data)
```

Conditionals

Conditionals or "if" statements (called tests in the Jinja2 documentation) allow you to make decisions in your template. We use the {% if <condition> %} construct, which is concluded with the {% endif %} construct. If you want an "else", you can use the {% else %} construct. Further, you may chain conditions with the {% elif <condition> %}. You typically use variables or form elements in the conditions and can use the common comparators (for a list of tests, see http://jinja.pocoo.org/docs/2.10/templates/#builtin-tests).

For example, you may want to change the label of a submit field depending on some event. You may want to define one submit button for adding or updating data. That is, when the web page is used to add a new data item, the text should read "Add" but when you update the data using the same web page, we want the text to read "Update". This is one of the keys to reusing the template for both GET and POST requests (read and write). The following shows an example of a conditional used in this manner.

```
{% if form.create_button.label.text == "Update" %}
  {{ form.new_note.label }}
  {{ form.new_note(rows='2',cols='100') }}
{% endif %}
```

```
{% if form.del_button %}
   {{ form.del_button }}
{% endif %}
```

There are two conditions in this example. The first demonstrates how to check the text of a label on the form. Note that here we reference the element on the form with `form.create_button`, which is the name of the field class we defined in the form class, which was instantiated prior to rendering the template (we will see how to do this in a later section). The form variable is passed to the template in the `render_template("book.html", form=form)` call. In this case, we only display the `new_note` field and its label if the button text was set to "Update."

The second example shows a simple test that if the `delete_button` on the form is active (not hidden or deleted), we display it. This is an example of how to display optional submit fields.

Variables and Variable Filters

Variables are a way to save data values for later processing. The most common use of variables is referencing data passed to the template from the view function (via the `render_template()` function). We can also use variables in our templates to save data such as counters, for loop data values, and more. Recall we reference a variable by enclosing it in curly braces `{{ variable }}` or in the case of the for loop, it is defined in the for loop construct. Note that when referenced inside HTML tags, the spaces inside the construct are ignored.

You can also use a filter in your template to change the values in variables. Variable filters are a way to programmatically change values for use in your presentation logic. You can change the case, remove whitespace, and even strip HTML tags or use the raw text directly. In this last case, we use the safe filter, which tells the template to use the text even if it has HTML tags. This is a little tricky because it could open a path for exploitation but if you use the special security feature of WTForms (shown in the next section), it is normally okay to do this but do so sparingly. Table 8-3 shows the commonly used variable filters.

Table 8-3. *Variable Filters*

Filter	Description
Capitalize	Converts the first character of the text to uppercase
Lower	Converts the text to lowercase characters
Safe	Renders the text without escaping special characters
Striptags	Removes HTML tags from text
Title	Capitalizes each word in the string
Trim	Removes leading and trailing whitespace
Upper	Converts the text to uppercase

Tip   For a more in-depth look at Jinja2 template constructs, see
`http://jinja.pocoo.org/`.

Now that we have an overview of how templates work and have defined a base template for the library application, let's look at how to use the base template to form the HTML files for our web pages. As you will see, it involves three concepts we've been discussing and will bring the discussion to a conclusion of how Flask works when building web pages and sending them to the client. We will look at getting data from the client in a later section.

HTML Files Using Templates

Now we are ready to see how to manifest the field classes we defined in our form classes. Let's begin the discussion with a walkthrough of how to present data for the publisher data in the library application. We begin with the form class and the field classes defined to the view function, which renders the template and finally the template itself.

Recall, that the form class is where we define one or more form fields. We will use these field class instances to access the data in our view functions and in the template. Listing 8-6 show the form class (without database access).

Listing 8-6. Publisher Form Class (No Database Code)

```
class PublisherForm(FlaskForm):
    publisherid = HiddenField('PublisherId')
    name = TextField('Name', validators=[
            Required(message=REQUIRED.format("Name")),
            Length(min=1, max=128, message=RANGE.format("Name", 1, 128))
        ])
    city = TextField('City', validators=[
            Required(message=REQUIRED.format("City")),
            Length(min=1, max=32, message=RANGE.format("City", 1, 32))
        ])
    url = TextField('URL/Website')
    create_button = SubmitField('Add')
    del_button = SubmitField('Delete')
```

Note that the form class creates three fields: one for the publisher name (name),
one for the city in which the publisher is based (city), and another for the publisher
URL (url). We also see two submit fields (buttons): one for creating new publisher data
(create_button), and one for deleting publisher data (del_button). We also have a
hidden field for the publisher id.

We pass the form data to the template when it is rendered after instantiating it in
the view function. Listing 8-7 shows the view function for the publisher data. Here, we
instantiate the publisher form class first then pass it to the template.

Listing 8-7. Publisher View Function

```
#
# Publisher
#
# This page allows creating and editing publisher records.
#
@app.route('/publisher', methods=['GET', 'POST'])
@app.route('/publisher/<int:publisher_id>', methods=['GET', 'POST'])
def publisher(publisher_id=None):
    form = PublisherForm()
```

```
    if request.method == 'POST':
            pass
    return render_template("publisher.html", form=form)
```

Note here that we see the routes we've defined for the view. Note also that we have set the methods for requests to include both GET and POST. We can check to see if the request is a POST (submission of data). It is in this condition that we can retrieve data from the form class instance and save it to the database. We'll look at that a bit more when we add database capabilities.

Finally, note that we instantiate an instance of the publisher form class (form) and later pass that as a parameter to the render_template("publisher.html", form=form) call. In this case, we now render the publisher.html template stored in the templates folder.

Ok, now we have our form class and view function. The focus now is what happens when we render the HTML template file. Listing 8-8 shows the HTML file (template) for the publisher data.

Listing 8-8. Publisher HTML File

```
{#
  Introducing the MySQL 8 Document Store

  This template defines the publisher template for use in the MyLibrary
application
  using the base template.

  Dr. Charles Bell, 2017
#}
{% extends "base.html" %}
{% block title %}MyLibrary Search{% endblock %}
{% block page_content %}
  <form method=post> {{ form.csrf_token }}
    <fieldset>
      <legend>Publisher - Detail</legend>
      {{ form.hidden_tag() }}
      <div style=font-size:20pz; font-weight:bold; margin-left:150px;s>
        {{ form.name.label }} <br>
        {{ form.name(size=64) }} <br>
        {{ form.city.label }} <br>
```

```
        {{ form.city(size=48) }} <br>
        {{ form.url.label }} <br>
        {{ form.url(size=75) }} <br><br>
        {{ form.create_button }}
        {% if form.del_button %}
           {{ form.del_button }}
        {% endif %}
      </div>
    </fieldset>
  </form>
{% endblock %}
```

Note that the template begins with extending (inheriting) the base.html template file that we discussed earlier. We see a block defining the title and another block defining the page content. In that block, we see how to define the fields on the page referencing the field class instances from the form class instance (form). Indeed, note that we reference the label of the field as well as the data. The label is defined when you declare that the field class and the data is where the values are stored. When we want to populate a form (GET) we set the data element to the value and when we want to read the data (POST), we reference the data element.

Note that we also added the CSRF token for security, rendered the hidden fields with the form.hidden_tag() function, and included the submit fields conditionally by including the delete submit field (del_button).

Whew! That's how Flask works to present a web page. Once you're used to it, it is a nifty way to separate several layers of functionality and make it easy to get data from the user or present it to the user.

Now, let's look at how to build custom error handlers into our application and later how to redirect control in our application to the correct view functions.

Error Handlers

Recall I mentioned it was possible to create your own error handling mechanisms for errors in your application. There are two such error mechanisms you should consider making: one for the 404 (not found) error, and another for 500 (application errors). To define each, we first make a view function decorated with @app.errorhandler(num), a view function, and an HTML file. Let's look at each example.

Not Found (404) Errors

To handle 404 (not found) errors, we create a view function with the special error handler routing function, which renders the HTML file. Flask will automatically direct all not found error conditions to this view. The following shows the view function for the 404 not found error handler. As you can see, it is simple.

```
@app.errorhandler(404)
def page_not_found(e):
    return render_template('404.html'), 404
```

The associated error handler HTML code is in the file named 404.html as shown in the following. Note that we inherit it from the base.html file so the resulting web page looks the same as any other in the application complete with the menu from the bootstrap component. Note that we also can define the text for the error message and a title. Feel free to embellish your own error handlers to make things more interesting for your users.[7]

```
{% extends "base.html" %}
{% block title %}MyLibrary ERROR: Page Not Found{% endblock %}
{% block page_content %}
<div class="page-header">
    <h1>Page not found.</h1>
</div>
{% endblock %}
```

Application (500) Errors

To handle 500 (application) errors, follow the same pattern as before. The following is the error handler for the application errors.

```
@app.errorhandler(500)
def internal_server_error(e):
    return render_template('500.html'), 500
```

---

[7]An example of great custom error handlers can be found on Github. They have a custom background and style sheet that puts the boring 404 errors of other websites to shame.

The associated error handler HTML code is in the file named 500.html as shown in the following. Note that we inherit it from the base.html file so the resulting web page looks the same as any other in the application complete with the menu from the bootstrap component.

```
{% extends "base.html" %}
{% block title %}MyLibrary ERROR{% endblock %}
{% block page_content %}
<div class="page-header">
    <h1>OOPS! Application error.</h1>
</div>
{% endblock %}
```

Creating these basic error handlers is highly recommended for all Flask applications. You may find the application error handler most helpful when developing your application. You can even augment the code to provide debug information to be displayed in the web page.

Redirects

At this point, you may be wondering how a Flask application can programmatically direct execution from one view to another. The answer is another simple construct in Flask: redirects. We use the redirect() function (imported from the flask module) with a URL to redirect control to another view. For example, suppose you had a list form and, depending on which button the user clicks (submitting the form via POST), you want to display a different web page. The following demonstrates how to use the redirect() function to do this.

```
if kind == 'book' or not kind:
    if request.method == 'POST':
        return redirect('book')
    return render_template("list.html", form=form, rows=rows,
                           columns=columns, kind=kind)
elif kind == 'author':
    if request.method == 'POST':
        return redirect('author')
    return render_template("list.html", form=form, rows=rows,
```

```
                        columns=columns, kind=kind)
elif kind == 'publisher':
    if request.method == 'POST':
        return redirect('publisher')
    return render_template("list.html", form=form, rows=rows,
                        columns=columns, kind=kind)
```

Here, we see there are three redirects after a POST request. In each case, we are using one of the routes defined in our application to tell Flask to call the associated view function. In this way, we can create a menu or a series of submit fields to allow the user to move from one page to another.

The redirect() function requires a valid route and for most cases, it is simply the text you supplied in the decorator. However, if you need to form a complex URL path, you can use the url_for() function to validate the route before you redirect. The function also helps avoid broken links if you reorganize or change your routes. For example, you can use redirect(url_for("author")) to validate the route and form a URL for it.

Additional Features

There is much more to Flask than what we've seen in this crash course. Some of the things not discussed that you may be interested in learning more about include the following (these are just a few of them). If these interest you, consider looking them up in the online documentation.

- *Application and request context*: There are variables you can use to capture application context such as session, global, request, and more. For more information, see http://flask.pocoo.org/docs/0.12/appcontext/.

- *Cookies*: You can work with cookies if you require. For more information, see http://flask.pocoo.org/docs/0.12/quickstart/#cookies.

- *Flask-Moment—Localization of dates and times*: If you need to work with localization of date and time, see the Flask-Moment extension at https://github.com/miguelgrinberg/Flask-Moment.

Flask Review: Sample Application

Now that we've had a brief primer on Flask, let's see how all of this works. In this section, we review what we have learned in the form of a basic layout for a typical Flask web application. We will be using this as a guide for writing the library application later in this chapter. Don't worry too much about executing this code as it doesn't do much and is intended as a jumpstart for the chapter project. However, it does demonstrate how all the parts we've learned are pieced together to get the Flask web application running with no forms defined.

Listing 8-9 shows the sample application layout for the library application. Take a moment to read it through. You should find all the topics we've discussed thus far with placeholders for field classes, form classes, and view functions.

Listing 8-9. Sample Flask Application Template

```
#
# Introducing the MySQL 8 Document Store - Template
#
# This file contains a template for building Flask applications. No form
# classes, routes, or view functions are defined but placeholders for each
# are defined in the comments.
#
# Dr. Charles Bell, 2017
#
from flask import Flask, render_template, request, redirect, flash
from flask_script import Manager
from flask_bootstrap import Bootstrap
from flask_wtf import FlaskForm
from wtforms import (HiddenField, TextField, TextAreaField, SelectField,
                     SelectMultipleField, IntegerField, SubmitField)
from wtforms.validators import Required, Length

#
# Setup Flask, Bootstrap, and security.
#
app = Flask(__name__)
app.config['SECRET_KEY'] = "He says, he's already got one!"
```

```
manager = Manager(app)
bootstrap = Bootstrap(app)

#
# Utility functions
#
def flash_errors(form):
    for error in form.errors:
        flash("{0} : {1}".format(error, ",".join(form.errors[error])))

#
# Customized fields for skipping prevalidation
#
<custom field classes go here>

#
# Form classes - the forms for the application
#
<form classes go here>

#
# Routing functions - the following defines the routing functions for the
# menu including the index or "home", book, author, and publisher.
#
<routing functions (view functions) go here>

#
# Error handling routes
#
@app.errorhandler(404)
def page_not_found(e):
    return render_template('404.html'), 404

@app.errorhandler(500)
def internal_server_error(e):
    return render_template('500.html'), 500

#
# Main entry
```

```
#
if __name__ == '__main__':
    manager.run()
```

Note that there is one thing in this template we haven't talked about yet—utility functions. These are your own functions to support your application. One function you may want to consider including in all your Flask applications is a function to loop through the errors on a form and display them in a flash message. Recall flash messages are displayed as popup boxes on the web page. The following presents the utility function for clarity. Note that we use a for loop to loop through the errors array of the form instance flashing each message. This permits you to display multiple messages on the web page.

```
def flash_errors(form):
    for error in form.errors:
        flash("{0} : {1}".format(error, ",".join(form.errors[error])))
```

Feel free to use this template when creating your own Flask applications. We will also be using it in the next section to define the user interface for the library application.

Tip   For more information about Flask and how to use it and its associated packages, the following book is an excellent reference on the topic: *Flask Web Development: Developing Web Applications with Python* 2nd ed., Miguel Grinberg, (O'Reilly Media, 2018).

Now that we've setup the Flask environment and discovered Flask and its extensions, let's look at the user interface common to the three versions of the application.

Library Application User Interface Design

Now that we know a lot more about Flask and how to build Flask applications, let's look at the library application user interface. As you may surmise, we build the database access as a separate set of classes but the user interface can be built nearly completely without it. Examining the user interface separate from the database access mechanisms makes it easier to focus on each part. We will discuss the database access mechanisms in the next section.

The user interface for the library application is the same code for all three versions of the application with some modifications to the code to adapt to the different database mechanisms. In particular, we have the full interface as presented here in version 1 (relational database), a reduced user interface for version 2 (hybrid: relational database with JSON), and version 3 will be more concise (document store). Therefore, we will write the form classes, view functions, and templates for all the web pages hosted in the user interface.

However, before we embark on writing the form classes, view functions, and templates for the application, we need to create a few directories.

Preparing the Directory Structure

Before we embark on implementing the three versions of the library application, we need to make a few folders (directories). Recall from the Flask Primer, we need folders to contain the .html files (form templates). We also place the code for interfacing with MySQL in a folder named database. Finally, we need a separate folder for each version of the application. Listing 8-10 shows the folder structure you will need. You can name the version folders however you wish, but the database and templates folder must be named as shown. Note we also have a folder named "base" that will contain the base user interface design without the database folder as discussed in the next section.

Listing 8-10. Directory Structure

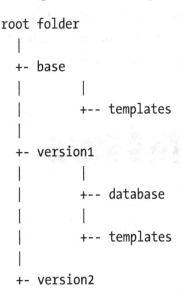

```
root folder
  |
  +- base
  |        |
  |        +--- templates
  |
  +- version1
  |        |
  |        +--- database
  |        |
  |        +--- templates
  |
  +- version2
```

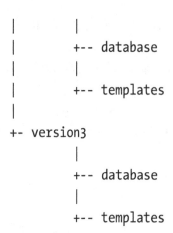

```
|          |
|          +-- database
|          |
|          +-- templates
|
+- version3
           |
           +-- database
           |
           +-- templates
```

User Interface Features

The library application will host three types of data: books, authors, and publishers linking them to form a library of books. The default view of the application will be a list of the books, which presents all the books in the form of an abbreviated bibliography. There will also be views for all the authors and all the publishers. Users will also be able to view the data for a specific book, author, or publisher allowing them to update or delete data items. Thus, the library application demonstrates the basic create, read, update, and delete (CRUD) operations for data.

Recall we will be using the bootstrap navigation bar, which has menu items for each of the views: books, authors, and publishers. Let's look at the default view—the list of books. Figure 8-3 shows the default view (without data). Note that the navigation bar and the choices for each of the views. Recall also that we specified the default view (reached by clicking on MyLibrary Base) is the same view of the books. In other words, it's the typical index.html or home of other web applications.

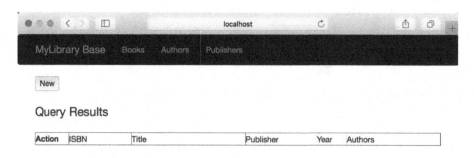

Figure 8-3. *MyLibrary application book list (default view)*

Although there is no data in this example, we will write the code to make a link for each item in the list that the user can click on to edit the data in the row. You will see how that is done in a later section. Note also the New button. Users can use this to create a new view as shown in Figure 8-4. This uses the same form class, view function, and template for viewing and editing the data. Recall also we will place a delete button on the view to allow users to delete the data as an option when editing it. This extra step—edit first, then delete—is a way to avoid the tired "are you sure?" question common to most applications for verifying delete operations. This way allows the user to edit the data and view it before deleting it. You be the judge as to whether it is better than the "are you sure?" prompt.

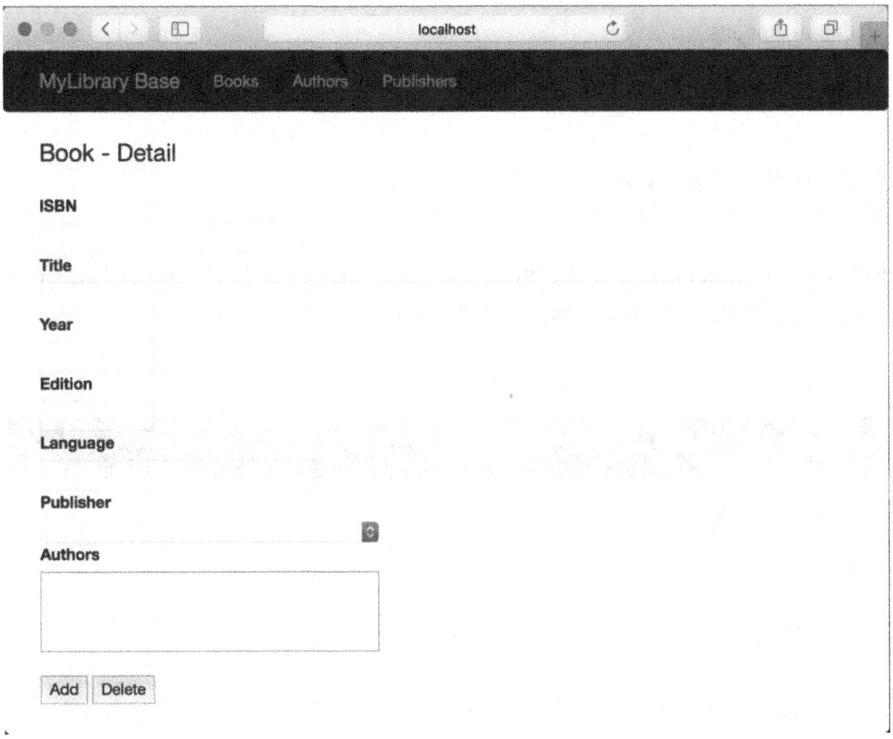

Figure 8-4. Book detail view

Note that on the form there is a select (dropdown) field. This field is populated with the names of the publishers in the database. Likewise, there is a multiselect field that allows users to select one or more authors in the database. As you will see when we discuss the database design, this layout is somewhat forced on us when using relational data. We will populate these lists in the view function. Note also we see both the Add and Delete submit fields (buttons). Recall, we will disable the Delete button in the template—it would not normally be enabled when adding a new data item.

Next is the author view. Here, as with the books view, is a list of the authors in the database complete with links for editing rows and a new button for creating new authors. Figure 8-5 shows the author view.

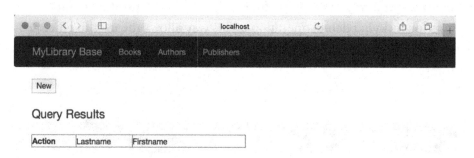

Figure 8-5. *Author list view*

When the user clicks on New (or later, the edit link in the list), the author detail view is shown. Figure 8-6 shows the author detail view.

Figure 8-6. *Author detail view*

Note that the form is very short. It shows only the two fields along with the Add and Delete button, which will be controlled in the template.

Finally, we have the publisher view, which displays a list of all the publishers in the database. Figure 8-7 shows the publisher view.

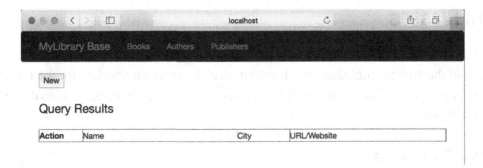

Figure 8-7. *Publisher view*

Finally, when users click on New or the edit link in the list, the publisher detail view is displayed as shown in Figure 8-8. Note here we have the three fields for the publisher data along with the Add and Delete buttons.

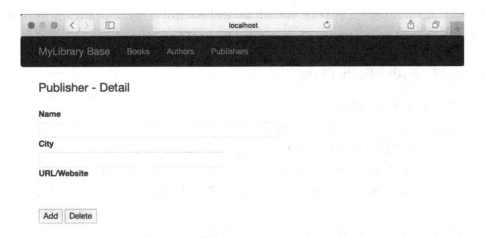

Figure 8-8. *Publisher detail view*

Now that we have had a look at the basic user interface, let's look at how to build the form classes for the three form classes for the detail views and a single form class for presenting the list, which uses inheritance and a bit of template constructs to share the form class and template among all three list views. Cool, eh?

Form Classes

The form classes for the library application require three form classes. There will be one for each of the author, publisher, and book views along with a form class for the reusable list view. Let's begin with the simplest form class (author) and work our way to the more complex (book).

Author Form Class

The author form is very simple and requires only three fields: one to store the primary key for the row using a HiddenField field class, one for the first name, and one for the last name. Both name fields use a TextField field class. Validation for the name fields set both to required (hint: they're defined as NOT NULL in the database table) along with minimal and maximum length checks. We also need two SubmitField field classes: one for Add and another for Delete. Recall, we will control programmatically the delete button in the template. Listing 8-11 shows the AuthorForm form class.

Listing 8-11. AuthorForm Class

```
class AuthorForm(FlaskForm):
    authorid = HiddenField('AuthorId')
    firstname = TextField('First name', validators=[
            Required(message=REQUIRED.format("Firstname")),
            Length(min=1, max=64, message=RANGE.format("Firstname", 1, 64))
        ])
    lastname = TextField( 'Last name', validators=[
            Required(message=REQUIRED.format("Lastname")),
            Length(min=1, max=64, message=RANGE.format("Lastname", 1, 64))
        ])
    create_button = SubmitField('Add')
    del_button = SubmitField('Delete')
```

Publisher Form Class

The publisher form also is very simple and requires only four fields: one to store the primary key for the row using a HiddenField field class, one for the publisher name, one for the publisher city of origin, and another for the URL for the publisher. All three visible fields use a TextField field class. Validation for the name and city fields set both to required (hint: they're defined as NOT NULL in the database table) along with minimal and maximum length checks. The URL field as no validators because it is an optional field for the data (it can be NULL in the database table). We also see the two SubmitFields() for the Add and Delete buttons. Listing 8-12 shows the PublisherForm form class.

Listing 8-12. PublisherForm Class

```
class PublisherForm(FlaskForm):
    publisherid = HiddenField('PublisherId')
    name = TextField('Name', validators=[
            Required(message=REQUIRED.format("Name")),
            Length(min=1, max=128, message=RANGE.format("Name", 1, 128))
        ])
    city = TextField('City', validators=[
            Required(message=REQUIRED.format("City")),
            Length(min=1, max=32, message=RANGE.format("City", 1, 32))
        ])
    url = TextField('URL/Website')
    create_button = SubmitField('Add')
    del_button = SubmitField('Delete')
```

Book Form Class

The book form is a bit more complex with many fields for the data. In fact, there are 10 fields. Table 8-4 lists the fields needed for the book form class. Included are the name of the field, the field class used, and validation choices.

Table 8-4. *Field Classes for the Book Form Class*

Field Name	Field Class	Validation
ISBN	TextField()	Required(), Length()
Title	TextField()	Required()
Year	IntegerField()	Required()
Edition	IntegerField()	None
Language	TextField()	Required(), Length()
Publisher	NewSelectField()	Required()
Authors	NewSelectMultipleField()	Required()
create_button	SubmitField()	N/A
del_button	SubmitField()	N/A
new_note	TextAreaField()	None

Before we discuss the form class for the book detail view, there is a small issue that needs to be overcome. There is a commonly known catch when using the SelectField() and SelectMultipleField() field classes. The prevalidation code can present some unusual results when validated if there is no default selected or if you set the default programmatically. To overcome these limitations, we can create our own derived field class and override the prevalidation code. Listing 8-13 shows the code used to create custom versions of these field classes to overcome the limitation. You will need to place these in your code if you want to use either of these field classes.

Listing 8-13. Creating Custom Field Classes

```
class NewSelectMultipleField(SelectMultipleField):
    def pre_validate(self, form):
        # Prevent "not a valid choice" error
        pass

    def process_formdata(self, valuelist):
        if valuelist:
            self.data = ",".join(valuelist)
        else:
            self.data = ""
```

```python
class NewSelectField(SelectField):
    def pre_validate(self, form):
        # Prevent "not a valid choice" error
        pass

    def process_formdata(self, valuelist):
        if valuelist:
            self.data = ",".join(valuelist)
        else:
            self.data = ""
```

Note that in each case, we override the pre_validate() and process_formdata() methods allowing us to ignore prevalidation and make it easier to update the values. Now let's look at the code for the book form class. Listing 8-14 shows the code for the BookForm form class. Note that we use the new field classes for the authors and publisher fields. We also see the two SubmitFields() for the Add and Delete buttons.

Listing 8-14. BookForm Class

```python
class BookForm(FlaskForm):
    isbn = TextField('ISBN ', validators=[
            Required(message=REQUIRED.format("ISBN")),
            Length(min=1, max=32, message=RANGE.format("ISBN", 1, 32))
        ])
    title = TextField('Title ',
                    validators=[Required(message=REQUIRED.format("Title"))])
    year = IntegerField('Year ',
                      validators=[Required(message=REQUIRED.format("Year"))])
    edition = IntegerField('Edition ')
    language = TextField('Language ', validators=[
            Required(message=REQUIRED.format("Language")),
            Length(min=1, max=24, message=RANGE.format("Language", 1, 24))
        ])
    publisher = NewSelectField('Publisher ',
                    validators=[Required(message=REQUIRED.format("Publisher"))])
    authors = NewSelectMultipleField('Authors ',
                    validators=[Required(message=REQUIRED.format("Author"))])
```

```
create_button = SubmitField('Add')
del_button = SubmitField('Delete')
new_note = TextAreaField('Add Note')
```

List Form Class

To save duplicate code, we will create a simple form class that we can use to create a simple list of rows in the form of an HTML table. The code for this is very simple because all the presentation code will be in the template file. The following is the code for the ListForm form class.

```
class ListForm(FlaskForm):
    submit = SubmitField('New')
```

Now that we've seen all the form classes for the library application, we now examine the associated view functions.

View Functions

View functions are where and how Flask applications direct execution. Together with the routes we define, we can build our application without loops or polling. Let's dive in starting with the simplest view function. We will see the view functions with the routes defined (via decorators). The basic code for the author, publisher, and book view functions are the same and need no additional discussion. The only differences are the routes and the population or the select and multiselect fields in the book view function. Each function is show in Listing 8-15 (named author), Listing 8-16 (named publisher), and Listing 8-17 (named book).

Listing 8-15. Author View Function

```
@app.route('/author', methods=['GET', 'POST'])
@app.route('/author/<int:author_id>', methods=['GET', 'POST'])
def author(author_id=None):
    form = AuthorForm()
    if request.method == 'POST':
        pass
    return render_template("author.html", form=form)
```

Listing 8-16. Publisher View Function

```
@app.route('/publisher', methods=['GET', 'POST'])
@app.route('/publisher/<int:publisher_id>', methods=['GET', 'POST'])
def publisher(publisher_id=None):
    form = PublisherForm()
    if request.method == 'POST':
            pass
    return render_template("publisher.html", form=form)
```

Listing 8-17. Book View Function

```
@app.route('/book', methods=['GET', 'POST'])
@app.route('/book/<string:isbn_selected>', methods=['GET', 'POST'])
def book(isbn_selected=None):
    notes = None
    form = BookForm()
    form.publisher.choices = []
    form.authors.choices = []
    new_note = ""
    if request.method == 'POST':
        pass
    return render_template("book.html", form=form, notes=notes)
```

The list view function is more complicated. Recall, we want to create a list that we can reuse. Thus, we will need to be able to create an HTML table with a list of column names and the rows we want to display. We can pass the columns and rows using parameters in the render_template() function. We also want to define the size of the columns. We can do this by passing HTML code to the template. In this case, we define them as HTML tags for the column names and in the template, use the safe filter to display it without translation.

We also want to create a link for each row that contains the primary key for the row, which we will pass as the first data item in each row. For authors and publishers, it is the auto increment primary key. For books, it is the ISBN. Thus, ISBN will be listed twice in the row. To determine which data we want, we use a variable in the list route. For example, if we want books, our URL would be localhost:5000/list/book. Cool.

Finally, because this view function is a default view, the routes are simple: the default (index) and list. Listing 8-18 shows the complete code for the list view function named `simple_list`. Take some time to read through it so you understand the code.

Listing 8-18. List View Function

```python
@app.route('/', methods=['GET', 'POST'])
@app.route('/list/<kind>', methods=['GET', 'POST'])
def simple_list(kind=None):
    rows = []
    columns = []
    form = ListForm()
    if kind == 'book' or not kind:
        if request.method == 'POST':
            return redirect('book')
        columns = (
            '<td style="width:200px">ISBN</td>',
            '<td style="width:400px">Title</td>',
            '<td style="width:200px">Publisher</td>',
            '<td style="width:80px">Year</td>',
            '<td style="width:300px">Authors</td>',
        )
        kind = 'book'
        # Here, we get all books in the database
        return render_template("list.html", form=form, rows=rows,
                               columns=columns, kind=kind)
    elif kind == 'author':
        if request.method == 'POST':
            return redirect('author')
        # Just list the authors
        columns = (
            '<td style="width:100px">Lastname</td>',
            '<td style="width:200px">Firstname</td>',
        )
        kind = 'author'
        # Here, we get all authors in the database
```

```
    return render_template("list.html", form=form, rows=rows,
                            columns=columns, kind=kind)
elif kind == 'publisher':
    if request.method == 'POST':
        return redirect('publisher')
    columns = (
        '<td style="width:300px">Name</td>',
        '<td style="width:100px">City</td>',
        '<td style="width:300px">URL/Website</td>',
    )
    kind = 'publisher'
    # Here, we get all publishers in the database
    return render_template("list.html", form=form, rows=rows,
                            columns=columns, kind=kind)
else:
    flash("Something is wrong!")
    return
```

Now that we've seen the code for the form classes and view functions, let's look at the remaining piece of the puzzle: templates.

Templates

Templates are where we place all our HTML and template constructs for building our web pages (in the context of a database application, a data view or simply view[8]). The templates are presented with short descriptions and are provided for reference so that you can see all the parts together. Because we have four view functions, we will create four template files all of which will use the base template explained earlier. Recall, the base template defines the bootstrap navigation bar and a for loop for displaying an array of flash messages.

Note   Remember, template files are in the templates folder and named XXX.html by convention.

---

[8]Which is unfortunate because it can easily be confused with Flask view functions.

Author Template

The author template creates a form for viewing, editing, and creating author data. As such, we give the page a legend, host the hidden field (for the auto increment primary key), and place the label and form field on the form for each of the fields. We keep it simple by listing the fields vertically (but you can use any format you want). We also set the size of the fields using the form fields default function. For example, to set the size for the first name field to 75 characters, we use form.firstname(size=75). Finally, we see the logic to turn on the delete button if it is defined (we will see how to disable it later). Listing 8-19 shows the completed template for the author data (named author.html).

Listing 8-19. Author Template (author.html)

```
{% extends "base.html" %}
{% block title %}MyLibrary Search{% endblock %}
{% block page_content %}
  <form method=post> {{ form.csrf_token }}
    <fieldset>
      <legend>Author - Detail</legend>
      {{ form.hidden_tag() }}
      <div style=font-size:20pz; font-weight:bold; margin-left:150px;s>
        {{ form.firstname.label }} <br>
        {{ form.firstname(size=75) }} <br>
        {{ form.lastname.label }} <br>
        {{ form.lastname(size=75) }} <br><br>
        {{ form.create_button }}
        {% if form.del_button %}
          {{ form.del_button }}
        {% endif %}
      </div>
    </fieldset>
  </form>
{% endblock %}
```

Publisher Template

The publisher template creates a form for viewing, editing, and creating publisher data. As such, we give the page a legend, host the hidden field (for the auto increment primary key), and place the label and form field on the form for each of the fields. We keep it simple by listing the fields vertically (but you can use any format you want). We also set the size of the fields. Finally, we see the logic to turn on the delete button if it is defined (we will see how to disable it later). Listing 8-20 shows the completed template for the publisher data (named publisher.html).

Listing 8-20. Publisher Template (publisher.html)

```
{% extends "base.html" %}
{% block title %}MyLibrary Search{% endblock %}
{% block page_content %}
  <form method=post> {{ form.csrf_token }}
    <fieldset>
      <legend>Publisher - Detail</legend>
      {{ form.hidden_tag() }}
      <div style=font-size:20pz; font-weight:bold; margin-left:150px;s>
        {{ form.name.label }} <br>
        {{ form.name(size=64) }} <br>
        {{ form.city.label }} <br>
        {{ form.city(size=48) }} <br>
        {{ form.url.label }} <br>
        {{ form.url(size=75) }} <br><br>
        {{ form.create_button }}
        {% if form.del_button %}
          {{ form.del_button }}
        {% endif %}
      </div>
    </fieldset>
  </form>
{% endblock %}
```

Book Template

The book template is a bit more complex. We start out with a legend and the hidden tag, which stores the ISBN for the current data, then build the form listing the labels and the fields vertically setting the size of the fields as we go. So far, this is similar to how we built the author and publisher templates.

Things get a bit more interesting when we try to set the field size for the select fields. In this case, we need to use the style parameter passing in the width parameter using units in pixels. This is one of the very few nuances of Flask templates that can be a bit tricky because the size parameter doesn't apply to the select fields (but now you know how to get around it). As with the previous templates, we see the logic to turn on the delete button if it is defined (we will see how to disable it later).

After that, we see some additional logic for working with notes. The notes feature allows users to add notes to the book after it has been created. Thus, we need to both show any existing notes and provide a means to add a new note, but only when the page is used for update operations. You can see how this is done near the bottom of the file.

Listing 8-21 shows the completed template for the publisher data (named book.html). Take some time to read through the file until you are confident you understand how it works.

Listing 8-21. Book Template (book.html)

```
{% extends "base.html" %}
{% block title %}MyLibrary Search{% endblock %}
{% block page_content %}
  <form method=post> {{ form.csrf_token }}
    <fieldset>
      <legend>Book - Detail</legend>
      {{ form.hidden_tag() }}
      <div style=font-size:20pz; font-weight:bold; margin-left:150px;>
        {{ form.isbn.label }} <br>
        {{ form.isbn(size=32) }} <br>
        {{ form.title.label }} <br>
        {{ form.title(size=100) }} <br>
        {{ form.year.label }} <br>
        {{ form.year(size=10) }} <br>
        {{ form.edition.label }} <br>
```

```
        {{ form.edition(size=10) }} <br>
        {{ form.language.label }} <br>
        {{ form.language(size=34) }} <br>
        {{ form.publisher.label }} <br>
        {{ form.publisher(style="width: 300px;") }} <br>
        {{ form.authors.label }} <br>
        {{ form.authors(style="width: 300px;") }}
        {# Show the new note text field if this is an update. #}
        {% if form.create_button.label.text == "Update" %}
          <br>{{ form.new_note.label }} <br>
          {{ form.new_note(rows='2',cols='100') }}
        {% endif %}
        <br><br>
        {{ form.create_button }}
        {% if form.del_button %}
          {{ form.del_button }}
        {% endif %}
        <br><br>
      </div>
      {# Show the list of existing notes if there is a list. #}
      {% if notes %}
        <div>
          <table border="1" cellpadding="1" cellspacing="1">
            <tr><td><b>Notes</b></td></tr>
            {% for note in notes %}
              <tr><td style="width:600px"> {{ note }} </td></tr>
            {% endfor %}
          </table>
          <br>
        </div>
      {% endif %}
    </fieldset>
  </form>
{% endblock %}
```

List Template

Despite the rather complex view function for the list feature, the template for the list view is rather straightforward. We simply add the New button (submit field) at the top, provide a legend, and then format the table using the columns array from the view function. We then build the HTML table using the rows also provided from the view function. Listing 8-22 shows the completed template for the list data (named list.html).

Listing 8-22. List Template (list.html)

```
{% extends "base.html" %}
{% block title %}MyLibrary Query Results{% endblock %}
{% block page_content %}
  <form method=post> {{ form.csrf_token }}
    <fieldset>
      {{ form.submit }} <br><br>
    </fieldset>
  </form>
  <legend>Query Results</legend>
  <table border="1" cellpadding="1" cellspacing="1">
    <tr>
      <td style="width:80px"><b>Action</b></td>
      {% for col in columns %}
        {{ col|safe }}
      {% endfor %}
    </tr>
    {% for row in rows %}
      <tr>
        <td><a href="{{ '/%s/%s'%(kind,row[0]) }}">Modify</a></td>
        {% for col in row[1:] %}
          <td> {{ col }} </td>
        {% endfor %}
      </tr>
    {% endfor %}
  </table>
{% endblock %}
```

Other Templates

Recall, there are three other templates that we've seen previously that we will be using: the 404 and 500 error handlers (404.html, 500.html) as described in the section, "Error Handlers" and the base template (base.html) as shown in Listing 8-5.

Application Code

Now, let's put these concepts together in the application code completing the basic layout presented previously. Listing 8-23 shows the application code for the library application. Because this is the base version of the library application, we name the file mylibrary_base.py. We can use it as the basis for the three versions of the library application (named mylibrary_v1.py, mylibrary_v2.py, and mylibrary_v3.py).

The listing is presented for completeness without additional discussion. The portions of the code previously discussed are marked with [...] placeholders to avoid duplication. Rather, the listing is provided as reference for later sections that discuss the three versions. Feel free to read through the code to ensure you understand all the parts of the code and refer to it when reading the sections on the different versions.

Listing 8-23. Base MyLibrary Application Code

```
#
# Introducing the MySQL 8 Document Store - Base
#
# This file contains the sample Python + Flask application for
demonstrating
# how to build a simple relational database application. Thus, it relies on
# a database class that encapsulates the CRUD operations for a MySQL
database
# of relational tables.
#
# Dr. Charles Bell, 2017
#
from flask import Flask, render_template, request, redirect, flash
from flask_script import Manager
from flask_bootstrap import Bootstrap
from flask_wtf import FlaskForm
```

```python
from wtforms import (HiddenField, TextField, TextAreaField, SelectField,
                     SelectMultipleField, IntegerField, SubmitField)
from wtforms.validators import Required, Length

#
# Strings
#
REQUIRED = "{0} field is required."
RANGE = "{0} range is {1} to {2} characters."

#
# Setup Flask, Bootstrap, and security.
#
app = Flask(__name__)
app.config['SECRET_KEY'] = "He says, he's already got one!"
manager = Manager(app)
bootstrap = Bootstrap(app)

#
# Utility functions
#
def flash_errors(form):
[...]

#
# Customized fields for skipping prevalidation
#
class NewSelectMultipleField(SelectMultipleField):
[...]

class NewSelectField(SelectField):
[...]

#
# Form classes - the forms for the application
#
class ListForm(FlaskForm):
[...]
```

```python
class PublisherForm(FlaskForm):
[...]

class AuthorForm(FlaskForm):
[...]

class BookForm(FlaskForm):
[...]

#
# Routing functions - the following defines the routing functions for the
# menu including the index or "home", book, author, and publisher.
#

#
# Simple List
#
# This is the default page for "home" and listing objects. It reuses a
# single template "list.html" to show a list of rows from the database.
# Built into each row is a special edit link for editing any of the rows,
# which redirects to the appropriate route (form).
#
@app.route('/', methods=['GET', 'POST'])
@app.route('/list/<kind>', methods=['GET', 'POST'])
def simple_list(kind=None):
[...]

#
# Author
#
# This page allows creating and editing author records.
#
@app.route('/author', methods=['GET', 'POST'])
@app.route('/author/<int:author_id>', methods=['GET', 'POST'])
def author(author_id=None):
[...]
```

```python
#
# Publisher
#
# This page allows creating and editing publisher records.
#
@app.route('/publisher', methods=['GET', 'POST'])
@app.route('/publisher/<int:publisher_id>', methods=['GET', 'POST'])
def publisher(publisher_id=None):
[...]

#
# Book
#
# This page allows creating and editing book records.
#
@app.route('/book', methods=['GET', 'POST'])
@app.route('/book/<string:isbn_selected>', methods=['GET', 'POST'])
def book(isbn_selected=None):
[...]

#
# Error handling routes
#
@app.errorhandler(404)
def page_not_found(e):
[...]

@app.errorhandler(500)
def internal_server_error(e):
[...]

#
# Main entry
#
if __name__ == '__main__':
    manager.run()
```

Now that we have a firm foundation in Flask and how the user interface is designed, we are ready to begin writing the code for each of the versions of the application starting with the relational database version.

Summary

Building MySQL applications using a good framework for not only the database access, but more important for the user interface. Deciding on a language and platform to use can sometimes become a science project or even an academic exercise or perhaps a mandate that cannot be overridden. Presenting concepts such as the document store with examples can be even more complicated as you must choose a language and framework that is easy to use and easy to understand. Perhaps even more challenging, choosing an application that illustrates the concepts in a meaningful manner.[9]

In this book, the choice for these technologies is Python, the Flask framework, and of course the MySQL Connector/Python database connector and the X DevAPI. Python is easy to read and anyone—even those who don't write a lot of code—can understand it. Plus, it is a very powerful language. However, user interfaces in Python are limited to command-line (terminal) output unless you use a user interface framework. Once again, choosing one can be a challenge. However, frameworks for web applications are just the ticket to help build a decent looking example that readers can use as the basis for their own experiments and applications.

In this chapter, we learned a new web application library for Python named Flask. We also saw how Flask is built as an extensible framework that is easily augmented with components to make your application more robust. We also covered an introduction to the user interface for the library application building on the foundations of what we learned about Flask.

In the next chapter, I look at three versions of the application: a pure relational database solution that uses the old protocols, a relational database with JSON (hybrid) that uses the X DevAPI and SQL statements, and a pure document store version. Each version presents foundations on how to build the application using a different database access mechanism. As you will see, there is a profound transition from the old to the new.

---

[9]Sadly, most well-documented tutorials rarely have an example you can actually use to build on. "Hello, World!" examples only go so far after all.

CHAPTER 9

Library Application: Database Implementations

Now that we have a firm foundation in Flask and how the user interface is designed, we are ready to begin writing the code for each of the versions of the application starting with the relational database version.

As you will see, the evolution of the application from a pure relational model to a document model demonstrates how we can avoid some of the messier aspects of using relational data—even in the hybrid example. One element that may surprise you is the length and complexity of the code for the document store version is considerably shorter and easier to understand. What better reason to consider writing all your future applications using the MySQL Document Store!

The following sections describe the three versions of the library application. Because they all use the same user interface code, we omit discussions of the user interface for brevity and present only snapshots of the application executing where appropriate to illustrate the differences. The following briefly recaps the versions. Each version implements a different form of data storage.

- *Version 1—relational database*: implements a traditional relational database model using only the nondocument store features.

- *Version 2—relational database + JSON fields (hybrid)*: implements a relational database model augmented with JSON fields.

- *Version 3—document store*: implements a pure document store (NoSQL) solution.

The following sections present the entire code for the database components for each version along with the appropriate changes to the user interface. Rather than present snippets of code potentially out of context, the entire code for each version is presented for clarity and completeness. As a result, this chapter is a bit longer.

C. Bell, *Introducing the MySQL 8 Document Store*, https://doi.org/10.1007/978-1-4842-2725-1_9

Note   Recall from Chapter 8 that we used a directory structure to organize the code. For example, we have folders named `version1`, `version2`, and `version3` for each version of the application. If you are following along, be sure to place the files discussed in the appropriate folder.

Version 1: Relational Database

This version implements a traditional relational database solution in which we model the data based on the views or data items. For the purposes of demonstration, we will implement the database code in a code module that we can import into the application code. This code module will use the older MySQL Connector/Python protocol and API. That is, we will not be using the X DevAPI and will rely on SQL statements to work with the data.

Let's start with a brief overview of the database design. Because relational database is familiar to most readers interested in the MySQL Document Store, we will skip any lengthy discussions and present the database with a brief introduction and a look at the SQL `CREATE` statements.

Database Design

The database for this version is named library_v1. In the spirit of good relational database design, we will create a table to store the data in discrete tables for authors, publishers, and books. We will also create a separate table to store the notes because this data is referenced less often and could be potentially long strings. We will use foreign keys to ensure consistency between these three tables. Because we can have more than one author for each book, we need to create a join table to manage the many-to-many relationship between books and authors. Thus, we will create five tables in total. Figure 9-1 shows the Entity Relationship Diagram (ERD) for the library_v1 database complete with indexes and foreign keys.

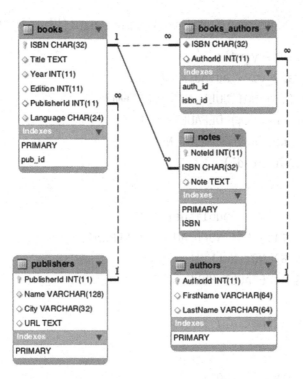

Figure 9-1. *ERD diagram—library database (version 1)*

We also need a way to retrieve the primary keys from the authors table for a given
book via the ISBN column. We use this data when we query the database for the
data for a given book. To make it easier to maintain, we will create a stored routine
(function) to retrieve a comma-separated list of the AuthorId column in the authors
table. We use this to populate the SelectMultipleField in the book template. Finally,
we will need another stored routine (function) that retrieves the author names for a
given book via the ISBN column. We then will use this data to populate the list view of
the books table.

Listing 9-1 shows the CREATE statements for all seven of these objects. If you want to
follow along building this version of the application as you read, you should create a file
named library_v1.sql so you can recreate the database later if needed. The database
uses only tables and stored routines to keep the discussion short.

Listing 9-1. Library Version 1 Database Create Script (library_v1.sql)

```sql
CREATE DATABASE `library_v1`;
CREATE TABLE `library_v1`.`authors` (
    `AuthorId` int(11) NOT NULL AUTO_INCREMENT,
    `FirstName` varchar(64) DEFAULT NULL,
    `LastName` varchar(64) DEFAULT NULL,
    PRIMARY KEY (`AuthorId`)
) ENGINE=InnoDB;

CREATE TABLE `library_v1`.`publishers` (
  `PublisherId` int(11) NOT NULL AUTO_INCREMENT,
  `Name` varchar(128) NOT NULL,
  `City` varchar(32) DEFAULT NULL,
  `URL` text,
  PRIMARY KEY (`PublisherId`)
) ENGINE=InnoDB;

CREATE TABLE `library_v1`.`books` (
  `ISBN` char(32) NOT NULL,
  `Title` text NOT NULL,
  `Year` int(11) NOT NULL DEFAULT '2017',
  `Edition` int(11) DEFAULT '1',
  `PublisherId` int(11) DEFAULT NULL,
  `Language` char(24) NOT NULL DEFAULT 'English',
  PRIMARY KEY (`ISBN`),
  KEY `pub_id` (`PublisherId`),
  CONSTRAINT `books_ibfk_1` FOREIGN KEY (`PublisherId`)
    REFERENCES `library_v1`.`publishers` (`publisherid`)
) ENGINE=InnoDB;

CREATE TABLE `library_v1`.`notes` (
  `NoteId` int(11) NOT NULL AUTO_INCREMENT,
  `ISBN` char(32) NOT NULL,
  `Note` text,
  PRIMARY KEY (`NoteId`,`ISBN`),
  KEY `ISBN` (`ISBN`),
```

```
  CONSTRAINT `notes_fk_1` FOREIGN KEY (`ISBN`)
    REFERENCES `library_v1`.`books` (`isbn`)
) ENGINE=InnoDB;

CREATE TABLE `library_v1`.`books_authors` (
  `ISBN` char(32) NOT NULL,
  `AuthorId` int(11) DEFAULT NULL,
  KEY `auth_id` (`AuthorId`),
  KEY `isbn_id` (`ISBN`),
  CONSTRAINT `books_authors_fk_1` FOREIGN KEY (`ISBN`)
    REFERENCES `library_v1`.`books` (`isbn`),
  CONSTRAINT `books_authors_fk_2` FOREIGN KEY (`AuthorId`)
    REFERENCES `library_v1`.`authors` (`authorid`)
) ENGINE=InnoDB;

DELIMITER //
CREATE FUNCTION `library_v1`.`get_author_ids`(isbn_lookup char(32))
  RETURNS varchar(128) DETERMINISTIC
  RETURN (
    SELECT GROUP_CONCAT(library_v1.authors.AuthorId SEPARATOR ', ')
    AS author_ids
      FROM library_v1.books_authors JOIN library_v1.authors
        ON books_authors.AuthorId = authors.AuthorId
      WHERE ISBN = isbn_lookup GROUP BY library_v1.books_authors.ISBN
)//

CREATE FUNCTION `library_v1`.`get_author_names`(isbn_lookup char(32))
  RETURNS varchar(128) DETERMINISTIC
    RETURN (
    SELECT GROUP_CONCAT(library_v1.authors.LastName SEPARATOR ', ') AS
    author_names
      FROM library_v1.books_authors JOIN library_v1.authors
        ON books_authors.AuthorId = authors.AuthorId
      WHERE ISBN = isbn_lookup GROUP BY library_v1.books_authors.ISBN
)//
DELIMITER ;
```

Now that the database has been created, let's see the code for the database class.

Tip   There is a database creation script for each version in the sample code for this book. See the Apress web site for this book to download the source code.

Database Code

The code for working with the database is placed in a file named `library_v1.py` in the database folder under the `version1` folder as described in Chapter 8 under the section, "Preparing the Directory Structure." Because most of the code is common to older Python applications that use the MySQL Connector/Python connector, we discuss only the salient points for each portion of the code.

That said the code implements four classes: one for each of the data views (author, publisher, book) and another class for interfacing with the server. These classes are named `Author`, `Publisher`, `Book`, and `Library`, respectfully.

Note   To use the library placed in the `database` folder, you must create an empty file named `__init__.py` in the `database` folder.

SQL Strings

To make the code easier to maintain and to modify it if any changes are needed for the SQL statements, we place these in the preamble of the code module as strings that we can reference later in the code. Doing this also helps keep code line lengths shorter. Listing 9-2 shows the preamble for the `library_v1.py` code module. Note that it begins with importing the MySQL Connector/Python library.

Listing 9-2. Initialization and SQL Statements (library_v1.py)

```
import mysql.connector

ALL_BOOKS = """
    SELECT DISTINCT book.ISBN, book.ISBN, Title, publisher.Name as Publisher,
                    Year, library_v1.get_author_names(book.ISBN) as Authors
    FROM library_v1.books As book
```

```
            INNER JOIN library_v1.publishers as publisher ON
                    book.PublisherId=publisher.PublisherId
            INNER JOIN library_v1.books_authors as book_author ON
                    book.ISBN = book_author.ISBN
            INNER JOIN library_v1.authors as a ON book_author.AuthorId = a.AuthorId
        ORDER BY book.ISBN DESC
"""

GET_LASTID = "SELECT @@last_insert_id"


#
# Author SQL Statements
#
INSERT_AUTHOR = """
    INSERT INTO library_v1.authors (LastName, FirstName) VALUES ('{0}','{1}')
"""

GET_AUTHORS = "SELECT AuthorId, LastName, FirstName FROM library_v1.authors {0}"
UPDATE_AUTHOR = """
    UPDATE library_v1.authors SET LastName = '{0}',
    FirstName='{1}' WHERE AuthorId = {2}
"""

DELETE_AUTHOR = """
    DELETE FROM library_v1.authors WHERE AuthorId = {0}
"""


#
# Publisher SQL Statements
#
INSERT_PUBLISHER = """
    INSERT INTO library_v1.publishers (Name, City, URL) VALUES ('{0}','{1}','{2}')
"""

GET_PUBLISHERS = "SELECT * FROM library_v1.publishers {0}"
UPDATE_PUBLISHER = "UPDATE library_v1.publishers SET Name = '{0}'"
DELETE_PUBLISHER = "DELETE FROM library_v1.publishers WHERE PublisherId = {0}"
```

```
#
# Book SQL Statements
#
INSERT_BOOK = """
    INSERT INTO library_v1.books (ISBN, Title, Year, PublisherId, Edition,
    Language) VALUES ('{0}','{1}','{2}','{3}',{4},'{5}')
"""

INSERT_BOOK_AUTHOR = """
    INSERT INTO library_v1.books_authors (ISBN, AuthorId) VALUES ('{0}', {1})
"""

INSERT_NOTE = "INSERT INTO library_v1.notes (ISBN, Note) VALUES ('{0}','{1}')"
GET_BOOKS = "SELECT * FROM library_v1.books {0}"
GET_NOTES = "SELECT * FROM library_v1.notes WHERE ISBN = '{0}'"
GET_AUTHOR_IDS = "SELECT library_v1.get_author_ids('{0}')"
UPDATE_BOOK = "UPDATE library_v1.books SET ISBN = '{0}'"
DELETE_BOOK = "DELETE FROM library_v1.books WHERE ISBN = '{0}'"
DELETE_BOOK_AUTHOR = "DELETE FROM library_v1.books_authors WHERE ISBN = '{0}'"
DELETE_NOTES = "DELETE FROM library_v1.notes WHERE ISBN = '{0}'"
```

That's a lot of SQL, isn't it? If it seems daunting, consider that most relational database applications have a similar set of SQL statements. Consider also that this example application is purposefully small and limited. Taking those into account, imagine the number and complexity of SQL statements for a much larger application. Wow.

Next, let's look at the Author class.

Author Class

The Author class is the least complicated and forms a model for how the other data classes are constructed. In particular, we save an instance of the Library class via the constructor and reference this instance whenever we execute queries (or use any of the methods in the Library class). We then build four functions—one each for create, read, update, and delete. Listing 9-3 shows the Author class code. The read operation is designed to return one row if the primary key is passed as a parameter or all rows if no parameter is supplied.

Note that we use the Library class function `sql()` to execute queries. For example, `self.library.sql("COMMIT")` executes the COMMIT SQL command. We use the strings created previously using the `format()` function to fill in the optional parameters. We will see this function in more detail later in this section. Take some time to read through the code to ensure you understand it.

Listing 9-3. Author Class (library_v1.py)

```python
class Author(object):
    """Author class

    This class encapsulates the authors table permitting CRUD operations
    on the data.
    """
    def __init__(self, library):
        self.library = library

    def create(self, LastName, FirstName):
        assert LastName, "You must supply a LastName for a new author."
        assert FirstName, "You must supply a FirstName for a new author."
        query_str = INSERT_AUTHOR
        last_id = None
        try:
            self.library.sql(query_str.format(LastName, FirstName))
            last_id = self.library.sql(GET_LASTID)
            self.library.sql("COMMIT")
        except Exception as err:
            print("ERROR: Cannot add author: {0}".format(err))
        return last_id

    def read(self, AuthorId=None):
        query_str = GET_AUTHORS
        if not AuthorId:
            # return all authors
            query_str = query_str.format("")
        else:
            # return specific author
```

```
            query_str = query_str.format("WHERE AuthorId = '{0}'".format(AuthorId))
        return self.library.sql(query_str)

    def update(self, AuthorId, LastName, FirstName):
        assert AuthorId, "You must supply an AuthorId to update the author."
        assert LastName, "You must supply a LastName for the author."
        assert FirstName, "You must supply a FirstName for the author."
        query_str = UPDATE_AUTHOR
        try:
            self.library.sql(query_str.format(LastName, FirstName, AuthorId))
            self.library.sql("COMMIT")
        except Exception as err:
            print("ERROR: Cannot update author: {0}".format(err))

    def delete(self, AuthorId):
        assert AuthorId, "You must supply an AuthorId to delete the author."
        query_str = DELETE_AUTHOR.format(AuthorId)
        try:
            self.library.sql(query_str)
            self.library.sql("COMMIT")
        except Exception as err:
            print("ERROR: Cannot delete author: {0}".format(err))
```

Next, let's look at the Publisher class.

Publisher Class

The Publisher class is very similar to the Author class and is implemented in the same manner. The only difference is in the SQL statements used. To be complete, Listing 9-4 shows the complete code for the Publisher class.

Listing 9-4. Publisher Class (library_v1.py)

```
class Publisher(object):
    """Publisher class

    This class encapsulates the publishers table permitting CRUD operations
    on the data.
    """
```

```python
def __init__(self, library):
    self.library = library

def create(self, Name, City=None, URL=None):
    assert Name, "You must supply a Name for a new publisher."
    query_str = INSERT_PUBLISHER
    last_id = None
    try:
        self.library.sql(query_str.format(Name, City, URL))
        last_id = self.library.sql(GET_LASTID)
        self.library.sql("COMMIT")
    except Exception as err:
        print("ERROR: Cannot add publisher: {0}".format(err))
    return last_id

def read(self, PublisherId=None):
    query_str = GET_PUBLISHERS
    if not PublisherId:
        # return all authors
        query_str = query_str.format("")
    else:
        # return specific author
        query_str = query_str.format(
            "WHERE PublisherId = '{0}'".format(PublisherId))
    return self.library.sql(query_str)

def update(self, PublisherId, Name, City=None, URL=None):
    assert PublisherId, "You must supply a publisher to update the author."
    query_str = UPDATE_PUBLISHER.format(Name)
    if City:
        query_str = query_str + ", City = '{0}'".format(City)
    if URL:
        query_str = query_str + ", URL = '{0}'".format(URL)
    query_str = query_str + " WHERE PublisherId = {0}".format(PublisherId)
    try:
        self.library.sql(query_str)
        self.library.sql("COMMIT")
```

```
    except Exception as err:
        print("ERROR: Cannot update publisher: {0}".format(err))

def delete(self, PublisherId):
    assert PublisherId, "You must supply a publisher to delete the
    publisher."
    query_str = DELETE_PUBLISHER.format(PublisherId)
    try:
        self.library.sql(query_str)
        self.library.sql("COMMIT")
    except Exception as err:
        print("ERROR: Cannot delete publisher: {0}".format(err))
```

Next, a look at the Book class.

Book Class

The Book class has the same methods as the last two, but the code for create, update, and delete is a little more complex. This is because we must execute multiple statements to work with the data. Therefore, we implicitly start a transaction inside a try block and if any of the queries fail, we rollback the transaction. This is very common for relational database solutions. Listing 9-5 shows the complete code for the Book class. Take your time to read through the code to understand how it was constructed.

Listing 9-5. Book Class (library_v1.py)

```
class Book(object):
    """Book class

    This class encapsulates the books table permitting CRUD operations
    on the data.
    """
    def __init__(self, library):
        self.library = library

    def create(self, ISBN, Title, Year, PublisherId, Authors=[], Edition=1,
               Language='English'):
        assert ISBN, "You must supply an ISBN for a new book."
```

```
    assert Title, "You must supply Title for a new book."
    assert Year, "You must supply a Year for a new book."
    assert PublisherId, "You must supply a PublisherId for a new book."
    assert Authors, "You must supply at least one AuthorId for a new book."
    last_id = ISBN
    #
    # We must do this as a transaction to ensure all tables are updated.
    #
    try:
        self.library.sql("START TRANSACTION")
        query_str = INSERT_BOOK.format(ISBN, Title, Year, PublisherId,
                                       Edition, Language)
        self.library.sql(query_str)
        query_str = INSERT_BOOK_AUTHOR
        for AuthorId in Authors.split(","):
            self.library.sql(query_str.format(ISBN, AuthorId))
        self.library.sql("COMMIT")
    except Exception as err:
        print("ERROR: Cannot add book: {0}".format(err))
        self.library.sql("ROLLBACK")
    return last_id

def read(self, ISBN=None):
    query_str = GET_BOOKS
    if not ISBN:
        # return all authors
        query_str = query_str.format("")
    else:
        # return specific author
        query_str = query_str.format("WHERE ISBN = '{0}'".format(ISBN))
    return self.library.sql(query_str)

def read_notes(self, ISBN):
    assert ISBN, "You must supply an ISBN to get the notes."
    query_str = GET_NOTES.format(ISBN)
    return self.library.sql(query_str)
```

```python
def read_author_ids(self, ISBN):
    assert ISBN, "You must supply an ISBN to get the list of author ids."
    query_str = GET_AUTHOR_IDS.format(ISBN)
    return self.library.sql(query_str)

def update(self, old_isbn, ISBN, Title=None, Year=None, PublisherId=None,
           Authors=None, Edition=None, Language=None, Note=None):
    assert ISBN, "You must supply an ISBN to update the book."
    last_id = None
    #
    # Build the book update query
    #
    book_query_str = UPDATE_BOOK.format(ISBN)
    if Title:
        book_query_str += ", Title = '{0}'".format(Title)
    if Year:
        book_query_str += ", Year = {0}".format(Year)
    if PublisherId:
        book_query_str += ", PublisherId = {0}".format(PublisherId)
    if Edition:
        book_query_str += ", Edition = {0}".format(Edition)
    book_query_str += " WHERE ISBN = '{0}'".format(old_isbn)
    #
    # We must do this as a transaction to ensure all tables are updated.
    #
    try:
        self.library.sql("START TRANSACTION")
        #
        # If the ISBN changes, we must remove the author ids first to
        # avoid the foreign key constraint error.
        #
        if old_isbn != ISBN:
            self.library.sql(DELETE_BOOK_AUTHOR.format(old_isbn))
        self.library.sql(book_query_str)
        last_id = self.library.sql(GET_LASTID)
        if Authors:
```

```
                # First, clear the author list.
                self.library.sql(DELETE_BOOK_AUTHOR.format(ISBN))
                query_str = INSERT_BOOK_AUTHOR
                for AuthorId in Authors:
                    self.library.sql(query_str.format(ISBN,AuthorId))
            if Note:
                self.add_note(ISBN, Note)
            self.library.sql("COMMIT")
        except Exception as err:
            print("ERROR: Cannot update book: {0}".format(err))
            self.library.sql("ROLLBACK")
        return last_id

    def delete(self, ISBN):
        assert ISBN, "You must supply a ISBN to delete the book."
        #
        # Here, we must cascade delete the notes when we delete a book.
        # We must do this as a transaction to ensure all tables are updated.
        #
        try:
            self.library.sql("START TRANSACTION")
            query_str = DELETE_NOTES.format(ISBN)
            self.library.sql(query_str)
            query_str = DELETE_BOOK_AUTHOR.format(ISBN)
            self.library.sql(query_str)
            query_str = DELETE_BOOK.format(ISBN)
            self.library.sql(query_str)
            self.library.sql("COMMIT")
        except Exception as err:
            print("ERROR: Cannot delete book: {0}".format(err))
            self.library.sql("ROLLBACK")

    def add_note(self, ISBN, Note):
        assert ISBN, "You must supply a ISBN to add a note for the book."
        assert Note, "You must supply text (Note) to add a note for the book."
        query_str = INSERT_NOTE.format(ISBN, Note)
```

```
    try:
        self.library.sql(query_str)
        self.library.sql("COMMIT")
    except Exception as err:
        print("ERROR: Cannot add publisher: {0}".format(err))
```

Finally, we look at the Library class.

Library Class

Recall, the Library class is used to encapsulate working with the MySQL server. Thus, we create functions for working with the connection (connect, disconnect, is_connected). We also create a function that we can use to execute queries. This is mainly for convenience and not generally required. The function is named sql() and handles returning result sets or errors as necessary. The last function is used to return an abbreviated dataset of the books in the database, which is used to populate the book list page. Listing 9-6 shows the code for the Library class. As you will see, it too is very straightforward.

Listing 9-6. Library Class (library_v1.py)

```python
class Library(object):
    """Library master class

    Use this class to interface with the library database. It includes
    utility functions for connections to the server as well as running
    queries.
    """

    def __init__(self):
        self.db_conn = None

    def connect(self, username, passwd, host, port, db=None):
        config = {
            'user': username,
            'password': passwd,
            'host': host,
            'port': port,
            'database': db,
        }
```

```
    try:
        self.db_conn = mysql.connector.connect(**config)
    except mysql.connector.Error as err:
        print("CONNECTION ERROR:", err)
        self.db_conn = None
        raise

#
# Return the connection for use in other classes
#
def get_connection(self):
    return self.db_conn

#
# Check to see if connected to the server
#
def is_connected(self):
    return (self.db_conn and (self.db_conn.is_connected()))

#
# Disconnect from the server
#
def disconnect(self):
    try:
        self.db_conn.disconnect()
    except:
        pass

#
# Execute a query and return any results
#
# query_str[in]     The query to execute
# fetch             Execute the fetch as part of the operation and
#                   use a buffered cursor (default is True)
# buffered          If True, use a buffered raw cursor (default is False)
#
# Returns result set or cursor
```

```python
    #
    def sql(self, query_str, fetch=True, buffered=False):
        # If we are fetching all, we need to use a buffered
        if fetch:
            cur = self.db_conn.cursor(buffered=True)
        else:
            cur = self.db_conn.cursor(raw=True)

        try:
            cur.execute(query_str)
        except Exception as err:
            cur.close()
            print("Query error. Command: {0}:{1}".format(query_str, err))
            raise

        # Fetch rows (only if available or fetch = True).
        if cur.with_rows:
            if fetch:
                try:
                    results = cur.fetchall()
                except mysql.connector.Error as err:
                    print("Error fetching all query data: {0}".format(err))
                    raise
                finally:
                    cur.close()
                return results
            else:
                # Return cursor to fetch rows elsewhere (fetch = false).
                return cur
        else:
            return cur

    #
    # Get list of books
    #
    def get_books(self):
```

```
try:
    results = self.sql(ALL_BOOKS)
except Exception as err:
    print("ERROR: {0}".format(err))
    raise
return results
```

Now that we have the database code module, let's look at the application code.

Application Code

There are only a few areas in the application code from the base code we saw earlier where we need to add more code. This includes adding the import statement for the database code module, setting up the Library class instance, and adding code to the author, publisher, and book view functions to use the classes in the database code module. It is fortunate that the template files we created in the user interface discussion can be used without modification.

To build this version of the application, you should copy the base/mylibrary_base. py file to version1/mylibrary_v1.py and either enter the code below or retrieve it from the Apress book web site.

Although the code may appear to be long, it isn't complicated. Further, except for the book view function, the logic is the same pattern for the author and publisher view. The book view has more logic to enable the add note feature. The following sections discuss the changes needed for each area. Recall, we need the mylibrary_base.py code we saw in an earlier section.

Setup and Initialization

The code for setup and initialization for the Library class is simple. We need only import the classes from the code module and then create an instance of the Library class and call the connect() function as shown in the following. The import statement goes at the end of the other import statements and the Library setup code can go anywhere after that. In the example code, this code is placed before the first form class function.

```
from database.library_v1 import Library, Author, Publisher, Book
[...]
#
# Setup the library database class
#
library = Library()
# Provide your user credentials here
library.connect(<user>, <password>, 'localhost', 3306)
```

Note   Be sure to change the `<user>` and `<password>` entries to match your MySQL configuration. These are placeholders for the user account and password.

List View Function

The list view function requires only a few modifications. We will use the `Library` class instance (named `library`) to get the data from the database to be displayed in the list on the page. For books, this is simply calling the `library.get_books()` function. For authors, we instantiate an instance of the `Author` and `Publisher` classes then call the `read()` function without any parameters. Recall from the previous sections, this results in reading all the rows in the table. Listing 9-7 shows the changes needed for the `simple_list()` view function. The new lines of code are in bold. As you can see, we're only adding five lines of code. Simple!

Listing 9-7. List View Function (Version 1)

```
def simple_list(kind=None):
    rows = []
    columns = []
    form = ListForm()
    if kind == 'book' or not kind:
        if request.method == 'POST':
            return redirect('book')
```

```
    columns = (
        '<td style="width:200px">ISBN</td>',
        '<td style="width:400px">Title</td>',
        '<td style="width:200px">Publisher</td>',
        '<td style="width:80px">Year</td>',
        '<td style="width:300px">Authors</td>',
    )
    kind = 'book'
    # Here, we get all books in the database
    rows = library.get_books()
    return render_template("list.html", form=form, rows=rows,
                            columns=columns, kind=kind)
elif kind == 'author':
    if request.method == 'POST':
        return redirect('author')
    # Just list the authors
    columns = (
        '<td style="width:100px">Lastname</td>',
        '<td style="width:200px">Firstname</td>',
    )
    kind = 'author'
    # Here, we get all authors in the database
    author = Author(library)
    rows = author.read()
    return render_template("list.html", form=form, rows=rows,
                            columns=columns, kind=kind)
elif kind == 'publisher':
    if request.method == 'POST':
        return redirect('publisher')
    columns = (
        '<td style="width:300px">Name</td>',
        '<td style="width:100px">City</td>',
        '<td style="width:300px">URL/Website</td>',
    )
    kind = 'publisher'
```

```
    # Here, we get all publishers in the database
    publisher = Publisher(library)
    rows = publisher.read()
    return render_template("list.html", form=form, rows=rows,
                                columns=columns, kind=kind)
else:
    flash("Something is wrong!")
    return
```

Author View Function

The changes for the author view function are a bit more complicated. Because the author, publisher, and book view functions follow the same pattern, we will discuss the pattern in general first then see the code for view each function. Because the concept of GET and POST operations may be new to you, we will take a moment and discuss the differences.

We want to use this view function for both GET and POST operations. In particular, when the user clicks on an author in the list, we want to display the data from that row in the table. Or, if the user clicks on the New button, we want to present an empty HTML form for the user to complete. So far, these are GET operations. If the user then clicks on the submit field (either Add, Update, or Delete), we then want to take the data from the user and either create, update, or delete the data. These are POST operations. How this works in a view function is not immediately obvious. However, it makes sense once you get used to it. Let's run through the conditions for how a view function is called. Table 9-1 lists the different conditions (or mode).

Table 9-1. *Operations (Modes) for View Functions*

Operation	Type	Action
Add	GET	Present an empty form and provide a submit field named Add
Create	POST	Save data to the database for one data item
Read	GET	Show data from the database for one data item and provide submit fields named Update and Delete
Update	POST	Save updated data to the database for existing data item
Delete	POST	Remove the data item from the database

Note that there are two GET operations and three POST operations. The GET operations are to present either an empty form or to read from a row in the table. The POST operations are events that occur when the user clicks on one of the submit fields resulting in either a create, update, or delete.

Returning the to the author view function, we need to add code for the operations listed above. Rather than discuss the code at length then present it, Listing 9-8 shows the completed code for the author view function. Line numbers have been added to make it easier to see the lines of code discussed. Detailed discussions of the database code are included after the listing.

Listing 9-8. Author View Function (Version 1)

```
01    def author(author_id=None):
02        author = Author(library)
03        form = AuthorForm()
04        # Get data from the form if present
05        form_authorid = form.authorid.data
06        firstname = form.firstname.data
07        lastname = form.lastname.data
08        # If the route with the variable is called, change the create
              button to update
09        # then populate the form with the data from the row in the table.
              Otherwise,
10        # remove the delete button because this will be a new data item.
11        if author_id:
12            form.create_button.label.text = "Update"
13            # Here, we get the data and populate the form
14            data = author.read(author_id)
15            if data == []:
16                flash("Author not found!")
17            form.authorid.data = data[0][0]
18            form.firstname.data = data[0][1]
19            form.lastname.data = data[0][2]
20        else:
21            del form.del_button
22        if request.method == 'POST':
```

```
23              # First, determine if we must create, update, or delete when form posts.
24              operation = "Create"
25              if form.create_button.data:
26                  if form.create_button.label.text == "Update":
27                      operation = "Update"
28              if form.del_button and form.del_button.data:
29                  operation = "Delete"
30              if form.validate_on_submit():
31                  # Get the data from the form here
32                  if operation == "Create":
33                      try:
34                          author.create(LastName=lastname, FirstName=firstname)
35                          flash("Added.")
36                          return redirect('/list/author')
37                      except Exception as err:
38                          flash(err)
39                  elif operation == "Update":
40                      try:
41                          author.update(AuthorId=form_authorid,
                                LastName=lastname,
42                                          FirstName=firstname)
43                          flash("Updated.")
44                          return redirect('/list/author')
45                      except Exception as err:
46                          flash(err)
47                  else:
48                      try:
49                          author.delete(form_authorid)
50                          flash("Deleted.")
51                          return redirect('/list/author')
52                      except Exception as err:
53                          flash(err)
54              else:
55                  flash_errors(form)
56      return render_template("author.html", form=form)
```

The first thing we do is add an instance of the Author class and pass it to the Library class instance as shown in line 2. Next, to cover operations where we need the data from the form, we place code at the top of the view function to copy data from the form to local variables as shown in lines 4-7. This ensures if the view function is called again for a POST operation that we capture any data entered by the user. If we hadn't done this, we could not use the view function for new and existing data.

Next, we must cover the route where we pass in the primary key (in this case author_id). If the author_id is present, we change the label of one of the submit fields (add) to Update. We also know we must read data from the database, which we do with the author.read(author_id) call on line 14 and if we retrieve the row without errors, we place the data from the table into the fields in lines 17—19. If the author_id variable is not present, we remove the delete submit field on line 21.

At this point, we've covered the operations of add and read shown in Table 9-1. The create, update, and delete operations are executed only when the request is a POST. To determine this, we check the value of the request.method attribute on line 22. If it is POST, we then must decide which operation is active. We can do this by checking the text of the submit fields. We use a default of create but change it to update or delete based on which submit field was clicked. You can see these operations in lines 24-29.

In particular, if a submit field is clicked, on POST, the data attribute will be True. Thus, we can see which operation we need to perform based on which button was clicked. In the case of the create button, we know it is create unless the label was changed to update and in that case the operation matches—update. On the other hand, if the delete button was not removed and it was clicked, the operation is delete. This is one method of how you can reuse a view function for multiple operations.

Now that we know which operation is active, we execute the action. However, we only do so if the fields have all passed their validation checks. The code on line 30 will return True if all fields have been validated. Thus, we only execute the active operation if the form fields are validated.

The create operation is shown in lines 33-38. Note that we use a try block to detect errors. To create a new author, we simply call the author.create() function with the data from the form. Likewise, the update operation is shown in lines 40-45. Once again, we use a try block to detect errors. To update an existing author, we call the author.update() function with the data from the form. Finally, the delete operation is shown in lines 46-53. Again, we use a try block to detect errors. To delete an existing author, we call the author.delete() function with the author_id from the form.

Now, let's look at the publisher view function, which is very similar.

Publisher View Function

Because the publisher view function is very similar to the author view function (it is
the same design or pattern), I only summarize the code describing only the database
operations in detail. Listing 9-9 shows the completed code for the publisher view
function. Line numbers have been added to make it easier to see the lines of code
discussed. Detailed discussions of the database code are included after the listing.

Listing 9-9. Publisher View Function (Version 1)

```
01    def publisher(publisher_id=None):
02        publisher = Publisher(library)
03        form = PublisherForm()
04        # Get data from the form if present
05        form_publisherid = form.publisherid.data
06        name = form.name.data
07        city = form.city.data
08        url = form.url.data
09        # If the route with the variable is called, change the create
              button to update then populate the form with the data from the
10        # row in the table. Otherwise, remove the delete button because
11        # this will be a new data item.
12        if publisher_id:
13            # Here, we get the data and populate the form
14            form.create_button.label.text = "Update"
15            # Here, we get the data and populate the form
16            data = publisher.read(publisher_id)
17            if data == []:
18                flash("Publisher not found!")
19            form.publisherid.data = data[0][0]
20            form.name.data = data[0][1]
21            form.city.data = data[0][2]
22            form.url.data = data[0][3]
23        else:
24            del form.del_button
25        if request.method == 'POST':
```

```
26          # First, determine if we must create, update, or delete when
               form posts.
27          operation = "Create"
28          if form.create_button.data:
29              if form.create_button.label.text == "Update":
30                  operation = "Update"
31          if form.del_button and form.del_button.data:
32              operation = "Delete"
33          if form.validate_on_submit():
34              # Get the data from the form here
35              if operation == "Create":
36                  try:
37                      publisher.create(Name=name, City=city, URL=url)
38                      flash("Added.")
39                      return redirect('/list/publisher')
40                  except Exception as err:
41                      flash(err)
42              elif operation == "Update":
43                  try:
44                      publisher.update(PublisherId=form_publisherid,
                        Name=name,
45                                          City=city, URL=url)
46                      flash("Updated.")
47                      return redirect('/list/publisher')
48                  except Exception as err:
49                      flash(err)
50              else:
51                  try:
52                      publisher.delete(form_publisherid)
53                      flash("Deleted.")
54                      return redirect('/list/publisher')
55                  except Exception as err:
56                      flash(err)
57          else:
58              flash_errors(form)
59      return render_template("publisher.html", form=form)
```

A with the author view function, line 2 instantiates an instance of the `Publisher` class and lines 4–8 fetch data from the form for use later. Line 12 begins the section to read data from the database, line 14 changes the label of the add submit button to update, and lines 16–22 store that data in the form. Finally, lines 27–32 determine the active operation for a `POST` request and line 33 ensures the form fields are validated before we execute the database operations.

The create operation is shown in lines 36–41. To create a new publisher, we simply call the `publisher.create()` function with the data from the form. Likewise, the update operation is shown in lines 43–49. To update an existing publisher, we call the `publisher.update()` function with the data from the form. Finally, the delete operation is shown in lines 51–56. To delete an existing publisher, we call the `publisher.delete()` function with the `publisher_id` from the form.

POP QUIZ

Did you notice a small difference in how we handled the publisher_id? Instead of using the variable from the route, we get the publisher id from the hidden field on the form. This was done intentionally to show an alternative way to save data to the form.

But there is a good reason to use this technique even though it does duplicate a small bit of data. For example, it is possible the user will want to change the ISBN. Because the ISBN is the primary key for the table, if we use the ISBN from the GET request (the /book/978-1-4842-2724-4 route), the database operation will fail to located the row because the ISBN was changed on the form.

This also demonstrates how surrogate primary keys such as auto increment fields can help save you from this potential data land mine.

Now, let's look at the book view function, which follows the same pattern but requires a bit more logic.

Book View Function

The book view function is more complicated than the author or publisher view function for three reasons: 1) it has more fields, 2) there are select fields that require populating, and 3) there is an additional feature for update operations to add notes to the database for the book.

However, the code follows the same pattern as the previous view functions. Listing 9-10 shows the book view function code in its entirety. Once again, line numbers have been added to enhance readability and discussion of the code follows the listing.

Listing 9-10. Book View Function (Version 1)

```
01    def book(isbn_selected=None):
02        notes = None
03        book = Book(library)
04        form = BookForm()
05        # Get data from the form if present
06        isbn = form.isbn.data
07        title = form.title.data
08        year = form.year.data
09        authorids = form.authors.data
10        publisherid = form.publisher.data
11        edition = form.edition.data
12        language = form.language.data
13        #
14        # Here, we get the choices for the select lists
15        #
16        publisher = Publisher(library)
17        publishers = publisher.read()
18        publisher_list = []
19        for pub in publishers:
20            publisher_list.append((pub[0], '{0}'.format(pub[1])))
21        form.publisher.choices = publisher_list
22        author = Author(library)
23        authors = author.read()
24        author_list = []
25        for author in authors:
26            author_list.append((author[0],'{0}, {1}'.format(author[2],
                  author[1])))
27        form.authors.choices = author_list
28        new_note = form.new_note.data
```

```
29          # If the route with the variable is called, change the create
                button to update then populate the form with the data from
30          # the row in the table. Otherwise, remove the delete button
31          # because this will be a new data item.
32          if isbn_selected:
33              # Here, we get the data and populate the form
34              data = book.read(isbn_selected)
35              if data == []:
36                  flash("Book not found!")
37
38              #
39              # Here, we populate the data
40              #
41              form.isbn.data = data[0][0]
42              form.title.data = data[0][1]
43              form.year.data = data[0][2]
44              form.edition.data = data[0][3]
45              form.publisher.process_data(data[0][4])
46              form.language.data = data[0][5]
47              #
48              # Here, we get the author_ids for the authors
49              #
50              author_ids = book.read_author_ids(isbn_selected)[0][0]
51              form.authors.data = set(author_ids)
52
53              # We also must retrieve the notes for the book.
54              all_notes = book.read_notes(isbn_selected)
55              notes = []
56              for note in all_notes:
57                  notes.append(note[2])
58              form.create_button.label.text = "Update"
59          else:
60              del form.del_button
61          if request.method == 'POST':
```

```
62          # First, determine if we must create, update, or delete when
                form posts.
63          operation = "Create"
64          if form.create_button.data:
65              if form.create_button.label.text == "Update":
66                  operation = "Update"
67          if form.del_button and form.del_button.data:
68              operation = "Delete"
69          if form.validate_on_submit():
70              # Get the data from the form here
71              if operation == "Create":
72                  try:
73                      book.create(ISBN=isbn, Title=title, Year=year,
74                              PublisherId=publisherid,
                            Authors=authorids,
75                              Edition=edition, Language=language)
76                      flash("Added.")
77                      return redirect('/list/book')
78                  except Exception as err:
79                      flash(err)
80              elif operation == "Update":
81                  try:
82                      book.update(isbn_selected, ISBN=isbn,
                        Title=title, Year=year,
83                              PublisherId=publisherid,
                            Authors=authorids,
84                              Edition=edition, Language=language,
85                              Note=new_note)
86                      flash("Updated.")
87                      return redirect('/list/book')
88                  except Exception as err:
89                      flash(err)
90              else:
91                  try:
92                      book.delete(isbn)
```

```
93                          flash("Deleted.")
94                          return redirect('/list/book')
95                  except Exception as err:
96                          flash(err)
97          else:
98                  flash_errors(form)
99      return render_template("book.html", form=form, notes=notes)
```

First, you may notice we have a new variable named *notes*, which is set to None. We do this here because we will use this variable to contain all the notes for the book as read from the database. More on that later.

As with the author and publisher view functions, line 3 instantiates an instance of the Book class and lines 6–12 fetch data from the form for use later. Next is the code for populating the select fields with values from the database. We do this because the book table is dependent on the authors (technically via the books_authors join table, and publishers tables. Thus, we need to fetch the rows from both tables to populate the dropdown and multiple select lists.

Lines 16–21 are for the publisher data. Here, we first instantiate an instance of the Publisher class then retrieve all the data from the table. Next, we loop through the rows adding the publisher id and name to a list, which is then assigned to the data attribute for the select field choices attribute (form.publisher.choices). Why do we include the publisher id? Because the publisher id is only stored in the book table.

Likewise, lines 22–27 do the same for author data creating an instance of the Author class retrieving all the rows then looping through the data to add the author id, and concatenated last and first name. As with the select field, we populate the field data with the new array. At this point, we have both select fields populated. How to set the value to match the rows comes next along with retrieving the data from the database.

Line 32 begins the section to read data from the database. Lines 34–57 retrieve the data from the database and populates for form. For the select fields, setting the data attribute ensures the values are selected. In the case of the publisher, we set the select field data and the item that matches is selected by default. In the case of the select multiple field, we pass a comma-separated list as shown in lines 50–51 where we retrieve a list of author ids from the database. Next, we retrieve the notes for the book and populate an array we use in the template to populate the HTML table.

Wow! That's a lot of work, isn't it? All of that work was to setup the form for the add and read operations. Fortunately, the create, update, and delete setup is the same as the other view functions. You can see this in lines 63–9.

The database operations thankfully are familiar. The create operation is shown in lines 72–79. To create a new book, we simply call the book.create() function with the data from the form. Likewise, the update operation is shown in lines 81–89. To update an existing book, we call the book.update() function with the data from the form. Finally, the delete operation is shown in lines 91–96. To delete an existing book, we call the book.delete() function with the isbn from the form.

Templates

There were no changes to the template files from the base version. All you need to do is create a new folder and copy the files from the base. In particular, copy base/templates/* to version1/templates/.

The only change you need to make is to change the "base" text in the base.html file to "V1" as shown in the difference example in the following where the line with the "-" is removed and the line with the "+" is added.

```
-           <a class="navbar-brand" href="/">MyLibrary Base</a>
+           <a class="navbar-brand" href="/">MyLibrary v1</a>
```

Now that we have the code updated, let's see how it works!

Executing the Code

Now that the code is written, let's give it a test drive. Be sure to create the database and any tables necessary first. If you saved the previous SQL statements in a file named library_v1.sql, you can use the SOURCE command in the mysql client as follows.

```
mysql> SOURCE <path>/version1/library_v1.sql;
```

To execute the application, you can launch it with the Python interpreter specifying the runserver command. The following shows an example of executing the application. Note that we used the port option to specify the port. You should enter this command from the version1 folder. Note that we specify the port as 5001. We will use 5002 for version 2 and 5003 for version 3. This will allow you to run all three versions simultaneously.

```
$ cd version1
$ python ./mylibrary_v1.py runserver -p 5001
 * Running on http://127.0.0.1:5001/ (Press CTRL+C to quit)
```

The application will launch and run but there isn't any data in the database yet. You should start by grabbing a couple of your favorite books and enter the authors and publishers first then enter the book data. Don't worry about the notes just yet. Once you've added a few books, you should see them in the default view (by clicking on MyLibrary v1 or Books in the navigation bar. Figure 9-2 shows an example of what you should see. The other views are similar and are left as an exercise for the reader to explore.

Action	ISBN	Title	Publisher	Year	Authors
Modify	978-1449339586	MySQL High Availability	OReilly	2014	Bell, Kindahl, Thalmann
Modify	978-1-4842-3122-7	MicroPython for the Internet of Things	Apress	2017	Bell
Modify	978-1-4842-2724-4	Introducing the MySQL 8 Document Store	Apress	2018	Bell
Modify	978-1-4842-2107-5	Windows 10 for the Internet of Things	Apress	2017	Bell
Modify	978-1-4842-1294-3	MySQL for the Internet of Things	Apress	2016	Bell

Figure 9-2. *Library application book list (version 1)*

Next, try out the notes feature. Click on the *Modify link* in the list for one of the books in the books list and then add a note and click *Update*. When you next view the data by clicking on the *Modify link*, you will see the note appear. Figure 9-3 shows an excerpt of the notes list for a book.

Notes
Covers the Arduino and Raspberry Pi.
Has a walk-through for installing MySQL on Windows.
Demonstrates how to use MySQL with Python.

Figure 9-3. *Notes list example (version 1)*

Before we move on to version 2, let's take a moment to discuss some observations about this version of the application.

Observations

The following are some observations about this version of the application. Some are consequences of the database design, others are from the code, and others are things we may want to change to make the application a bit better. The observations are presented in the form of an unordered list. If you want to experiment with this version of the application, you can consider some of these are challenges for improving the application. Otherwise, consider this list something to think about for the next version.

- *Lengthy code*: The code for the application is quite long (over 400 lines).

- *Lengthy database code module*: The code for the database code module is also quite long (over 400 lines).

- *Over-designed tables*: The many-to-many table is unnecessarily complicated, which makes working with SQL a bit more difficult.

- *Database design can be improved*: Savvy database administrators will undoubtedly spot areas that can be improved in the database design. For example, the use of a view can replace the query used in the get_books() function of the Library class.

- *Over-analyzed data*: One of the banes of relational database design is overuse of normal forms in the face of usability. In this case, it is unlikely the user will care to know a list of authors because there is no additional meaningful information—just the author's first and last name.

- *Simplistic read*: The default mechanism to view data is a list. Although this works fine for authors and publishers, it is restrictive for books because you must click on the Modify link to see the notes for the book. This can be improved with a simple read-only mode rather than update.

- *Older protocols*: There is no X DevAPI integration.

Now, let's look at the next version of the application.

Version 2: Relational Database + JSON Fields (Hybrid)

This version implements a relational database augmented with JSON fields. We model the data based on the views or data items but use a JSON field to eliminate one of the issues of traditional relational database solutions: many-to-many joins. For the purposes of demonstration, we will implement the database code in a code module that we can import into the application code. Although we will use MySQL Connector/Python as in version 1, we will be using the X DevAPI using SQL statements to work with the data. The goal is to demonstrate how to migrate to using the X DevAPI but preserving the SQL interface. Thus, this version presents a hybrid solution.

The many-to-many relationship in the version 1 database was so that we could make a link from a book to one or more authors and that we may have more than one book with the same authors. However, like most applications, the database design has revealed a case where we have more sophistication than what is needed. In particular, we have a table for authors but find that we only store (or care about) the first and last name. Further, use of the application has shown we have no use cases for querying author data other than to list them with the book.

Therefore, we can eliminate the many-to-many relationship storing the list of author names in a JSON field instead. This has led to other minor changes such as the stored routines and other additions.

Let's start with a brief overview of the database design after the changes. Because the database is the same as version 1 with minor changes, we will present a brief overview concentrating only on the differences.

Database Design

The database for this version is named library_v2. Because the goal is to remove the many-to-many relationship, we removed the books_authors join table replacing it with a JSON field in the books table and removed the authors table. Thus, we have reduced the database from five tables to three. Figure 9-4 shows the ERD for the library_v2 database complete with indexes and foreign keys.

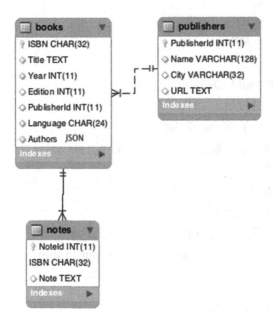

Figure 9-4. *ERD diagram—library database (version 2)*

By eliminating the many-to-many relationship, we can remove the select multiple field for the authors on the book view. We can replace it with a simple comma-separated list, which is easy to convert to JSON. Thus, we need a way to retrieve the names from the JSON field returning the comma-separated list. We can do this with a stored routine (function).

Listing 9-11 shows the CREATE statements for all the objects. If you want to follow along building this version of the application while you read, you should create a file named library_v2.sql so that you can recreate the database later.

Listing 9-11. Library Version 2 Database Create Script (library_v2.sql)

```
CREATE DATABASE `library_v2`;
CREATE TABLE `library_v2`.`publishers` (
  `PublisherId` int(11) NOT NULL AUTO_INCREMENT,
  `Name` varchar(128) NOT NULL,
  `City` varchar(32) DEFAULT NULL,
  `URL` text,
  PRIMARY KEY (`PublisherId`)
) ENGINE=InnoDB;
```

```
CREATE TABLE `library_v2`.`books` (
  `ISBN` char(32) NOT NULL,
  `Title` text NOT NULL,
  `Year` int(11) NOT NULL DEFAULT '2017',
  `Edition` int(11) DEFAULT '1',
  `PublisherId` int(11) DEFAULT NULL,
  `Language` char(24) NOT NULL DEFAULT 'English',
  `Authors` JSON NOT NULL,
  PRIMARY KEY (`ISBN`),
  KEY `Pub_id` (`PublisherId`),
  CONSTRAINT `books_fk_1` FOREIGN KEY (`PublisherId`)
    REFERENCES `library_v2`.`publishers` (`publisherid`)
) ENGINE=InnoDB;

CREATE TABLE `library_v2`.`notes` (
  `NoteId` int(11) NOT NULL AUTO_INCREMENT,
  `ISBN` char(32) NOT NULL,
  `Note` text,
  PRIMARY KEY (`NoteId`,`ISBN`),
  KEY `ISBN` (`ISBN`),
  CONSTRAINT `notes_fk_1` FOREIGN KEY (`ISBN`)
    REFERENCES `library_v2`.`books` (`isbn`)
) ENGINE=InnoDB;

DELIMITER //
CREATE FUNCTION `library_v2`.`get_author_names`(isbn_lookup char(32))
  RETURNS text DETERMINISTIC
BEGIN
  DECLARE j_array varchar(255);
  DECLARE num_items int;
  DECLARE i int;
  DECLARE last char(20);
  DECLARE first char(20);
  DECLARE csv varchar(255);
  SET j_array = (SELECT JSON_EXTRACT(Authors,'$.authors')
                FROM library_v2.books WHERE ISBN = isbn_lookup);
```

```
  SET num_items = JSON_LENGTH(j_array);
  SET csv = "";
  SET i = 0;
  author_loop: LOOP
    IF i < num_items THEN
      SET last = CONCAT('$[',i,'].LastName');
      SET first = CONCAT('$[',i,'].FirstName');
      IF i > 0 THEN
        SET csv = CONCAT(csv,", ",JSON_UNQUOTE(JSON_EXTRACT(j_array,last)),' ',
                         JSON_UNQUOTE(JSON_EXTRACT(j_array,first)));
      ELSE
        SET csv = CONCAT(JSON_UNQUOTE(JSON_EXTRACT(j_array,last)),' ',
                         JSON_UNQUOTE(JSON_EXTRACT(j_array,first)));
      END IF;
      SET i = i + 1;
    ELSE
      LEAVE author_loop;
    END IF;
  END LOOP;
  RETURN csv;
END//
DELIMITER ;
```

Note the new function named get_author_names(). The function retrieves the JSON document from the row matching the ISBN and creates a comma-separated list of authors. This is used in the presentation of the author data to make it easier for users to view.

Now that we've got the database created, let's see the code for the database class.

Database Code

The code for working with the database is placed in a file named library_v2.py in the database folder under the version2 folder as described in Chapter 8 under the section, "Preparing the Directory Structure." The code is based on version 1 converted to use the X DevAPI, and there is no longer a need for a class for the authors table. That said the code implements three classes: one for each of the data views—publisher and book— and another class for interfacing with the server. These classes are named Publisher, Book, and Library, respectfully.

However, because the code is based on version 1, I discuss the changes rather than another lengthy discussion on the classes and how they work. The following summarizes the changes.

- The ALL_BOOKS query is considerably shorter and easier to maintain.

- A new GET_PUBLISHER_NAME query is added to populate the book list.

- The INSERT_BOOK query needs an additional column for the authors JSON document.

- All the queries for the authors table are removed.

- We change GET_AUTHOR_IDS to GET_AUTHOR_NAMES since we're only working with names in the JSON document.

- The database name changes from library_v1 to library_v2.

To create the file, you can simply copy the file from version1/database/library_v1.py to version2/database/library_v2.py.

Code Deleted

Begin by deleting the Authors class and the SQL statements for the author table. They will not be needed.

SQL Strings

Because this version also uses SQL statements, place these in the preamble of the code module as strings that can be referenced later in the code. Listing 9-12 shows the preamble for the library_v2.py code module, which replaces what was used for the first version. Note that it begins with importing the MySQL Connector/Python X DevAPI library. The changes listed earlier (aside from the version 1 to 2 rename) are shown in bold in the listing.

Listing 9-12. Initialization and SQL Statements (library_v2.py)

```
import mysqlx

ALL_BOOKS = """
    SELECT DISTINCT book.ISBN, book.ISBN, Title, PublisherId, Year,
                    library_v2.get_author_names(book.ISBN) as Authors
```

```
    FROM library_v2.books As book
    ORDER BY book.ISBN DESC
"""

GET_PUBLISHER_NAME = """
    SELECT Name
    FROM library_v2.publishers
    WHERE PublisherId = {0}
"""

GET_LASTID = "SELECT @@last_insert_id"

INSERT_PUBLISHER = """
    INSERT INTO library_v2.publishers (Name, City, URL) VALUES ('{0}','{1}','{2}')
"""

GET_PUBLISHERS = "SELECT * FROM library_v2.publishers {0}"
UPDATE_PUBLISHER = "UPDATE library_v2.publishers SET Name = '{0}'"
DELETE_PUBLISHER = "DELETE FROM library_v2.publishers WHERE PublisherId = {0}"

INSERT_BOOK = """
    INSERT INTO library_v2.books (ISBN, Title, Year, PublisherId, Edition,
    Language, Authors) VALUES ('{0}','{1}','{2}','{3}',{4},'{5}','{6}')
"""

INSERT_NOTE = "INSERT INTO library_v2.notes (ISBN, Note) VALUES ('{0}','{1}')"
GET_BOOKS = "SELECT * FROM library_v2.books {0}"
GET_NOTES = "SELECT * FROM library_v2.notes WHERE ISBN = '{0}'"
GET_AUTHOR_NAMES = "SELECT library_v2.get_author_names('{0}')"
UPDATE_BOOK = "UPDATE library_v2.books SET ISBN = '{0}'"
DELETE_NOTES = "DELETE FROM library_v2.notes WHERE ISBN = '{0}'"
DELETE_BOOK = "DELETE FROM library_v2.books WHERE ISBN = '{0}'"
```

If you recall the length of this same code from version 1, note that we've reduced the number of strings quite a lot. This is largely due to removing the authors table and the many-to-many relationship. So, adding a single JSON field has had a huge impact!

Before we discuss the changes to the Publisher and Book classes, let's discuss the changes to the Library class.

Library Class

The library class is based on version 1, but because we're using the X DevAPI, things will work quite differently. In particular, we will open a session to make a connection to the MySQL server on port 33060 (the default for the X Protocol), and we will use a SQLStatement object for executing SQL statements. The following summarizes the changes to the Library class.

The following lists a summary of the changes for the Library class.

- We use a session object instead of a connection object.

- The connect() function is changed to retrieve a session from the mysql_x library.

- The sql() function is vastly simplified to only return the result from session.sql()—a SQLStatment object.

- We add a make_rows() function to convert the row results from the SQLStatement object into an array.

- The get_books() function calls the make_rows() function chaining the SQLStatement execute() function (passed as a parameter).

Note   The changes to the Library class are designed to demonstrate how to migrate from the old protocol to using the X DevAPI. As you will see, it is possible to minimize changes to existing database libraries as well as dependent code by using the same methods but with different database access methods.

Listing 9-13 shows the modified Library class. The changes from version 1 are shown in bold. Note that we have the same methods as the first version but instead of a connection object, we use a session object and the renamed functions to get and check the session. These are always good functions to include as you may need them as you develop more advanced features.

Listing 9-13. Library Class (library_v2.py)

```python
class Library(object):
    """Library master class

    Use this class to interface with the library database. It includes
    utility functions for connections to the server and returning a
    SQLStatement object.
    """

    def __init__(self):
        self.session = None

    #
    # Connect to a MySQL server at host, port
    #
    # Attempts to connect to the server as specified by the connection
    # parameters.
    #
    def connect(self, username, passwd, host, port):
        config = {
            'user': username,
            'password': passwd,
            'host': host,
            'port': port,
        }
        try:
            self.session = mysqlx.get_session(**config)
        except Exception as err:
            print("CONNECTION ERROR:", err)
            self.session = None
            raise

    #
    # Return the session for use in other classes
    #
    def get_session(self):
        return self.session
```

```python
#
# Check to see if connected to the server
#
def is_connected(self):
    return (self.session and (self.session.is_open()))

#
# Disconnect from the server
#
def disconnect(self):
    try:
        self.session.close()
    except:
        pass

#
# Get an SQLStatement object
#
def sql(self, query_str):
    return self.session.sql(query_str)

#
#  Build row array
#
#  Here, we cheat a bit and give an option to substitute the publisher name
#  for publisher Id column.
#
def make_rows(self, sql_res, get_publisher=False):
    cols = []
    for col in sql_res.columns:
        cols.append(col.get_column_name())
    rows = []
    for row in sql_res.fetch_all():
        row_item = []
        for col in cols:
            if get_publisher and (col == 'PublisherId'):
                query_str = GET_PUBLISHER_NAME.format(row.get_string(col))
```

```
                name = self.session.sql(query_str).execute().fetch_one()[0]
                row_item.append("{0}".format(name))
            else:
                row_item.append("{0}".format(row.get_string(col)))
        rows.append(row_item)
    return rows

    #
    # Get list of books
    #
    def get_books(self):
        try:
            sql_stmt = self.sql(ALL_BOOKS)
            results = self.make_rows(sql_stmt.execute(), True)
        except Exception as err:
            print("ERROR: {0}".format(err))
            raise
        return results
```

Note how much shorter the sql() function is compared to version 1. Recall, the sql() function from version 1 was 30 lines in length. Using the SQLStatement object instance has saved us a lot of coding! We will see this theme continue in version 3. In fact, we see the get_books() function is also a bit shorter. Nice.

There is a new function as previously mentioned. The function, make_rows() takes the result object, fetches all of the rows, and converts it to a list. There may be more effective ways to do this, but this demonstrates some of what you may need to do to transition your existing code to use the X DevAPI.

Next, let's look at the Publisher class.

Publisher Class

The Publisher class is nearly the same as the version 1 code except we adapt it for use with the X DevAPI. In particular, because we are getting a SQLStatement object returned from the sql() function in the Library class, we can chain that with the execute() function of the SQLStatement instance and get the result. We also utilize the make_rows() function of the Library class to make an array for the rows in a result. Listing 9-14 shows the complete code for the Publisher class with the changes shown in bold for clarity.

Listing 9-14. Publisher Class (library_v2.py)

```python
class Publisher(object):
    """Publisher class

    This class encapsulates the publishers table permitting CRUD operations
    on the data.
    """

    def __init__(self, library):
        self.library = library

    def create(self, Name, City=None, URL=None):
        assert Name, "You must supply a Name for a new publisher."
        query_str = INSERT_PUBLISHER
        last_id = None
        try:
            self.library.sql(query_str.format(Name, City, URL)).execute()
            last_id = self.library.make_rows(
                self.library.sql(GET_LASTID).execute())[0][0]
            self.library.sql("COMMIT").execute()
        except Exception as err:
            print("ERROR: Cannot add publisher: {0}".format(err))
        return last_id

    def read(self, PublisherId=None):
        query_str = GET_PUBLISHERS
        if not PublisherId:
            # return all authors
            query_str = query_str.format("")
        else:
            # return specific author
            query_str = query_str.format(
                "WHERE PublisherId = '{0}'".format(PublisherId))
        sql_stmt = self.library.sql(query_str)
        return self.library.make_rows(sql_stmt.execute())
```

```python
def update(self, PublisherId, Name, City=None, URL=None):
    assert PublisherId, "You must supply a publisher to update the author."
    query_str = UPDATE_PUBLISHER.format(Name)
    if City:
        query_str = query_str + ", City = '{0}'".format(City)
    if URL:
        query_str = query_str + ", URL = '{0}'".format(URL)
    query_str = query_str + " WHERE PublisherId = {0}".format(PublisherId)
    try:
        self.library.sql(query_str).execute()
        self.library.sql("COMMIT").execute()
    except Exception as err:
        print("ERROR: Cannot update publisher: {0}".format(err))

def delete(self, PublisherId):
    assert PublisherId, "You must supply a publisher to delete the publisher."
    query_str = DELETE_PUBLISHER.format(PublisherId)
    try:
        self.library.sql(query_str).execute()
        self.library.sql("COMMIT").execute()
    except Exception as err:
        print("ERROR: Cannot delete publisher: {0}".format(err))
```

As you can see, the changes are minimal and once again demonstrate how easy it is to migrate code to the new X DevAPI.

Now let's look at the Book class, which has a similar short list of changes.

Book Class

The Book class, like the Publisher class, has few changes from the version 1 code. We have the same changes for using the X DevAPI but we also need to handle converting the comma-separated list of authors to a JSON document. We will use a helper function for this. We also reduce the complexity of the code by removing the join table. The following summarizes the changes to this version of the Book class.

- We use the sql() function of the Library class chaining the execute() function to execute the SQL statement.

- We prepare the SQLStatement object instance before we call the make_rows() function of the Library class.

- We add a function make_authors_json() to convert a comma-separated list of author names to a JSON document.

- We remove the code for working with the books_authors table.

Listing 9-15 shows the complete code for the Book class for clarity with the changes shown in bold. As you will see, despite adding more lines for working with JSON documents, the code is a bit shorter than the previous version.

Listing 9-15. Book Class (library_v2.py)

```python
class Book(object):
    """Book class
    This class encapsulates the books table permitting CRUD operations
    on the data.
    """

    def __init__(self, library):
        self.library = library

    def make_authors_json(self, author_list=None):
        from json import JSONEncoder

        if not author_list:
            return None
        author_dict = {"authors":[]}
        authors = author_list.split(",")
        for author in authors:
            try:
                last, first = author.strip(' ').split(' ')
            except Exception as err:
                last = author.strip(' ')
                first = ''
            author_dict["authors"].append({"LastName":last,"FirstName":first})
        author_json = JSONEncoder().encode(author_dict)
        return author_json
```

```python
def create(self, ISBN, Title, Year, PublisherId, Authors=[], Edition=1,
           Language='English'):
    assert ISBN, "You must supply an ISBN for a new book."
    assert Title, "You must supply Title for a new book."
    assert Year, "You must supply a Year for a new book."
    assert PublisherId, "You must supply a publisher for a new book."
    assert Authors, "You must supply at least one Author for a new book."
    query_str = INSERT_BOOK
    last_id = ISBN
    try:
        author_json = self.make_authors_json(Authors)
        self.library.sql(query_str.format(ISBN, Title, Year, PublisherId,
                                          Edition, Language,
                                          author_json)).execute()
        self.library.sql("COMMIT").execute()
    except Exception as err:
        print("ERROR: Cannot add book: {0}".format(err))
        self.library.sql("ROLLBACK").execute()
    return last_id

def read(self, ISBN=None):
    query_str = GET_BOOKS
    if not ISBN:
        # return all authors
        query_str = query_str.format("")
    else:
        # return specific author
        query_str = query_str.format("WHERE ISBN = '{0}'".format(ISBN))
    sql_stmt = self.library.sql(query_str)
    return self.library.make_rows(sql_stmt.execute())

#
# Get the notes for this book
#
def read_notes(self, ISBN):
    assert ISBN, "You must supply an ISBN to get the notes."
```

```
        query_str = GET_NOTES.format(ISBN)
        sql_stmt = self.library.sql(query_str)
        return self.library.make_rows(sql_stmt.execute())

    #
    # Get the authors for this book
    #
    def read_authors(self, ISBN):
        assert ISBN, "You must supply an ISBN to get the list of author ids."
        query_str = GET_AUTHOR_NAMES.format(ISBN)
        sql_stmt = self.library.sql(query_str)
        return self.library.make_rows(sql_stmt.execute())

    def update(self, old_isbn, ISBN, Title=None, Year=None, PublisherId=None,
               Authors=None, Edition=None, Language=None, Note=None):
        assert ISBN, "You must supply an ISBN to update the book."
        last_id = None
        #
        # Build the book update query
        #
        book_query_str = UPDATE_BOOK.format(ISBN)
        if Title:
            book_query_str += ", Title = '{0}'".format(Title)
        if Year:
            book_query_str += ", Year = {0}".format(Year)
        if PublisherId:
            book_query_str += ", PublisherId = {0}".format(PublisherId)
        if Edition:
            book_query_str += ", Edition = {0}".format(Edition)
        if Authors:
            author_json = self.make_authors_json(Authors)
            book_query_str += ", Authors = '{0}'".format(author_json)
        book_query_str += " WHERE ISBN = '{0}'".format(old_isbn)
        #
        # We must do this as a transaction to ensure all tables are updated.
        #
```

```python
        try:
            self.library.sql("START TRANSACTION").execute()
            self.library.sql(book_query_str).execute()
            if Note:
                self.add_note(ISBN, Note)
            self.library.sql("COMMIT").execute()
        except Exception as err:
            print("ERROR: Cannot update book: {0}".format(err))
            self.library.sql("ROLLBACK").execute()
        return last_id

    def delete(self, ISBN):
        assert ISBN, "You must supply a ISBN to delete the book."
        #
        # Here, we must cascade delete the notes when we delete a book.
        # We must do this as a transaction to ensure all tables are updated.
        #
        try:
            self.library.sql("START TRANSACTION").execute()
            query_str = DELETE_NOTES.format(ISBN)
            self.library.sql(query_str).execute()
            query_str = DELETE_BOOK.format(ISBN)
            self.library.sql(query_str).execute()
            self.library.sql("COMMIT").execute()
        except Exception as err:
            print("ERROR: Cannot delete book: {0}".format(err))
            self.library.sql("ROLLBACK").execute()

    #
    # Add a note for this book
    #
    def add_note(self, ISBN, Note):
        assert ISBN, "You must supply a ISBN to add a note for the book."
        assert Note, "You must supply text (Note) to add a note for the book."
        query_str = INSERT_NOTE.format(ISBN, Note)
        try:
```

```
        self.library.sql(query_str).execute()
        self.library.sql("COMMIT").execute()
    except Exception as err:
        print("ERROR: Cannot add note: {0}".format(err))
```

Note the new function, make_author_json(), which demonstrates how to build a JSON document. In this case, it is a simple JSON array built using the Python JSON encoder. We also see in the update() function how to incorporate the JSON document into our UPDATE SQL statement. Sweet!

That wasn't too bad, was it? Now, let's look at the changes to the application code.

Application Code

There are some minor changes in the application code from the version 1 code we saw earlier. This includes adapting the user interface to remove the authors view and add the authors list to the book view form. Fortunately, most of the code from version 1 can be used without modification.

To build this version of the application, you should copy the version1/mylibrary_v1.py file to version2/mylibrary_v2.py and either enter the code below or retrieve it from the Apress book web site. The following lists the changes for the application code. Although this looks like a long list, most are trivial changes. The following sections describe the changes in more detail.

- Remove the Author class from the import statement.

- Change the port from 3306 to 33060.

- Remove the NewSelectMultipleField class as it is no longer needed (it was used in the book view form to show a list of authors to choose).

- Remove the author view function and template.

- Replace the multiple select field on the book detail page to a text field.

- Remove the author list from the list view function.

- Change the code to read a list of author names rather than ids.

- Add the author list to create and update calls to the Book class.

- Pass the list of author names from the new text field to the render_template() function in the book view function.

- No changes are needed for the publisher view function, form class, or template.

- No changes are needed for the list form class or template.

- The base template was changed to indicate version 2 of the application.

We look at the changes starting with the changes to setup and initialization.

Setup and Initialization

Changes to the setup and initialization are trivial. We need only remove the Author class from the imports, change library_v1 to library_v2, and change the default port in the connect() function as shown in the following.

```
from database.library_v2 import Library, Publisher, Book
...
library.connect(<user>, <password>, 'localhost', 33060)
```

Form Classes

First, we can remove the AuthorForm and NewSelectMultipleField classes because we don't need them. It is fortunate that there are no changes needed for the PublisherForm class. Even the BookForm class has only a minor change to switch the multiple select field to a text field. Listing 9-16 shows the modified BookForm class code with the changes in bold. As you will see, it is only one line of code to change.

Listing 9-16. Book Form Class (Version 2)

```
class BookForm(FlaskForm):
    isbn = TextField('ISBN ', validators=[
            Required(message=REQUIRED.format("ISBN")),
            Length(min=1, max=32, message=RANGE.format("ISBN", 1, 32))
        ])
    title = TextField('Title ',
                    validators=[Required(message=REQUIRED.format("Title"))])
```

```
year = IntegerField('Year ',
                    validators=[Required(message=REQUIRED.format("Year"))])
edition = IntegerField('Edition ')
language = TextField('Language ', validators=[
        Required(message=REQUIRED.format("Language")),
        Length(min=1, max=24, message=RANGE.format("Language", 1, 24))
    ])
publisher = NewSelectField('Publisher ',
                    validators=[Required(message=REQUIRED.format("Publisher"))])
authors = TextField('Authors (comma separated by LastName FirstName)',
                    validators=[Required(message=REQUIRED.format("Author"))])
create_button = SubmitField('Add')
del_button = SubmitField('Delete')
new_note = TextAreaField('Add Note')
```

View Functions

First, we can remove the author() view function as it is no longer needed. It is fortunate that there are no changes needed for the publisher view function.

However, we need to modify the simple_list() view function to remove the author list option. Listing 9-17 shows the modified template with the area where code was removed as shown in bold.

Listing 9-17. List View Function (Version 2)

```
def simple_list(kind=None):
    rows = []
    columns = []
    form = ListForm()
    if kind == 'book' or not kind:
        if request.method == 'POST':
            return redirect('book')
        columns = (
            '<td style="width:200px">ISBN</td>',
            '<td style="width:400px">Title</td>',
            '<td style="width:200px">Publisher</td>',
            '<td style="width:80px">Year</td>',
```

```
            '<td style="width:300px">Authors</td>',
        )
        kind = 'book'
        # Here, we get all books in the database
        rows = library.get_books()
        return render_template("list.html", form=form, rows=rows,
                              columns=columns, kind=kind)
    elif kind == 'publisher':
        if request.method == 'POST':
            return redirect('publisher')
        columns = (
            '<td style="width:300px">Name</td>',
            '<td style="width:100px">City</td>',
            '<td style="width:300px">URL/Website</td>',
        )
        kind = 'publisher'
        # Here, we get all publishers in the database
        publisher = Publisher(library)
        rows = publisher.read()
        return render_template("list.html", form=form, rows=rows,
                              columns=columns, kind=kind)
    else:
        flash("Something is wrong!")
        return
```

We also need to modify the book view function. There are more changes needed in this section because the authors for a book are now a JSON document and we use a comma-separated list to specify them in the book detail form. The following lists the changes needed for this code.

- We change the authorids list of ids to author_list to contain the comma-separated list.

- We remove the Author() class code.

- We change fetching a list of author ids to a list retrieving the comma-separated list.

- We do not need the author list for the template file.

453

Listing 9-18 shows the changes to the book view function with the changes shown in bold.

Listing 9-18. Book View Function (Version 2)

```
def book(isbn_selected=None):
    notes = None
    book = Book(library)
    form = BookForm()
    # Get data from the form if present
    isbn = form.isbn.data
    title = form.title.data
    year = form.year.data
    author_list = form.authors.data
    publisherid = form.publisher.data
    edition = form.edition.data
    language = form.language.data
    #
    # Here, we get the choices for the select lists
    #
    publisher = Publisher(library)
    publishers = publisher.read()
    publisher_list = []
    for pub in publishers:
        publisher_list.append((pub[0], '{0}'.format(pub[1])))
    form.publisher.choices = publisher_list
    new_note = form.new_note.data
    # If the route with the variable is called, change the create button to update
    # then populate the form with the data from the row in the table. Otherwise,
    # remove the delete button because this will be a new data item.
    if isbn_selected:
        # Here, we get the data and populate the form
        data = book.read(isbn_selected)
        if data == []:
            flash("Book not found!")
```

```
        #
        # Here, we populate the data
        #
        form.isbn.data = data[0][0]
        form.title.data = data[0][1]
        form.year.data = data[0][2]
        form.edition.data = data[0][3]
        form.publisher.process_data(data[0][4])
        form.language.data = data[0][5]
        form.authors.data = book.read_authors(isbn_selected)[0][0]

        # We also must retrieve the notes for the book.
        all_notes = book.read_notes(isbn_selected)
        notes = []
        for note in all_notes:
            notes.append(note[2])
        form.create_button.label.text = "Update"
else:
    del form.del_button
if request.method == 'POST':
    # First, determine if we must create, update, or delete when form posts.
    operation = "Create"
    if form.create_button.data:
        if form.create_button.label.text == "Update":
            operation = "Update"
    if form.del_button and form.del_button.data:
        operation = "Delete"
    if form.validate_on_submit():
        # Get the data from the form here
        if operation == "Create":
            try:
                book.create(ISBN=isbn, Title=title, Year=year,
                            PublisherId=publisherid, Authors=author_list,
                            Edition=edition, Language=language)
                flash("Added.")
                return redirect('/list/book')
```

```
            except Exception as err:
                flash(err)
        elif operation == "Update":
            try:
                book.update(isbn_selected, isbn, Title=title, Year=year,
                            PublisherId=publisherid, Authors=author_list,
                            Edition=edition, Language=language,
                            Note=new_note)
                flash("Updated.")
                return redirect('/list/book')
            except Exception as err:
                flash(err)
        else:
            try:
                book.delete(isbn)
                flash("Deleted.")
                return redirect('/list/book')
            except Exception as err:
                flash(err)
    else:
        flash_errors(form)
    return render_template("book.html", form=form, notes=notes,
                            authors=author_list)
```

No additional changes are needed for the application code. Once again, that wasn't so bad. We're not done just yet. There are some minor changes needed for the templates.

Templates

The changes to the template files are minor. If you haven't already done so, copy the templates from version 1 to version 2. For example, copy all the files from version1/ templates/* to version2/templates. Once copied, you can remove the author.html template as we no longer need it.

We also need to make two small changes to the base.html file to change the version number and remove the author list from the navigation bar. Listing 9-19 shows an excerpt from the base.html file with the changes shown in bold.

Listing 9-19. Base Template (Version 2)

```
<div class="navbar navbar-inverse" role="navigation">
    <div class="container">
        <div class="navbar-header">
            <button type="button" class="navbar-toggle" data-
            toggle="collapse" data-target=".navbar-collapse">
                <span class="sr-only">Toggle navigation</span>
                <span class="icon-bar"></span>
                <span class="icon-bar"></span>
                <span class="icon-bar"></span>
            </button>
            <a class="navbar-brand" href="/">MyLibrary v2</a>
        </div>
        <div class="navbar-collapse collapse">
            <ul class="nav navbar-nav">
                <li><a href="/list/book">Books</a></li>
            </ul>
            <ul class="nav navbar-nav">
                <li><a href="/list/publisher">Publishers</a></li>
            </ul>
        </div>
    </div>
</div>
```

We must also make two small changes to the book.html template to show a text field for the comma-separated list of authors. Listing 9-20 shows an excerpt of the modified template with the changes in bold.

Listing 9-20. Book Template (Version 2)

```
{% extends "base.html" %}
{% block title %}MyLibrary Search{% endblock %}
{% block page_content %}
  <form method=post> {{ form.csrf_token }}
    <fieldset>
      <legend>Book - Detail</legend>
      {{ form.hidden_tag() }}
```

```
<div style=font-size:20pz; font-weight:bold; margin-left:150px;>
  {{ form.isbn.label }} <br>
  {{ form.isbn(size=32) }} <br>
  {{ form.title.label }} <br>
  {{ form.title(size=100) }} <br>
  {{ form.year.label }} <br>
  {{ form.year(size=10) }} <br>
  {{ form.edition.label }} <br>
  {{ form.edition(size=10) }} <br>
  {{ form.language.label }} <br>
  {{ form.language(size=34) }} <br>
  {{ form.publisher.label }} <br>
  {{ form.publisher(style="width: 300px;") }} <br><br>
  {{ form.authors.label }} <br>
  {{ form.authors(size=100) }} <br>
  {# Show the new note text field if this is an update. #}
  {% if form.create_button.label.text == "Update" %}
    <br>{{ form.new_note.label }} <br>
    {{ form.new_note(rows='2',cols='100') }}
  {% endif %}
```
...

Ok, that's it for the changes now let's see the code in action.

Executing the Code

Now that we've got the code written, let's give it a test drive. To execute the application, you can launch it with the Python interpreter specifying the runserver command. The following shows an example of executing the application. Note that we used the port option to specify the port. You should enter this command from the version2 folder.

```
$ cd version2
$ python ./mylibrary_v2.py runserver -p 5002
 * Running on http://127.0.0.1:5002/ (Press CTRL+C to quit)
```

The application will launch and run but there isn't any data in the database yet. You should start by grabbing a couple of your favorite books and enter the authors and publishers first then enter the book data. Don't worry about the notes just yet. Once you've added a few books, you should see them in the default view (by clicking on MyLibrary v2 or Books in the navigation bar. Figure 9-5 shows an example of what you should see. The other views are similar and are left as an exercise for the reader to explore.

MyLibrary v2   Books   Publishers

New

Query Results

Action	ISBN	Title	Publisher	Year	Authors
Modify	978-1449339586	MySQL High Availability	OReilly	2014	Bell Charles, Kindahl Mats, Thalmann Lars
Modify	978-1-4842-3122-7	MicroPython for the Internet of Things	Apress	2017	Bell Charles
Modify	978-1-4842-2724-4	Introducing the MySQL 8 Document Store	Apress	2018	Bell Charles
Modify	978-1-4842-2107-5	Windows 10 for the Internet of Things	Apress	2017	Bell Charles
Modify	978-1-4842-1294-3	MySQL for the Internet of Things	Apress	2016	Bell Charles
Modify	978-1-4842-1174-8	3D Printing with Delta Printers	Apress	2015	Bell Charles

Figure 9-5. *Library application book list (version 2)*

Note that we removed the author entry in the navigation bar because we no longer have a detailed view. Rather, the author list is stored in a JSON document with the book. Figure 9-6 shows the new form.

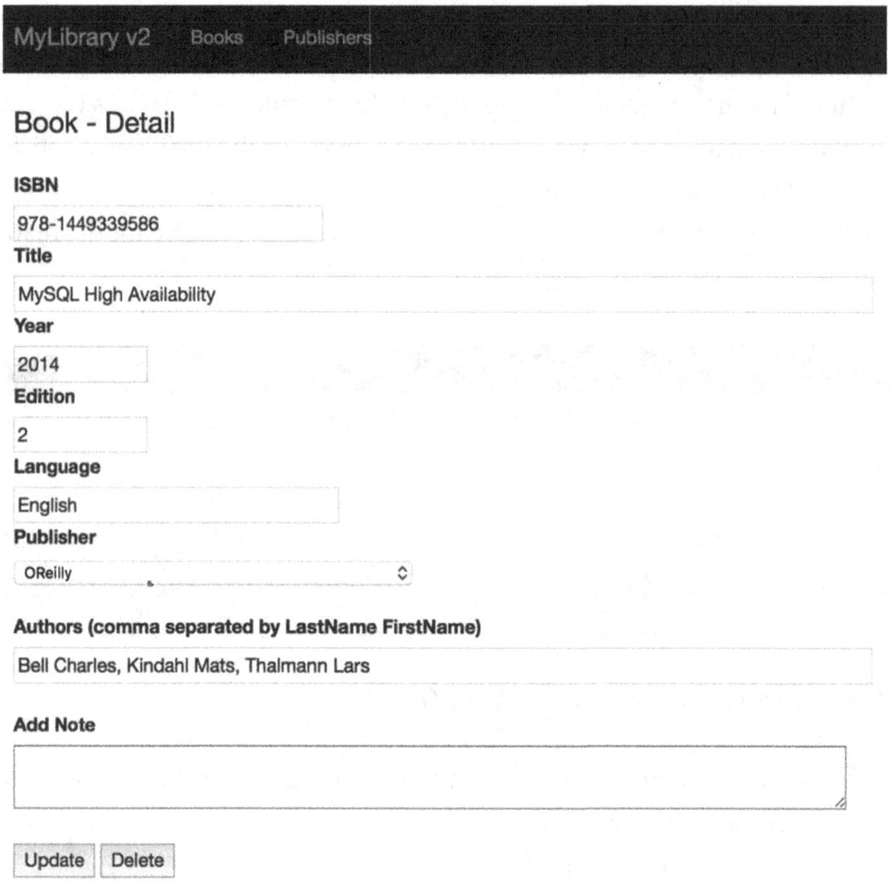

Figure 9-6. *Book detailed view (version 2)*

Note that the authors entry is now a text field instead of a multiple select list. Some may see this as more intuitive while others may feel the multiple select list is better. The comma-separated list was chosen for demonstration purposes, but feel free to experiment with your own ideas for how to collect and display information about the authors for a book.

The publisher view is unchanged from version 1.

Before we move on to version 3, let's take a moment to discuss some observations about this version of the application.

Observations

The following are some observations about this version of the application. Some are consequences of the database design, others are from the code, and others are things we may want to change to make the application a bit better. The observations are presented in the form of an unordered list. If you want to experiment with this version of the application, you can consider some of them challenges for improving the application. Otherwise, consider this list something to think about for the next version.

- *Further simplify database with JSON*: The notes table also can be converted to a JSON field in the books table because there is no need to query the notes table without viewing it in context with a book and one row in the notes table matches one and only one row in the books table.

- *The database code is shorter*: We need less code in the database code module to implement the application.

- *The application code is shorter*: We need less code in the application.

- *Some conversion code is needed for JSON*: Although Python provides a library for working with JSON and it is possible to use JSON documents directly in Python as data structures, we need to add code to convert JSON to a more human readable form. In this case, it was working with a list of author names.

- *Author list may need to be improved*: Although designed for demonstration purposes, the comma-separated list may not be the best choice for novice users.

Now, let's look at the last version of the application.

Version 3: Document Store

This version implements a pure document store version of the data. For the purposes of demonstration, we will implement the database code in a code module that we can import into the application code. We will be using the X DevAPI managing a collection to store and retrieve the data. The goal is to demonstrate how to migrate to using JSON documents instead of the SQL interface.

To do this, we will flatten the database from multiple tables to a single collection of documents—more specifically, a collection of books. Let's start with a brief overview of the design of the database.

Database Design

Calling this a database design is a little archaic as we aren't working with a database logically but a schema in the X DevAPI terminology. Implementation wise it is still a database in MySQL and will show as such in the SHOW DATABASES command as shown in the following (`library_v3`) in the output from the MySQL Shell.

```
$ mysqlsh root@localhost:33060 -mx --sql
Creating an X protocol session to 'root@localhost:33060'
...
 MySQL  localhost:33060+ ssl  SQL > SHOW DATABASES;
+--------------------+
| Database           |
+--------------------+
| animals            |
| information_schema |
| library_v1         |
| library_v2         |
| library_v3         |
| mysql              |
| performance_schema |
| sys                |
+--------------------+
8 rows in set (0.00 sec)
```

The database (schema) contains only one table, which was created as a collection. You can do this using the commands shown here in the MySQL Shell.

```
$ mysqlsh root@localhost:33060 -mx --py
Creating an X protocol session to 'root@localhost:33060'
...
```

```
MySQL  localhost:33060+ ssl  Py > import mysqlx
MySQL  localhost:33060+ ssl  Py > session = mysqlx.get_
                                    session('root:password@localhost:33060')
MySQL  localhost:33060+ ssl  Py > schema = session.create_schema('library_v3')
MySQL  localhost:33060+ ssl  Py > collection = schema.create_collection('books')
```

Note that we get a session then create the schema and finally create the collection. This new collection will appear in the library_v3 database as a table named books, but its CREATE statement looks very different. The following shows the CREATE statement for the table. You should never need to use this statement and should always use the MySQL Shell and X DevAPI to create schemas, collections, or any object in the X DevAPI pantheon.

```
MySQL  localhost:33060+ ssl  SQL > SHOW CREATE TABLE library_v3.books \G
*************************** 1. row ***************************
       Table: books
Create Table: CREATE TABLE `books` (
  `doc` json DEFAULT NULL,
  `_id` varchar(32) GENERATED ALWAYS AS (json_unquote(json_extract(`doc`,
  _utf8mb4'$._id'))) STORED NOT NULL,
  PRIMARY KEY (`_id`)
) ENGINE=InnoDB DEFAULT CHARSET=utf8mb4
1 row in set (0.00 sec)
```

Don't worry that the CREATE statement looks strange. It's supposed to look this way. After all, it is a collection implemented as a table of rows containing a document id and a JSON field. Note that there is a primary key defined so that will make lookups by id fast. Cool.

Now that we've got the schema (database) and collection (table) created, let's see the code for the database class.

Database Code

The changes to the database code for this version of the application are a bit longer than the last version. Although we switched to using the X DevAPI in version 2, we were still using an SQL interface. This version uses a pure X DevAPI interface.

The code for working with the database is placed in a file named `library_v3.py` in the `database` folder under the `version3` folder as described in Chapter 8 under the section, "Preparing the Directory Structure." The code is based on version 2 converted to use the X DevAPI, and we no longer need a class for the publishers table. However, because the code is based on version 2, we will discuss the changes rather than another lengthy discussion on the classes and how they work. The following summarizes the changes.

- Add the `JSONEncoder` import statement.

- Remove all the SQL statements (yes!).

- Remove the `Publisher` class.

- Rename the `Book` class to `Books`.

- Change the `Books` class to use session, schema, and collection object instances.

- Remove the `make_authors_json()` function.

- Remove the `Library` class moving the utility functions to the `Books` class.

- The database name changes from `library_v2` to `library_v3`.

To create the file, you can simply copy the file from `version2/database/library_v2.py` to `version3/database/library_v3.py`.

Code Deleted

Begin by deleting the `Publishers` class and all the SQL statements. We won't need those. You also will need to delete the `Library` class, but we will still use some of the methods in that class. See the section on the Books class for more details.

Setup and Initialization

Once you've deleted the SQL statements, we need to add an import statement to import the Python JSON encoder class. The following code should be placed at the end of the imports section.

```
from json import JSONEncoder as encoder
```

Books Class

This class is where the rest of the code changes appear. The following sections briefly describe each of the changes followed by a complete listing of the modified class. Note that the first thing we do is change the class name from Book to Books because we are modeling a collection of books rather than a single book.

Tip   This is one of the fundamental "think" changes one must make when working with collections. Although you can model a single document, most will gravitate naturally to modeling a collection of document (things).

Class Declaration

The following shows the modified class declaration. Note that we renamed the class and comments to reflect the changes to the class model. Note we also declare two more class variables in the constructor; book_schema and book_col. The class variable book_schema is used to store an instance of the schema object and the book_col variable is used to store an instance of the collection object. These will be initialized in the connect() function.

```
#
# Books collection simple abstraction (document store)
#
class Books(object):
    """Books class

    This class encapsulates the books collection permitting CRUD operations
    on the data.
    """

    def __init__(self):
        self.session = None
        self.book_schema = None
        self.book_col =  None
```

Create Function

Next, we change the `create()` function to work better with a collection. In this case, we change the parameter list to include the three pieces of data for the publisher; name, city, and URL. We also use a function we will write to make the JSON complex document. The new function is named `make_book_json()` and will be described later. You also can remove the `make_authors_json()` function. Finally, we change the code to use the `book_col` class variable to add the book to the collection followed by a lookup for the document id of the new book. Recall, the document id is assigned by the server so retrieving it this way allows us to use it to quickly locate the document. Listing 9-21 shows the modified create() statement with the changed areas in bold.

Note   The indentation for the functions in the library class should be indented 4 spaces. Spaces are omitted in the listings for readability.

Listing 9-21. Create Function (Version 3)

```
def create(self, ISBN, Title, Pub_Year, Pub_Name, Pub_City, Pub_URL,
           Authors=[], Notes=[], Edition=1, Language='English'):
    assert ISBN, "You must supply an ISBN for a new book."
    assert Title, "You must supply Title for a new book."
    assert Pub_Year, "You must supply a Year for a new book."
    assert Pub_Name, "You must supply a Publisher Name for a new book."
    assert Authors, "You must supply at least one Author Name for a new book."
    last_id = None
    try:
        book_json = self.make_book_json(ISBN, Title, Pub_Year, Pub_Name,
                                        Pub_City, Pub_URL, Authors, Notes,
                                        Edition, Language)
        self.book_col.add(book_json).execute()
        last_id = self.book_col.find(
            "ISBN = '{0}'".format(ISBN)).execute().fetch_all()[0]["_id"]
    except Exception as err:
        print("ERROR: Cannot add book: {0}".format(err))
    return last_id
```

Read Function

The read() function is greatly simplified now that we are using the collection object. Indeed, all we need to do is call the find() function passing in the document id and then fetch the document—all in one line of code! Auxiliary read functions from version 2 are removed, see the "Utility Functions" section later for more details.

```
def read(self, bookid=None):
    return self.book_col.find("_id = '{0}'".format(bookid)).execute().
    fetch_one()
```

Update Function

The update function is where a lot of code is changed. This is due to how we form the chain of modify() clauses for updating a collection. More specific, the code has been changed to detect when a data element is changed and if it has changed, call the modify().set().execute() chain to modify the data. Because we are doing more than one set of these changes potentially, we use the session class variable to start a transaction then if all statements succeed, commit it to the collection. If not, we rollback the changes.

The other changes have to do with how we handle the notes and author arrays. The publisher data is easy because we will place text boxes on the web page to hold the data. Listing 9-22 shows the modified create() function. Most of this code differs from version 2.

Listing 9-22. Update Function (Version 3)

```
def update(self, book_id, book_data, ISBN, Title, Pub_Year, Pub_Name, Pub_City,
           Pub_URL, Authors=[], New_Note=None, Edition=1, Language='English'):
    assert book_id, "You must supply an book id to update the book."
    try:
        bkid = "_id = '{0}'".format(book_id)
        self.session.start_transaction()
        if ISBN != book_data["ISBN"]:
            self.book_col.modify(bkid).set("ISBN", ISBN).execute()
        if Title != book_data["Title"]:
            self.book_col.modify(bkid).set("Title", Title).execute()
```

```python
            if Pub_Year != book_data["Pub_Year"]:
                self.book_col.modify(bkid).set("Pub_Year", Pub_Year).execute()
            if Pub_Name != book_data["Publisher"]["Name"]:
                self.book_col.modify(bkid).set("$.Publisher.Name", Pub_Name).
                execute()
            if Pub_City != book_data["Publisher"]["City"]:
                self.book_col.modify(bkid).set("$.Publisher.City", Pub_City).
                execute()
            if Pub_URL != book_data["Publisher"]["URL"]:
                self.book_col.modify(bkid).set("$.Publisher.URL", Pub_URL).
                execute()
            if Edition != book_data["Edition"]:
                self.book_col.modify(bkid).set("Edition", Edition).execute()
            if Language != book_data["Language"]:
                self.book_col.modify(bkid).set("Language", Language).execute()
            if New_Note:
                #
                # If this is the first note, we create the array otherwise,
                # we append to it.
                #
                if not "Notes" in book_data.keys():
                    mod_book = self.book_col.modify(bkid)
                    mod_book.set("Notes", [{"Text":New_Note}]).execute()
                else:
                    mod_book =  self.book_col.modify(bkid)
                    mod_book.array_append("Notes", {"Text":New_Note}).execute()
            if Authors and (Authors != self.make_authors_str(book_data['Authors'])):
                authors_json = self.make_authors_dict_list(Authors)
                self.book_col.modify(bkid).set("Authors", authors_json).execute()
            self.session.commit()
        except Exception as err:
            print("ERROR: Cannot update book: {0}".format(err))
            self.session.rollback()
```

Take some time to read through this code to ensure you see how we've gone from simply updating the entire data row to checking to see what items need to change and to set those. The nature of the X DevAPI is such that it enables (and encourages) such behavior as we only want to change what has changed and nothing else to save processing time (and more).

Delete Function

The delete() function also undergoes some change, but much less than the create() function. As with the read() function, the X DevAPI makes it much easier for us to perform a delete operation. Instead of having to execute a series of deletes as we did in version 1 and 2, we only need to use the remove_one() convenience function of the collection to find the book by document id and delete it. Nice! The following shows the modified delete() function.

```
def delete(self, book_id):
    assert book_id, "You must supply a book id to delete the book."
    try:
        self.book_col.remove_one(book_id).execute()
    except Exception as err:
        print("ERROR: Cannot delete book: {0}".format(err))
        self.session.rollback()
```

Utility Functions

There are also a number of changes to the utility functions. The following summarizes the changes needed and later paragraphs provide more details on the change.

- Remove functions no longer needed.

- Move the connect() and get_books() functions from the old Library class to the Books.

- Add new functions for working with JSON documents.

There are a lot of extra functions that are not needed for a pure document store code module. We deleted the make_authors_json(), read_notes(), add_note(), read_authors(), get_session(), is_connected(), disconnect(), make_rows(), and sql() functions from the library class as we do not need them anymore. Because the author and publisher data is part of the document, we treat the collection as an object rather than a gateway to a database server.

The connect() function requires some minor changes to allow us to work with the session object. Listing 9-23 shows the modified connect() function with the changes in bold. This function is moved to the Books class. Here, we attempt to get a session using the connection parameters passed (note there is no database parameter), then get the schema object for the library_v3 schema and finally get the collection object for the books collection.

Listing 9-23. Connect( ) Function (Version 3)

```
def connect(self, username, passwd, host, port):
    config = {
        'user': username,
        'password': passwd,
        'host': host,
        'port': port,
    }
    try:
        self.session = mysqlx.get_session(**config)
        if self.session.is_open():
            self.book_schema = self.session.get_schema("library_v3")
            self.book_col = self.book_schema.get_collection("books")
    except Exception as err:
        print("CONNECTION ERROR:", err)
        self.session = None
        raise
```

The get_books() function is simplified over version 2 because instead of issuing an SQL statement read a book, we use the collection object to find all of the books. We also use a rewrite of an older function to return an array of documents that we can use in Python. This new function is named make_row_array() and will be explained in the next sections.

```
def get_books(self):
    rows = []
    try:
        book_docs = self.book_col.find().sort("ISBN").execute().fetch_all();
        rows = self.make_row_array(book_docs)
    except Exception as err:
```

```
        print("ERROR: {0}".format(err))
        raise
    return rows
```

Finally, there are a number of new functions we need to add to make working with the JSON documents a bit easier. The following lists and summarizes the new functions. We leave the code for these to the next section where we list the complete code for the Books class. As you will see, there are no surprises in how these functions were coded.

- `make_authors_str(<array>)`: Given an array of authors, return a comma-separated list of first name last name.

- `make_authors_dict_list(<string>)`: Given a comma-separated list of author names, return a list (array) of dictionaries containing author first and last names.

- `make_book_json(<params>)`: Given a parameter list of the data from the fields on the web page, return a JSON document populated with the data.

- `make_row_array(<array or JSON documents>)`: Given an array of JSON documents, return an array of dictionaries containing a subset of the JSON document elements. Note that this is used to show the list of books in the collection.

Completed Code

Because there are a lot of changes necessary to this version of the database code and the Books class in particular, it is a good idea to see the completed code in its entirety. Listing 9-24 shows the complete code for the Books class. You can study this code to see how the many changes above were implemented.

Listing 9-24. Books Class (Version 3)

```
class Books(object):
    """Books class

    This class encapsulates the books collection permitting CRUD operations
    on the data.
    """
```

```python
    def __init__(self):
        self.session = None
        self.book_schema = None
        self.book_col =  None

    def create(self, ISBN, Title, Pub_Year, Pub_Name, Pub_City, Pub_URL,
               Authors=[], Notes=[], Edition=1, Language='English'):
        assert ISBN, "You must supply an ISBN for a new book."
        assert Title, "You must supply Title for a new book."
        assert Pub_Year, "You must supply a Year for a new book."
        assert Pub_Name, "You must supply a Publisher Name for a new book."
        assert Authors, "You must supply at least one Author Name for a new book."
        last_id = None
        try:
            book_json = self.make_book_json(ISBN, Title, Pub_Year, Pub_Name,
                                            Pub_City, Pub_URL, Authors, Notes,
                                            Edition, Language)
            self.book_col.add(book_json).execute()
            last_id = self.book_col.find(
                "ISBN = '{0}'".format(ISBN)).execute().fetch_all()[0]["_id"]
        except Exception as err:
            print("ERROR: Cannot add book: {0}".format(err))
        return last_id

    def read(self, bookid=None):
        return self.book_col.find("_id = '{0}'".format(bookid)).execute().
        fetch_one()

    def update(self, book_id, book_data, ISBN, Title, Pub_Year, Pub_Name, Pub_City,
               Pub_URL, Authors=[], New_Note=None, Edition=1, Language='English'):
        assert book_id, "You must supply an book id to update the book."
        try:
            bkid = "_id = '{0}'".format(book_id)
            self.session.start_transaction()
            if ISBN != book_data["ISBN"]:
                self.book_col.modify(bkid).set("ISBN", ISBN).execute()
            if Title != book_data["Title"]:
```

```
            self.book_col.modify(bkid).set("Title", Title).execute()
        if Pub_Year != book_data["Pub_Year"]:
            self.book_col.modify(bkid).set("Pub_Year", Pub_Year).execute()
        if Pub_Name != book_data["Publisher"]["Name"]:
            self.book_col.modify(bkid).set("$.Publisher.Name",
            Pub_Name).execute()
        if Pub_City != book_data["Publisher"]["City"]:
            self.book_col.modify(bkid).set("$.Publisher.City",
            Pub_City).execute()
        if Pub_URL != book_data["Publisher"]["URL"]:
            self.book_col.modify(bkid).set("$.Publisher.URL", Pub_URL).
            execute()
        if Edition != book_data["Edition"]:
            self.book_col.modify(bkid).set("Edition", Edition).execute()
        if Language != book_data["Language"]:
            self.book_col.modify(bkid).set("Language", Language).execute()
        if New_Note:
            #
            # If this is the first note, we create the array otherwise,
            # we append to it.
            #
            if not "Notes" in book_data.keys():
                mod_book = self.book_col.modify(bkid)
                mod_book.set("Notes", [{"Text":New_Note}]).execute()
            else:
                mod_book =  self.book_col.modify(bkid)
                mod_book.array_append("Notes", {"Text":New_Note}).execute()
        if Authors and (Authors != self.make_authors_str(book_
        data['Authors'])):
            authors_json = self.make_authors_dict_list(Authors)
            self.book_col.modify(bkid).set("Authors", authors_json).execute()
        self.session.commit()
    except Exception as err:
        print("ERROR: Cannot update book: {0}".format(err))
        self.session.rollback()
```

```python
    def delete(self, book_id):
        assert book_id, "You must supply a book id to delete the book."
        try:
            self.book_col.remove_one(book_id).execute()
        except Exception as err:
            print("ERROR: Cannot delete book: {0}".format(err))
            self.session.rollback()

    #
    # Connect to a MySQL server at host, port
    #
    # Attempts to connect to the server as specified by the connection
    # parameters.
    #
    def connect(self, username, passwd, host, port):
        config = {
            'user': username,
            'password': passwd,
            'host': host,
            'port': port,
        }
        try:
            self.session = mysqlx.get_session(**config)
            if self.session.is_open():
                self.book_schema = self.session.get_schema("library_v3")
                self.book_col = self.book_schema.get_collection("books")
        except Exception as err:
            print("CONNECTION ERROR:", err)
            self.session = None
            raise

    def make_authors_str(self, authors):
        author_str = ""
        num = len(authors)
        i = 0
        while (i < num):
```

```
        author_str += "{0} {1}".format(authors[i]["LastName"],
                                        authors[i]["FirstName"])
        i += 1
        if (i < num):
            author_str += ", "
    return author_str

def make_authors_dict_list(self, author_list=None):
    if not author_list:
        return None
    author_dict_list = []
    authors = author_list.split(",")
    for author in authors:
        try:
            last, first = author.strip(' ').split(' ')
        except Exception as err:
            last = author.strip(' ')
            first = ''
        author_dict_list.append({"LastName":last,"FirstName":first})
    return author_dict_list

def make_book_json(self, ISBN, Title, Pub_Year, Pub_Name, Pub_City, Pub_URL,
                   Authors=[], Notes=[], Edition=1, Language='English'):
    notes_list = []
    for note in Notes:
        notes_list.append({"Text":"{0}".format(note)})
    book_dict = {
        "ISBN": ISBN,
        "Title": Title,
        "Pub_Year": Pub_Year,
        "Edition": Edition,
        "Language": Language,
        "Authors": self.make_authors_dict_list(Authors),
        "Publisher": {
            "Name": Pub_Name,
            "City": Pub_City,
```

```
                "URL": Pub_URL,
            },
            "Notes": notes_list,
        }
        return encoder().encode(book_dict)

    #
    #  Build row array
    #
    def make_row_array(self, book_doc_list):
        rows = []
        for book in book_doc_list:
            book_dict = book
            # Now, we build the row for the book list
            row_item = (
                book_dict["_id"],
                book_dict["ISBN"],
                book_dict["Title"],
                book_dict["Publisher"]["Name"],
                book_dict["Pub_Year"],
                self.make_authors_str(book_dict["Authors"]),
            )
            rows.append(row_item)
        return rows

    #
    # Get list of books
    #
    def get_books(self):
        rows = []
        try:
            book_docs = self.book_col.find().sort("ISBN").execute().fetch_all();
            rows = self.make_row_array(book_docs)
        except Exception as err:
            print("ERROR: {0}".format(err))
            raise
        return rows
```

Wow, that was a lot of changes! This version shows how much different the code for working with collections is from even a hybrid solution. Now, let's look at the changes to the application code.

Application Code

The changes to the application code for this version are not as long as the database code module changes. In essence, we remove the publisher list and detail view and convert the book view function to work the JSON document. There are a number of other small changes as well. The following summarizes the changes. Later sections describe the changes in more detail.

- Import the Books class from the library_v3 module.

- Switch the Library class to the Books class and call the connect() function.

- Remove the NewSelectField() class.

- Remove the PublisherForm() class.

- Change the BookForm class to list the publisher data as fields.

- Change the BookForm class to add hidden fields for the document id and JSON string.

- Remove the publisher option from the ListForm template.

- Remove the publisher view function.

- Modify the book view function to work with the JSON document.

The following sections show the details of the three major areas for changes: setup and initialization, form class, and view functions. To create the file, you can simply copy the file from version1/database/library_v2.py to version2/database/library_v3.py.

Setup and Initialization

The changes to the setup and initialization sections are minor. We must import the Books class from the `library_v3` code module and change the code to use the `Books()` object instead of the `Library()` object in version 2. The following shows the changes in bold.

```
from wtforms import (HiddenField, TextField, TextAreaField,
                     IntegerField, SubmitField)
from wtforms.validators import Required, Length
from database.library_v3 import Books
...
#
# Setup the books document store class
#
books = Books()
# Provide your user credentials here
books.connect(<user>, <password>, 'localhost', 33060)
```

Form Classes

The form classes changes are also minor. First, we delete the `NewSelectField()` and `PublisherForm()` classes as we don't need them anymore. Second, we must modify the `BookForm()` form class to use text fields for the publisher data. Recall, this is name, city, and URL. We also want to add two hidden fields: one for the document id, and another for the JSON document.

The document id will be critical in making it easy to retrieve or update the JSON document and the JSON document stored in the form will allow us to detect when data has changed. Recall from the discussion of the `Books` class in the database code module we do exactly that in the `update()` function. Using hidden fields to contain data like this is common, but you should use the technique sparingly because data in hidden fields are like any other field—you must ensure you update the data in your code otherwise you could be working with stale data.

Listing 9-25 shows the updated `BookForm` for class with changes shown in bold.

Listing 9-25. Book Form Class (Version 3)

```python
class BookForm(FlaskForm):
    isbn = TextField('ISBN ', validators=[
            Required(message=REQUIRED.format("ISBN")),
            Length(min=1, max=32, message=RANGE.format("ISBN", 1, 32))
        ])
    title = TextField('Title ',
                    validators=[Required(message=REQUIRED.format("Title"))])
    year = IntegerField('Year ',
                        validators=[Required(message=REQUIRED.
                        format("Year"))])
    edition = IntegerField('Edition ')
    language = TextField('Language ', validators=[
            Required(message=REQUIRED.format("Language")),
            Length(min=1, max=24, message=RANGE.format("Language", 1, 24))
        ])
    pub_name = TextField('Publisher Name', validators=[
            Required(message=REQUIRED.format("Name")),
            Length(min=1, max=128, message=RANGE.format("Name", 1, 128))
        ])
    pub_city = TextField('Publisher City', validators=[
            Required(message=REQUIRED.format("City")),
            Length(min=1, max=32, message=RANGE.format("City", 1, 32))
        ])
    pub_url = TextField('Publisher URL/Website')
    authors = TextField('Authors (comma separated by LastName FirstName)',
                        validators=[Required(message=REQUIRED.
                        format("Author"))])
    create_button = SubmitField('Add')
    del_button = SubmitField('Delete')
    new_note = TextAreaField('Add Note')
    # Here, we book id for faster updates
    book_id = HiddenField("BookId")
    # Here, we store the book data structure (document)
    book_dict = HiddenField("BookData")
```

479

Book View Function

The view functions area is where most of the changes to the application take place. This is because we must modify the function to use JSON documents (data). It is fortunate that JSON objects translate to code nicely allowing us to use path expressions in the form of array and dictionary key lookups. Cool! The following lists the changes needed to the book view function. Later paragraphs explain the changes in more detail.

- Change publisher list to fields.

- Remove populating the publisher select field.

- Change the variable for the route from the ISBN to document id.

- Use the books() instance instead of book().

- When retrieving data from the collection, use the JSON document directly in Python accessing data items by array index and dictionary keys.

- Detect when data elements are missing for optional fields.

- Call the CRUD functions with the modified parameter lists adding the publisher fields.

As mentioned, the book view function requires modification to include publisher data that is now represented as fields, so we no longer have to populate a select field thereby simplifying the code a bit.

Because the data is now in JSON, we can use the document id as the key thereby eliminating the concern over users changing the primary key (e.g. the ISBN). In fact, using JSON documents allows users to change any field (or add new ones) without creating problems with keys and indexes. Neat!

When retrieving information from the books collection, we have a JSON document that we can access the data in Python as if it were a big dictionary. For example, we can access data items by name like **data["ISBN"]** where ISBN is the key in the dictionary, data. Nice! We see these changes in the section after the **if id_selected:** conditional. For those fields that are optional, we can check the dictionary (JSON object) to see if the key exists and if it does, retrieve the data.

We also see where we've added assignments to save the document id and the original JSON document to the hidden fields. Finally, we must also make a small change to how we call the CRUD functions as we have the extra parameters for the publisher data. Listing 9-26 shows the complete, modified code for the book view function with the modified sections in bold.

Listing 9-26. Book View Function (Version 3)

```
def book(id_selected=None):
    notes = []
    form = BookForm()
    # Get data from the form if present
    bookid = form.book_id.data
    isbn = form.isbn.data
    title = form.title.data
    year = form.year.data
    author_list = form.authors.data
    pub_name = form.pub_name.data
    pub_city = form.pub_city.data
    pub_url = form.pub_url.data
    edition = form.edition.data
    language = form.language.data
    new_note = form.new_note.data
    # If the route with the variable is called, change the create button to update
    # then populate the form with the data from the row in the table. Otherwise,
    # remove the delete button because this will be a new data item.
    if id_selected:
        # Here, we get the data and populate the form
        data = books.read(id_selected)
        if data == []:
            flash("Book not found!")

        #
        # Here, we populate the data
        #
        form.book_dict.data = data
        form.book_id.data = data["_id"]
```

```
form.isbn.data = data["ISBN"]
form.title.data = data["Title"]
form.year.data = data["Pub_Year"]
#
# Since edition is optional, we must check for it first.
#
if "Edition" in data.keys():
    form.edition.data = data["Edition"]
else:
    form.edition.data = '1'
form.pub_name.data = data["Publisher"]["Name"]
#
# Since publisher city is optional, we must check for it first.
#
if "City" in data["Publisher"].keys():
    form.pub_city.data = data["Publisher"]["City"]
else:
    form.pub_city = ""
#
# Since publisher URL is optional, we must check for it first.
#
if "URL" in data["Publisher"].keys():
    form.pub_url.data = data["Publisher"]["URL"]
else:
    form.pub_url.data = ""
#
# Since language is optional, we must check for it first.
#
if "Language" in data.keys():
    form.language.data = data["Language"]
else:
    form.language.data = "English"
form.authors.data = books.make_authors_str(data["Authors"])
```

```
        # We also must retrieve the notes for the book.
        if "Notes" in data.keys():
            all_notes = data["Notes"]
        else:
            all_notes = []
        notes = []
        for note in all_notes:
            notes.append(note["Text"])
        form.create_button.label.text = "Update"
else:
    del form.del_button
if request.method == 'POST':
    # First, determine if we must create, update, or delete when form posts.
    operation = "Create"
    if form.create_button.data:
        if form.create_button.label.text == "Update":
            operation = "Update"
    if form.del_button and form.del_button.data:
        operation = "Delete"
    if form.validate_on_submit():
        # Get the data from the form here
        if operation == "Create":
            try:
                books.create(ISBN=isbn, Title=title, Pub_Year=year,
                            Pub_Name=pub_name, Pub_City=pub_city,
                            Pub_URL=pub_url, Authors=author_list,
                            Notes=notes, Edition=edition,
                            Language=language)
                flash("Added.")
                return redirect('/list/book')
            except Exception as err:
                flash(err)
        elif operation == "Update":
```

```
            try:
                books.update(id_selected, form.book_dict.data, ISBN=isbn,
                            Title=title, Pub_Year=year, Pub_Name=pub_name,
                            Pub_City=pub_city, Pub_URL=pub_url,
                            Authors=author_list, Edition=edition,
                            Language=language, New_Note=new_note)
                flash("Updated.")
                return redirect('/list/book')
            except Exception as err:
                flash(err)
        else:
            try:
                books.delete(form.book_id.data)
                flash("Deleted.")
                return redirect('/list/book')
            except Exception as err:
                flash(err)
    else:
        flash_errors(form)
    return render_template("book.html", form=form, notes=notes,
                        authors=author_list)
```

Finally, we can remove the `publisher()` view function and the publisher section in the `simple_list()` view as we don't need those either.

Templates

The changes to the template files are minor. If you haven't already done so, copy the templates from version 2 to version 3. For example, copy all the files from `version2/templates/*` to `version3/templates`. Once copied, you can remove the `publisher.html` template as it is no longer needed.

We also need to make two small changes to the base.html file to change the version number and remove the publisher list from the navigation bar. Listing 9-27 shows an excerpt from the base.html file with the changes shown in bold.

Listing 9-27. Base Template (Version 3)

```
<div class="navbar navbar-inverse" role="navigation">
    <div class="container">
        <div class="navbar-header">
            <button type="button" class="navbar-toggle" data-toggle="collapse"
            data-target=".navbar-collapse">
                <span class="sr-only">Toggle navigation</span>
                <span class="icon-bar"></span>
                <span class="icon-bar"></span>
                <span class="icon-bar"></span>
            </button>
            <a class="navbar-brand" href="/">MyLibrary v3</a>
        </div>
        <div class="navbar-collapse collapse">
            <ul class="nav navbar-nav">
                <li><a href="/list/book">Books</a></li>
            </ul>
        </div>
    </div>
</div>
```

We also must make small changes to the book.html template to show a text field for the comma-separated list of authors. Listing 9-28 shows an excerpt of the modified template with the changes in bold.

Listing 9-28. Book Template (Version 3)

```
...
{% block page_content %}
  <form method=post> {{ form.csrf_token }}
    <fieldset>
      <legend>Book - Detail</legend>
      {{ form.hidden_tag() }}
      <div style=font-size:20pz; font-weight:bold; margin-left:150px;>
        {{ form.isbn.label }} <br>
        {{ form.isbn(size=32) }} <br>
```

```
{{ form.title.label }} <br>
{{ form.title(size=100) }} <br>
{{ form.year.label }} <br>
{{ form.year(size=10) }} <br>
{{ form.edition.label }} <br>
{{ form.edition(size=10) }} <br>
{{ form.language.label }} <br>
{{ form.language(size=34) }} <br>
{{ form.pub_name.label }} <br>
{{ form.pub_name(style="width: 300px;") }} <br>
{{ form.pub_city.label }} <br>
{{ form.pub_city(style="width: 300px;") }} <br>
{{ form.pub_url.label }} <br>
{{ form.pub_url(style="width: 300px;") }} <br><br>
{{ form.authors.label }} <br>
{{ form.authors(size=100) }} <br>
```

. . .

Ok, that's it for the changes; now let's see the code in action.

Executing the Code

Now that we've got the code written, let's give it a test drive. To execute the application, you can launch it with the Python interpreter specifying the `runserver` command. The following shows an example of executing the application. Note that we used the port option to specify the port. You should enter this command from the `version3` folder.

```
$ cd version3
$ python ./mylibrary_v3.py runserver -p 5003
 * Running on http://127.0.0.1:5003/ (Press CTRL+C to quit)
```

The application will launch and run but there isn't any data in the database yet. You should start by grabbing a couple of your favorite books and enter the book data. Don't worry about the notes just yet. Once you've added a few books, you should see them in the default view (by clicking on *MyLibrary v3* or *Books* in the navigation bar. Figure 9-7 shows an example of what you should see.

MyLibrary v3   Books

New

Query Results

Action	ISBN	Title	Publisher	Year	Authors
Modify	978-1-4842-1174-8	3D Printing with Delta Printers	Apress	2015	Bell Charles
Modify	978-1-4842-1294-3	MySQL for the Internet of Things	Apress	2016	Bell Charles
Modify	978-1-4842-2107-5	Windows 10 for the Internet of Things	Apress	2017	Bell Charles
Modify	978-1-4842-2724-4	Introducing the MySQL 8 Document Store	Apress	2018	Bell Charles
Modify	978-1-4842-3122-7	MicroPython for the Internet of Things	Apress	2017	Bell Charles
Modify	978-1449339586	MySQL High Availability	OReilly	2014	Bell Charles, Kindahl Mats, Thalmann Lars

Figure 9-7. *Library application book list (version 3)*

If this is starting to look a little familiar, you're right, it is. This version implements the same interface except without the publisher and author views. As in the other versions, you can click on the *Modify link* for any book and see the book details. Figure 9-8 shows the updated book detail view. Note that the publisher entry is now a set of three text fields instead of a dropdown list. The author list is unchanged from version 2.

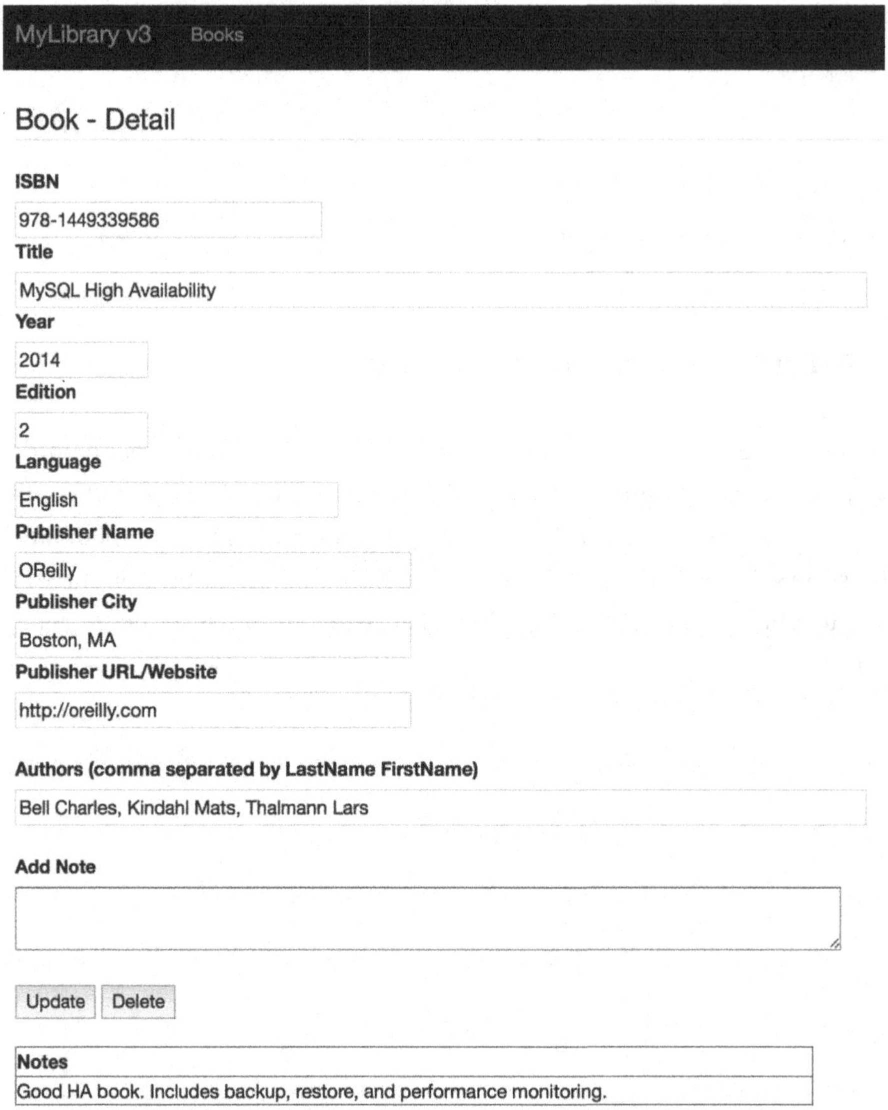

Figure 9-8. *Book detailed view (version 3)*

Now, let's take a moment to discuss some observations about this version of the application.

Observations

The following are some observations about this version of the application. Some are consequences of the database design, others are from the code, and others are things we made a bit better. The observations are presented in the form of an unordered list. This list is shorter than the previous versions because we have achieved a better application! So, this is a list of successes rather than improvements.

- *Database code much shorter*: We need less code for working with collections and documents using the X DevAPI.

- *Database code easier to understand*: Working with JSON documents are a natural extension of Python (and other languages).

- *Application code significantly shorter*: We need less code for the application because we simplified the user interface. In fact, the code is almost 50% of the size of version 1.

There is one other observation that bears discussing. The changes to the user experience using the three versions of the application are minor. In fact, one of the goals was to keep the user interface changes to a minimum to demonstrate that migrating from a traditional relational database model to a hybrid and ultimately a pure document store model does not mean one must redesign the entire user interface!

Although there may be some changes necessary to facilitate changes in how the data is stored and retrieved—like what we saw with the authors and books_authors join tables, the changes often help solve problems with the database design or in this case help eliminate a false premise that the specific author and publisher data is meaningful outside the context of a book. In this example application, it was not. So, designing separate tables (or documents) for storing the information wasn't necessary and added complexity we didn't need. Such are the challenges and rewards of a designing your data around JSON documents and the MySQL document store engine.

Challenges

The application in either version is very basic in functionality. If you find the application is a good fit for further experimentation or even to base another effort, there are a few areas where you may want to consider improving the design and code. The following includes a brief list of things that can be improved.

- *ISBN lookup service*: Add the ability to retrieve information about books using an ISBN lookup service such as isbntools (http://isbntools.readthedocs.io/en/latest/) or SearchUPC (http://www.searchupc.com). Some services require creating accounts while others may be fee-based services.

- *Separate library modules*: Break the library file into separate code modules (book, author, publisher, library) for version 1 and 2.

- *Separate code modules*: Larger Flask applications typically break out the views (form classes) in the main code file into separate code modules.

- *Remove hardcoded values*: Make the user, password, host, and port data for the MySQL parameters rather than hard coded values (hint: use argparse).

- *Expand the data*: Modify the database or document store to store additional media such as magazines, articles, and online references.

Summary

There is no doubt that the new MySQL 8 release is set to be the biggest, most significant release in MySQL history. The addition of the JSON data type and the X DevAPI is simply groundbreaking for MySQL applications.

In this chapter, we explored the differences between a relational database solution and a relational database solution augmented with JSON fields, and finally a pure document store solution. As we discovered, the new X DevAPI makes developing MySQL solutions easier, faster, and with less code than a relational database solution. This gives us many reasons to start adopting the document store going forward.

In Chapter 10, I conclude my exploration of the MySQL 8 Document Store with a look at how you can prepare your existing and future application plans to incorporate the document store. This includes notes about upgrading to MySQL 8 and tips for how to migrate to document store solutions.

CHAPTER 10

Planning for MySQL 8 and the Document Store

This book has covered a lot of material including a brief overview of some of the newest features of MySQL 8. I focused on the MySQL Document Store including all its components: the X Protocol, X DevAPI, MySQL Shell, and changes to the server with the MySQL X Plugin. Not only that, but I also gave a walkthrough on how to develop applications using the X DevAPI—from SQL-based to hybrid to NoSQL solution. These technologies are fantastic additions to the server features and promise far more return on your development resources than traditional relational database application development. It is clear that there is a lot to MySQL 8 than just a new, jaunty jump in version numbering.

Recall, we received a glimpse of some new high availability features such as Group Replication and InnoDB Cluster. But it doesn't end there, does it? We also have new authentication mechanisms, the new data dictionary, and many small but significant updates. So, where does one start considering the implications of migrating and upgrading to MySQL 8? In this chapter, I look at some strategies for migrating to MySQL 8 including considerations and best practices for migrating applications to use the document store with another example of migrating existing database applications. I explore some tips and tricks for working with MySQL 8.

Let's begin by briefly discussing some strategies for considering upgrading to MySQL 8 from MySQL 5.7 and earlier.

© Charles Bell 2018
C. Bell, *Introducing the MySQL 8 Document Store*, https://doi.org/10.1007/978-1-4842-2725-1_10

Upgrading from MySQL 5.7 and Earlier

Although this book is not a tutorial on how to upgrade to MySQL 8, there are some things you should consider before adopting the MySQL Document Store, which will likely result in upgrading your existing MySQL servers.

There are several ways you can go about learning how to do an upgrade. The most obvious and recommended route is to read the online MySQL reference manual, which contains a section on upgrading MySQL (providing critical information you must know). However, there are some higher-level or general practices that apply to any form of upgrade or migration. This section presents upgrade practices that will help you avoid some of the trouble with upgrading a major system like MySQL.

In this section, we look at the types of upgrades you will encounter with MySQL then discuss some general practices for planning and executing the upgrade. We conclude the section with a brief discussion about reasons for performing the upgrade. We discuss the reasons for doing an upgrade last so that you will have a better understanding of what is involved including implied risks.

Let's begin by looking at the types of upgrades you are likely to encounter.

Types of Upgrades

The online MySQL reference manual and similar publications describe two basic upgrade methods, which are strategies and procedures for how to do the upgrade. The following is a summary of the methods.

- *In-Place*: MySQL server instances are upgraded with binaries using the existing data dictionary. This method employs various utilities and tools to ensure a smooth transition to the new version.

- *Logical*: The data is backed up before installing the new version over the old installation and data is restored after the upgrade.

Although these describe two general strategies for upgrading MySQL, they don't cover all possible options. In fact, we will see another method in a later section. After all, your installation is likely to be slightly different—especially if you've been using MySQL for a long time or have a lot of MySQL servers configured for high availability or are using third-party applications and components with your own applications. These factors can make following a given, generic procedure problematic.

Rather than try to expand on the upgrade methods, let's look at it from the point of view of a system administrator. In particular, what do we do if we have version x.y.z and want to upgrade to a.b.c? The following sections describe upgrades based on versions.

Caution   Oracle only recommends upgrades of GA versions. Upgrading other releases is not recommended and may require accepting additional time to migrate and accepting potential incompatibilities. Upgrade non-GA releases at your own risk.

MYSQL VERSION NUMBER TERMINOLOGY

MySQL uses a 3-digit version number in the form of major, minor, and revision (odd that it is also called the *version* in the documentation). This is often expressed with dot notation. For example, version 5.7.20 defines the major version as 5, the minor version as 7, and the revision as 20. Often, the version number is followed by text (called the *suffix* in the documentation) indicating additional version history, stability, or alignment such as general availability (GA), release candidate (RC), and so forth. For a complete explanation of the version number in MySQL, see `https://dev.mysql.com/doc/refman/8.0/en/which-version.html`.

Revision Upgrade

The simplest form of upgrade is when upgrading when only the revision number is changed. This is commonly referred to the Z in the X.Y.Z version number or simply "the version of the major.minor release." For example, version 5.7.20 is revision 20 or version 20 of 5.7.

Upgrading at this version level is generally safe and, although not guaranteed to work flawlessly, is low risk. However, you still should take the precaution of reading the release notes before executing the upgrade. This is especially true if you are working with nongeneral availability (GA) releases. If the release is not a GA release, you must pay attention to the release notes and upgrade section in the online MySQL reference manual. Although it is rare, sometimes there are special considerations you must plan for and overcome to achieve the upgrade. Fortunately, Oracle does an excellent job of communicating any necessary steps and procedures—you just need to read the documentation!

Minor Upgrade

The next form of upgrade is upgrading when the minor number is changed. This is commonly referred to the *Y* in the X.Y.Z version number—for example, upgrading from 5.6 to 5.7.

Upgrades are generally acceptable and documented for single digit increment of the minor version. For example, the upgrade from 5.6 to 5.7 is supported, but an upgrade from 5.0 to 5.7 is not directly supported. This is because there are too many differences between the versions to make an upgrade viable (but not impossible).

Nevertheless, you can upgrade minor version changes with manageable risk if you plan accordingly. More about managing the risk in later sections.

Major Upgrade

The next form of upgrade is when upgrading when the major number is changed. This category—aside from the incompatible versions—is the one with the most risk and potentially the most likely to require more work.

Upgrades of versions at the major version are rare and only occur when Oracle has released a new, major set of changes (hence the name) to the server. MySQL 8 server contains many improvements over MySQL 5—most have been tremendous increases in performance, advanced features, and stability. However, there have been a few changes that have rendered some features in older versions incompatible.

For example, once MySQL 8.0 is released as GA, upgrading from MySQL 5.7 to MySQL 8.0 is supported but you may have to migrate certain features to complete the upgrade.

It is fortunate that Oracle has documented all the problem areas in detail with suggestions on how to migrate to the new features. We've even seen this extend beyond major versions—the MySQL Document Store is a very good example.

Incompatible Upgrades

As you may have surmised, there are some upgrades that are not recommended either due to lack of features to support the upgrade or major incompatibilities. For example, you should not consider upgrading from MySQL 5.0 to MySQL 8.0. This is simply because there is no support for some of the older 5.0 features in 8.0. Because these types of upgrades are not common, we summarize some of the incompatible upgrades in the following list. The subject of the incompatibility isn't the new version to which you want to upgrade, it is the old version that you want to upgrade.

- *Skipping major versions*: Upgrading major versions may introduce incompatible changes.

- *Skipping minor versions*: Some upgrades of minor versions may introduce incompatible changes.

- *Upgrading incompatible hardware*: Upgrading hardware of one endianness may not be compatible with another. For example, big-endian to little-endian may not be compatible.

- *Versions that change the InnoDB format*: There have been some changes where the InnoDB storage engine internals have changed. Most have been planned for compatible minor.revision upgrades (e.g. 5.7.3 to 5.7.12), but some have required a few extra steps to prepare the data.

- *New features*: Less frequently, there are new features introduced that may introduce incompatibilities. For example, the data dictionary was added rendering the .FRM metadata obsolete.

- *Platform changes*: Some upgrades that include changing platforms may require additional work or introduce potential incompatibilities. For example, moving from a platform without case sensitivity support in the file system to one that does support case sensitivity.

- *Upgrading non-GA releases*: Upgrades from a non-GA to a GA, GA to non-GA, and among non-GA releases is not recommended.

Without a doubt, the incompatibilities are dependent on certain features, hardware, or internal storage mechanisms. In most cases, the online documentation outlines what you can do to ensure success. Sometimes this requires following a specific upgrade path such as first upgrading to one version before upgrading to your target version.

WHAT IF I MUST UPGRADE AN INCOMPATIBLE VERSION?

If you find your upgrade strategy falls into this section listing incompatible upgrades, do not despair. You may still be able to perform the upgrade, but it may be costlier and require more work. For example, you could perform a logical upgrade by backing up your data using SQL statements with `mysqldump` or `mysqlpump`, installing the new version, then working with the SQL files to adjust them to remove any incompatibilities. Although this does introduce considerable risk that you can still import all your data cleanly, it is still possible. If you find yourself in this situation, be sure to spend more time on addressing risks using such strategies as parallel installation and extended periods of testing.

Now that we have a good idea of what types of upgrades are possible, let's look at some best practices for performing the upgrade.

Upgrade Practices

When upgrading any system, there are some general practices you should adhere to or you should at least use as a guide. This section describes some of the fundamental practices you should consider for upgrading your MySQL servers. Again, some of these may be familiar and some may not be the one you would consider to use with upgrading MySQL. Further, some of these are not outlined in the online MySQL reference manual.

As you will see, these practices are not necessarily sequential or even a prerequisite for the next. For example, planning also should include time for testing. Therefore, the practices discussed here are in a general order of importance but should not be considered or implemented in this order.

Check Prerequisites

The first thing you should do when upgrading MySQL is to check the documentation for any prerequisites. Sometimes this is simply safely backing up your data, but also can include things such as which utilities and tools you need to use to migrate certain features (or data). Be sure you have all the prerequisites met before you being the upgrade.

The upgrade documentation also will include incompatibility issues. Most often, this occurs when upgrading major versions but sometimes this happens for minor versions. It is fortunate that these are outlined in the online MySQL reference manual. Checking the prerequisites also can help you by providing details you can use to plan the upgrade.

Caution   The online MySQL reference manual section on upgrading should be your first stop, not your last when things go wrong. "Fore read" means being forewarned.

Once you've read through the documentation, one of the things you will want to do as a prerequisite is to use the mysqlcheck utility to check your MySQL installation for compatibilities. For example, one of the prerequisites for upgrading to MySQL 8 is that, per the section entitled, "**MySQL Upgrade Strategies**" in the online MySQL reference manual, "*there must be no tables that use obsolete data types, obsolete functions, orphan .frm files, InnoDB tables that use nonnative partitioning, or triggers that have a missing or empty definer or an invalid creation context.*" We can use the mysqlcheck utility to identify any of these conditions as shown in Listing 10-1.

Listing 10-1. Using mysqlcheck to Identify Upgrade Issues

```
$ mysqlcheck -u root -p --all-databases --check-upgrade
Enter password:
library_v1.authors                        OK
library_v1.books                          OK
library_v1.books_authors                  OK
library_v1.notes                          OK
library_v1.publishers                     OK
library_v2.books                          OK
library_v2.notes                          OK
library_v2.publishers                     OK
library_v3.books                          OK
...
mysql.user                                OK
sys.sys_config                            OK
```

For best results, you should use the mysqlcheck utility from the version you are upgrading. This will ensure the utility is the most up to date and should identify more upgrade issues.

Plan the Upgrade

Once you have all the prerequisites mapped out and have identified any features that require special handling to solve incompatibilities, it is time to plan for upgrading your server. This may be an obvious thing to do if you have thousands of servers, but less obvious to those with only a few (or even one) server to upgrade.

You should resist the temptation to simply run the upgrade without planning what you are going to do. Recall, we want to ensure the upgrade goes smoothly by reducing (or eliminating) risk. This is much more critical for production environments, but any potential loss of availability, performance, or data can result in loss of productivity.

You can get most of what you need to plan from the documentation, but the documentation won't be specific to your installation, servers, platform, and so forth. Therefore, you must fill in those blanks and adapt the procedures suggested in the documentation to your own installation. However, you can learn quite a lot by reading the section, "What's New in MySQL 8.0," paying attention to any subsections labeled "Ramifications for Upgrades" in the online MySQL reference manual. There you will find tips that may help you avoid some complicated decisions, or better to avoid complex repairs.

This also includes making sure you have the right personnel on hand to do the upgrade or to be ready to jump in case something goes wrong.[1] For example, don't forget your developers, web administrators, and other critical roles.

The form of the plan is up to you; however, I suggest that you write what you plan to do and share it with others. This way, everyone in the chain of ownership of the upgrade will know what is to be done. You will be surprised how much a little communication can do to reduce risk of things going wrong.

Caution   If you are using or plan to use a platform that supports automatic updates and those facilities include repositories that monitor MySQL, you may want to consider excluding MySQL from automatic updates. This is especially true for production environments. You should never automatically update MySQL in a production environment for any mission critical data.

---

[1]It is always shocking for a database or web administrator to get a call (often in the middle of the night) to fix something that has gone wrong in an upgrade—especially when they have no knowledge that such an upgrade was planned! Yes, it does happen—far too often.

Consider Parallel Deployment

One practice that can help the most when upgrading systems that require more than a trivial amount of work is installing the new version parallel to the existing version. This is a practice known to software engineering and is designed to ensure the existing data and applications remain unchanged while the new system is being installed and configured. The new version (installation) would be considered a development platform and often goes into production once sufficient testing of the migration is complete.

Although this isn't an upgrade per se (it's a new installation), having a new parallel version of MySQL running gives considerable freedom in how to attack the migration of your existing data and applications. After all, if something goes wrong, your data is still operational on the old system.

This practice also provides you another benefit: you can change platforms or other major hardware without having to risk your existing data. Therefore, if your existing servers have hardware that is to be updated at the same time, you can use a parallel installation to install MySQL on the new hardware thus isolating the risks with the new hardware.

Finally, employing a parallel installation may help with scheduling and planning your migration by ensuring the existing systems are fully capable. And, better, you can always go back to the old system if during the migration something goes wrong.

Parallel deployment often includes keeping both systems running for some period. The length of time may depend on the amount of risk you're willing to take or it may be based on how long it takes to fully switchover all your applications.

It is unfortunate that some may not have the resources available to consider parallel deployments. As having two installations of MySQL running at the same time may place a greater burden on developers, administrators, and support personnel. Given the benefits of parallel development, it may be worth adding extra resources or accepting less productivity of some personnel for a short period.

However, even this safety net is tenuous if you don't perform enough testing.

Test, Test, Test!

This practice, along with planning, is often overlooked or given far less importance. Sometimes this is due to external forces such as not having the right personnel available or failures in planning that results in no time for extensive testing. Regardless of the excuse, failing to adequately test your upgrade increases risk beyond what most would be willing to endure.

Testing should include that you ensure all the data has been migrated, all applications work completely, and all access (user accounts, permissions, etc.) are functional. However, don't stop there. You should also ensure all your operational practices have been modified for the new version. More specific, your maintenance scripts, procedures, and tools all work correctly with the new version.

Furthermore, your testing should result in a go/no go decision to accept the upgrade. If things are not working or there are too many issues, you may need to decide to keep or reject the upgrade. The parallel installation practice can help in this manner because you don't destroy the existing data or installation until you are certain everything is working. Make sure that you write those criteria into your plan and to ensure success.

Tip   Be sure to test all existing operational procedures as part of your acceptance criteria.

Production Deployment Strategies

If you have a production and development (or test) environment, you also should consider how to move the development or test deployments to production. If you are using parallel installations, it may be simply switching application routers and similar appliances and applications. If you are using in place installations, it may be more involved. For example, you may need to plan for a period of downtime to complete the migration.

For parallel installations, planning the downtime may be more precise and involve a shorter period because you have more time to test things. However, for in place upgrades, you may need to set aside a period to complete the migration. As expected, you will want to minimize the downtime by doing as much of the migration as you can. But in the base of MySQL, this may be nothing more than forming a plan and gathering resources. The bottom line is, don't forsake including production deployment in your plan.

Now that we've discussed upgrade practices, let's take a moment to discuss some reasons we may want to consider performing the upgrade, which clearly can be a very involved process with a certain amount of risk.

Reasons for Upgrading

If you're like most avid users of platforms or systems, you will want to upgrade to the latest and greatest versions whenever a new one is released. Savvy administrators and planners know there is little room in a production database environment for such behavior. Thus, reasons for upgrading will require some genuine bang for the buck. That is, it must be worth your while. The main driving reasons for upgrading MySQL include the following.

- *Features*: A new feature is released that can improve your applications or data, examples include the Document Store, Group Replication, and InnoDB Cluster

- *Performance*: The newer version improves performance making your applications better. For example, the latest 5.7 release is many times faster than previous versions and MySQL 8 promises to improve on that.

- *Maintenance*: There are new features that help you maintain the system better. Examples include the new data dictionary, Group Replication, and ancillary tools such as MySQL Enterprise Backup.

- *Bug fixes*: There may be defects in older versions that required workarounds or limitations. Newer versions may contain fixes for critical bugs so you can remove the workarounds and limitations caused by the defect.

- *Compliance*: Your platform, standard operating procedures, or external entities require the upgrade for compliance. For example, you may be required to run a specific version of MySQL for contractual agreements.

The bottom line is you must answer the question, "Why should I upgrade?" and that answer must result in some benefit for you, your data, clients, workforce, and the company's future. It makes little sense to spend resources on an upgrade that has little or no benefit, which is another reason companies often skip version upgrades. Alas, skipping too many upgrades can make later upgrades more problematic. However, given how much improvement MySQL 8.0 is over MySQL 5.7 and earlier, many will want to plan to upgrade to MySQL 8.

Tip   For more details about migrating to MySQL 8 including platform-specific steps, see `http://dev.mysql.com/doc/refman/8.0/en/upgrading-from-previous-series.html`.

SO, SHOULD I UPGRADE TO MYSQL 8 OR NOT?

The discussion in this section may cast some doubt on whether you should upgrade to MySQL 8. That is not the case. In fact, this book should convince you to upgrade to MySQL 8 as soon as you can do so in a safe, risk-free manner. Thus, in this section I suggest that you need to plan your upgrade and execute it carefully to ensure success.

Considerations for Upgrading to MySQL 8

There are several compatibility issues identified in the online MySQL reference manual MySQL 8.0. The following are a few that you should be aware of when planning your MySQL 8.0 upgrade.

- *Data dictionary*: The new metadata, transactional storage mechanism is a major change in the architecture. If you have DevOps that work with `.frm` files and other metadata, you may need to make changes to migrate to using the data dictionary.

- *Authentication plugin*: The default authentication plugin has changed. This may result in connection issues for those that use older authentication mechanisms.

- *Error codes*: Some error codes have changed. If you to have applications that use error codes, you will want to explore these changes to avoid application errors after upgrading.

- *Partitioning*: The default partitioning storage engine support has been removed. If you are using a custom storage engine (or an old one), you will need to ensure there exists an upgraded version for use with MySQL 8.

- *INFORMATION_SCHEMA*: Minor changes to the views. If your applications or devops use these views, be sure to check to see if any of the views you are using have been removed or changed.

- *SQL commands*: There are some new and obsolete SQL commands. Be sure to check your SQL statements to see if you are using some of the older, removed commands.

- *Default charset*: The default character set (charset) has been changed to utf8mb4. If you have character set support in your applications, you may need to test with the new default to ensure compatibility.

Once again, be sure to read the online MySQL reference manual section, "Verifying Upgrade Prerequisites for Your MySQL 5.7 Installation" and the section, "Changes Affecting Upgrades to MySQL 8.0" for the most up-to-date information about these and other prerequisites and migration tasks needed to upgrade to MySQL 8.0.

Another excellent resource is the engineering blogs at `https://mysqlserverteam.com/`. These blogs often discuss new features before they are released as GA and are a fount of knowledge about how the feature works as well as any upgrade issues that the engineering team has identified or are working to overcome. Watching the blogs will give an excellent early warning of changes.

Tip   See the engineering blogs at `https://mysqlserverteam.com/` for early announcements about new features and how to work with them.

Now that we've discussed upgrading MySQL in general and some specifics about upgrading to MySQL 8.0, let's discuss a very important development concept you should spend some time to understand before adopting the MySQL Document Store fully.

Migrating to Schemaless Documents

What does *schemaless* mean? It simply means that we don't restrict our data storage to rigid formats with specific fields with a give type. The key factor to remember in adopting a schemaless mindset is play to the strengths of JSON documents: the ability to store only the data needed including the ability to add document elements where needed and keep all meaningful data together. This is also known as flexibility and is the cornerstone of designed schemaless documents.

For example, if a developer finds a new field must be added, it can. Or, if the developer discovers embedding information results in faster, easier code, the decision is one of weighing benefits of the application and the user experience rather than strict data storage rules.

Flexibility has another angle. Relational databases are typically designed using the same set of rules and tools. So much so that what applies to one database will show up in another. In schemaless designs, having data in separate collections or embedded are largely made based on how the data will be used and thus can vary from one application to another.

However, you should not conclude from this that developers have a free ride and can run amuck whenever they choose. Rather, you should consider flexibility a tool that you can use if warranted after due process to evaluate the change.

Another benefit of the schemaless mindset is the ability to scale the data without retrofitting. For example, if our applications gain more features resulting in more data in the documents, there is no need to go back and force older documents into a new structure. We simply scale the document as the application features mature. If we do need to go back and add data to the old documents, it's a simple coding affair.

Although reducing unnecessary complexity and ambiguities should be goals in any data store design, a schemaless mindset should be more willing to accept responsibility of the tradeoffs and to work to minimize their impact rather than adhering to a set of fixed rules.

Thus, the schemaless mindset should be one of flexibility and scalability where we emphasize these qualities over data structure and conformity. Remember, we're striving to keep the data together to reduce the number of times it must be retrieved.

The following sections identify some of the areas you may need to consider thinking about when adopting a schemaless mindset

Normalization vs. Denormalization

One of the most fundamental mindset challenges is recognizing the difference between normalization and denormalization. In basic terms, normalization is a goal that relational database designers strive to reduce the amount of data stored without the possibility of duplication or ambiguity. Denormalization is a goal for document store designers to strive to make the data as local as possible by describing an entity in its fullest with duplication a much lower concern.

In a schemaless world, we use denormalization to remove the need for joins thereby possibly increasing performance. However, it doesn't end there. The goal is to make the data models store data that is used as a unit. In other words, the document should contain all the data pertinent.

In some cases, this may result in embedding data in the document that would normally be stored in a separate collection (or table). Denormalizing the data therefore may introduce some duplication. For example, we saw this in the last chapter where we stored the author name in the book document. In this case, the author names were indeed duplicated among books that had the same authors. However, the way the data is used—to view bibliography information—meant there was no practical need to search or perform queries on the author data. By simply listing authors was all that was need. Thus, the cost of retrieving the normalized author data was an artificial application of fixed rules.

When approaching the question of normalization or denormalization, take some time to analyze your data not only from the standpoint of how it is organized but also in how it is used. Sometimes you may find your reasons for isolating data may not be important. For example, if there is no need to have a child table and some duplication is acceptable, you can embed the information in one or more JSON fields thereby applying enough denormalization to get the benefits of having the data in one place (retrieved with one pass).

Formal Rules vs. Heuristics

Another area to consider working on is how data storage is designed or, more appropriately, what mechanisms are used to drive the development. In the relational database world, we have a set of rules we use (e.g., unyielding and sometimes unforgiving[2] rules called *normal forms*) that guide designers to achieve the least redundant, most accurate retrieval solution possible. In the schemaless world, we use heuristics or rules of thumb when designing the data storage to achieve the storage that best optimizes describing the things we're modeling and to make the data accessible.

The difference is not in how the data is designed so much as how the data is revealed. In the relational database world, the data store is designed largely by how to store it whereas in the schemaless world, the documents are designed based on how it will be used and how the users will view the data.

Therefore, we can predict reasonably well how a relational database will be accessed and how to form the queries (often in advance of the application) and with the right tools even how the queries will perform. However, in a schemaless solution, we cannot tell by examining the document how it will perform. We must test it with the application to learn how to access it more effectively. Sometimes, this can result in making minor changes, which can be in the code or in the document itself. It is fortunate that the process in which to make the modifications is much easier than in a relational database. Thus, in the schemaless world we must adapt a more change friendly attitude.

This is one of the things that sets the two apart. For example, in a relational database, when we need to change a table (or set of tables), we often must plan well in advance as changing the strict schema often forces application developers to change their applications. On the other hand, changing a document doesn't require a lengthy retooling effort. In fact, developers can simply add the new data item in code never stressing the database administrator. Let's look at an example.

Consider a solution where we are storing addresses. We all know what they look like—street1, street2, city, state, and zip code. But what if you had to make your database available for international data? Now, we're looking at the possibility of adding a country name at the very least if not additional fields for country-specific addresses. Without a doubt, this would require modifying the table (as well as the code). Now, consider a document that stores addresses. If we need new fields, we just add them in code and write the code to detect the new fields.

---

[2]Watch out for the normal form zealots! Their whole world revolves around reaching a Zen-like state of fifth normal form. It is sad that they will likely miss the point of denormalization.

View Data as Code

One of the hardest concepts about schemaless designs for those who have worked with relational databases is that the data (document) should (can) be viewed as code. Consider the JSON structure—it's code! Thus, thinking about your data as part of your code will help you design better documents.

For example, if you know your document contains elements that are lists, and you need to iterate over the items in those lists, code to do this is typically some form of loop or iterator mechanism such as *a* for each or for *X* in *Y* construct. Thus, you can view the document has having data that is used in those looping constructs. Yes, this is akin to thinking in result sets (arrays of rows), but in this case, we're much closer to the real code. In fact, due to the uniqueness of how JSON works, we can write code to reference the elements of the document rather than an abstraction layer as we see in result set processing. That is, we access the field by name rather than asking a library to give us the "*n*th" field. This results in code that is easier to read and is described by the data (and vice-versa).

Take Storage for Granted

This may sound a little odd, but the storage mechanism—placing a document in the document store—can largely be ignored by schemaless designers and code developers. For instance, we aren't concerned about table rows, fields, and so forth. The schema is flexible, and the focus is on collecting documents.

The APIs for document stores in general and the X DevAPI make these operations ubiquitous thereby freeing the designers and developers to focus on how the document is used rather than how it is stored.

As expected, there are cases where we want to ensure we're not over denormalizing and in those cases, we will need to think logically about how to organize the data in collections, but this too is a higher level and not directly liked to storage mechanisms.

Embed or Separate?

Knowing when to embed data is one of the skills you will learn as you design more schemaless documents. However, there are some general rules to follow to help answer the question "to embed or not?" The following lists a few conditions under which you may need to decide to embed or separate the data.

507

- *Integrity*: The embedded data applies only to this document. It is not used elsewhere and is seldom changed (or viewed) without the document. If it can be used in other documents and changes must apply to all references or it is a separate entity, it should not be embedded.

- *Limited growth*: The embedded data is not likely to grow in length. For example, if the embedded data is an array, the size of the array (number of items) will remain small (or few). If there is a chance to grow beyond a reasonable size, it should be made a separate collection.

- *Containership*: If a relationship exists where one document contains another document and the documents are only accessed as a set, you may want to embed. However, if the documents can be accessed or changed separately (and it makes sense to do so), you may want to consider not to embed the document.

- *Frequency of edits*: If there is data in a document that is seldom changed, you can embed it. However, if the data can change frequently either from another access point (view) or mechanism in the application that does not use the original document; you may want to consider moving the data to its own collection.

- *Links*: If the data you want to embed is only ever referenced infrequently from one document, you can consider embedding it. However, if it is referenced by more than one document and the data must be the same for all references, you should place the linked data in its own collection.

Strategies for Migrating to a Document Store

Now that we have a better understanding of a schemaless mindset, let us review some strategies you can employ for migrating existing relational database to a document store. This section reinforces the lessons learned thus far in the book using another example of migrating to a document store.

As we saw in Chapter 9, we do not have to migrate all our database and data in one go—although you can do that if you have the resources, time, and sufficient needs.

However, most will want to migrate slowly to a document store. In may also be the case that a pure document store may not meet your needs or may be too costly making a migration a longer-term goal.

Let's use a commonly known database solution for a contact list. Here, we are storing names, addresses, and phone numbers. A typical relational database solution for a contact list would group all the data in a single database with one-to-many relationships for addresses, phone numbers, email addresses, and so forth. This because we know each contact will have one or more of these data items. Figure 10-1 shows an entity relationship diagram (ERD) for such a relational database design.

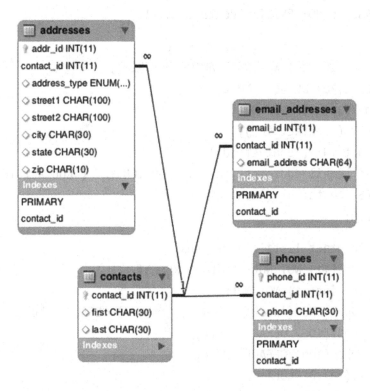

Figure 10-1. Contact list (relational database)

First, note this database design is not completely normalized. For example, it is possible that a contact list could include two or more people who have the same work or home address as well as the same phone number. Without a doubt, we could make many-to-many relationships but that is taking normalization too far. More specific, we do not store addresses and phone numbers separately from the contact data—it doesn't make any sense to use the data in that way.

Second, note that the database does support storing multiple email, address, and phone numbers for each contact. That is, there exists a one-to-many relationship among the contacts table and email_addresses, addresses, and phones tables. We will use the database name contact_list1 so that we can migrate this to other forms for comparison.

In this example, there are foreign key constraints as well as primary keys on all the tables. Listing 10-2 shows the SQL statements for the tables in the database.

Listing 10-2. Contact List Relational Database

```
CREATE DATABASE IF NOT EXISTS `contact_list1`;

CREATE TABLE `contact_list1`.`contacts` (
    `contact_id` int(11) NOT NULL AUTO_INCREMENT,
    `first` char(30) DEFAULT NULL,
    `last` char(30) DEFAULT NULL,
    PRIMARY KEY (`contact_id`),
    KEY `contact_id` (`contact_id`),
    CONSTRAINT `email_addresses_ibfk_1` FOREIGN KEY (`contact_id`)
    REFERENCES `contacts` (`contact_id`)
) ENGINE=InnoDB;

CREATE TABLE `contact_list1`.`addresses` (
    `addr_id` int(11) NOT NULL AUTO_INCREMENT,
    `contact_id` int(11) NOT NULL,
    `address_type` ENUM('work', 'home', 'other') DEFAULT 'home',
    `street1` char(100) DEFAULT NULL,
    `street2` char(100) DEFAULT NULL,
    `city` char(30) DEFAULT NULL,
    `state` char(30) DEFAULT NULL,
    `zip` char(10) DEFAULT NULL,
    PRIMARY KEY (`addr_id`,`contact_id`),
    KEY `contact_id` (`contact_id`),
    CONSTRAINT `addresses_ibfk_1` FOREIGN KEY (`contact_id`) REFERENCES
    `contacts` (`contact_id`)
) ENGINE=InnoDB;
```

```
CREATE TABLE `contact_list1`.`email_addresses` (
    `email_id` int(11) NOT NULL AUTO_INCREMENT,
    `contact_id` int(11) NOT NULL,
    `email_address` char(64) DEFAULT NULL,
    PRIMARY KEY (`email_id`,`contact_id`)
) ENGINE=InnoDB;

CREATE TABLE `contact_list1`.`phones` (
    `phone_id` int(11) NOT NULL AUTO_INCREMENT,
    `contact_id` int(11) NOT NULL,
    `phone` char(30) DEFAULT NULL,
    PRIMARY KEY (`phone_id`,`contact_id`),
    KEY `contact_id` (`contact_id`),
    CONSTRAINT `phones_ibfk_1` FOREIGN KEY (`contact_id`) REFERENCES
`contacts` (`contact_id`)
) ENGINE=InnoDB;
```

Note   Savvy database designers will note the phone number field is denormalized too far. Can you spot the issue?[3]

Now that we have seen the database design, let's consider some things that a document store designer would notice and want to change. That is, let's look at this design a bit more critically. Note that for any contact we want to view, we have potentially up to three additional queries to retrieve all the data. This is because we have broken out the phone, email, and address into separate tables. We could issue a single join query to get all the data, but that will result in extra data (unless you use an outer join or similar tricks).

To keep things simple, let's stick with the one query per dependent table. Even so, that gives us a total of four queries to execute to retrieve all the data for a given contact. Listing 10-3 shows the queries we would need to execute to get the data for a contact named 'Bill Smith.'

---

[3]Hint: What if you need to find all contacts that live in a certain area code? How would you write the query?

Listing 10-3. Queries to Retrieve a Contact (Relational Database)

```
MySQL  localhost:33060+  SQL > SELECT * FROM contact_list1.contacts WHERE
first = 'Bill' AND last = 'Smith';
+------------+-------+-------+
| contact_id | first | last  |
+------------+-------+-------+
|          1 | Bill  | Smith |
+------------+-------+-------+
1 row in set (0.00 sec)

 MySQL  localhost:33060+  SQL > SELECT * FROM contact_list1.addresses WHERE
contact_id = 1;
+---------+------------+--------------+-----------------+---------+
---------+-------+-------+
| addr_id | contact_id | address_type | street1         | street2 |
city     | state | zip   |
+---------+------------+--------------+-----------------+---------+
---------+-------+-------+
|       1 |          1 | home         | 123 Main Street | NULL    |
Anywhere | VT    | 12388 |
+---------+------------+--------------+-----------------+---------+
---------+-------+-------+
1 row in set (0.00 sec)

 MySQL  localhost:33060+  SQL > SELECT * FROM contact_list1.email_addresses
WHERE contact_id = 1;
+----------+------------+---------------------------+
| email_id | contact_id | email_address             |
+----------+------------+---------------------------+
|        1 |          1 | bill@smithmanufacturing.co |
|        2 |          1 | bill.smith@gomail.com     |
+----------+------------+---------------------------+
2 rows in set (0.00 sec)
```

```
MySQL  localhost:33060+  SQL > SELECT * FROM contact_list1.phones WHERE
contact_id = 1;
+-----------+------------+-----------------+
| phone_id  | contact_id | phone           |
+-----------+------------+-----------------+
|         1 |          1 | (301) 555-1212  |
+-----------+------------+-----------------+
1 row in set (0.00 sec)
```

As you can see, this involves several trips to the database server to get the data. If your application is designed to use tabs or some other user interface mechanism to hide the phone, address, and emails until the user clicks to reveal the information, having four queries might be okay and might save you some effort. However, almost every contact list solution includes name, address, and phone number. So, we're not saving much in the general terms of round trips to the database.

Note also it requires us to keep track of the contact_id passing to each of the three dependent queries. A good relational database designer would say, "so what?" at these observations. However, the schemaless mindset tells us to try to minimize joins and to keep all the data together. Let's see how we can apply a schemaless mindset to migrate the database to a hybrid solution keeping the base table but incorporating JSON fields.

Note   I don't go into how to create, update, and delete operations because these are very familiar in relational database systems.

Migrating to a Hybrid Solution

Removing joins is a good strategy for improving performance in retrieving data. It also plays to one of the standards of schemaless design; keep the data together. Both are strategies that fall under denormalizing the data. The example contact list database in the last section was normalized to include four tables: one for the contact name, and one each to contain all the addresses, phone numbers, and email addresses.

The goal wasn't to make the separate tables searchable or even accessible and presented on their own. After all, what use would anyone have to see a list of phone numbers without any connection to the owner? Rather, the normalization was meant to keep like data together and remove duplication.

For example, it is possible if you know several people who work at the same place that their work address and phone numbers will be the same. Likewise, members of the same family may have the same address and phone numbers.[4] Normalization then results in a main table with three dependent tables in a one-to-many relationship.

However, if you consider that we will seldom need to query the phone number, email address, or address table separately and that the data in those tables is associated with a contact and that it only makes sense to view the data as a set, we can denormalize the data by embedding it in the contact data.

We can do this easily by simply adding three fields to the contacts table using JSON fields to embed the data and still maintain the structure. Recall, we can use a JSON document in code and thus all the field names from the original tables can be used. When you do it this way, migrating the code is easier because you will be referring to the same data names. The following shows a redesign of the database to use a hybrid solution.

```
CREATE DATABASE IF NOT EXISTS `contact_list2`;

CREATE TABLE `contact_list2`.`contacts` (
    `contact_id` int(11) NOT NULL AUTO_INCREMENT,
    `first` char(30) DEFAULT NULL,
    `last` char(30) DEFAULT NULL,
    `addresses` json DEFAULT NULL,
    `email_addresses` json DEFAULT NULL,
    `phones` json DEFAULT NULL,
    PRIMARY KEY (`contact_id`)
) ENGINE=InnoDB;
```

Here, we eliminated the three tables by adding the relations as JSON arrays. But wait, how do we format those JSON documents? Isn't that going to be a problem? No, not really. To migrate to a hybrid solution you would carry over the field names from the embedded data using them as keys in the JSON document.

---

[4]It is not unusual to encounter two or more generations (or members there of) living in the same home. With the rising costs of medical and long-term care, this can only become more prevalent.

We can also improve the data for the phone numbers by adding keys to reference the area code, exchange, and phone number. Better, if we later find that we need to add a country code value, we can do so for those contacts that require them. Remember, the beauty of JSON documents is that they are mutable and you can add or leave out fields as needed. The only catch is your code must be written to expect the omissions and new fields. Thus, there is no reason to retool your data to add a country code to new contacts.

The following shows how this is done for the create operation using the same contact shown in the last section.

```
INSERT INTO contact_list2.contacts VALUES(
  NULL, 'Bill', 'Smith',
  '{"addresses":[{"address_type":"home", "street1":"123 Main Street",
  "street2":"","city":"Anywhere","state":"VT","zip":12388}]}',
  '{"email_addresses":["bill@smithmanufacturing.co","bill.smith@gomail.
  com"]}',
  '{"phones":[{"area_code":301,"exchange":555,"number":1212}]}'
);
```

This results in an interesting row returned from a SELECT query. We see the result in the following.

```
MySQL  localhost:33060+  SQL > SELECT * FROM contact_list2.contacts WHERE
first = 'Bill' AND last = 'Smith' \G
*************************** 1. row ***************************
    contact_id: 1
         first: Bill
          last: Smith
     addresses: {"addresses": [{"zip": 12388, "city": "Anywhere", "state":
    "VT", "street1": "123 Main Street", "street2": "", "address_type":
    "home"}]}
email_addresses: {"email_addresses": ["bill@smithmanufacturing.co", "bill.
smith@gomail.com"]}
        phones: {"phones": [{"number": 1212, "exchange": 555, "area_code":
        301}]}
1 row in set (0.00 sec)
```

Here, see that we've used the same names as the fields in the original tables. Accessing the data is made easier as we can migrate our code from looking for columns in row objects to using the field names directly in code. For example, to display the embedded lists of addresses, phones, and emails, we can use loops. Listing 10-4 shows an example script to do this.

Listing 10-4. Sample Read Operation for Contact List (Hybrid)

```python
import mysqlx
from json import JSONDecoder

GET_BILL = """
SELECT * FROM contact_list2.contacts
WHERE last = 'Smith' AND first = 'Bill'
"""

# Connect to database
session = mysqlx.get_session("root:password@localhost:33060")

# Read the row
row = session.sql(GET_BILL).execute().fetch_one()

# Convert JSON strings to Python dictionaries
addresses = JSONDecoder().decode(row["addresses"])["addresses"]
phones = JSONDecoder().decode(row["phones"])["phones"]
email_addresses = JSONDecoder().decode(row["email_addresses"])
["email_addresses"]

# Display the data
print("Contact List (Hybrid)")
print("---------------------")
print("Name: {0} {1}".format(row["first"],row["last"]))
print("\nAddresses:")
for address in addresses:
    print("\t({0})".format(address["address_type"].upper()))
    print("\t{0}".format(address["street1"]))
    if address["street2"]:
        print("\t{0}".format(address["street2"]))
    print("\t{0}, {1} {2}".format(address["city"],
                                   address["state"],
                                   address["zip"]))
```

```python
print("\nPhones:")
for phone in phones:
    print("\t({0}) {1}-{2}".format(phone["area_code"],
                                   phone["exchange"],
                                   phone["number"]))
print("\neMail Addresses:")
for email in email_addresses:
    print("\t{0}".format(email))

print("")
```

Note that the code reads well and we can see exactly which data we're accessing in the loops. However, there is some duplication when converting the JSON strings to Python dictionaries. This is because we have a field in the table and a key in the JSON string with the same name. For example, there is an addresses field and the key in the JSON document is addresses. This might look a little odd, but it is precisely how you would access the JSON document in the fields. Some may want to rename the field or JSON key to make it a bit less ambiguous.

The following shows this code executing. Note the output does resemble how you would expect to see the data by reading the code. The use of tabs (\t) is helpful for printing strings to a console.

```
$ python ./hybrid_read.py
Contact List (Hybrid)
---------------------
Name: Bill Smith

Addresses:
    (HOME)
    123 Main Street
    Anywhere, VT 12388

Phones:
    (301) 555-1212

eMail Addresses:
    bill@smithmanufacturing.co
    bill.smith@gomail.com
```

This solution is better and does solve the issue of removing joins and keeping the data together, but what if we need to store a surname, suffix, title, or if there are contacts with more than two names? Likewise, what if you found you needed to find all contacts that live or work in a certain area code? The data is there, but because the phone number is a single string, it's harder to search for the data (but not impossible).

We can solve this problem (and similar issues) by simply altering the table to break out the data into separate fields. That will work and that is what most developers will do. However, what do you do with any existing data? Do you go back and reformat using special tools you create yourself? You don't have any choice and if there is a lot of data, the conversion can be painful and time consuming.

Sadly, hybrid solutions with relational parts (table, fields) are still fixed and thus hybrid solutions are not immune to changes. What we need is to achieve mutability—to be able to change the structure whenever we need to do so without having to retool. If you're thinking, "there's got to be a better way," you are correct—there is. Let's see how to overcome these issues by converting the database to a pure document store.

Converting to a Document Store

Perhaps the best attribute of document store solutions is mutability. That, along with the "data as code" concept makes working with document stores so much easier than relational databases. Although we saw some improvements in a hybrid solution for the contacts database, we are not quite to the point where mutability is possible.

To be specific, we still have fixed fields in the hybrid solution. If these fields were the complete set (for all time), we might be satisfied with a hybrid solution. But if you work in an international setting, you will find that storing first and last names are far too casual and, in some cases, insufficient.

For example, Geraldo Jose Miguel Gomez. What do you do with such a name? Split the name arbitrarily placing the parts in the two fields? What if the individual uses Miguel as his first name? Now, your database will list his name as "Miguel", "Geraldo Jose Gomez", which is not correct. Furthermore, if you do split the name in such a manner, any queries on first name or last name for that matter are subject to incorrect results or at least additional parsing after the query to sort out these anomalies.

If we used a document store, we can add whatever fields we need. We just need to keep our code and data synchronized. That is, when we add new fields, we must also add code in our CRUD operations to compensate. For example, adding a nickname field to the document is easy, but the code that reads the data and displays it must allow for working with the nickname. Best of all, we can add the change and don't have to rework any existing data.

This, then, is the goal: to make your data schemaless and integrated tightly with the code. Once you adopt this mindset, you will find the stigma of normalization easy to cast off. Although that doesn't mean all schemaless solutions will outperform their relational counterparts (unlikely in fact), it does mean you can make the data work for you instead of against you. Developers especially will appreciate the freedom.

As we learned in Chapter 9 and earlier in the book, we can create a collection easily in code. Recall, this includes connecting to the server, getting a schema object instance, and creating the collection. We can then create, read, update, or delete documents in the collection. Figure 10-2 shows a snapshot of using the MySQL Shell to create the schema and collection for the contact list. We also add the row we've been using as an example.

```
MySQL  Py > session = mysqlx.get_session('root:root@localhost:33060')
MySQL  Py > schema = session.create_schema('contact_list3')
MySQL  Py > contacts = schema.create_collection('contacts')
MySQL  Py > contacts.add({"first":"Bill","last":"Smith","title":"Salesman","suf
fix":"Jr","addresses":[{"address_type":"home","street1":"123 Main Street","city"
:"Anywhere","state":"VT","zip":12388}],"email_addresses":["bill@smithmanufacturi
ng.co","bill.smith@gomail.com"],"phones":[{"area_code":301,"exchange":555,"numbe
r":1212}]}).execute()
Query OK, 1 item affected (0.00 sec)

MySQL  Py > contacts.find().execute()
[
    {
        "_id": "58CDFA7D85228504E811FB35560F1EB6",
        "addresses": [
            {
                "address_type": "home",
                "city": "Anywhere",
                "state": "VT",
                "street1": "123 Main Street",
                "zip": 12388
            }
        ],
        "email_addresses": [
            "bill@smithmanufacturing.co",
            "bill.smith@gomail.com"
        ],
        "first": "Bill",
        "last": "Smith",
        "phones": [
            {
                "area_code": 301,
                "exchange": 555,
                "number": 1212
            }
        ],
        "suffix": "Jr",
        "title": "Salesman"
    }
]
1 document in set (0.00 sec)

MySQL  Py > []
```

Figure 10-2. *Creating a document store*

Here, we see we have migrated our rigid relational database model to a mutable JSON document with embedded data that keeps all the data together for each contact.

Now, let's look at the code to perform a read operation on the document store. Listing 10-5 shows the code to read the document from the collection and print it to the console.

Listing 10-5. Sample Read Operation for Contact List (Document Store)

```python
import mysqlx

# Connect to server
session = mysqlx.get_session("root:password@localhost:33060")

# Get the schema
schema = session.get_schema("contact_list3")

# Get the collection
contacts = schema.get_collection("contacts")

# Read the row
row = contacts.find("first = '{0}' and last = '{1}'".format('Bill',
                                                'Smith')).execute()

contact = row.fetch_one()

addresses = contact["addresses"]
phones = contact["phones"]
email_addresses = contact["email_addresses"]

# Display the data
print("Contact List (DocStore)")
print("-----------------------")
suffix = ""
if "suffix" in contact.keys():
    suffix = ", {0}".format(contact["suffix"])
print("Name: {0} {1}{2}".format(contact["first"],contact["last"],suffix))
if "title" in contact.keys():
    print("Title: {0}".format(contact["title"]))
print("\nAddresses:")
for address in addresses:
```

```python
    print("\t({0})".format(address["address_type"].upper()))
    print("\t{0}".format(address["street1"]))
    if "street2" in address.keys():
        print("\t{0}".format(address["street2"]))
    print("\t{0}, {1} {2}".format(address["city"],
                                  address["state"],
                                  address["zip"]))
print("\nPhones:")
for phone in phones:
    print("\t({0}) {1}-{2}".format(phone["area_code"],
                                   phone["exchange"],
                                   phone["number"]))
print("\neMail Addresses:")
for email in email_addresses:
    print("\t{0}".format(email))

print("")
```

Note that the code is very similar to the hybrid solution. In fact, the print sections are the same. The difference is seen early on when retrieving the data. In this case, we can retrieve the document and then store the addresses, phones, and email addresses as dictionaries, which makes the code even easier to read. Very nice!

The following shows the code executing. As you can see, the output is the same as the hybrid solution.

```
$ python ./docstore_read.py
Contact List (DocStore)
-----------------------
Name: Bill Smith, Jr
Title: Salesman

Addresses:
    (HOME)
    123 Main Street
    Anywhere, VT 12388

Phones:
    (301) 555-1212
```

eMail Addresses:
    bill@smithmanufacturing.co
    bill.smith@gomail.com

Now that we've discussed what a schemaless mindset is, let's review some tips and tricks for working with the MySQL Document Store.

Document Store Tips and Tricks

The following contain several best practices for planning, developing, and managing applications using MySQL Document Store. Some may seem intuitive whereas others may simply remind you to do those things we all know we should do but sometimes short cut for brevity. They are presented in a bulleted list and are intended to be a resource you can use to refer to periodically at the start of a migration or development effort.

- *Minimize joins*: Joins can be expensive. Reducing how many places you need to join data can help speed up your queries. Removing joins may result in some level of denormalization but can result in faster access to the data.

- *Plan for mutability*: Schemaless designs are focused on mutability. Build your applications with the ability to modify the document as needed (and within reason).

- *Remove many-to-many relationships*: Use embedded arrays and lists to store relationships among documents. This can be as simple as embedding the data in the document or embedding an array of document ids in the document. In the first case, the data is available as soon as you read the document and in the second, it takes only one additional step to retrieve the data. In cases of seldom read (used) relationships, having the data linked with an array of ids can be more efficient (less data to read on the first pass).

- *Avoid over denormalizing*: It is possible to take denormalization too far. If you denormalize your data by embedding things in your document at the expense of duplication, you may at some point discover you need to change the duplicated data. If this happens, you've crossed the line and now your data update nightmares commence. Thus, whenever you denormalize always consider how (or if) the data will be updated. If it can be updated in isolation (say only for one or more documents) and those changes do not need to exist in other documents, your denormalization should be fine. However, if you think even for a moment that you will need to update all occurrences of the embedded data, you must consider moving the data to another collection and using embedded lists to link the documents by id.

- *Know your data*: This may sound obvious, but you must understand the data you are using in your design. Not just what it can (or must) contain, but also how it will be used. Often, relational database designers are only concerned about the ability to retrieve any part of data at the expense of how the data is used. Thus, in the relational database world we often find ourselves optimizing queries after the application and data are designed. In the schemaless world, we must focus on how the data will be used from the start so that we can store the pertinent data together in a single or sometimes linked document. Knowing how your data will be used in the application can make a difference to how you form your document. It also can help you determine how to write the code to retrieve the data before you start to write the code.

- *Avoid large documents*: Storing all the data in a single document is indeed one of the goals of schemaless design, but this too must be used with some judgment behind it. If your document ends up being very large, you could encounter performance problems trying to retrieve more than a single document (say for a list or to perform an operation over a set of documents). Thus, you should consider what parts of the document are used and when. You may find that you can split your document into several smaller documents (each in their own collection). This way, you can optimize retrieval for most of operations retrieving the less frequently used data only when you need it.

- *Use JSON columns for embedding data in tables*: If you want to improve your existing relational database by reducing the number of joins, you can use a JSON field to embed the data. For example, use a JSON field to collapse many-to-many join tables by storing an array of pointers (keys) to the dependent table. One obvious candidate is the text of BLOB fields that have encoded data.

Summary

The MySQL Document Store and the latest incarnation of the server, MySQL 8, represent a huge leap forward in functionality, reliability, and availability. Best of all, MySQL 8 doesn't force you into a new paradigm. The NoSQL option via the X DevAPI perfectly complements the advanced clustering and availability of NDB Cluster. But unlike NDB Cluster, you can use your existing MySQL servers.[5]

What this means is you don't have to learn and completely retool your infrastructure and applications to use the newest features. What we saw in this book and in practice in Chapter 9 is that you can choose to use MySQL 8 as a traditional relational database store, migrate your applications to a hybrid of relational data with one or more JSON fields, or completely rethink your data by migrating to a pure Document Store solution.

In fact, MySQL makes it easy to migrate your applications because the X DevAPI supports both an SQL and NoSQL interface. Thus, the first step is to migrate to the X DevAPI for all your SQL interface-based applications then you have the option of migrating those to a hybrid or pure document store solution.

This is an exciting time for MySQL users. Oracle continues to keep it's promise to not only continue developing MySQL but also pouring resources into improving and expanding the feature set. Keep a close watch on more excellent features and further refinement and updates. MySQL 8 is here and now is the time to jump on board. Look for more titles from Apress on MySQL 8!

---

[5]NDB Cluster requires several servers with the NDB Cluster server installed. See the NDB Cluster section in the online MySQL reference manual for more details.

Index

Printed in the United States
By Bookmasters